THE JEWISH HIT SQUAD

Jewish Hit Squad

The Łukawiecki Partisans Unit of the Polish Armia Krajowa, 1941–1944

Simon Lavee (Łukawiecki)

This book was published with the support of:

Yad Vashem
The Holocaust Martyrs' and Heroes' Remembrance Authority
The Foundation for Support of Survivors' Memoirs

The Azrieli Group

The Azrieli Foundation

Claims Conference
The Conference on Jewish Material Claims Against Germany

Copyright © Simon Lavee (Łukawiecki)
Jerusalem 2015/5775

All rights reserved. No part of this publication may be translated, reproduced, stored in a retrieval system or transmitted, in any form or by any means, electronic, mechanical, photocopying, recording or otherwise, without express written permission from the publishers.

Cover Design: Leah Ben Avraham/Noonim Graphics
Typesetting: Raphaël Freeman, Renana Typesetting

ISBN: 978-965-229-608-5

1 3 5 7 9 8 6 4 2

Gefen Publishing House Ltd.
6 Hatzvi Street
Jerusalem 94386, Israel
972-2-538-0247
orders@gefenpublishing.com

Gefen Books
11 Edison Place
Springfield, NJ 07081
516-593-1234
orders@gefenpublishing.com

www.gefenpublishing.com

Printed in Israel

Send for our free catalog

LIBRARY OF CONGRESS CATALOGING-IN-PUBLICATION DATA

Lavee, Simon, author.
 Jewish hit squad: the Lukawiecki partisans unit of the Polish Armia Krajowa, 1941–1944 / Simon Lavee.
   pages cm
 Includes bibliographical references.
 ISBN 978-965-229-608-5
 1. Lukawiecki, Edmund, 1921–2004. 2. Jews – Poland – Biography. 3. World War, 1939-1945 – Underground movements – Poland – Lubacz?w – Biography. 4. World War, 1939-1945 – Jewish resistance – Poland – Lubacz?w – Biography. 5. Holocaust, Jewish (1939-1945) – Poland – Biography. 6. Poland. Polskie Sily Zbrojne. Armia Krajowa – Biography. 7. Lubacz?w (Poland) – Biography. I. Title.
 DS134.72.L85L38 2015
 940.54'12438 – dc23

2015002941

In the darkness of day, the foe reigned.
"Give me your life," he claimed.
The lioness stood up, her body forged for fight.
She roared deafeningly, "Nay!" The foe stood paralyzed in fright.
"I will defeat you and shut on you my door!
Stop there; I will take no more!"

He stared at the lioness,
Saw her strength and decisiveness,
Saw her vigor and readiness.
With eyes downcast, he left without repentance.

– Simon Lavee

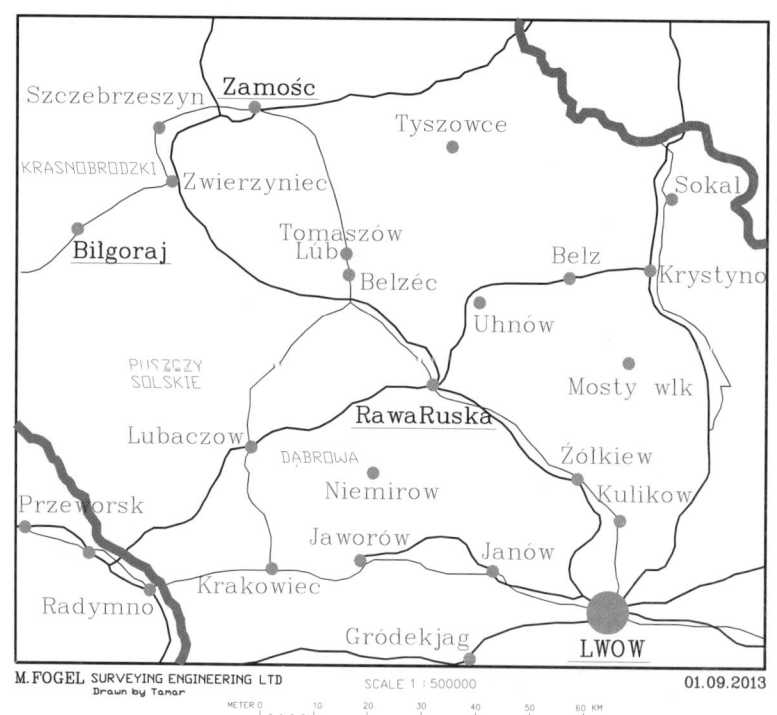

General map of area of operations

Contents

	Preface	ix
	Acknowledgments	xvii
1	A Bottle of Vodka and a Kilogram of Sugar	1
2	The Jackals Are Howling	19
3	*Czyn*	40
4	A World Turned Upside Down	51
5	Camp Lipowa	61
6	The Death of Humanity	68
7	Sokolniki Death Camp	72
8	Return to the Underground Movement	79
9	Relocation to Ostrowiec	85
10	Partisan Fighting Company	88
11	The Establishment of the Lubaczów Ghettos	97
12	Rape	107
13	Vus Macht der Urel Du?	114
14	Leica Camera No. 334164	120
15	Mother Maria	125
16	Partisan Land	135
17	Jewish Partisans in Southeast Lublin	156
18	Susiec	172
19	Forming the Jewish Hit Squad	178
	Berish Brand	181
	Isaac Helman	183
	Anshel Bogner	185
	Maurie Hoffman and His Brother Tobias	188

20	Bunker 1	193
21	If I Am Not for Myself, Then Who Will Be for Me? And if Not Now, When?	200
22	Operations of the Jewish Hit Squad	204
23	Bunker 2	208
24	Jaworów	216
25	Chana's Pledge	222
26	The Bridge	229
27	Hitlerjugend	232
28	Air and Canon Bombardment	235
29	Scorched Earth	238
30	Caught with Trousers Down	246
31	Qualms	251
32	From AK to UB	261
	Epilogue	281
	Bibliography	283
	Primary Sources	283
	Documents	284
	Maps	287
	Testimonies	287
	Personal Interviews	288
	Personal Correspondence	289
	Archives and Museums	289
	Sources in English	290
	Sources in German	293
	Sources in Hebrew	295
	Sources in Polish	295
	Sources in Ukrainian	300
	Index	301

Preface

In the summer of 2009, the late Lula Weiner Baum – a very old family friend – invited me to join her and her family on their visit to her mother Ora Haiman Regev, whose mother had survived WWII as a young girl. She had just completed a thorough investigation into her family roots. After Ora's presentation, we all praised her for her hard work. Lola replied, "With all due respect to her family," she said, pointing her finger at me, "your father's story is a much more compelling and brave story than her mother's."

Despite the bold approach, her comment triggered my inquisitiveness and led me to try to understand what she was talking about. I decided to look into it. One of the Jewish hit squad survivors – Maurie Hoffman – had written a book entitled *Keep Yelling: A Survivor's Testimony* (Richmond, Australia: Spectrum, 1995). It had remained untouched on my bookshelf since I received it from him in 1995. I read it the night I came back. The way he described my mother struck a chord in me. That night, at the not-so-tender age of sixty-two, I discovered that my mother had been a sex slave for a Ukrainian policeman at the beginning of WWII. This completely staggered me. This kind and gentle woman, who had been raised in a very religious Jewish family, was so loving, compassionate, and patient. I had never imagined she had been so severely abused.

The pangs of conscience prevented me from sleeping for several nights. It was torture – without mercy. I, her own son, had never considered the inferno that raged inside her all those years ago. She raised me with love and care. She seemed to have managed to put her journey through hell behind her. During those long, restless nights, I often dreamt about the cruel, brutal life she led. And how she seemed so well balanced throughout my youth.

Her voice was always soft and calm. She never raised her hand in anger. She never lost her temper and was always concerned about the well-being of the family. She was never depressed, though she was sad on occasion. She rarely smiled or laughed. Her emotions were kept inside and were not externalized for the world to see. This meant no hugs, no kisses, no display of affection. In fact, I never knew that hugs and kisses were a normal part of a mother-son relationship. Based upon false information, she was sure that I had been killed during the 1967 Six-Day War, in which I was at the front in Sinai, in the division commanded by General Ariel Sharon. When I arrived home unharmed, she kissed me on my forehead and said, without a tear or the slightest display of emotion, "Welcome home." But she changed dramatically with the birth of her grandchildren. Smiles, kisses, and hugs abounded. Happiness had returned to her life.

Being a mischievous boy growing up, I did not really take her past into account. On the contrary, I often added new grief and misery to her life. But in 2009, I finally grasped who my mother was. I admired her. My conscience was in turmoil. Where had I been during her short life? Why hadn't I learned more about what she'd gone through during WWII? Her refusal to talk about it was not an adequate excuse and did not ease the pain in my heart.

Even though she passed away twenty-four years ago, I have been asking her for forgiveness since I read Maurie Hoffman's book; we've had endless conversations in my sleep.

A few days after my dramatic discovery about my mother's past, I had a court hearing at the Supreme Court of Justice in Jerusalem. While I was in the area, I decided to stop in to Yad Vashem, the Holocaust Martyrs' and Heroes' Remembrance Authority. My parents had completed forms at Yad Vashem as the family of victims of the Holocaust. For the first time I decided to study my family tree – my grandfathers, my grandmothers, my uncles and aunts.

While at Yad Vashem, I was told that my father had been interviewed there in 1993. Yad Vashem had recorded it. I suddenly heard my father's voice, speaking fluent Polish as if he were alive. Tears streamed from my eyes and I could barely get out the words as I asked them to stop playing the interview. I felt like I was going to faint.

Yad Vashem kindly provided me with a copy of the recording, together with a transcript and a short Hebrew translation. That night, I read the translation a hundred times. My father's voice played in my head, over and over again. But it was only after a couple of months that I was really able to listen to the interview. It was the first time my parents' story as partisans was presented to me clearly and comprehensively.

As a child, I had heard stories from my parents' life as partisans. A story here, an incident there. Most of it was told in a humorous way. For example, there was my father's story of pretending to be a carpenter at the Sokolniki concentration camp. The light-hearted story did not reflect the fact that his life was at stake and that he was miraculously saved. The only stories we ever heard were ones that had an element of humor in them. What did come through, however, was my father's palpable resentment and enmity toward the Ukrainians. They were portrayed in my father's stories as people who happily and willingly slaughtered Jews.

Life with my father was not easy. He managed the family with an iron fist. Discipline was very strict. We were punished often when he thought we had disobeyed his orders. Any breach of rules drew an angry reaction. In fact, there were times when life at home with my father was unbearable and almost impossible. Nonetheless, my mother refused to divorce him even though we, her sons, suggested it. She forgave him time and time again and would advocate for my brother and me. She would try to protect us with love and soft words, attempting to calm his outbreaks and uncontrollable rage. She would always tell us that we must forgive him, since he was treated very cruelly by the Nazis at Sokolniki. Our protector and savior was always our mother.

But despite his raging temper and iron-fisted rule over the household, my father had a sensitive, artistic temperament, and seconds after an outburst he was fully capable of taking up his violin and filling the house with the heavenly tunes of famous composers, his agile fingers dancing over the strings as he conjured a pathway to the divine.

After reading (and finally listening to) his Yad Vashem interview, I now understood his preoccupation with WWII and how his struggle to survive had shaped his personality. His soul was tortured by the thought that he could have saved his family, but did not. He saw his family executed in Dachnów by a German-Ukrainian firing squad. He later refused compensation from Germany, feeling that his family's blood could not be bought by money. There were "other ways" to avenge their deaths.

At the time, I did not know what he meant by "other ways." But after reading his interview and then doing research, I came to understand. As a partisan and member of the Communist-controlled secret police organization the Urząd Bezpieczeństwa (UB; Department of Security) and the Stalinist Korpus Bezpieczeństwa Wewnetrznego (KBW; Internal Security Corps), he followed his drive – to pay back the Nazis and their collaborators – and then fulfilled it. As a member of a non-religious Jewish family, he had completely assimilated and identified with Polish-German society in Lemberg/Lwów. He had deep nationalistic ties to Poland. Even his family name was changed to a Polish one. Yet all this pretense turned out to be for nothing. The family was persecuted as Jews.

So he adopted Jewish nationalism. He had been involved with a right-wing youth movement before the war and then the ZWZ (which later became the AK) Polish nationalist organization during the war. The preoccupation with retaliation for his family brought him to cross lines and join the UB and the KBW.

His unique brilliance during WWII was his ability to adapt to living in the woods, together with his superior fighting methods and his knack for anticipating the enemy's way of thinking. He developed "night combat" techniques. He used his knowledge of the German language as a fighting tool. He fought from the woods, at the woods, and to the woods. He was known as a very brave, almost fearless soldier and had incredible physical strength. He also had the survival and hunting instincts of an animal. As a leader, he demanded unquestioning obedience. As he said himself, everybody knew not to mess with him because he was something of a madman. On the one hand he was a genius; on the other he was slightly crazy.

All of this I learned about him through painstaking research: for more than three years after the fateful discovery of my father's interview with Yad Vashem, I immersed myself in his story. I could not find any documentation about the ZWZ's/AK's Jewish partisan fighting units. My father's combat activities were partially mentioned in some of my Polish research, especially in the Lubaczów area. But they were totally ignored by non-Polish researchers.

The more I learned in the course of more than three years of research, the more I was able to document and verify my father's story (and continue to do so, as I regularly come across new facts and sources). I started this research from a very pessimistic point of view, believing that my father's memories included a mixture of fact and fiction, but very quickly I realized my mistake and how accurate his memories actually were. It is impossible to point out even a single mistake in my father's story.

During my first visit to the Lubaczów area in February 2010, I was with my son, Or. He joined the trip to help me get through it emotionally. We went to my grandfather's farm in Ostrowiec (not the town on the Kamienna River southwest of Lublin, but a tiny suburb by the same name two kilometers southeast of Lubaczów). Mrs. Maria Podporska-Szutka, now an elderly lady, was a neighbor of my grandfather's. She pointed at my son, ignoring me, and shouted as if she had seen a ghost, "Mundek, Mundek!" We realized that Or looked like my father when he was in his twenties.

Receiving the decoration, the medal, and the certificate of honor of Righteous Among the Nations from the Israeli ambassador to Poland, H.E. Zvi Rav-Ner, in Rzeszów, Poland, January 17, 2012. Receiving the certificate are Józef Kulpa's grandchildren. Left to right: Mr. Jacek Kulpa, Mr. Janusz Kulpa, Mrs. Ewa Wasilewska, the author and survivor's son Simon Lavee (Łukawiecki).

On that trip Or and I also met with the family of Józef Kulpa, who helped save my parents. The meeting was exciting, touching, and inspiring. I learned that my father had reestablished contact with them in 1997 and expressed his intention to nominate Józef Kulpa as a "Righteous among the Nations." However, his illness prevented him from completing this. I was gratified to be able to do this on his behalf, and in January 2012 the medal was posthumously awarded.

The relationship of trust and friendship between Józef Kulpa and my father is widely illustrated, as shown in the pictures in this book (presented here as a full collection for the first time). All these pictures were taken either by my father or his partisan colleagues during WWII with the Leica camera my father

The Righteous Among the Nations certificate awarded posthumously to Józef Kulpa

was always carrying around with him during this time. He would snap pictures whenever it was possible. These pictures of course were taken on a negative strip, which would have to be developed later on and printed, unlike today's digitalized system. The responsibility of making these pictures available was in the hands of Józef Kulpa, and his involvement carried a very high risk. The process of taking these pictures from the moment of capture to the final development involved steps in which at any given time the people doing this could be caught and the information might have been disclosed to the Gestapo.

My parents survived the war because of good people like Józef Kulpa and Marian Warda, the local ZWZ commanding officer, who disobeyed ZWZ rules and allowed Jews to join the ZWZ's ranks. He started guerrilla combat operations against the Nazis to prevent the Germans from repatriating the Zamość area. To achieve that goal, Warda even cooperated with Soviet partisans. Born March 31, 1931, Warda died September 22, 2007, and was buried in the largest cemetery in Lublin, next to Państwowe Muzeum na Majdanku (Majdanek State Museum, the former Majdanek concentration camp).

There were also geographical advantages of Zamość that helped save my parents' lives. It was a heavily covered wood with ravine-like terrain. This made it difficult for regular military forces to conduct engagements. But it was perfectly suited for guerrilla warfare. And my father always planned his "hit-and-run" operations far from his hideout in the Janowskie woods ("A thief should not steal in his own neighborhood," he used to say).

My father was an adept military leader with high-level tactical ability and was devoted to actively fighting the Nazis and their collaborators. And yet, he was unable to save his own family. He watched with his own eyes as Germans and Ukrainians executed them. He even saw a German soldier kick their bodies to the bottom of a ditch. He could not understand what sins they could have committed – especially his youngest sister Judith – to deserve such a fate.

Tragically, in his own harsh self-criticism, he felt he had not even attempted to save them, being busy with his own survival at the time. This is what tortured him his entire life; he never stopped asking himself why he had not tried harder to save his own family. (In fact, he did try – he tried to save many people who refused to risk going out into the woods, but he blamed himself for not having been more stubborn with his family.) He did save my mother, along with many others. And that was the reason she always forgave him for his "madness." She owed her life to him, for better or worse. Most probably, it was his very "madness" that saved his life and the lives of others.

This is the father I grew up with: a man indelibly marked by WWII. I always ignored it. I did not try to see the world through his eyes. On the contrary, I just covered mine. I remember being ten years old and going to the attic to look for something with him. It was here that he had stored all his partisan gear and artifacts from WWII. I said, "Daddy, throw this stuff away. You don't need it anymore in Israel." He stared at me for very long time, without saying a word. But he did end up throwing it out. I did not understand at the time that it was a part of his soul, a part of him, and a part of my family. But as a "new" Israeli, I did not want to know about that past. It conflicted with my new identity in our new-old homeland.

I deliberately refused to speak Polish or German. I wasn't interested in learning about my family members and our history. I despised it and him. I despised everything linked to the Diaspora. Not only had he refused to talk about his experiences in WWII, I was also not interested in hearing about them. I thought that in order to be Israeli, I must put the past behind me, and this started with my family roots and the Holocaust.

At the height of my self-created "Israeli" identity, my parents hosted our cousins the Pomerantz family when they first arrived in Israel in 1958. Abraham and Rozalia Pomerantz and their three children Miriam, Zvi, and Shmuel, fresh off the boat, stayed with us for their first days as new *olim* (immigrants). None of them spoke Hebrew. The children were my age. As newcomers they saw me as an experienced Israeli. For my part I simply ignored them. I wanted nothing to do with with them and did not want to be identified with them in any way.

My challenge was to be purely Israeli, untainted by the European continent, untainted by the war. Only years later did I realize how much my father had wrestled with his own identity. All his life, he struggled to overcome the horrors of WWII. And now, he was struggling for his place in the present. He won the first battle on foreign soil, but lost the second in his homeland. And during his lifetime, I never understood him.

This book is my plea for forgiveness and absolution.

Acknowledgments

As I was completing the writing of this book, I received a DVD copy of a Hebrew interview conducted with my father in May 1997 by Steven Spielberg's USC Shoah Foundation Institute. It was a very valuable part of my research.

The on-the-ground research for this book was conducted in Poland, Ukraine, Germany, Great Britain, Canada, and the United States, whenever I could find free time from my career as a lawyer. I conducted interviews with everybody who was connected to my parents. That included ZWZ/AK members in Poland, family relatives, acquaintances, friends, and therapists who assisted them. I would like to thank all of them for their valuable information and knowledge to help relay the heroic story of my parents and their partisan group.

I had endless conversations with the two remaining survivors, Maurie Hoffman and Isaac Helman (who unfortunately passed away in March 2012), and I thank them for that. Maurie Hoffman told me that for many years they were afraid to tell anyone about their wartime activities, for fear there could still be consequences. The first time his daughter was exposed to his story was an interview he did on October 7, 2012, that she attended. I heard the same from the families of Isaac Helman, Berish Brand, and Anshel Bogner.

Józef Kulpa played a key role in saving my parents, the partisan group, and an unknown number of Jews. The meeting with his family enriched my knowledge and I would like to thank all of them and their families: Janusz Kulpa, Jacek Kulpa, Ewa Wasilewska, and Władysław Burek. The contact with the Kulpa family was made possible thanks to Father Andrzej Legowicz and Father Janusz Sokołowski from Łukawiec.

My heartfelt gratitude goes out to Chana Cieszanówer Diner (my grandfather's cousin), to the late Lula Weiner Baum (who passed away on July 10, 2014, during the writing of this book), Joe Warner, Miriam Marcus, Aliza Segal (who transcribed my father's story), Dahlia Levin (who assisted my mother during her illness), Dr. Adam Bauman, and Dr. Isaac Weinberg.

Thanks also to AK members Czesław Podporski and his mother Maria Szutka. Special thanks to the late Mieczysław Argasiński and his wife Lidia, who spent long hours with me sharing information.

I was advised by outstanding historians, and their knowledge paved the way for my research. Those historians include Tomasz Róg, Steve Campbell, Edward Westermann, and Colonel Mark Worell, Defense Section, British Embassy Tel Aviv.

I would also like to thank Richard Tyndorf, a fellow lawyer from Toronto, Canada, for his outstanding advice concerning not only accuracy of Polish terminology, but also historical facts, events, and chronology. With his outstanding knowledge he resolved many questions.

I also very much appreciate the assistance I received from Stanisław Piotr Makara, Barbara Woch, Patek Razon and Zenon Swatek, all from Muzeum Kresów in Lubaczów. And further thanks to Peter Gohle of the Bundesarchiv Ludwigsburg, and Dr. Thomas Menzel of the Military Archive, Bundesarchiv Freiburg.

Special thanks to the historian Dr. Volker Riess from Ludwigsburg, whose expert knowledge contributed greatly to this work. He shared with me very important information and documents. He also read this entire work and gave me many valuable comments and corrections (both factual and linguistic), all of which I accepted.

I received invaluable insight into nationalistic Ukrainian ideology and information about the village from which my mother's rapist came from the historian of Nowe Sioło, Sikum Władek. A comprehensive description of how the village welcomed the Nazis was outlined by Josefa Kolodziej.

A very big thanks to Deborah Kottiner and Nicha Fishgrund, as well as the Bais Yaacov Central Museum in Jerusalem, who allowed me to better understand Bais Yaacov and the religious world in which my mother grew up.

Since my father crossed the lines after WWII from the AK to the Polish UB and KBW, this book couldn't be completed without analyzing that aspect. It was of utmost importance to see the entire picture. I want to thank Mr. Tomasz Gołdyn and Ms. Anna Kęszycka of Instytut Pamięci Narodowej Kraków (IPN,

Institute of National Remembrance), who showed a lot of goodwill and patience in revealing my father's personal file to me.

Judge Artur Brosz from Lubaczów enabled me to piece together the history of my family in Kraków.

I would not have been able to fully comprehend the Polish documents without the assistance and excellent interpretation of Miriam Nachmias, Adam Meshel, Agatha Winograd, Ayelet Shafir, and the outstanding goodwill of Joseph Karmin, from Kibbutz Negba, on the border of the Gaza Strip. In addition, Aleksandra Rawska checked the Polish spellings in the manuscript.

I spent endless amounts of time and effort trying to locate the surviving members of my father's partisan group. Yaron Enosh and his producer Magi Ochayon managed to locate Isaac Helman, which was an amazing breakthrough. Mr. Menachem Dolinski managed to locate the Berish Brand family. I thank them very much for their dedication and hard work.

Throughout my entire time researching, I received assistance from Robert Golis from Łukawiec, Poland, and Sergey Erofeev from Lwów (today called Lviv), Ukraine. Their knowledge, interpretation, and ability to overcome obstacles and barriers were unparalled. Without them, my research would have stalled time and time again.

Finally, I would like to thank Mrs. Maria Magon, the mayor of Lubaczów – my grandparents' hometown. Her accommodating assistant Ms. Ania Jarosławiec provided all possible assistance and support. Lubaczów itself should be proud that Józef Kulpa was one of its residents; throughout the dark, endless night of WWII, he stood as a shining beacon of humanity.

I am obliged to thank my cousin (none of us know how we are related, but we are) Varda Givoly Ringler-Zum for her generous and patient assistance and support in translating Polish documents.

Many thanks to my secretary, Rachel Cohn Efrat.

I would like to thank my nephew, Tal Lavee (Łukawiecki), for going over the book in detail and giving many excellent suggestions, which really made this book possible. I am forever in his debt.

The dark subject matter of this book and the intensely personal nature of my relationship to the material were at times overwhelming. In those dark moments I was inspired by my life partner, Dafna Elnatan-Abramowitz, who was a beacon to me throughout this difficult process. Her very wise advice, sharp mind and suggestions, always given with a smile and good humor, gave me the strength to carry on. This book was completed due to Dafna's spirit and help. My love for and debt to her is infinite.

Chapter 1
A Bottle of Vodka and a Kilogram of Sugar

Mundek Łukawiecki in military gear, summer 1943

The Janowskie woods, which were part of the Puszcza Solska forest about forty kilometers (twenty-five miles) north of the small town of Lubaczów, Poland, consisted of young pine trees. The trees were small, no more than two meters tall. Since it was a relatively new wood, the trees and vegetation were sparse and scattered. No animals inhabited the woods, except for birds such as crows and sparrows. It was easy to move through these woods without leaving a trace. Because the wood was newer than other woods in the area, Mundek – the young

Mundek in military gear, summer 1943

commander of the partisans – thought it an ideal hiding place. He suspected that the Gestapo and their Ukrainian collaborators wouldn't think of searching here for people in hiding.[1]

One morning in the winter of 1943, the prevailing peaceful atmosphere was suddenly overturned when a fully armed Mundek, in his half-Polish, half-Russian partisan uniform, rushed into the center of the partisan hideout. A tall, slim man standing at about six feet two, he wore a uniform consisting of a long-sleeved coat with two flap pockets on the front, riding pants, and high black leather boots. Slung across each shoulder were two bandoliers holding 7.92 mm bullets for his

---

[1] Gestapo branch IV of the German Security Police had the task of fighting all enemies of the German Reich, especially the Jews. The Security Police was part of the German police (which also included the Gendarmerie, the Polish police, the Ukrainian police, etc.). In the General Government area, the Security Police officers and units were deployed in big cities, while the German gendarmerie and their local helpers were present in the country. In this book, the term *Gestapo* is used as a synonym for all the German police.

Česká zbrojovka rifle. He also had with him four AGD-33 Russian hand grenades. On his belt he carried field binoculars and a Leica camera.

It was just before dawn when Mundek arrived. He started shouting and screaming, demanding that everyone stand in the center of the hideout. The partisans scurried to the center of the hideout dressed in their civilian clothes, coats, and boots. The winter cold penetrated their clothing, making them feel frozen stiff. Only the falling, wet snow could be felt and the only sound was the wind. It was twenty degrees below zero Celsius (minus four Fahrenheit).

Chana Bern in the woods, spring 1944

Mundek, who had just returned from a meeting with Józef Kulpa, a local countryman and partisan supporter, looked possessed; his pale, unshaven face radiated pure hatred and unmitigated fury. Breathlessly, he ordered everyone to change into their partisan uniforms, take their weapons and gear, and stand in a circle in the center of the hideout.

On this unusual morning, there were two women in the partisan group. The first, twenty-year-old Chana Bern, a blonde with blue eyes, was Mundek's girlfriend. The second girl, nineteen-year-old Zisa Stein, had been found by the partisans running in the woods. When they found her, she had told them she was running from the Nazis.

Chana Bern armed with a Parabellum pistol, spring 1944

A furious Mundek now dragged Zisa by her hair, which was covered by a scarf, and threw her into the center of the circle. "You hand over Jews to the Germans and Ukrainians," he screamed, "for a bottle of vodka and a kilogram of sugar?!"[2]

It was the first time Mundek had ever displayed such a loss of control and such wild behavior. The rest of the partisans stood frozen, their mouths agape in shock. Zisa was sitting in front of Mundek weeping uncontrollably. Her once colorful flower-patterned dress was now dirty and torn.

"You are a Jew from the same town as we are – you know all of us!" Mundek yelled. "We know who you are! We all went to the same school and have some of the same rabbis! You know who our parents are. We know your parents. Your older brother Morris[3] was my best friend! How dare you collaborate with them?

---

2. Based on Mundek Łukawiecki's early oral descriptions of operations, later confirmed by Maurie Hoffman, *Keep Yelling: A Survivor's Testimony* (Richmond, Australia: Spectrum Publications, 1995), 122–23. This encounter between the Jewish hit squad and Zisa was probably not the first. Hoffman writes in his book that Zisa was a prostitute in Biłgoraj.
3. Pseudonym.

You betrayed us all: your family, your friends, your faith, your people – all of us! Where is your responsibility as a Jew?"

Mundek continued to scream at Zisa. His stance was very threatening and his face was turning red. The more he screamed, the worse his temper became.

"The payment, the prize, the reward that you got from them was one bottle of vodka and one kilogram of sugar for every Jew you handed over! You should be executed as a traitor! You're a bitch's daughter! You are the devil herself!"

All the while, Mundek was circling Zisa and aiming a Parabellum pistol – which he had borrowed from Chana Bern – at her face.

Zisa had been brought to the hideout by the partisan team led by Berish Brand. They had found her during a routine patrol. Berish Brand told Mundek that when they came across Zisa, she had seemed like a crazy person. One of Brand's team members, Isaac Helman, recognized Zisa as a Jewish girl from Lubaczów. She was the daughter of Rabbi Sholom Shochet,[4] a teacher at the local synagogue. She had a ten-month-old son, Fishel, and a husband named Lazar,[5] who was a blacksmith. When she was spotted by Berish Brand's team, she was talking to herself, making noises and singing Jewish prayers, almost as if she wanted to be caught.

Berish Brand and his team watched her as a precaution. They knew that the Gestapo and Ukrainian nationalists had undercover agents that infiltrated partisan groups. These undercover "partisans" were former Russian, Belorussian, and Ukrainian soldiers who were now attached to the German military, the so-called Waffen-SS. They were active in finding and turning over Jews.[6] The Gestapo also hired country men and women to infiltrate groups in hiding and turn them over.

---

4. Pseudonym.
5. Pseudonym.
6. See Dieter Pohl, *Nationalsozialistische Judenverfolgung in Ostgalizien, 1941–1944: Organisation und Durchführung eines staatlichen Massenverbrechens* [National Socialist persecution of the Jews in Eastern Galicia, 1941–1944: Organization and implementation of a state mass crime] (Munich: Oldenbourg Verlag, 1997), pp. 368–73. Pohl describes in detail the complex situation of the Jews after deportation, from autumn 1942 until liberation. He writes that the Jewish partisans faced nearly total isolation while patrols and roundups of German gendarmerie (a militarized police force) and so-called *Truppenpolizei* (mobile police units) searched for Jews in the forests. Polish criminal police and Ukrainian Auxiliary Police did the same. If discovered, Jews were usually killed on the spot. The searches were mostly sparked by denunciations. Other Jews were killed within the framework of the general war on the partisans, also in collaboration with the Wehrmacht units.

Zisa Stein serving food to the partisans group, summer 1944. This is the only extant picture of Zisa.

As a reward, they were given one kilogram of sugar[7] and one bottle of vodka for every Jew that was brought in, as was also the practice of the German police.[8]

Brand's team followed Zisa for a couple of days before approaching her. When they finally spoke to her, she told them that her parents, siblings, and husband had been shot down by the Germans and Ukrainians. They were killed as part of a massacre on January 6, 1943, near Dachnów. She explained that she and her son had escaped by pretending to be dead in a ditch. They had stayed there all day, covered by the bodies of Jews who had just been murdered. Every time she heard the words *"Feuer! Feuer!"* (Fire! Fire!),[9] more bodies came rolling down into the ditch. The bodies that fell on her and the blood that spilled on her kept her and little Fishel warm. It helped to keep them alive, although at the time she wasn't sure if Fishel was still breathing. She didn't dare move for what seemed like an eternity. The air was full of screaming, crying, shouting, and gunfire. She thought this must be what hell sounded like.

---

7. For more on sugar as a reward, see also Isaac Kowalski, ed., *Anthology on Armed Jewish Resistance, 1939–1945* (New York: Jewish Combatants Publishers House, 1991), vol. 4, p. 63.
8. The German police under the General Government also paid rewards for Jews.
9. The command for the firing squad to open fire.

Zisa continued her story and told the partisans how she had escaped at nightfall. After overhearing some women who were looking for loot, she realized that the massacre was over. Zisa stood up, pushed the dead bodies off herself, and realized that Fishel was still alive! They hid in her town, Lubaczów, for a little while, until a Polish neighbor informed the Gestapo of her whereabouts. The Gestapo imprisoned her, but she escaped, leaving Fishel behind. She now told the partisans that she didn't care about being caught. She just wanted Fishel to be safe. She missed him more than anyone could understand.

Berish and his team were unsure whether to believe Zisa or not. Parts of her story, which she stuck to consistently, sounded true, and other parts sounded like a bunch of lies. What mother would escape prison but leave her little boy behind?

Isaac Helman left the group to inform Mundek about Zisa. Upon hearing that she was Jewish, Mundek ordered that she be brought to the hideout. To Mundek, the thought that a Jew could work for the Gestapo was unimaginable.

Zisa was starving when the partisans found her. Upon arriving at the camp, they immediately fed her potatoes and bread and gave her something to drink. The next morning Mundek, Berish Brand, and his deputy Anshel Bogner questioned her. This time Mundek heard her entire story. Although she didn't change her story once, Zisa could tell that they didn't believe her.

Mundek wanted to find out if she was telling the truth, so he left that night to speak to one of his contacts. Before leaving, Mundek told Chana to make Zisa help with the food preparation and that he would be gone for two nights. He left Bogner in charge until his return, instructing him not to let Zisa out of his sight and not to let her escape; if she tried, he was to shoot her.

Józef Kulpa was Mundek's contact in the Polish resistance group Związek Walki Zbrojnej (ZWZ; Union of Armed Struggle), which later became the Armia Krajowa (AK; Home Army), and was the person who had enlisted Mundek into the ZWZ.[10] He was a Polish nationalist who opposed Communism, the USSR, and the Germans. Kulpa was thirty-five years old. Although not a tall man, he nevertheless gave an impression of sturdiness; he had wide shoulders with a

---

10. Kulpa enlisted Mundek in the AK's predecessor organization, the Związek Walki Zbrojnej (ZWZ; Union for Armed Struggle), in 1940, prior to the formation of the AK. See chapter 3, "*Czyn*."

Józef Kulpa, 1940

square-shaped head, a firm jaw, and a high, wide forehead. His smooth, black hair was combed back.

Kulpa was a Polish-Christian peasant and a family friend and business associate of Mundek's grandparents, Hersh and Dora Łukawiecki, who owned a farm not far away from Kulpa's farm in Ostrowiec. Kulpa was a hard worker and had a very successful farm. Life as a farmer had hardened Kulpa's character and developed his courage and tolerance for risk. He was guided by a sense of justice, honesty, and fairness. Kulpa was also a much-respected member of his community and acted as the head of the Ostrowiec community. As a result, he had an excellent relationship with the German-established local authorities of Lubaczów, formed by the administration of the General Government as well as the Gestapo. At the same time, Kulpa was considered to have true Polish loyalties because he hated the Germans, Ukrainians, and Soviets. Moreover, he was a member of the Polish underground and the ZWZ.

Mundek left on his own for Kulpa's farm that evening. This was standard procedure. No one in Mundek's partisan group knew who Kulpa was; they only knew his name.

Józef Kulpa at his farm in Ostrowiec, 1933

Kulpa's farm, in Ostrowiec, was about forty kilometers (twenty-five miles) southwest of Mundek's location in the Janowskie woods. Mundek had to walk alone through the woods the entire night to reach it. The trees were not much taller than Mundek. He took extra precaution as he walked, stepping very gently but with long, fast, quiet steps. He barely left a footprint; it was as if he never actually touched the snow but merely hovered above it. He also never used the same path twice. He used all the skills he had learned as a teenager when, for two summers, he underwent military training with the Polish Sixth Corps, a regular corps of the pre-WWII Polish military force, whose headquarters were deployed in Lwów.

Mundek was fully armed. Due to the snowy winter, he wore an additional heavy Russian military overcoat. The moon was out and there were no clouds in the sky, making it easier to see. From time to time, he would stop and scan the area with his binoculars. It was a very quiet night, apart from the sound that his footsteps made in the melting snow. The Gestapo no longer dared to walk in these woods. The Ukrainians and other civilians preferred to keep warm on such a night, rather than be outside in the forest. Mundek moved as fast as was humanly possible in order to reach Kulpa's farm by dawn. He felt that sunrise was the best time to speak with Kulpa. As he continued his long journey, Mundek imagined drinking a nice, warm glass of fresh milk from one of Kulpa's cows.

After six strenuous hours, Mundek finally arrived at Kulpa's farm. It was still dark. Mundek stood about seven hundred meters away, at the edge of the Niwki woods. He did not want the dogs and other animals to smell him and give away his location.

The farm had two buildings, a house and a barn, which were about fifty meters from each other. The house was at the front of the farm while the barn was south,

Wedding photo of Józef Kulpa and his wife Rozali, 1920

toward the forest. The house was relatively small, with three rooms. Kulpa and his wife occupied one room, while his mother had a room to herself. The last room was shared by Kulpa's three teenaged sons, Czesław, Jan, and Stanisław. There was a narrow hallway that led to the rooms. Behind the house was an outhouse – a small hut with a toilet.

The barn was a very long building used to store equipment and to house six cows and two horses. Both the house and the barn were brown-gray and made entirely of mud, straw, and wooden logs. The buildings consisted of a single floor and a roof layered with straw and covered in mud and *papa*. *Papa* was the local name for a sort of tar paper that prevented water from seeping into the building. The hinges were made by the local blacksmith. There was no electricity or running water.

At this hour, the house was very quiet and dark, with gray smoke rising from the chimney. Mundek scoured the area to make sure there were no Gestapo or police around. He saw Kulpa's wife and mother carrying two buckets of water. The sky started to get brighter and then the door opened and Kulpa left the house, holding a gasoline lamp. As Kulpa walked energetically to the cowshed, Mundek knocked on the barrel of his Česká zbrojovka rifle once with a bullet. He paused and then knocked twice. He paused again and knocked once more. This was their agreed signal.

Kulpa didn't appear to recognize the knocking. He didn't freeze or show any reaction at all. He just continued walking to the cowshed. He opened the cowshed gate and went inside. After a few moments, he returned with a bucket and placed it upside down next to the gate before disappearing back into the cowshed. It looked as if the bucket was meant to block the gate. This was the sign Mundek had been waiting for; it was Kulpa's acceptance of his signal.

Mundek ran through the shadows quickly and slipped into the cowshed. Kulpa was waiting for him deep inside it. They hugged like a father and son who hadn't seen each other for years. Kulpa gave Mundek a change of dry clothes and took the wet ones from him to be dried. He gave Mundek a huge jug of fresh milk. It was warm just as Mundek had imagined, and he drank it in one gulp. Kulpa gave Mundek food from the cowshed so that his family, who were waiting for him to get breakfast, would not become suspicious.

Mundek did not waste any time telling Kulpa about Zisa. He needed confirmation. Mundek asked if Kulpa could verify her story. Kulpa promised to visit the Ukrainian chief of auxiliary police in Lubaczów that day after the morning work on the farm was done. He instructed Mundek to stay at the farm and wait for him to return. After Kulpa left, Mundek made himself comfortable and fell into a deep sleep at the back of the barn.

Kulpa returned in the late afternoon with an answer. He had met with the chief of police, who told him that Zisa was an informer for the German Gestapo in Sokal, whose jurisdiction also included Lubaczów. She had been released from prison in Sokal under the condition that she bring back Jews who were hiding in the woods. Kulpa also learned that Zisa had been a prostitute for the Germans for the past two years in Bilgoraj.[11] Zisa was out on her second mission as an informer. On her first mission, she had successfully brought back a family of five – the Steinbruchs – who were hiding in the Płazów forest. For each family member, she received a bottle of vodka and a kilogram of sugar.

The Ukrainian chief of police also told Kulpa that the Gestapo had promised to keep Zisa's son Fishel safe and unharmed as long as she continued to be their informer. The chief of police told Kulpa that he knew all of this information because Fishel was currently staying with one of his Ukrainian Auxiliary Police officers, and the officer had handed in some of the baby's clothes, saying he did not want himself or his family to be contaminated by bad spirits. This time, however, Zisa's orders were to infiltrate a big, dangerous, and aggressive group of Jewish partisans, consisting mainly of Jews from Lubaczów, who were avoiding contact with Russian partisans that supported Germany[12] and with the Ukrainian Bandera partisans.[13] Kulpa added that the Gestapo chief had promised to release her and Fishel if she provided enough information to lead the authorities to this Jewish group, but emphasized that promises made by the police, such as this one, were not always kept.[14]

Mundek sat in shock and bewilderment. Kulpa couldn't look at him. After some time, Mundek became restless and started asking questions. He was not aware that he kept repeating, "How could she do it?" out loud. He seemed to have lost his mind.

---

11. Hoffman, *Keep Yelling*, 123.
12. Russian soldiers who were in German service as counter-partisan groups aimed to hunt down partisans. They were of much concern to Mundek Łukawiecki. There is a German combat report concerning the Lublin area in which an "accident" is mentioned; German police shot at their own *Gegenbande* (counter-partisan group).
13. Stepan Andriyovych Bandera (Організація Українських Націоналістів) was the Ukrainian head of the nationalist Organization of Ukrainian Nationalists (OUN). Apart from its nationalist ideology, it was antisemitic and cooperated fully with the Nazis, carrying out many atrocities against Jews. To describe the OUN, Mundek Łukawiecki used the word *Banderowcy* (Bandera's men), which was widely used as a term of disgrace.
14. For more on Jewish collaboration, see Richard C. Lukas, *Forgotten Holocaust: The Poles under German Occupation, 1939–1944*, rev. ed. (New York: Hippocrene Books, 2005), 118. For another type of cooperation, see Brian Mark Rigg, *Hitler's Jewish Soldiers: The Untold Story of Nazi Racial Laws and Men of Jewish Descent in the German Military* (Lawrence: University Press of Kansas, 2002).

"Are you absolutely sure of this?" Mundek asked.

"He showed me the baby clothes that Zisa left," Kulpa answered. "One of the items had a small yarmulke, with the Star of David embroidered on it."

"Who is taking care of the baby?"

"The wife of the Ukrainian Auxiliary Police officer," Kulpa replied in a whisper. "She is breastfeeding her own baby as well."

"Why, when they will kill both of them anyway?" Mundek wondered.

"Yes, but they want to use her as long as possible," Kulpa explained. "So they will keep him alive as long as she is instrumental to them. They cannot force her without the baby. When she dies, they will kill him as well."

Mundek realized that his group might have already been massacred by the Germans and Ukrainians. Partisan life was extremely difficult. There was constant fear of being killed at any moment.[15] He quickly changed back into his uniform and told Kulpa that he must return to his hideout immediately. It was already dark out when Mundek ran into the woods. He alternated between running and walking as fast as he possibly could. His heart was beating like a drum. He was crying and kept mumbling, "What have I done? I must save them." Mundek kept imagining that his group had all been killed. He felt that he had betrayed their trust and let them down. He pictured them having all been captured and executed by the Nazis, imagining that Zisa had been awarded thirteen kilograms of sugar and thirteen bottles of vodka.

Mundek was no longer hiking. He took the shortest path possible back to the hideout, ignoring all the usual precautions.

It was slightly drizzling and a little before dawn when Mundek finally approached his hideout. The only thing he could think was, "Are they all right? Or have they already been captured by the Nazis?" He did not make the usual owl calls but rushed into the center of the hideout. How relieved he was when he saw a Česká zbrojovka rifle aiming at him! His group was unharmed! The partisan who was on guard started yelling in shock, "I almost killed you!" before swearing at Mundek in uncontrollable anger.

Mundek headed straight for Zisa and grabbed her by the hair. He dragged her to the center of the circle. Between her whimpers, she tried to answer Mundek's

---

15. Personal interview with Miriam Marcus, March 27, 2012, quoting Chana Bern. Miriam, a Holocaust survivor, met Mundek Łukawiecki in Israel.

questions. But Zisa could barely speak; she was sobbing hysterically to the point where she was having trouble breathing. On her knees before Mundek and the rest of the group, she began pleading.

"I am sorry! I beg your pardon. I deserve to die, but they are holding my boy, my Fishel. I had no choice. They killed my husband and my family. They were going to kill Fishel if I didn't cooperate!"

Her sobbing was heartbreaking, but it was not helping her cause. The partisans felt no sympathy or sadness for her.

Suddenly, Mundek snapped, "What about the Steinbruch family?" Mundek didn't wait for an answer; he continued to scream at her, blaming her for disclosing information to the Gestapo about the Steinbruch family in the Płazów forest that led to their capture and execution.

Zisa looked as if she had seen a ghost as Mundek told the group about her first mission and explained that this was her second. He also told them about her reward for informing the Gestapo of their whereabouts. She collapsed and fainted momentarily. The partisans were paralyzed and speechless. They realized that they were on the verge of death because of Zisa. They also realized that the Gestapo had sent somebody to find and capture them, using a Jewish girl to try to fulfill their goal. They now realized that they were a direct target of the Gestapo.

Mundek lost control as though he was possessed by a demon. Normally, he adopted the manners and politeness of a Polish nobleman. But when he lost his temper, another side of his character was exposed.[16]

He started screaming, "You told us the story of Dachnów to get our sympathy. My family was massacred there. Chana's family was shot down there. We saw it with our own eyes, from the woods. After the Germans killed my brother, they kicked his body down the trench because it didn't roll fast enough. I saw it. I saw it! We couldn't help them. Now, when we can help each other, you're handing us over to the Nazis and the Ukrainians. They will kill you and your son anyway! You stupid Jew. You are a disgrace to Jews. You are worse than the Germans and the Ukrainians. They are our enemies. But you, you are part of our blood! You are not true blood. You are poison, intoxicating us from the inside secretly. I will kill you. I will kill you, you bitch!"

---

16. Personal interview with Miriam Marcus, March 27, 2012.

As time passed, it became colder and colder. Mundek turned to the group and asked hysterically, "What should we do with her? Should we kill her?"

Zisa spoke up and started begging for her life. Everyone was still in shock as the sun rose with its penetrating rays, accompanied by clouds, and not long after, heavy gray rain. It was a new morning as the cold wind blew. Zisa lay down in the mud with her body stretched out, her face in her hands and her chest heaving up and down.

"Please save my life. I will not tell them I found you. I will conceal this secret for the rest of my life. I will keep it with me even if I have to give my life for it!" she begged.

But nobody trusted her empty promises.

After some silence, Anshel Bogner asked her, "How can we trust your promise?"

"For your safety, you can also change the forest you are hiding in," she suggested.

Anshel's question dramatically influenced Mundek. Being the leader of the group, Mundek felt a huge relief. Somebody was sharing the responsibility for their lives. Mundek sat down in the mud and started to cry out of anger and sorrow. He couldn't bear the fact that a Jewish girl had collaborated with the Nazis.

The partisans were amazed that their captain was crying. Suddenly, all of their attention turned to Mundek. Zisa also stared at Mundek disbelievingly. She then realized that no one was paying attention to her. In a split-second decision, she sprang up and started running as fast as she could! Mundek and the partisans reacted quickly and chased after her. Mundek's pistol and Anshel Bogner's and Berish Brand's Česká zbrojovka rifles were all pointed in her direction as she fled. When Zisa was about twelve meters in front of them, Mundek aimed and fired a single shot. Zisa collapsed. She was dead. They approached her, out of breath and speechless as blood poured out of her head. After a few moments, they returned to the group and reported her death.

The group crawled into their tents and those on guard duty started to patrol the area again. The silence in the camp could be cut with a knife. The atmosphere turned very gray.

Mundek didn't get any rest that morning. At noon, he left his tent and told the group to pack everything up; they were relocating. The Nazis probably knew of the Puszcza Solska forest hideout now because of Zisa. He also told them that on the way to the new hideout, they would give Zisa a proper Jewish burial.

Mundek's orders were always obeyed without question. He was a very accomplished and efficient leader, and he expected everyone to be flawless in executing his commands because they could not afford to make a single mistake. He told Berger to prepare a stretcher for Zisa. He then crawled back into his shelter. He kept thinking about the morning's events over and over again in his mind. He could not come to terms with the fact that he had taken two lives: Zisa's and her baby's. He suddenly felt confused and remorseful. He began thinking of his little sister, Judith. For the second time that day, tears streamed down his face as he cried out loud. He was only twenty-two years old, yet he had already seen so much horror.

Chana, who shared the tent with Mundek, hugged him silently. She didn't say a single word. Her life experience had taught her to be strong. She did not feel anything for Zisa. After a few moments, with no more tears to shed and utterly exhausted, Mundek fell asleep. Chana left their shelter and started to pack up all their gear and equipment before joining the others. Everyone in the group had their private belongings, as well as group items. No conversations took place as everything was packed. Before Berger completed his packing, he prepared the stretcher.

Two hours later, Mundek awoke from his restless sleep. He jumped out of the shelter and looked around to see what his partisans were doing. Without a word, he went to Chana and started to help her pack. In the late afternoon, Mundek went to Anshel and informed him that they would be marching in combat formation. Mundek and Anshel would be leading the group to protect them from any attacks. Departure was set for five o'clock in the afternoon and that meant they would need to scout the area at four o'clock to make sure that it was safe to leave. They would also need to camouflage any signs of the fact that they had ever been there.

Mundek's orders were executed precisely. Two partisans carried Zisa's body. She was underweight and therefore easy to carry. The rest of the partisans lined up behind the stretcher. Nobody asked where they were going; they trusted that Mundek knew what he was doing.

The weather that evening was awful. It was a fierce and blustery cold snowstorm. After walking for an hour in complete silence, Mundek heard someone singing softly behind him. It was Isaac Helman, one of the youngest members of the partisan group, and one of those holding the stretcher. Isaac was familiar

Chana's siddur

Title page of Chana's siddur

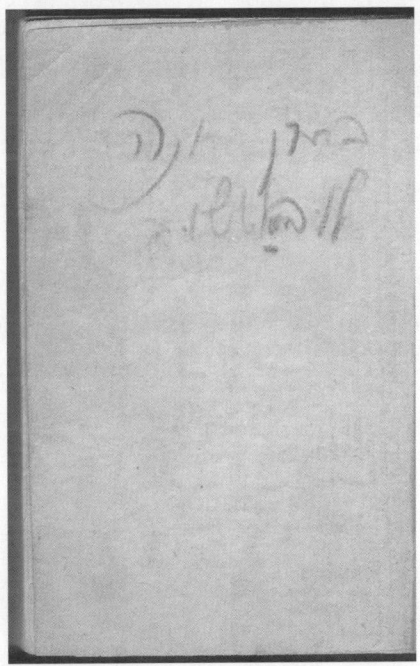

Chana's handwriting in Yiddish on the inside of the siddur: "Bern Chana, Lubaczów"

with Jewish prayers. He was whispering the Kaddish, a Jewish mourning prayer. Mundek stopped and listened for a moment. The familiar tune touched him and he thought, "Using Jewish funeral prayers might be a proper way to tell Zisa that we aren't judging her, nor blaming her, and that she is forgiven." And so, in spite of the fact that he was unfamiliar with the words of the prayer, Mundek hummed along with the tune as best as he could.[17] That night, during a blinding snowstorm, a parade of Jewish partisans carried a Jewish spy who had collaborated with the Nazis, in order to give her a proper Jewish burial in a Jewish cemetery.

After walking for eight hours from the Janowskie woods, the partisans arrived at the Jewish cemetery of Lubaczów on Tadeusza Kościuszki Street. Mundek and Bogner made sure that the cemetery was clear. Then the partisans went in. One of them knew where Zisa's family was buried. They found the area and a small, empty plot to bury her beside them.

The soil was frozen and as hard as rock when Mundek began to dig. They all took turns digging. After about two hours, at around four o'clock in the morning, the grave was ready. Isaac Helman, being the most knowledgeable in Jewish ceremonies, conducted the service the best he could. After burying the body, Isaac hummed the Yizkor prayer, imploring God to remember the soul and protect it, and asking for forgiveness for Zisa's soul. He then asked for forgiveness on behalf of the group if they had insulted or abused her. A wooden sign with Zisa's name, prepared by Chana, was placed on Zisa's grave by Chana herself. Then, to the surprise of everyone, Chana stood and quoted a sentence from the Bible: "Every man shall be put to death for his own sin."[18]

By four thirty, the ceremony was over. It was a half hour that none of them would ever forget. And it was what all of them thought about as they began the journey to their next location in the Mariarmia woods.[19]

---

17. Personal interview with Isaac Helman, February 3, 2010.
18. 2 Kings 16:6.
19. From Mundek's biographical information form in his UB file, filled out by Mundek Łukawiecki on April 6, 1946. UB personal file of Mundek Łukawiecki, IPN/OBUiAd/Kraków, Sygn IPN 16 057/1028.

Chapter 2
The Jackals Are Howling

Shimon Bern was born Szymon Cieszanówer[1] in Narol, a small town very close to Lubaczów. His father Benjamin (Binem) was religious and a follower of the Rabbi of Belż.[2] Benjamin married Chana and the couple had three children: Shimon, the eldest, followed by a second son, Wolf (Zeev), and a mute daughter, Gittel (Tova).[3]

During World War I, Shimon wanted to be drafted into the Austro-Hungarian Imperial Army in line with the Jewish law that requires a person to be faithful to his country of residence, and also in light of the German origin of his family. He was rejected due to poor health, but his younger brother Wolf was enlisted. Shimon then decided to emigrate to the United States, as he felt that he had no future under the Austro-Hungarian monarchy. To ease his anticipated integration into the United States, he changed his surname from Cieszanówer to Bern. When seeing him off at the train station, however, his mother Chana fainted. Shimon got off the train and cancelled his emigration plans. He did not return to Narol, but remained in Lubaczów.

After World War I, Wolf Cieszanówer returned safely home from the army and went back to Narol. He and his brother Shimon both married and named their first daughters after their beloved mother, Chana, who by then had passed away at a very young age.[4] Their father remarried a widow from the nearby town

---

1. The anglicized form is Czeszanower.
2. Interview of Isaac Helman, on February 6, 2011. Belz is a Hasidic dynasty named after the town of Belz, today within Ukraine, about eighty-five kilometers (fifty-five miles) from Lubaczów.
3. Personal interview with Chana Diner, January 29, 2011.
4. Chana Cieszanówer, Wolf's daughter and the first cousin of Chana Bern, married Joseph Zvi Diner in Germany in 1946, and her name became Chana Diner.

of Cieszanów, who also had two boys and a daughter. The name of one of the boys was Isaac.[5]

Shimon Bern married Gittel Katz from Lubaczów in 1919.[6] Born in 1890 to Jonas Katz and Henye (Henny) Reichenthal from Ludwigburg, Germany, Gittel was the only daughter among four sons:[7] Herman, who was born in Lubaczów on December 22, 1880;[8] Isaac, who was born on January 27, 1886;[9] Moritz,[10] who was born on February 19, 1896;[11] and Abraham, who was born in 1900 and died of epilepsy on May 5, 1918.[12] The family ran a shoe shop.[13]

After their marriage, Shimon and Gittel bought a small, two-story building

---

5. Personal interview with Chana Diner, January 29, 2011.
6. Oddly the municipal records in Lubaczów indicate that Shimon Bern declares that he married Gittel in 1938. The Jews regularly gave false information to the authorities for various reasons.
7. Lubaczów municipal records death record no. 37, December 1, 1921, recording the death of Herman's first wife Henia.
8. Stuttgart municipal records FR-Bd. 27-200.
9. Stuttgart municipal records FR-Bd. 25-52; Esslingen municipal records Fam. Reg. 25 B-52.
10. Despite what is written in Maria Zelzer, *Weg und Schicksal der Stuttgarter Juden* [The path and fate of Stuttgart's Jews] (Stuttgart: Ernst Klett Verlag, 1964), p. 478, he escaped to the US in 1938.
11. Stuttgart municipal records FR-Bd. 27-198, Bd. 232 5.304; Esslingen municipal records Fam. Reg. 27 198.
12. Lubaczów municipal records.
13. They lived in the Stuttgart area in southwest Germany, first in the city of Karlsruhe and after that in Esslingen on Moerike Street; after a while they moved twenty-five kilometers (fifteen miles) north to Ludwigsburg, where they lived at 14 Martin Luther Strasse and ran shoe shops at 18/1 Seesstrasse and 8/1 Koerner Strasse. Herman Katz and his second wife Selma were deported at the end of October 1938 by the Gestapo to the German-Polish border and forced to cross. In Poland they went to Lubaczów and lived with Herman's sister Gittel Katz Bern's family until all of them were executed in Dachnów in January 1943. Morris (Moritz) Katz managed to escape to the US and Isaac emigrated to Palestine in 1937. The Polenaktion, the deportation of twelve to seventeen thousand Polish Jews to the German-Polish border, dispatched deportation trains ending in three cities in western Poland (Zbąszynek [called Neu Bentschen in German], Bytom [Beuthen], and Chojnice [Konitz]). The Jews had to walk further into Poland. Polish authorities assisted the distribution of the deportees within Poland or to other countries. The action was stopped by the German government after Poland threatened to deport Polish Germans to Germany. From Stuttgart, Jews were deported by train to Zbąszynek. Most probably Jews of Ludwigsburg were part of this deportation. The Polish consul general in Munich protested in Stuttgart at the Staatsministerium in vain. The train left Stuttgart on the night of October 28, 1938. See Roland Müller, *Stuttgart zur Zeit des Nationalsozialismus* [Stuttgart in the time of National Socialism] (Tübingen: Konrad Theiss Verlag, 1988), p. 301.

Shimon Bern's former house, February 24, 2010. The current owners refused to reveal their name, but stated that they purchased the house from the Polish Center for Missing People.

in Lubaczów at 2 Józefa Piłsudskiego Street, on the corner of Adam Mickiewicza Street. Like the apartment the Łukawieckis would later rent, this property faced the local prison and court of law, and would eventually be part of the ghetto. The Berns operated a wholesale textile store on the ground floor and lived on the floor above it. They had four children: Abraham Joel, who was born on January 8, 1920, and died eight months later in September 1920; Chana, born July 15, 1921; Hanoch, born April 21, 1923; and Henye, born October 18, 1926.[14]

The mother tongue spoken by the Bern family was German. The family was well established and their textile business was successful. They imported textile goods and leather products from Germany and developed very strong commercial ties in Lwów, the old capital of Galicia in the foothills of the Carpathian Mountains and an important trade route between Vienna and Kiev. Because the family was well traveled, especially to Germany, the children became well aware of the world around them. At the same time, however, they strictly observed their religion. They obediently attended synagogue, which was opposite their

---

14. Lubaczów municipal records.

house on Adam Mickiewicza Street. Shimon also worked part-time as a religious studies teacher, while Gittel and Chana minded the shop.[15]

Shimon was always generous to the Jewish community and would routinely donate to it. The family commonly hosted guests on Friday nights for the Sabbath meal. Shimon kept himself in good condition and was known for his wispy blonde beard. His blue eyes were always smiling. He dressed in traditional male Jewish style with black trousers, a long black coat over a white shirt, a black tie, and a black hat. He followed the Belzer Rebbe[16] in word and in deed. Gittel and the other married women of the family wore their headscarves meticulously.

Gittel Katz Bern was a distant relative of the Łukawiecki family. They had originally been the Cohen family, but at the beginning of the nineteenth century, they had changed their name to Łukawiecki so that they would not be identified as Jews, particularly in business. There was already prevailing antisemitism even before the war, and they felt they must conceal their Jewish origin in order to keep their businesses viable. Moses and Chaja (née Weinberg) Cohen originally lived in the small German town of Luckau before moving to Rudzienko,[17] near Kałuszyn. From there they moved about fifty kilometers (thirty miles) east to Kopcie, in the Węgrowski region of Poland, a German-speaking area under the control of the Austro-Hungarian monarchy from 1875 until 1915, when the Russians took control of it. It was upon their arrival in Kopcie that the family changed their name to Łukawiecki[18] and started a successful wholesale trade business and chain of distilleries.

At the time, the family was religious and made sure to educate their children in the ways of Judaism. This strict education was passed on to the grandchildren as well. All of them attended the Yiddishe Schule (Jewish School)[19] regularly (although some of the youngsters were not enthusiastic and it was a constant fight). Their lives were immersed in religion and they participated in religious services in their synagogue and at home. As time passed, however, and the family's

---

15. Personal interview with Isaac Helman, June 2, 2011.
16. Personal interview with Isaac Helman, June 2, 2011.
17. Just southeast of Mińsk Mazowiecki.
18. In this region, there was a small town named Łuków. Therefore, the name change enabled them to perfectly camouflage themselves and not identify their Jewish origin. It was a coincidence that Hersh Wolf Łukawiecki later moved to a small farming area called Mielniki near a town called Łukawiec.
19. In German, *Schule* means "school," but in Yiddish *shul* translates into "synagogue."

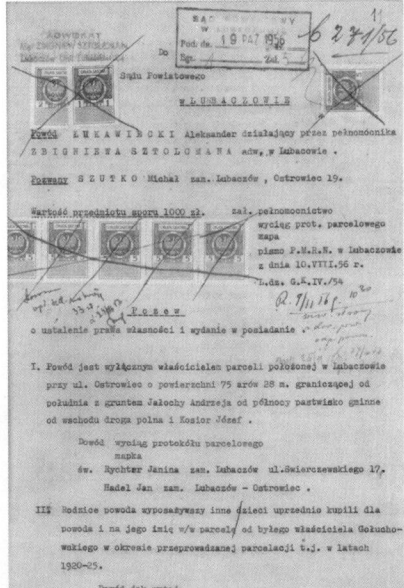 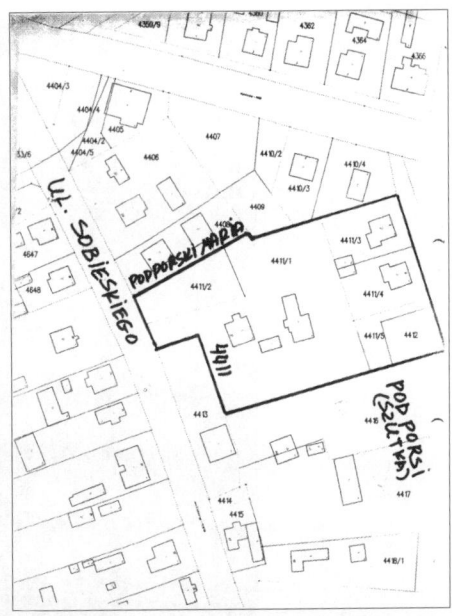

Court order of sale of farm in 1956 by Aleksander Łukawiecki to Michal Szutko. The court case concerned the removal of the ruins of the farmhouse.

Drawing of the location of the farm in Ostrowiec

wealth grew, some of the grandchildren rejected their strict religious upbringing. Bitter disputes ensued, resulting in an outright refusal to attend synagogue services anymore – and in one case, conversion to Christianity.

Of Moses and Chaja's sons, two of them – Hersh Wolf and Shmuel David – left the Węgrowski region to live elsewhere. The older son, Hersh Wolf (Velvale) Łukawiecki and his wife Dora went to live in Mielniki, which is next to Łukawiec, a small town south of Lubaczów. Their son Joseph was born there on February 2, 1892. A number of years later, Hersh bought a farm in the Ostrowiec suburb two kilometers southeast of Lubaczów – and moved there.[20] Being a wealthy family, the Łukawieckis adopted a son, Aleksander,[21] who was born in Sielce on July 4, 1901. Aleksander was adopted at a young age[22] and was treated like another son

---

20. Plot 17 located in Lubaczów, numbered 3492, 3493, of a total area of seventy-five dunam, or about a third of a square mile. Today it is plot number 4411, according to maps and documents concerning the sale.
21. His Jewish name was Menachem Mendel; he was called Mendel.
22. Court documents confirming the sale of the farm by Aleksander Łukawiecki identify him as "the son of Henryk and Dorota." Henryk is Hersh and Dorota is Dora.

Shmuel David Łukawiecki, brother of the author's great-grandfather Hersh Łukawiecki, with his first wife, Sara Mor Łukawiecki (1879–1919), and their daughter Leiba (Ahuva), born 1903

by Hersh and Dora, although it is unclear whether he was adopted formally and whether he was born to a Jewish family.

Hersh's younger brother, Shmuel David, and his first wife Sara ("Sarka," née Mor) went to live in the small town of Rudzienko, not far from Kałuszyn, and from there they moved to Grochów, a small town about six kilometers (just under four miles) from the center of Warsaw.[23] After a few years in Grochów, they moved nearby to another small town just outside of Warsaw called Gocław, where they lived on Grzybowska Street.[24] From there, they moved again to the Praga suburb of Warsaw, residing at 10 Brzeska Street.

Shmuel David's son, also named Joseph, was born in Praga on November 11, 1896. His parents married him off when he was twenty, but he subsequently left his wife when she was pregnant. In 1917, he was conscripted into the Polish army. He was one of a number of Jewish recruits who were loaded onto a truck and

---

23. Today it is a northeastern suburb of Warsaw.
24. It was a small town; today it is within the Warsaw district.

sent to an army camp. The trip was very long and they were not given any food or water the entire journey. They arrived at the camp in complete darkness. Two lines of soldiers forced the new recruits to run for hours on end, while other soldiers beat them.

Before entering their barracks, the recruits were informed that there were mattresses on the floor. When they entered, however, they discovered that all the mattresses had been stolen and therefore they would have to spend the night sleeping on the cold floor. Joseph sat against the wall in the dark. He spent his time thinking, analyzing his situation. He decided that army life wasn't for him. If Polish soldiers abused them, he thought, just imagine what enemy soldiers would do if he were captured.

So, in the middle of the night, he crept through a hole in the fence and disappeared into the darkness. He spent the next four months making his way to his Uncle Hersh's house in Mielniki. Because he was a deserter, he had to travel by night and hide during the day.

Hersh and Dora Łukawiecki took care of their nephew until he regained his strength. When he was ready to make his way, he procured some money from his uncle and bought a ticket to Palestine. In 1920, he made his way across the Black Sea aboard a ship named the *Aloan* via Turkey and Egypt (Alexandria), finally landing at the port of Haifa on January 27, 1920. The first thing he did when he arrived was to change his name from Łukawiecki back to Cohen.

In Palestine, Joseph Cohen became a successful businessman. He ran a metal bed factory at 34 Hashuk Street in Tel Aviv and owned other real estate properties throughout the city. Early on, he lived on the premises of his factory, but later he bought a brand-new apartment on 53 Herzl Street in Tel Aviv.[25]

By 1928, he had convinced his father Shmuel David Łukawiecki, his brother Zvi Łukawiecki,[26] and his sister Leiba Łukawiecki (now Zilberman) to bring their families to Palestine and settle there as well. On June 28, 1935, his young son Moshe, who was born from his short marriage to his first wife, also sailed

---

25. Then Palestine.
26. He left for England with his wife Shoshanna, the daughter of Mr. Narodiczky, a respected Zionist in London who owned a printing business and printed the reports of the Jewish Congress. After several years he returned to Palestine. In Haifa, he adopted a boy, David, May 23, 1934, while on the ship *Sphinx*.

there on the aptly named ship *Palestine*. Upon their arrival, all of them changed their names from Łukawiecki back to Cohen.

Throughout this time, Shmuel David's branch of the family strictly kept the Jewish laws, while Hersh Wolf's branch became more secular and Polish national in line with the spirit of liberalism that prevailed at the time.

Hersh Wolf Łukawiecki was a trained chemical engineer. During World War I, he served as an officer in the Austro-Hungarian Imperial Army, which had combined with the Polish army; he was wounded in battle and lost one of his legs. Two of his sons also served in the Polish army during World War I; Joseph served as an officer, and another son was killed in the line of duty.

After the war, Hersh was rewarded for his service by being allowed to own and operate a chain of distilleries.[27] This was a remarkable privilege for a Jewish family. The business grew and the family soon owned distilleries in Lwów

Certificate issued by the Institute of the Fermentation Industry in Warsaw on July 17, 1925, stating that Joseph Wolf Łukawiecki, born in 1892 in the Lubaczów district, attended a three-week course in alcohol distillery management

(the center of operations), Mielniki, Ostrowiec, Cieszanów, Oleszyce, and Stryj, where they also owned a sawmill.

Hersh's son Joseph Łukawiecki followed in his father's footsteps and completed university in Vienna, majoring in chemistry and biochemistry. He also

---

27. The family's nickname was Gorzelnicy, from the Polish word meaning "the owner of distilleries."

studied distillery plant management and subsequently became an engineer. In addition to helping his father run the various distilleries that the family owned, Joseph Łukawiecki became director-general of a distillery in Ruda Różaniecka that belonged to Baron Hugo Watmann,[28] a position he held from 1908 to 1914

Letter from Baron Hugo Watmann certifying on June 12, 1935, that Joseph Wolf Łukawiecki worked in his distillery in Ruda Różaniecka from 1908 to 1914 and 1923 to 1935 as manager of the distillery, to his complete satisfaction. The letter also states that Joseph is a qualified engineer of refining alcohol as well as grinding wheat and operating steam boilers.

and then again from 1923 to 1935. He also jointly owned a wholesale textile business with a partner named Mr. Rubin, located on 1 Furmańska Street in Lwów.[29]

The adopted son, Aleksander, attended elementóży school in Ostrowiec, where one of his classmates was the Łukawieckis' neighbor, Michał Szutka.[30] After completing his schooling, Aleksander did not at first continue in the same line of work as the Łukawieckis but worked as a town clerk in Lwów, where he lived alone at 36 Saint Theresa Street[31] in the fifth district of Lwów. However, after his marriage to Maria Skoropad in 1931, he moved to Kolonia Oficerska

---

28. The family of Baron Watmann was of Austrian origin from Vienna. They purchased a large area of land by auction in 1821. During the Austrian crown rule it belonged to the county of Lubaczów. Baron Watmann was the last owner of the land before it was nationalized in 1946. He passed away in Vienna that same year.
29. Lwów was the name at the time; today the city is Lviv, Ukraine.
30. I interviewed Maria Szutka, the daughter of Michał Szutka, in Ostrowiec on February 25, 2010.
31. Księga adresowa [phone book] Małopolski-Lwów-Stanisławów-Tarnopol Rocznik [for the years] 1935/1936, p. 239.

(the Officers' Colony), a district of Jarosław,[32] and joined the family business, managing the family distillery in Szówsko.[33]

Certificate issued on October 9, 1924, in Ruda Różaniecka by the inspectorate and control of steam boilers from Lwów that Joseph Łukawiecki, born in the Lubaczów district on February 2, 1892, completed a two-year practical internship course on Cornoval steam boilers and had passed the government examination on October 9, 1924, and he is certified to operate steam boilers.

Joseph Łukawiecki was a respected person. On Polish national holidays, he wore his officer's uniform, and after World War I, became a member of the right-wing Polish nationalist organization Strzelec,[34] which was part of the Legiony Polskie (Polish Legion). This was not unusual; Galicia was a stronghold of Jabotinsky's views, and Jews had a very positive attitude toward Polish patriotism.[35]

Joseph's wife Sarah Leah was born in a small town south of Lwów[36] named Żydaczów.[37] She was the daughter of Rebecca Nestel, who came from a very

---

32. Maria Szutka, at her taped interview in Ostrowiec on February 25, 2010, said that she visited them there.
33. Maria Szutka, taped interviews in Ostrowiec, February 25, 2010, and January 18, 2012.
34. Związek Strzelecki, a paramilitary organization. Its popular name was "Strzelec."
35. See Daniel Kupfert Heller, "The Rise of the Zionist Right: Polish Jews and the Betar Youth Movement, 1922–1935," a dissertation submitted to the Department of History and the Committee on Graduate Studies of Stanford University in partial fulfillment of the requirements for the degree of doctor of philosophy, August 2012, Stanford University, p. 246.
36. UB personal file of Mundek Łukawiecki – IPN/OBUiAd/Kraków, Sygn IPN 16 057/1028, and specifically the evaluation of Mundek Łukawiecki therein, dated October 12, 1945.
37. This is the Polish name by which the city was called pre-WWII. Today it is in Ukraine and the name is Zhydachiv. The Polish name means "place of Jews." The entire population was Jewish except for three policemen.

religious family, from her first marriage. It is unknown what happened to Rebecca's first husband, Sarah's father, but in any event Rebecca was remarried to the widower Jacob Gerstenfeld, and together they had a daughter, Ethel.[38] Sarah, like her mother, married twice; she had a first husband, Matityahu. It is unknown whether they divorced or he passed away; the only thing known about the union is that it produced no children, and that afterwards Sarah married Joseph Łukawiecki.[39] They lived in the small Subcarpathian town of Lubaczów, which begins on the banks of the Lubaczów River and merges with the Sołotwa River. Sarah was a housewife and her hobby was sewing. She was very friendly and helped Jewish women learn Polish whenever they were in need.

Edmund "Mundek" Łukawiecki was born on October 20, 1920,[40] and was given the Jewish name Matityahu.[41] The rest of Joseph and Sarah's children were born as follows: Zygmunt[42] on January 16, 1924; Rafael[43] on March 28, 1925; Mina[44] on September 30, 1926; and the youngest child, Judith-Ida,[45] on November 15, 1933.

---

38. Ethel Gerstenfeld's fate is unknown. The marriage between Rebecca Nestel and Jacob Gerstenfeld is something of a mystery, as Jacob Gerstenfeld did not come from a religious background, whereas Rebecca did, but details about their relationship (as well as Rebecca's first husband and his fate) are unknown.
39. If Sarah Leah was divorced from her first husband, her marriage to Joseph would be another proof that the Łukawieckis drifted from strict Jewish rules, as Joseph was a *cohen*, a member of the Jewish priestly class, who is forbidden to marry a divorcée. However, this seems unlikely, since Sarah Leah came from a religious family, and probably supports the theory that her first husband Matityahu died.
40. In the UB personal file of Mundek Łukawiecki – IPN/OBUiAd/Kraków, Sygn IPN 16 057/1028, March 8, 2011, CV dated 23.5.1945 and 6.4.1946 he stated that he was born on October 20, 1915. In his Israeli identification documents, however, he stated he was born on December 20, 1921.
41. The name's meaning is "gift of God." In Jewish history, the high priest Matityahu lent his name to the Maccabee dynasty, the rebels who led the revolt against the Seleucids in 165 BCE, as immortalized in the Chanukah story. The fact that the boy was named Mundek – the name of Sarah Leah's first husband – would seem to indicate that Sarah Leah's first husband passed away rather than that they divorced. Otherwise it seems surprising that her new husband wouldn't mind naming his son after his wife's ex-husband.
42. His Jewish name was Zalman.
43. His Jewish nickname was Fulek.
44. Her Jewish nickname was Minka and she was also called Onka.
45. Her Jewish nickname was Ida.

The Łukawieckis' former house on the farm in Ostrowiec, February 23, 2010. The left side was residential and the right the distillery. The land was divided into five parcels and now houses condominiums.

When he was young, Joseph Łukawiecki had worn *tzitzit*[46] and had *payot*,[47] but when he was older, he dropped everything and was no longer religious. This was in contrast to the Łukawiecki family in Warsaw, who were strictly religious and did not try to hide the fact that they were Jewish.

Joseph's wife Sarah was more observant than he was, as her father Jacob was very religious. She kept meat and milk separate in her kitchen and observed the Jewish festivals and holidays, such as Passover.[48] On Purim, she had Mundek deliver the traditional *mishloach manot* (special food packages) to family friends and associates, including her handmade triangular hamantaschen pastries.[49]

Nevertheless, the culture that prevailed at home was secular and Polish, and

---

46. A four-cornered garment with fringes worn by religious Jews in fulfillment of the requirement in Numbers 15:38 and Deuteronomy 22:12.
47. Sidelocks, in fulfillment of the order not to shave the "corners" of one's head, Leviticus 19:27.
48. They kept in the attic a special set of plates, cutlery, etc., for the Passover, not to be mixed with leavened food not permitted on Passover.
49. Food packages are sent to friends on the holiday of Purim in fulfillment of the verse in the Book of Esther 9:19.

the family were not religious. Joseph and Sarah spoke German between themselves but Polish with their children. The books that were read were written by authors such as Sienkiewicz and Mickiewicz. The children did attend the Jewish school, but only because it was near their house. On the Sabbath, Joseph Łukawiecki did not go to the synagogue unless his father-in-law Jacob Gerstenfeld was visiting. On the eve of Yom Kippur, the family all went to synagogue, and when Mundek tried to avoid going, he was slapped. Nevertheless, he did not fast all day long, but stopped fasting at noon.

The synagogue they attended was a progressive one named Synagoga Postępowa – also referred to as Synagoga Postępowa Tempel (Temple) – which was on Zołkiego Street in Lwów near the old *rynek*.[50] The services were conducted in a mix of Hebrew and German and the male and female congregants did not sit separately as in traditional synagogues. The family celebrated Mundek's bar mitzvah at the synagogue. He studied the prayers for two months with a special teacher. After the religious service, everybody had refreshments. Mundek continued to pray with tefillin[51] for two days and then stopped. This greatly upset his maternal step-grandfather Jacob Gerstenfeld, and his grandmother Rebecca, who often visited. Joseph's parents on the other hand were seldom there since Hersh was handicapped and the journey was difficult for him.

The Ostrowiec-Lwów Łukawieckis were also quite wealthy. In 1937, Joseph, his wife Sarah, and their five children moved from Lubaczów to the most upscale part of Lwów. They rented a flat on the upper floor of a two-story apartment building at 43 Kazimierzowska Street,[52] on the corner of Brajerowska Street and opposite the Brygidki Prison, with a view of Kazimierzowska Street. On the ground floor lived Jewish dignitaries, such as the families of the two most famous lawyers in Lwów, Dr. Lubliner and Dr. Bristinger, and the family of the Jewish scribe, Friedman.[53] On the Łukawieckis' floor, the inhabitants were mixed; there were both Gentile and Jewish families.

Mundek attended a Jewish elementary school called Czaczkes Elementary

---

50. It was a progressive synagogue near Stary Rynek (Stary Square), the old fish market.
51. Two small black leather boxes, containing scrolls inscribed with scriptural texts, worn by religious Jews during the morning prayer service.
52. Today Horodotska Street, Lviv, Ukraine.
53. Moshe Lavee (Edmund/Mundek Łukawiecki), recorded interview by USC Shoah Foundation Institute, interview code 31895, May 27, 1997.

School. He was not a good pupil, but he was a very good athlete. From the age of thirteen he attended a youth sports club called Hashmonaim.[54] He was a good runner, played table tennis and soccer, and finished in fifth place in the Lwów Bicycle Race.

For high school, Mundek refused to go to the Jewish school. He attended a Galician public secondary school for boys, the VIII Gimnazjum im. Kazimierza Wielkiego[55] There he made friends with fellow Polish students, as well as Ukrainians. However, Mundek did not complete his schooling there, as he was expelled after a fight with antisemitic pupils. There were another two Jewish students in his class, one of whom was named Joseph Tepper.[56] The Gentile pupils would often ask them, "Dirty Jews, what are you doing here? What are you doing among us?" Mundek could not hold back and had to respond. He got into several fistfights and the police were finally called. On another occasion, he was beaten on Akademicka Street because of his Jewish appearance. Ironically, Mundek was quite assimilated. He spoke four languages – Polish, Russian, Ukrainian, and German. The only commonly used language he could not speak was Yiddish. But that didn't matter to the antisemites.

During his time at the Gimnazjum, Mundek attended Przysposobienie Wojskowe, a military training program under the direction of the Sixth Corps of the Polish Army deployed in Lwów, during two summer vacations. This was a preparatory phase for youths before they were drafted into the Polish army. The paramilitary training consisted of courses and camps.[57] The training was established in 1927, but from 1937 onward it became compulsory.

This background sharpened Mundek's character and enhanced his knowledge of military procedure. It would later give him the ability to survive in the woods

---

54. The youth movement supporters of Jabotinsky's political work. See Heller, "The Rise of the Zionist Right," p. 48.
55. VIII Gimnazjum im. Kazimierza Wielkiego (Casimir the Great Eighth Middle School) was located on 17 Dwernickiego Street in an area known as Żelazna Woda in the southern part of Lwów. In the interview at the USC Shoah Foundation Institute, Mundek Łukawiecki called it by the slang name Ósma Buda (the Eighth Kennel).
56. Mundek had three additional very good friends – Zigo Friedman, a boy named Nadel who was the son of a poor carpenter, and Sasober Bertak, the son of the owner of a Jewish vegetarian restaurant.
57. For comprehensive background see Heller, "The Rise of the Zionist Right," pp. 165, 166, 246.

and to train his group of fifteen other partisans to do as well. It also helped to develop his leadership and command ability. He gained a solid understanding of military doctrine and learned the fighting tactics that he would go on to use against the Germans, conducting operational warfare and intelligence gathering, and exploiting the woods to his advantage.

Mundek had a multifaceted character. As a young man, he became enthusiastic about photography. After his time in the Gymnazjum, he asked for and received a simple box camera from his father. With that camera, he began to develop his photographic talent and strove to be a professional photographer. Mundek spent a long time learning about photography in the hopes of turning this hobby into a profession. He quickly realized that it was not enough to just be a good photographer; you also had to master the technical aspects of the picture you were taking.

Mundek had an artist's soul. He was not ashamed to cry in public when he could relate to the pain and suffering of others. This was in contrast to the rigid German education he had received at home. Photography helped him to develop his sense of beauty and grace, and it was this appreciation for the beauty of life that contributed to his optimism and gave him the strength to survive the difficult times in his life.

After being expelled from school, Mundek attended a bookkeeping school on Kołłątaja Street for two years. He studied Polish, German, and American bookkeeping. He completed this schooling with high marks, but did not work in this field despite the fact that he was accepted to start a job as the war broke out.

In September 1937,[58] Joseph Cohen and his second wife Zippora traveled from Palestine to Ostrowiec, to see Uncle Hersh – who had moved there in the meantime from Mielniki – and to see his cousin his age, Joseph Łukawiecki, who had recently moved to Lwów (Lemberg). Although the branch of the Łukawiecki family in Ostrowiec-Lwów were not religious, Joseph Cohen was indebted to them for helping him in his time of need. He went to Poland prior to World War II specifically to try to convince his family – and especially his cousin Joseph Łukawiecki and his wife – to join him in Palestine because of the rise of Nazism and its inherent threat to all Jews. He offered him a partnership in establishing the

---

58. Joseph Cohen, Palestine passport, no. 81472, dated March 3, 1937.

first distillery in Palestine with an initial investment of four thousand[59] British pounds,[60] which would be mainly contributed by the wealthy Łukawiecki family in Lwów. The plan was to open a distillery on 34 Hashuk Street in Tel Aviv that would produce spirits from oranges, a fruit that was plentiful in Palestine. There was also a promising market in the British army and the local population.

It was not complicated or difficult to convince them. The family already leaned toward the right, influenced by Ze'ev Jabotinsky's ideology. Mundek had attended Jabotinsky's speeches in 1936 and 1937 at the Coliseum on Słoneczna Street.

It was agreed. The anticipated reunion of the two brothers, Hersh and Shmuel David – who had emigrated to Palestine in 1928 – and their respective families was warmly accepted. It was decided that Joseph Łukawiecki's family from Lwów would be the pioneers and would prepare the ground for the arrival of the rest of the family.

After Joseph and Zippora Cohen's successful trip to Lwów, Mundek (who was seventeen at the time) and the rest of the family escorted the Cohens to the train station to say goodbye. As he was leaving, Mundek noticed that his uncle walked with a unique gait. He seemed to be imitating a deer when he walked – strangely elevating his thigh, moving it forward, and then lowering his leg gently to the ground. He then made the same motion with his other leg, and so on and so on. That was the one thing that Mundek remembered about his father's cousin Joseph.

Upon his return to Palestine, Joseph Cohen started to execute the new partnership and began to arrange the necessary papers for his relatives' arrival. The first step was to procure entry permits for the Łukawiecki family from Lwów, which he immediately applied for. The permits for Joseph Łukawiecki, his wife Sarah, and their six children were granted in early 1938, after the local Palestinian authorities had ensured that the needed investments for forming the distillery were secured and the jobs were waiting for the family so that they would not became a burden on the public in Palestine.[61] These papers meant that the entire Łukawiecki family could come legally to Palestine.

---

59. The monetary value today would be about one million USD.
60. The Central Zionist Archive, Jerusalem, s6p/1707/ל 1938.
61. The Central Zionist Archive, Jerusalem, s6p/1707/ל 1938.

In the meantime, following the Cohens' visit in July 1937,[62] the Łukawiecki family sold everything they owned and made all the necessary arrangements to emigrate to Palestine. However, as they were boarding the train to begin their journey to Palestine, Dora Łukawiecki, the grandmother, wife of Hersh Wolf Łukawiecki, suddenly decided not to go. She simply refused to board the train. She stated that she did not want to leave Poland for a deserted and remote place where only jackals thrived. She was not going to leave her established life for the sand dunes of Palestine after all.[63]

Dora was so persuasive in her arguments that she succeeded in talking all of the family out of their plans. In the days that followed, they diligently rebuilt their lives and reestablished their businesses in Poland. After some hard work and determination, not to mention payouts to government officials, they were able to go back to their old lives and were happy once again – for the time being.

At around the same time that the Bern and Łukawiecki families were raising their children and building their businesses, another family was flourishing in the town of Nowe Sioło, just nine kilometers (a little under six miles) north of Lubaczów.

The wide, agricultural plain of black, fertile soil that surrounded Nowe Sioło[64] was very plentiful for its three hundred farming families. All of them cultivated relatively big farms and a variety of livestock. The land blessed its owners and brought them economic prosperity. As a result, their houses were furnished with the most advanced technology for the time and they lived comfortably. This was their small, calm, relaxed, and tranquil paradise on earth.

About 70 percent of the Nowe Sioło population were Ukrainian families who had settled there about a hundred years earlier as part of an agricultural boom. Most of the families belonged to the Ukrainian Greek Catholic Church, although a small number were Polish Roman Catholics. Only five families were Jewish.

The peaceful landscape of Nowe Sioło, with its simple, one-story buildings, stretched along one road from east to west. Nowe Sioło was a stronghold of Ukrainian nationalism. The village identified itself with the supporters of Symon

---

62. Entries in Joseph Cohen's Palestine passport, no. 81472, dated March 3, 1937.
63. Joe Warner's e-mail to the author, on May 22, 2011. Joe Warner is the son-in-law of Joseph Cohen by marriage to Joseph's daughter Sarah.
64. Nowe Sioło is a Ukrainian name, meaning "the new village." In 1921, its population was 2,409 inhabitants, of which 1,636 were Ukrainians, 665 were Poles, and 108 were Jews.

Vasylyovych Petliura, a Ukrainian nationalist and anti-Jewish activist who was killed by a young Jew in Paris on May 25, 1926. After his death, Ukrainians in the village supported the more radical wing of the Organization of Ukrainian Nationalists (OUN),[65] led by Stepan Andriyovych Bandera. He became the head of the OUN-B, which cooperated with the Nazis even before World War II.

Many of the male villagers enthusiastically joined the OUN-B and were active members. Their living rooms proudly displayed the Tryzub,[66] the Ukrainian state coat of arms.[67] Although it was risky, they openly put up the Ukrainian flag and coat of arms and were devoted to publications such as *Ukrayinskaya zhyzn* (Ukrainian life).

After World War II began, the Polish partition between Germany and the USSR left Nowe Sioło on the Russian side, much to the townspeople's disappointment. They would have greatly prefered to be with the Germans under the General Government. This, however, did not stop them from cooperating with the Nazis. Since the border between Nowe Sioło and Cieszanów was less than five hundred meters away, it was easy to cross it and assist their German friends.

Much to the town's relief, however, the injustice was made right when the Third Reich invaded the USSR. It was then that Nowe Sioło was officially placed under German control. The Ukrainian population of Nowe Sioło welcomed the Germans by hanging their gold-and-blue flags together with the German swastika flag. On the evening of the official takeover, they celebrated the "liberation" by drinking and dancing together with Wehrmacht and SS officers. A common joke at the party was that the Russian commissar shot the Russian commander of Nowe Sioło because he was going to willingly surrender to the Germans anyway.

There was no white sand on the tiny banks of the narrow canal that ran between Nowe Sioło and Cieszanów. The canal gave the Nowe Sioło woods the look and feel of a jungle. Walking on the canal's banks was a very slippery pursuit, since they were very muddy and wet. It was easy to slip on the heavy, blackish

---

65. "Організація Українських Націоналістів" in Ukraininan.
66. This had been the Ukrainian national emblem since the first century CE. According to Władek Sikum, an elderly inhabitant of Nowe Sioło, the three prongs of its trident shape represent the Ukrainian flag, constitution, and anthem.
67. Testimony of Władek Sikum, who was acquainted with Sergeant Major Vasyl Kułczycki and is the unofficial historian of Nowe Sioło. The interview took place in Nowe Sioło on March 12, 2011.

soil and fall into the green stream. The banks were also fertile ground for trees, bushes, and other shrubs and plants. When winter came, snow covered the entire landscape. The only way to know that there was a canal there at all was by the line of trees and bushes, which was in direct contrast to the rest of the vast, shallow terrain. But beneath the whitish curtain of snow lay a freezing cold surprise.

This was the favorite playground of Vasyl Kułczycki, the son of a well-established family in Nowe Sioło; it was here that Vasyl created a fantasy world for himself. Here he did not need to speak, socialize, be polite, or feign interest in what others were saying. Here, he could focus on himself and his narrow world. It made him feel like the master of the universe. The property was actually a large agricultural farm owned by the Kułczycki family, on the outskirts of Nowe Sioło. Apart from the farm, the Kułczyckis owned a big mill, which was Vasyl's father's main business.

Vasyl was born on May 10, 1911, the same day on which Symon Petliura had been born in 1879. His father told him this on his seventh birthday, and it was an enormous source of pride to him for the rest of his life that he had something in common with the beloved secretary for military matters, who later became the Ukrainian head of state.

The Kułczyckis, like most other families in the area, were enthusiastic supporters of Ukrainian national movements, both morally and financially. On Sundays, the family attended religious services at the Greek Orthodox Church in Nowe Sioło, where the young Vasyl was a proud member of the local choir. One of his influences was a priest named Dudko,[68] who openly spread the falsehood that Poles and Jews were killing Ukrainians.

After services, the family normally had a traditional lunch with guests who shared their beliefs. The conversation would inevitably revolve around the political situation and the need to enlarge Ukrainian nationalist organizations. Antisemitism was also part of the regular dialogue, as Jews were thought to be representatives of the Moscow Bolsheviks and therefore behind the collectivization of land and property. Jews were deemed enemies of Ukraine and the Ukrainian nation and needed to be exterminated to preserve the welfare of the country.

---

68. Testimony of Józefa Kołodziej, an elderly inhabitant of Nowe Sioło. She was acquainted with Vasyl Kolosymski. The interview took place in Nowe Sioło on March 12, 2011.

Vasyl Kułczycki's land (current owner unknown), March 10, 2011

While lying on the banks of the tiny canal, Vasyl constantly dreamed about joining the Ukrainian national movement and one day becoming its leader. He wanted to form an independent Republic of Ukraine once again. These daydreams began to influence his behavior. He started to wear a military uniform and boots. He created military emblems, ranks, and medals. On May 25, 1926, when he was fifteen years old, the assassination of Petliura – his spiritual godfather – hit him hard. But it also fueled his imagination. He began to envision himself entering Kiev, the capital of the Ukraine, as its liberator. He was to be the successor of Petliura, like a Roman emperor worshipped by his people and decorated with olive branches.

Vasyl did not associate with many friends, as he considered it a waste of time. His interests involved solving universal political disputes and problems, and immersing himself in political essays and books. He was smart, so his ability to grasp political issues was remarkable.

Vasyl began to act on his beliefs. He started demonstrations and riots, and incited violence against Jews. His well-established and well-known family supported him and funded demonstrations in Nowe Sioło and other pro-Ukrainian centers. Belief in the Judeo-Bolshevist conspiracy led Vasyl to support Nazism, which was gaining a foothold in Germany and Austria.

In late 1939, young Ukrainians crossed the border into the General

Government, the newly occupied Nazi country, while in Germany the existing collaboration between Ukrainian nationalists and the Germans was intensified against the backdrop of planning a war against the Soviet Union. One result was the forming of the Ukrainian battalions Nachtigall and Roland by the Abwehr (German military intelligence), commanded by Admiral Wilhelm Canaris.

One of the volunteers was Vasyl. He crossed the border into the General Government and there offered his services and asked to join the Viiskovi Viddily Natsionalistiv (National Military Detachment), formed shortly before the invasion of Poland and commanded by Roman Sushko.[69] His request to join the six-hundred-soldier unit was turned down, as it consisted only of soldiers from the Karpatska Sich (Carpathian Guard) defense force and members of the Organizatsiya Ukrainskyh Natsionalistiv (Organization of Ukrainian Nationalists; OUN)[70] who lived in Germany. Disappointed and disillusioned, Vasyl returned to Nowe Sioło. He was in perfect physical condition for military service. He was single, well built, and of medium height, with brown hair and brown eyes. Beneath his straight, short nose was a Hitler-style moustache.

---

69. Roman Krokhmaliuk, *Zahrava na Skhodi: spohady i dokumenty z pratsi u Viis'koviĭ upravi "Halychyna" v 1943–1945 rokakh* (Toronto: Nakladom Bratstva, 1978), pp. 7–9.
70. There were different branches of this organization. The OUN-B was headed by Stephan Bandera and the OUN-M was headed by Andrei Melnyk.

Chapter 3
Czyn

In late August 1939, just a few days before the German invasion of Poland, Mundek Łukawiecki received orders to mobilize. He and other youths from Lwów were drafted into the Polish army and were given full military gear. When Germany invaded Poland on September 1, 1939, the commanding NCO of Mundek's unit, who had the rank of corporal, informed them that the following day, they would be transferred to the front line. When Mundek woke up the next morning, he was alone; all of Lwów's youth had deserted and disappeared, taking with them the military gear and weapons. Mundek therefore returned home.

Within a few days, the Polish army had retreated to Lwów and the Luftwaffe (the German air force) began a heavy air bombardment on September 7. The town was taken five days later, and Lubaczów was taken on September 12 and occupied by Nazi forces.

Two weeks later, however, Hitler and Stalin signed the Molotov-Ribbentrop Non-Aggression Pact, which divided Poland between the German Reich and the USSR. Parts of Poland that included many Polish and ethnic Germans were integrated into the German Reich itself, while the rest of the German-contolled area of Poland was named the General Government and was turned into a kind of colony euphemistically named Nebenland des Reiches (the borderland of the Reich). The rest of Poland was given to the Russians and became part of the Soviet Union.

The new border between Germany and the USSR was located about seven kilometers (a little over four miles) east of Lubaczów, with the result that *powiat Lubaczów* (the Lubaczów district) fell right on the dividing line; the town of Lubaczów itself and the majority of the former district became part of the USSR, while a smaller chunk of the area became part of the German district of Lublin.

On September 26, the Wehrmacht retreated and the Red Army entered

Front of former Łukawiecki residence in Lwów

Entrance to former Łukawiecki residence in Lwów, February 25, 2010. The home is currently owned by veterans of the Ukrainian army, who purchased it from the Polish Center for Missing People. Or Lavee is standing in the entrance.

Lubaczów.[1] After establishing their control, the Soviets immediately took steps to nationalize the economy and all private property, including banks, industries, and land.[2] In one day, the wealth of the Łukawiecki family vanished; the farm and distillery in Ostrowiec – a suburb of Lubaczów where Mundek's widowed grandmother Dora lived[3] – was nationalized, as were the family-owned distilleries in Lwów, Stryj, Szówsko, Jarosław, and Ruda Różaniecka, as well as their sawmills and retail textile stores in Lwów and Stryj. The Łukawiecki family had previously acquired the nickname "Gorzelnicy."[4] Now, all the distilleries were nationalized, and only the nickname remained. The Łukawiecki family was completely stripped of its wealth and assets.

Prior to the Molotov-Ribbentrop Pact[5] and the Russian invasion, Mundek's father, Joseph Łukawiecki, had been working as a chemical engineer in the Baczewski Distillery in Lwów.[6] In addition to the salary he received from the Baczewski Distillery, Joseph Łukawiecki also got monthly wages from the Polish army. As soon as the Russians entered Lubaczów, however, Joseph Łukawiecki was unable to work, as he was forced to hide himself in order to escape Russian persecution. This was because he had been an officer in the Polish army and was also a member of Strzelec,[7] which during World War I had formed part of the Polish Legion.[8]

---

1. The Red Army was reluctant to place this territory under Russian authority, as it was acquired as a result of its "non-aggression" pact with the Nazi regime.
2. Eliyahu Yones, *Smoke in the Sand: The Jews of Lvov in the War Years, 1939–1944* (Jerusalem: Gefen Publishing House, 2004), pp. 54–55.
3. During my research for this book, I was unable to establish when Hersh Łukawiecki passed away and how. Probably he passed away in 1938.
4. *Gorzelnia* means "distillery" in Polish. The nickname *gorzelnicy* (singular *gorzelnik*) means those who own distilleries or work in the distillery industry.
5. Moshe Lavee (Edmund/Mundek Łukawiecki), recorded interview by USC Shoah Foundation Institute, interview code 31895, May 27, 1997.
6. The Baczewski family owned the world-famous distillery in Lwów. The distillery was bombed by the Luftwaffe in the outbreak of WWII and destroyed. After Lwów was taken by the Red Army, a paper factory was built on the site.
7. Związek Strzelecki, a paramilitary organization.
8. Legiony Polskie. Joseph Łukawiecki bridged his Polish nationalist attitude and his Jewishness, as meny Jews in Galicia did at that time. See Heller, "The Rise of the Zionist Right," p. 196.

The site of the Łukawieckis' former wholesale textile shop in Lwów, February 25, 2010

The Soviet NKVD (secret police, later the KGB)[9] persecuted Polish officers and executed them, as they were regarded as subversive elements against the USSR.

Despite the fact that Joseph Łukawiecki was unemployed during the Russian period and the family faced severe economic difficulties as a result – even struggling to pay their rent – they were nevertheless grateful that they were not living in the area controlled by Germany. The German atrocities against Jews had been described by fugitives who had fled to Lwów and it was common knowledge.

One night, almost a year after the start of the Russian occupation of Lwów, Joseph Łukawiecki received a visit from one of his non-Jewish friends, Józef Kulpa of Ostrowiec. Born on July 14, 1899, in Ostrowiec, Kulpa was a member of the Polish underground organization Związek Walki Zbrojnej (ZWZ)[10] and had

---

9. The Narodny Komissariat Vnutrennikh Del (NKVD, People's Commissariat for Internal Affairs) was the public and secret police organization of the Soviet Union that was responsible for enforcing the Soviet ideology.

10. The Union of Armed Struggle. The ZWZ was formed on September 13, 1939, from the former organization Służba Zwycięstwu Polski (Service for Poland's Victory). In January 1940, the ZWZ was divided into two factions – the area under German occupation (commanded by Colonel Stefan Rowecki, headquartered in Warsaw) and the area under Soviet occupation (commanded by General Michał Tokarzewski-Karaszewicz, headquartered in Lwów), in

fought in World War I on the Italian front in the Polish 34th Infantry Regiment of the Austro–Hungarian Imperial Army. He was released from military duty on November 10, 1918[11] and upon his return to Lubaczów joined the Polish nationalist effort, mainly opposing the Ukrainians' activities. In 1937, he was decorated with the Polish Independence Medal.

Józef Kulpa was a former business associate of Joseph Łukawiecki and his family. In addition, the Łukawiecki family spent most of their summer vacations in Ostrowiec, where they operated a distillery as part of their chain. The families therefore knew each other well. They were more than neighbors, but rather like family.

Józef Kulpa was the same age as Joseph Łukawiecki. The relationship between the two men went beyond that of good neighbors and mutual assistance. They were like brothers. They shared a common ideology and common ideas. Joseph Łukawiecki was acquainted with Kulpa's Polish nationalist feelings and his anti-Ukrainian, German, and Soviet sentiments. During Kulpa's visits to Lwów, he spent time at the Łukawiecki residence and considered it a safe house, and the Łukawieckis gave him to understand that they too related to his underground activities. Moreover, Joseph Łukawiecki did not seal his pocket, and supported with what he could when asked. Kulpa, from his side, shared with him Polish nationalist thoughts and views. Both of them opposed the Soviets and the Communist system and were afraid of it. The idea of nationalized property meant bankruptcy to the Łukawieckis.[12] They also saw eye to eye on the dangers of Ukrainian nationalism; Kulpa saw the danger it posed toward Poles, and Joseph Łukawiecki feared the danger it would bring to Jews.

On June 12, 1940, Józef Kulpa was called by the ZWZ to go to Lwów to give an update and have a consultation with his superior. At that time, the ZWZ in Lwów, Lubaczów, and other areas under USSR control was under tremendous pressure and was being hammered severely by the NKVD. All ZWZ cells had effectively been destroyed. The majority of the ZWZ commanding echelon had been imprisoned and prosecuted. The rest, including regular members, were

---

which Lwów and Lubaczów belonged. In 1942 the Armia Krajowa (the Home Army or AK) was formed as a successor organization to the ZWZ.
11. Biographical sketch of Józef Kulpa written by his family.
12. Eventually the Soviets nationalized the distilleries and sawmills the family owned, as well as their fabric wholesale business; they lost all their wealth.

under constant pressure from the NKVD. Soviet oppression, suppression, and the activities of the Ukrainian nationalists greatly worried the ZWZ, but they had to find new supporters, since many of their leaders had been imprisoned by the USSR.

Beyond the havoc being wreaked on the ZWZ by the NKVD, the geographical boundaries of responsibility of the ZWZ in the Lubaczów-Ostrowiec area spread over areas controlled by Germany and areas controlled by the USSR. To cross the border between the areas was relatively easy at that time, but the ZWZ needed somebody who could operate on the German side. The problem was that they had no members or volunteers. The duty imposed on the young generation to join the Red Army prevented them from joining, and the continuous persecution against the ZWZ almost eliminated its existing members. In short, they desperately needed volunteers. It was understood that unless fresh recruits were drafted in and reorganization undertaken, the ZWZ would collapse.

That evening at the Łukawiecki's apartment, Joseph Łukawiecki and Józef Kulpa discussed the political and military situation over a cigarette and a glass of vodka. They were in mutual understanding that the situation was desperate and likely to deteriorate. Józef asked Mundek's father whether he would allow Mundek and his brother Zygmunt to join the Polish underground movement, and in so doing, increase his own chances of survival. At that moment, Joseph understood that his Jewish origin was a stain on the Polish nationalism.

Kulpa's idea to recruit Mundek made a lot of sense. Mundek would be a valuable addition to the underground movement. He spoke mother-tongue-level Polish, German, Ukrainian, and Russian. In high school, he had made friends with non-Jews from Lwów and nearby villages. Many of his classmates did not know he was Jewish.[13] He was a very poor pupil, preferring sport, and did not hesitate to resort to physical beatings and fistfights. He said about himself that he could easily be called a bully. In short, he was a perfect candidate for the underground movement, and his Polish name made him the perfect candidate to join the ZWZ and be a ZWZ operative in Nazi-controlled areas.

Joseph Łukawiecki agreed. Then Mundek was asked and he agreed as well.

---

13. Personal interview with Dr. Isaac Weinberg, May 30, 2011, quoting conversations with Mundek Łukawiecki. Dr Weinberg was a student to whom Mundek taught photography and who later became his personal friend.

So Mundek joined the Polish underground movement, without knowing that he was actually joining the ZWZ. Mundek was told not to reveal his Jewish faith.[14] He easily agreed; this was not difficult for him.

Mundek convinced his brother Zygmunt not to join at that time but to wait until he heard what Mundek's experience was like. However, Mundek asked his friend Zigo Friedman, whose family lived on the ground floor, if he would like to join him. Zigo, who came from a very religious family, refused, saying that he did not trust Gentiles.

Mundek was asked to travel to Ruda Różaniecka[15] in the German-controlled area and report to the *gajowy* (gamekeeper),[16] who was not familiar to Mundek. The ZWZ's reason for sending Mundek there was twofold: first, to see how he managed in a risky situation – crossing to the German side – and second, to see how he behaved in the midst of a clandestine activity. It was also an initial mission to deploy him and accustom him to this type of activity.

Mundek made his journey to Ruda Różaniecka without any problems and crossed the border, which was not marked or guarded, in the countryside. Mundek knew the area. His grandparents had had a farm in Ostrowiec, next to Kulpa's farm, where he used to visit them, and his father Joseph had managed the distillery of Baron Hugo Watmann in Ruda Różaniecka for many years.

The *gajowy* was a member of the ZWZ as well. Mundek knocked on the window of the cottage and a man opened it. Mundek told him that he had been sent by Józef Kulpa. The *gajowy* told Mundek that he would not immediately join those who were hiding in the woods; he must first wait by the woods for another member of the ZWZ, whose task it was to be the *łącznik* (liaison officer), who would instruct him.

The following night, the liaison officer arrived. Mundek could not see his face both because it was dark and because his face was hidden. The liaison officer

---

14. Maurie Hoffman, author of *Keep Yelling*, in written answers on May 21, 2009, to questions presented to him in a prior interview. This was confirmed by Dahlia Levin, a neighbor of the Łukawiecki family in Israel, who knew Mundek and Chana well. She was interviewed on June 6, 2011.
15. Part of the huge Puszcza Solska forest, about twenty kilometers (twelve miles) north of Lubaczów and 107 kilometers (sixty-six miles) northwest of Lwów.
16. This was someone assigned to supervise hunting in the area. He had a cottage (*gajówka*) at the entrance of the woods.

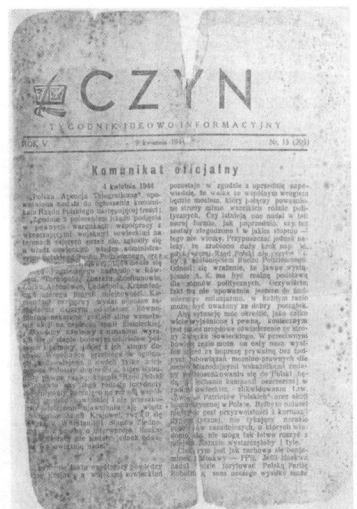 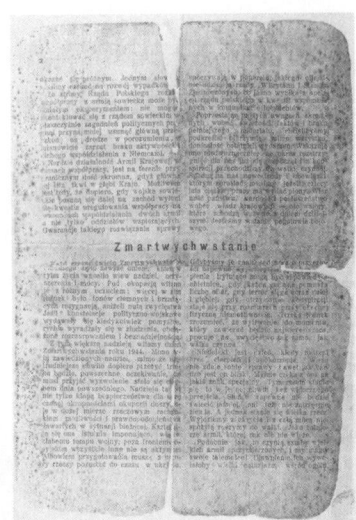

Sample page of the underground paper *Czyn*

was extremely impressed by the high level of Mundek's Polish and was sure that Mundek had had a high education.

The liaison officer informed Mundek that in the first stage he would not join the ZWZ members in the woods, but would distribute a fifteen-centimeter pamphlet titled *Czyn*,[17] which was printed in Jarosław and was brought to Lubaczów by a local ZWZ member. The ZWZ organization was well informed and was updated quickly when there were new developments. For foreign news, they relied mainly on the BBC.[18] The information was then widely circulated through *Czyn*. The pamphlet was dispatched under cover of night[19] free of charge in Cieszanów, Ruda Różaniecka, Płazów, Narol, and Lipsko – every night someplace different. It aimed to elevate Polish morale and to increase the ZWZ's influence over the population.

---

17. *Czyn* ("Deed" in Polish) was a weekly periodical published by AK on two-column newsprint; it was both ideological and informative. See also Mieczysław Argasiński, *Konspiracja w powiecie lubaczowskim w latach 1939–1947* [Conspiracy in Lubaczów county in the years 1939–1947] (Zwierzyniec: Ostoja, 2010), p. 55.
18. See War Cabinet Report of the Foreign Office, February 17, 1943, The National Archives (TNA) WP (43) 69, which describes a meeting with representatives of the Polish underground.
19. Tadeusz Bór-Komorowski, in his book *The Secret Army* (Nashville, TN: Battery Press, 1984), p. 121, says that each underground group had its own paper. By the time of Operation Barbarossa, there were already 168 underground newspapers being published. See also Lukas, *Forgotten Holocaust*, p. 106.

The liaison officer never revealed his identity to Mundek or to the pamphlets' readers. He took Mundek to fifteen or twenty addresses every night[20] but always stood far away, indicating to Mundek to whom he should give *Czyn*. Mundek never saw the operator, so that he would never be able to identify him. Mundek would approach the house and knock on the door or window, and then hand the pamphlet over to the person who opened it, while stating in Polish, "Niech będzie pochwalony" (It should be with blessing). After Mundek dispatched *Czyn* in one town or village, the liaison officer would connect Mundek to the next liaison officer from another town or village to dispatch the pamphlets there.

In the attic, with light shining through the timbers, summer 1942

During the day, Mundek hid. When nightfall approached, the liaison officer met Mundek in the hideout where he had spent the night. It might be the attic of a barn in a farm, or in the woods nearby. There was only one occasion when the liaison officer invited Mundek to sleep at his house for the night. He was

---

20. It must be emphasized that Mundek was dispatching *Czyn* prior to Operation Barbarossa. Therefore he was crossing the border from the USSR (the occupied area of Poland) into the German-occupied area of Poland, which was called the General Government. All his delivery addresses were in the German-controlled area.

Franek from Lipsko. He was living with his mother in a place that gave him the opportunity to escape if a raid took place.

The NKVD tried to discourage distribution of the pamphlets in the most severe way. The death penalty was imposed immediately on anyone who was involved: the printers, the writers, and the dispatchers.[21] The readers, however, were eager to get it and read it, as it sustained the Polish spirit.

On occasion, Mundek would visit his parents and stay with them for a few days. While there, he would look after their food and water supply.

The underground movement was very satisfied with Mundek's activities and achievements. Due to his ability to speak German and the possibility that he might be identified as a German, they decided to give him the necessary identification papers. That is how Mundek got false German identification from the son of Andrzej Zuchowski,[22] a Polish member of the Sejm.[23] Mundek could travel anywhere with these documents, and they provided a safeguard when he crossed the border to the General Government areas from the Russian-controlled areas to dispatch *Czyn*.

When the Nazis broke the Molotov-Ribbentrop pact and invaded the USSR on June 22, 1941, the ZWZ was not caught entirely by surprise,[24] in contrast to the Soviet defenders in the frontier zone, who were totally unprepared,[25] despite the fact that Soviet intelligence had formed a clear picture of German intentions.[26] With this, his sweeping Operation Barbarossa, Hitler started his plan for expanding German territory and providing a buffer against the Russians. He wanted not only to occupy Poland, but to destroy it. He said he would crush the Poles at the end of the campaign with relentless vigor. Those in the know understood that he meant the destruction of the Polish intelligentsia, and in particular the

---

21. Lukas, *Forgotten Holocaust*, p. 108.
22. Andrzej Zuchowski (1883–1935) was a Polish nationalist. In the twenties, he was the mayor of Lubaczów, and in 1928 was elected to the Sejm. He was acquainted with Józef Kulpa and with Joseph Łukawiecki, Mundek's father. In WWII his son Marian and other family were active members of the AK (see chapter 10, "Partisan Fighting Company").
23. On usage of false papers, see also Hoffman, *Keep Yelling*, pp. 123, 163.
24. Bór-Komorowski, *The Secret Army*, pp. 62–64.
25. Samuel W. Mitcham, Jr., *The Men of Barbarossa: Commanders of the German Invasion of Russia, 1941* (Havertown, PA: Casemate, 2009), p. 61.
26. Ibid., 25.

priesthood,[27] as the first killings of Jews, priests, and political leaders in Nazi-occupied areas had already taken place in 1939–1940.

Mundek was in Rawa Ruska at the time. Activities relating to the *Czyn* had ceased due to the awareness of the German preparation of the coming invasion. No new orders had been given to him. Immediately he rushed home to Lwów to be with his family. He knew that his place, at that time, was with his family at home. He was frantic. He thought of all the horrors the Germans were causing Jews in the part of Poland they already occupied. After he got approval from his commander, he left Rawa Ruska at sunset on June 21, 1941. He traveled the distance of sixty-five kilometers (forty miles) in one night, mainly walking and running close to the main road. He made his way as fast as he could. As he approched Lwów, at about 3:30 A.M. on June 22, 1941, he realized there was a bombardment and fighting going on. The Germans had invaded Russia. Ignoring the fighting between the Wehrmacht and the Red Army, he rushed home.

Mundek arrived in Lwów before the German Wehrmacht entered it. The family was terrified. They were trapped. They could not flee to the USSR, as they risked being persecuted by the NKVD, Polish nationalists, and members of the Polish army. On the other hand, remaining in Lwów meant being annihilated by the Germans. Joseph Łukawiecki could not decide which was the worse option. But on June 22, 1941, it was too late to make any more decisions. The Wehrmacht entered Lwów and the world as they had known it was over.

---

27. Richard Rhodes, *Masters of Death: The SS-Einsatzgruppen and the Invention of the Holocaust* (New York: Alfred A. Knopf, 2002), pp. 4–5.

Chapter 4
A World Turned Upside Down

In the early morning hours of June 22, 1941,[1] large numbers of German infantry units entered Lwów, Poland.[2] By sunrise, the entire city was occupied, bringing the twenty-month Soviet occupation to an end. The blitzkrieg-style onslaught bombarded them from all directions. Mundek stood on the balcony of the family apartment on Kazimierzowska Street watching as the Nazis rolled into the city at high speed with armored motorcycles carrying machine gun–toting soldiers. All the while, the Luftwaffe bombed the city heavily. The motorcycles were followed by a parade of clean-shaven soldiers in prim, neat uniforms singing military songs. Ukrainians stood on either side, welcoming them by throwing flowers. Mundek felt a terrible fear; he knew what was awaiting the Jews.

Completely caught off guard, the Russian Red Army was in a state of mass confusion. Only a small number of soldiers even tried to fight back. Some of them deserted or surrendered to the Germans. The rest were in complete disarray. Military camps were deserted, the armaments, ammunition, munitions, and uniforms left behind. Soldiers tried to escape as fast as they could, changing quickly into peasant attire in order to blend in, and begging peasants to hide them at their farms.

For the next five days, military convoys controlled Lwów's streets. Tanks, armored vehicles loaded with soldiers, regular military vehicles, and supply trucks dominated city streets. All intersections were monitored by the German military police, who directed traffic as they saw fit. The killing that ensued was unpredictable and entirely random. The Soviets mass-murdered all the prisoners in the Lwów prisons, including Poles, Ukrainians, and Jews, and also murdered

---
1. Yones, *Smoke in the Sand*, p. 75.
2. Today Lwów is called Lviv and is part of the Ukraine.

many civilians. Four thousand people were executed in this manner.³ At the same time, Ukrainian rooftop snipers shot down civilians, targeting Jews and non-Jews alike, and also fired at Red Army soldiers who were trying to retreat from the onslaught.⁴ The streets began to fill with hundreds of corpses. Human bodies littered the streets as passersby looked on with disinterest.

But it was primarily the Jews who were executed at an astonishing rate. A Jewish resident in Lwów wrote in a contemporary diary, "The devil's game began."⁵ Einsatzgruppe C⁶ and Ukrainian nationalists began to systematically murder Jews on a daily basis. During the first days of the occupation of Lwów, more than three thousand Jews were killed in the Lwów prisons. Among them was one of the best-known and most popular rabbis of Lwów, Dr. Yehezkel Levin, together with his brother Aaron Levin, the rabbi of Zheshkov.⁷ Every morning about a thousand Jews were brought and distributed among the three prisons. The Germans seized Jews in the streets or from their homes and forced them to work in the prisons.

For Vasyl Kułczycki, the eager Ukrainian nationalist from Nowe Sioło, it was a wonderful present when the German army triumphantly entered his hometown on June 22, 1941, shortly after his thirtieth birthday. He asked his uncle (the mayor of the village) to arrange a welcome party and ceremony for the "liberators." On behalf of the Nazi supporters in Nowe Sioło, Vasyl addressed the German general that evening by quoting Jarosław Stećko, who sent a letter to Hitler saying, "It is with an overwhelming feeling of gratitude and admiration for your heroic army that we are hereby sending Your Excellency our heartfelt wishes for complete victory." In addition, the priest Dudko enthusiastically welcomed the Nazis, encouraged by the archbishop of the metropolitan of Lwów, Andrzej Szeptycki.

---

3. Andrew Roberts, *The Storm of War: A New History of the Second World War* (New York: Harper Collins, 2011), p. 162.
4. See chapter 8 in Christoph Mick, *Kriegserfahrungen in einer multiethnischen Stadt: Lemberg 1914–1947* (Wiesbaden: Harrassowitz Verlag, 2010). See also Yones, *Smoke in the Sand*, p. 76, and see testimony of Edmund (Mundek) Łukawiecki (Moshe Lavee) to Yad Vashem, July 28, 1993, no. 03-6946, tape no. 033c/2757.
5. Rhodes, *Masters of Death*, p. 61.
6. Einsatzgruppe C consisted of several *Einsatzkomandos* or *Sonderkommandos* and was commanded by Dr. Otto Emil Rasch. The abbreviation of *Einsatzkommando* is EK or Ek and *Sonderkommando* is SK or Sk.
7. Rhodes, *Masters of Death*, p. 61.

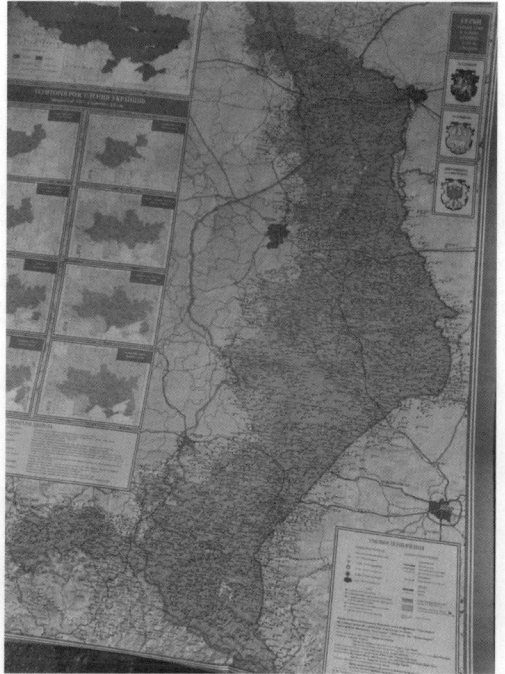

Map owned by Ukrainian nationalists in Nowe Sioło, showing Polish territory claimed by Ukrainian nationalists

The following day, the village published an advertisement written by Vasyl that encouraged the town's youth to join the Ukrainian Auxiliary Police. It was a preliminary step to Himmler's upcoming order,[8] which was formally announced on July 25, 1941.[9] The order formed Auxiliary Police units using reliable, non-Communist local inhabitants. These units were called Schutzmannschaften (defense units), or Schuma for short. Led by German officers, the Schuma was composed of individuals from Nazi-occupied countries. However, the Ukrainians made up the majority, with more than eighteen battalions and about nine thousand men willingly taking part.[10]

---

8. Stephen Campbell, *Police Battalions of the Third Reich*, Schiffer Military History (Atglen, PA: Schiffer, 2007), p. 34.
9. The first local Ukrainische Hilfspolizei (Ukrainian Auxiliary Police) was formed and commanded by the Wehrmacht in many places in the Ukraine in June and July 1941. Later many of their members were transferred to the local order police (Schutzmannschaft-Einzeldienst-Ukrainische Hilfspolizei) or to Ukrainian Schutzmannschafts (Schuma) battalions (Ukr. Schutzmannschafts Bataillone). These battalions often were deployed far away.
10. In Galicia, there were three thousand Ukrainian policemen.

54 · CHAPTER 4

Pictures of Ukrainian nationalists in *Here Was Our Village*, a memory book about Nowe Sioło and its UPA affiliations, written by one Vasyl Graywitz and published in 1950. Top: Wasyl Lekowitz, commander of the UPA (he was not from Nowe Sioło), captured by the NKVD and imprisoned for twenty-five years in Siberia. Bottom: two nationalist brothers, Omlan and Ivan Graywitz, nephews of the book's author. Bottom left: Ivan (nickname Grama), chairman of the UPA, was killed January 8, 1945. Bottom right: Omlan (nickname Batko), killed July 1945.

There was no difficulty in recruiting large numbers of youth from Nowe Sioło to volunteer for the Ukrainian units in Germany, and those who were twenty years or over were accepted. The local Ukrainians had established very good connections with the Germans in the General Government prior to Operation Barbarossa, and crossed the border into the General Government very easily and very often.[11] Furthermore these local Ukrainian police battalions revived the locals' aspiration for independence, which increased Ukrainian enthusiasm for the police battalions.

The following Nowe Sioło residents joined and served in the Lubaczów Ukrainian Police under the command of Vasyl Kułczycki,[12] participating in atrocities in the Lubaczów area:

- Vasyl Hul: Leader of the Ukrainian national movement in Nowe Sioło and also head of the village, he openly incited anti-Polish and anti-Jewish sentiments.[13]

---

11. Testimony of elderly Nowe Sioło resident Władek Sikum, March 12, 2011.
12. In the index of the Bundesarchiv in Ludwigsburg, Germany, there is no listing for Vasyl Kułczycki, nor for Lubaczów.
13. His son Sikum Władek (it is unclear why the two have different family names), whom we interviewed on March 12, 2011, is very proud of his Ukrainian national heritage, and actually is

- Jan (Ivan) Pałczyński: Commander in chief of the local police in Nowe Sioło, he actively took part in assisting the Nazis in the region when needed. After the war, he was a Russian fugitive of justice, but acquired fake Polish documents. He was eventually shot in the backyard of Nowe Sioło resident Sikum Władek by the NKVD (Soviet secret police).
- Jan Szymański: Commander in chief of the Ukrainian police in Cieszanów, he was responsible for the liquidation of the Jews of Cieszanów. In 1944, he led raids against Polish peasants in Cieszanów, which resulted in the evacuation of the AK.
- Kołosywski Teodor ("Kowalenko")
- Władysław Krasulak: Killed in Lubaczów during the war by the AK.
- Stefan Laszyk
- Vasyl Szczyrba: Together with Vasyl Kułczycki, he went to Germany to volunteer with the Ukrainian forces but was turned down because of his age. After the war, he committed suicide by detonating a hand grenade as the Russians were about to capture him.
- Hryhorij Czapacha: Police commander of the German administration in Lubaczów.
- Two Chrabec brothers: Members of the Ukrainian police in Lubaczów.

Vasyl Kułczycki was the first volunteer to join the Ukrainian Auxiliary Police (Ukrainische Hilfspolizei) and was given the rank of sergeant major, the highest rank that Ukrainians could be awarded in the German units. He was proud to wear the black uniform with the gray cuffs. His first course of action, in gratitude to the Nazis, was to organize the capture and execution of the five Jewish families living in Nowe Sioło.

Officers of the newly created Ukrainian Auxiliary Police also conducted arrests of Jews and forced Jews to clean the streets by clearing and burying the bodies. The Aryan residents of Lwów also participated in this brutal show. Crowds wandered along the prison corridors and courtyards, observing with satisfaction the suffering of the Jews. Here and there volunteers could be found helping the Germans to beat the Jews. The operation was over in three or four days.

---

the traditional keeper of the village tradition and legacy. He safeguards the village's emblems, maps, flags, and books. He is not ashamed to zealously tell the story, precisely revealing facts and details, including the execution of Jews.

56 · CHAPTER 4

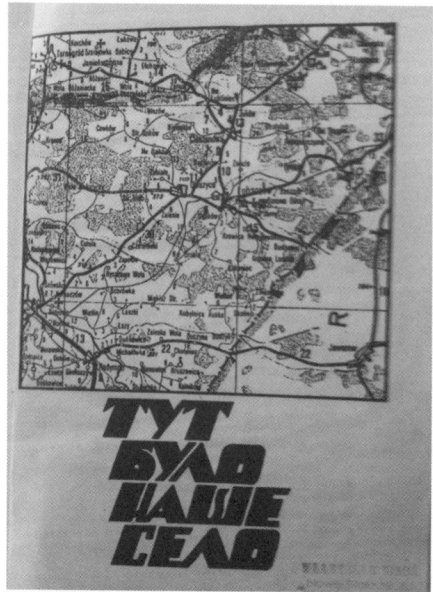

The book *Here Was Our Village*, by Vasyl Graywitz

The local Ukrainian historian, Sikum Władek, Nowe Sioło, March 10, 2011

The Nazis allowed the Ukrainians to form nationalist militias. These militias indulged in the mass killing of "Jews and Bolsheviks," and were responsible for about ten thousand deaths. To justify these murders and further incite hatred, the Nazis blamed the Jews for political killings inside Lwów prisons.

The staff of Einsatzgruppe C and its commandos, Sonderkommando 4b, Einsatzkommando 6, and Einsatzkommando 5, only stayed in Lwów for a few days before moving on. On July 2, 1941, the first unit of Einsatzkommando z.b.V.,[14] commanded by SS-Brigadeführer Karl Schöngarth, entered Lwów and commandeered the NKVD central building. The Nazis then incorporated Eastern Galicia into the General Government and named it "Distrikt Galizien."[15] This in turn led to a week of complete lawlessness and horrifying chaos.

---

14. *Zur besonderen Verwendung* (for special employment). This term was used to refer to killing squads or units.

15. Galicia was a former Austro-Hungarian territory, created as the result of the third division of Poland between Prussia, Russia, and Austria. The Third Reich's policy was to evacuate and deport the Polish population from the Lublin-Zamość area and to enforce a policy of "Germanisierung" (Germanization). After the German-Russian treaty and the division of Poland in 1939, nearly fifty thousand "Galiziendeutsche" (Galician Germans) were resettled in the German-occupied Poland in 1939–1940, and they had to stay there after the German

On the same day that the German invasion hit Lwów, June 22, 1941, the small town of Lubaczów was overrun by German troops for the second time since the start of the war. Three days later, on June 25, 1941, the city was officially occupied by the Germans. During those three days, Germans conducted mass executions in the Niwki woods, not far away from Kulpa's farm.

Lubaczów was a well-known Jewish center; almost one third of its population – approximately 2,300 people – was Jewish. In 1939 it had 6,582 inhabitants,[16] but by 1943 this had been reduced to 4,179.[17]

At first, the town was run by the German District Commander's Office (*Ortskommandantur*). The Jews were allowed to come and go relatively easily and were even allowed to go to work under the escort of a Ukrainian guard.[18] This lasted all of two weeks. From then on, the Jews' fate was sealed; their complete extermination was only a matter of time, and until then, their existence would be one of despair, hunger, and disease.

In August 1941, authority over Lubaczów was transferred. Rawa Ruska and Lubaczów were unified under one administrative regime – called a *Kreishauptmannschaft* – which was headed by a German *Kreishauptmann*.[19] The town[20] of Lubaczów and the new rural municipality,[21] including several villages of the

---

conquest of Galicia in summer 1941. As there were also Ukrainian inhabitants in the area, the situation became complicated for the German administration. Concerning the Jews, it was planned in the beginning to deport them to concentration camps and later on the plan was to execute them.

16. *Statistisches Gemeindeverzeichnis des bisherigen polnischen Staates, mit Berücksichtigung der am 28. September 1939 festgelegten Grenze der deutschen und sowjetrussischen Reichsinteressen* [Statistical community directory of the current Polish state, with consideration of the September 28, 1939, border set by the interests of the German and Soviet Russian states] (Berlin, 1939), p. 118.
17. *Amtliches Gemeinde- und Dorfverzeichnis für das Generalgouvernement auf Grund der summarischen Bevölkerungsbestandsaufnahme am 1. März 1943, herausgegeben vom statistischen Amt des Generalgouvernement* [Township and village directory for the General Government on the basis of the March 1, 1943, census, published by the Statistical Office of the General Government] (Krakow: Burgverlag Krakau, 1943), p. 11.
18. For a comprehensive description of the events of the Lubaczów ghetto, see Martin Dean, ed., *Ghettos in German-Occupied Eastern Europe*, vol. 2 in *Encyclopedia of Camps and Ghettos, 1933–1945*, ed. Geoffrey P. Megargee (Bloomington: Indiana University Press in association with the United States Holocaust Memorial Museum, 2012), pp. 800–802.
19. Argasiński, *Konspiracja w powiecie*, p. 146.
20. In German *Stadtgemeinde*.
21. In German *Landgemeinde*.

former Polish district of Lubaczów, became part of Kreishauptmannschaft Rawa Ruska,[22] of the district of Galicia.[23] The area included about fifty thousand Ukrainians, thirty-two thousand Poles, and ten thousand Jews. Other villages, such as Narol, remained part of the district of Lublin.

Most Ukrainians welcomed the Germans with flowers wrapped in blue-and-gold-colored ribbons. On June 22, 1941, an announcement by a member of the Ukrainian nationalists was broadcast on Radio Berlin proclaiming, "*Smert Zydam, smert Kummunistam, smert Kummunisrem!*" (Death to Jews, death to Communists, death to commissars!).[24] On June 30, 1941, Bandera's supporters declared Ukrainian independence and formed their own government. This was done without the consent of the Germans. The Nazis opposed the proclamation and reacted severely; within three days, those behind the declaration were arrested.

Some Jews believed that the Germans would behave as the Austrians had during their tenure in Lwów twenty years earlier.[25] These Jews refused to believe in the so-called Nazi atrocities that they had heard about. They couldn't understand why the Germans would want to kill Jews. But they soon discovered that there was no rhyme or reason to the Nazis' hatred of Jews. Killing and beating of Jews became a common phenomenon. No reason was needed. Before long, hundreds of corpses lined the streets.

Mundek's maternal grandmother, Rebecca Nestel, was spared this sight. Shortly before the Germans reached Rawa Ruska, she passed away.[26] On June

---

22. Dean, *Ghettos in German-Occupied Eastern Europe*, pp. 800–802.
23. See for example *Amtliches Gemeinde- und Dorfverzeichnis für das Generalgouvernement auf Grund der summarischen Bevölkerungsbestandsaufnahme am 1. März 1943, herausgegeben vom statistischen Amt des Generalgouvernement* [Township and village directory for the General Government on the basis of the March 1, 1943, census, published by the Statistical Office of the General Government] and see also *Statistisches Gemeindeverzeichnis des bisherigen polnischen Staates, mit Berücksichtigung der am 28. September 1939 festgelegten Grenze der deutschen und sowjetrussischen Reichsinteressen* [Statistical community directory of the current Polish state, with consideration of the September 28, 1939, border set by the interests of the German and Soviet Russian states].
24. B.F. Sabrin, ed., *Alliance for Murder: The Nazi-Ukrainian Nationalist Partnership in Genocide* (New York: Sarpedon, 1991), p. 7.
25. Yones, *Smoke in the Sand*, p. 79.
26. It is not known how she passed away or what was the cause of death.

28, 1941, the Germans entered and took possession of the town and immediately afterward, the Ukrainian police started to execute Jews.[27]

On Tuesday morning, July 1, 1941, two Ukrainian militiamen armed with sticks broke down the front door and entered the Łukawiecki flat.[28] They forced Joseph Łukawiecki and his two eldest sons – Mundek, who was twenty-one at the time, and Zygmunt, who was twenty – to join other Jews in clearing bodies from the streets. The Łukawieckis were taken to Brygidki Prison, where a group of Jews was assigned to load the corpses onto trucks and a second group was given the task of taking the bodies to a mass grave for burial. The Germans and the Ukrainians "motivated" the Jews to work more quickly by enthusiastically shooting down anyone they felt was working too slowly.

Joseph Łukawiecki and his two sons had the sense to jump into the prison basement and help to remove the corpses of those killed by the retreating Russians. This involved bringing the corpses upstairs to the prison's very large yard and loading them onto horse-drawn wagons. Around the yard, compressed to the walls on all sides, stood lines of bearded Jews with *payot* (sidelocks), all of them wearing black coats and black pants. Their faces were white and bloodless, utterly doomed to their bitter fate, as Gestapo officers armed with pistols stood in front of them and shot them down one row at a time.

For the rest of his life, Mundek would never forget the sounds of that terrible scene: the screams of the terrified Jews, their yelling, begging, and crying; the sound of the guns, *pak, pak, pak*; the German orders to the rest of the Jews queuing for their deaths, "*Schneller, Schneller!*" [Faster! Faster!]. And when the next victims had stepped forward and filled the line once again – *pak, pak, pak*, the bodies collapsed, and the Jews were ordered to load the corpses onto wagons. That was the way Rabbi Levin was killed.

Kazimierzowska Street, Grodecka Street, and Plac Głowackiego were soon filled with corpses. Joseph Łukawiecki and his two sons worked for three days from sunrise to four o'clock in the afternoon to clear the basement and yard of

---

27. Guy Miron and Shlomit Shulhani, eds., *The Yad Vashem Encyclopedia of the Ghettos during the Holocaust* (Jerusalem: Yad Vashem, 2010), vol. 2, p. 649.
28. Personal interview with Aliza Segal, May 30, 2011. Aliza Segal was a volunteer nurse who took personal care of Mundek Łukawiecki once a week in 1997 and 1998. Mundek dictated to her his memories, which were recorded in a notebook. Only four pages of this text have been found, however.

Brygidki Prison. After a long, grueling day, a German soldier shouted at them in German, "*Genug für heute*" (Enough for today). Immediately they dropped everything and ran home. To reach their building, they had only to go fifty meters, as it was directly opposite the Brygidki Prison, but in these fifty meters they were beaten by clubs, sticks, fists, and kicks. Nevertheless, nothing stopped them and they just continued running.

When Mundek's mother, Sarah Łukawiecki, opened the front door and saw her husband and two sons, tears of joy streamed down her face. There were countless other families who had already lost sizable contingents of their broods; for example, the Friedmans and another Jewish family called the Zisses, as well as the prominent owners of a religious Jewish bookstore in their neighborhood. The Łukawieckis' Jewish neighbors all came to see the miracle of their return.

The situation in Lwów was intolerable, impossible. Sergeant Felix Landau, a member of the *Einsatzkommandos*, wrote the following description of the horrible circumstances: "We continued going along the road. There were hundreds of Jews walking along the street with blood pouring down their faces, holes in their heads, their hands broken, and their eyes hanging out of their sockets. They were covered in blood. Some of them were carrying others who had collapsed."[29]

As a result of the terrible situation in Lwów, the Łukawiecki family decided to move to Joseph's parents' farm in Ostrowiec, next to Lubaczów. The possibility of going to Żydaczów, the hometown of Sarah Łukawiecki, was rejected, as it was a Jewish town and therefore likely to face severe Nazi atrocities. At sunset on July 8, 1941, Mundek left for Ostrowiec to seek help (such as a horse wagon) from Józef Kulpa for the transfer of the family. Upon his arrival at his late grandfather's farm on the morning of July 9, 1941, his grandmother Dora hugged him, crying inconsolably.

---

29. Rhodes, *Masters of Death*, pp. 61–63.

Chapter 5
Camp Lipowa

As a result of the disorganized Red Army's failure to successfully attack Finland in 1939–1940, Joseph Stalin had felt that Russia needed to avoid war with Germany at all costs, hence the signing of the treaty of non-aggression between Germany and the Union of Soviet Socialist Republics (the Molotov-Ribbentrop Pact). But due to his inherent distrust of Hitler, Stalin increased the size of his military nonetheless. By 1941, the Red Army had three million men enlisted (in three hundred divisions). This included children as young as fifteen years old who were conscripted into military service. The new Red Army recruits pledged to protect their Soviet homeland with their lives.

The Red Army's military barracks in Ostrowiec-Lubaczów were located in a clearing of the woods of Mazury forest, at the end of what is now known as Lipowa Street. It housed cavalry and infantry soldiers, who were supported by horse-drawn artillery. The Red Army was deployed in trenches and utilized military armor tanks, cavalry units, and towed canons, among other things. Only a few barracks were actually built. The entire division was dug into foxholes in between pine trees.[1]

This particular military outpost was primarily made up of teenagers and horses. Most of these youths were terrified of being soldiers. Their uniforms were oversized and made them look like walking scarecrows; their thin arms sank into their coat sleeves, and their overlapping trousers were stuffed into their leather boots. The "Children's Army" lacked basic training, as well as any real military experience. The officers and commanders did not provide them with much

---

[1]. Personal interview with Czesław Podporski and his mother Maria Szutka, September 24, 2010, in Ostrowiec. Maria knew this information from personal knowledge, and Czesław recounted his grandfather's stories.

guidance. There was an absence of political commissars,[2] whose job it was to instill soldiers with true loyalty to Russia's communist ideology and leadership. Enthusiasm to fight and defend Mother Russia to the death, and to die for the communist ideal, were not easily mustered up. Most of the Children's Army were recruited from families of laborers or peasants. Consequently, these soldiers were not convinced that they should die to defend Stalin's empire and did not enjoy being at the front, thousands of kilometers away from home.

The Children's Army was part of the Lwów defense line. Lubaczów was the external line in defending Lwów. The teenage soldiers were supposed to fight at the Dachnów antitank trench. The trench was designed by the Red Army engineering corps and dug by the Children's Army. They were instructed to fight from trenches rather than being given proper military training.

Nationalized by Russian authorities during the Soviet occupation, the Łukawiecki distillery in Ostrowiec produced purified vodka to meet the demands of the thirsty Children's Army. Part of pretending to be an adult meant consuming alcohol in mass quantities. As a result, most of their nights were spent getting drunk.

Despite receiving good intelligence that warned him ahead of time, Stalin had still been shocked when the Wehrmacht attacked and invaded the USSR during Operation Barbarossa.[3] After Colonel Zimmerman of the German Wehrmacht took control of Lubaczów[4] for the second time since the start of the war (on June 22, 1941), the demoralized Red Army had retreated, leaving confusion and chaos behind it, as well as abandoned military equipment, armament, weapons, food, and uniforms.[5]

The Children's Army at the Lipowa Camp had panicked at the overwhelming fury and efficiency of the Wehrmacht. Stunned, they ignored their orders and threw off their personal gear – a major breach of military code. The young men exchanged their uniforms for peasants' clothing. Those who did not have a change of clothes simply tore off any military insignias and fled before the arrival

---

2. An officer who was a voluntary member of the military structure for the purposes of enforcing ideology and education and to ensure the loyalty of soldiers.
3. Leopold Trepper, *The Great Game: The Story of the Red Orchestra*, trans. Helen Weaver (London: Michael Joseph, 1977). On June 10 and 11, British and American intelligence supplied the Russians with information about Operation Barbarossa. It confirmed information that Russian intelligence already had.
4. Hoffman, *Keep Yelling*, p. 37.
5. Ibid.

of the German troops. They tried to mingle with local peasants and sought refuge in their villages. In most cases, they were not accepted by the peasants. Local peasants did not much appreciate the intricacies of the Communist system. Terrified by what the Nazis might do to them if they found them, these desperate soldiers had run to the woods to hide. This is how the Red Army–affiliated partisans were established, who later became known as the Communist Partisans.

In the blink of an eye, the Lipowa Camp was deserted. It was as though some mysterious entity had caused all human life to evaporate. Uniforms and munitions were scattered everywhere. Offices were unlocked and files and papers were left unattended and in a mess. Food and kitchenware were left neatly organized for an upcoming meal. But there was no sign of human life. The Wehrmacht scouted the camp and after a quick search of the premises, ordered five Ukrainian Auxiliary Police officers to safeguard the deserted camp. The rest of the Wehrmacht rushed to Lwów with the goal of overrunning it.

One night soon afterwards, one of the deserters of the Lipowa Camp sought refuge at Józef Kulpa's farm. He was a young, terrified fifteen-year-old by the name of Piotr. He had one thing on his mind: avoid the Nazis. But he was also wary of being caught by his own Red Army. He was in real fear of being killed. The Germans did not generally kill prisoners of war, but in 1941–1942 there was in the Wehrmacht a *Kommissarbefehl* (order for commissars) that instructed that all captured political commissars of the Red Army had to be killed by the troops. Most of the troops therefore did so. The Wehrmacht captured more than three million members of the Red Army in World War II, and only a third of them survived. Piotr's well-grounded fear was that the Germans would most likely kill him.

On the other hand he was afraid that if the political commissars of the Red Army got their hands on him, he would be labeled a deserter and executed.

He was between a rock and a hard place.

In complete and utter desperation, Piotr crawled up to the front door of Kulpa's house and begged him to let him in. He was drenched with sweat from head to toe. The whites of his eyes had turned red from crying and his pupils were dilated, despite the daylight. The world had essentially collapsed in on him.

Kulpa agreed to provide him with shelter. Despite this fact, it still took Piotr a few hours to stop hyperventilating and crying. He shook for hours after being allowed into the farmhouse, but the possibility that he might be saved calmed him down slowly. Yet he still refused to eat and only drank water. His stomach was a bundle of nerves.

Kulpa learned that Piotr was born on the highlands of the Ural Mountains in a coal-mining town called Kemerovo. As a sign of gratitude to Kulpa, he informed his new host that his former camp was well equipped with military supplies, armaments, and munitions. Józef Kulpa immediately began to envision stocking up on military equipment and armaments for the ZWZ. He decided to act quickly, before the Wehrmacht organized itself and took possession of the Red Army's losses.

On the morning of July 9, 1941, Mundek Łukawiecki arrived in Ostrowiec at his grandmother's farm. Mundek went to see Józef Kulpa to ask for his assistance in transfering the Łukawiecki family from Lwów to Ostrowiec. Józef Kulpa immediately agreed and gave his consent. They decided that Kulpa would arrive in Lwów with a horse-drawn wagon to transport them on Sunday, August 3, 1941, thinking there would probably be less traffic and fewer SS patrols on a Sunday.

Kulpa briefed Mundek about the abandoned army outpost. Mundek was excited to finally get a chance to be involved in some real covert action and be able to support Józef Kulpa at the same time. At the end of the briefing, Kulpa told him that the operation was to take place that night, as the Germans were not completely oriented with the area and were also busy advancing through the Lwów region and eastward toward Russia. They agreed to meet in Ostrowiec at nine o'clock that evening at the intersection of what is now known as Lipowa and Sowińskiego Streets. This would give them the entire night to successfully complete their mission.

It was the beginning of summer and mild outside. The pine needles and tree branches were still wet from the previous day's rain and the mist hit Mundek's face as he walked to the meeting point, which was not far from his grandmother's farm. The only sound he could hear was the wind maneuvering its way through the treetops. Were it not for the reality of war, this excursion might have been an enjoyable walk through the woods.

It was Mundek's first assault against his oppressors. As he made his way to the designated meeting place, his thoughts wandered to his family. The fear of what might have happened to them since he had left overwhelmed him. Memories flooded his mind: his younger sister Judith's smile; his mother's farewell kiss; the easygoing yet tough nature of his father. He thought about the VIII Gimnazjum im. Kazimierza Wielkiego, where he had received his military training,[6] and about the upcoming raid, wondering if Kulpa would trust him enough to give him a weapon. Using it would signify the first step toward freedom. Not only his own freedom, but his family's and the entire Jewish nation's.

Mundek crept nearer to the edges of the woods. He knew the area by heart. Finally, he arrived at the meeting point at about 7:30 P.M. He was an hour and a half early. It was still daylight, so Mundek decided to scout the camp.

Because of the German invasion of Russia, all normal activities in the area had ceased. Nobody dared to go out without good reason. This included even getting food or harvesting crops. The residents just consumed what they had stored in their houses. Windows were sealed shut. Gates and doors were locked. Everything stood silent and still; there were literally no sounds from any of the houses or farms. It was as if a self-imposed curfew had been declared. The only movement came from German military vehicles, but aside from these military convoys, it was quiet and calm and the only people Mundek saw were refugees seeking shelter.

Kulpa arrived undetected with Piotr and his two sons, Stanisław and Jan. The Ukrainian guards at the gate were not particularly alert. One Ukrainian policeman stood close to the gate, while two other guards sat in front of the guards' post.

Darkness soon fell upon them. Kulpa made sure that everyone understood his role in the raid. Mundek and Kulpa would walk to the gate, wearing no uniform. Twenty-five meters before they reached it, Mundek was to stand in the middle of the road and shout in German, "*Wer ist dort? Wo ist die Wache? Ich bin Nachrichtenoffizier und unser Auto ist kaputt!*" (Who is here? Where are the guards? I am a German intelligence officer and our car broke down!). As the guards approached, Kulpa and Mundek were to shoot them. At this point, Kulpa's sons and Piotr would enter the camp with a two-wheeled cart and load up the armaments.

The two Ukrainian guards outside the gate immediately stood up as Mundek and Kulpa walked toward the gate. Fortunately, the gate area was not well lit. As they neared the gate, Mundek began speaking in German. The Ukrainian guards

---

6. See chapter 3, *Czyn*.

stood shocked and frozen with fear. All of a sudden, Mundek and Kulpa fired and killed all the guards in a flurry of gunfire.

Kulpa's sons arrived as the last gunshot was being fired. Kulpa opened the gate and the two-wheeled cart entered the Lipowa Camp. Piotr directed the group to the various storage areas where guns, munitions, uniforms, and boots were stored. They grabbed as much as they could, keeping them in their original boxes and cases.

Navigating quickly through the huge, well-stocked military camp, their only companion was the howling night wind. All of them put on Russian uniforms, hats, and boots, and armed themselves with guns, munitions, and hand grenades. In a matter of minutes, they were transformed from a ragtag group of guerillas to real soldiers. Their morale skyrocketed. When they had finished loading up the cart to capacity, they left to transport their newfound bounty to the Niwki woods.

It was after midnight when they arrived at Niwki. Kulpa gave each of them a shovel. Enthusiastically and vigorously, they began digging a three-by-three-meter hole for a cache, between two old pine trees. The soil was wet and starlight allowed them to see what they were doing, so it was not that hard to dig quickly. They finished digging their storage bunker within a couple of hours.

Shortly thereafter, Stanisław and Jan went to the farm and returned with a jerry can of water and a roll of tarpaper and canvas. They padded the bottom of the hole with canvas. First they put the armament boxes in, then the ammunitions in their original boxes. The third layer consisted of the uniforms and boots, and all of it was then covered with more canvas, wrapped in tarpaper. Finally, they covered the trench with soil and used pine needles to further camouflage it. Now they had Russian Vintovkas,[7] cavalry carbines, machine guns, bolts, hand grenades, pistols, binoculars, compasses, and uniforms safely stashed away!

It was almost four o'clock in the morning when Mundek left Kulpa and his sons and went back to his grandmother's farm. The sky was clear and the stars were still shining. Early daylight guided his short walk back. The pine trees were wet and the raindrops fell on his face. It looked like he was crying – but if there were any real tears, they were tears of joy.

---

7. The Vintovka Mosina (Винтовка Мосина) was a Russian military rifle, informally called the Mosin-Nagant after its two developers.

Kulpa instructed Mundek to return to Lwów and wait until he would arrive with the horse wagon on August 3, 1941. On the night of July 11, 1941 – after a day's rest at his grandmother's farm – Mundek left Dora, promising her to return with the whole family, as had been decided with Józef Kulpa. Before he left, Mundek changed out of his new Russian military uniform and back into peasant clothing. He wrapped the armament and weaponry he'd taken personally from the raid with the uniform and buried it near the farm.

The journey to Lwów was approximately eighty kilometers (fifty miles). Mundek avoided walking on the roads and instead stuck to the southeastern edge of the woods as he made his way in the general direction of Nowe Brusno and from there to the woods south of Rawa Ruska. He made it halfway and realized that sunrise was about an hour away. So Mundek decided to spend the day there and rest. It was cool and wet, but not freezing. He found refuge below a pine tree that was relatively dry. He took out a round loaf of black bread from his backpack, broke off a small part of it, and ate it with an onion.

Curled up close to the tree trunk, he fell asleep. He woke up at noon. Moving to the edge of the woods, he spotted the road to Lwów. Heavy German military movements were advancing toward Lwów. He decided to continue walking in the woods to Jaworów and then to Lwów. He left Rawa Ruska at dusk and arrived home later that night on July 16, 1941. His mother cried and hugged him, while caressing his wild, uncut black hair. Joseph, his father, did not say a word but in his quiet way, he was as happy as the day Mundek was born. His son was still alive. He thought that Mundek's return had paved the way for the family's survival.

But it was not to be.

Chapter 6
The Death of Humanity

On July 27, 1941, shortly after Mundek's return to Lwów, the Germans formed a Judenrat (Jewish council) headed by a man called Dr. Parnas. The Judenrat executed orders given by the Gestapo and the Ukrainians. To achieve this, the Judenrat built detention cells in the Judenrat building and formed a Jewish police unit that fully cooperated with the Gestapo and the Kriminalpolizei (criminal investigations agency – Kripo for short) section of the Ukrainian police. The Jewish Order Police wore hats with a yellow ribbon featuring a Star of David.

The newly recruited Jewish policemen almost all had criminal records and were the undesirables of the Jewish community. They were armed with clubs, which they used freely. To prove their worth, they often treated other Jews even more sadistically than the Nazis did. For example, during the clearing of the bodies that littered the streets on a daily basis, they would often beat unsuspecting Jews without reason – merely to impress the German guards and to demonstrate their loyalty and dedication to their newfound "profession." They were also the ones who made sure that all Jews wore the yellow Star of David. Those found not wearing it were shot down on the spot, no questions asked.

They blindly obeyed orders, no matter how cruel or heartless they were. In autumn 1941, a Jewish girl lost her mind and ran naked in the streets, shouting that it was her wedding day. She was beaten severely by two Jewish Order Policemen. They did this hoping that it would save them and their families' lives. They were mistaken, however. Cooperative Jews were still Jews, according to the Nazis. And all Jews needed to be exterminated for the Final Solution to be carried out effectively.

Very soon, the SS- und Polizeiführer (head of the SS and police of Galicia), General Fritz Katzmann,[1] ordered all Jews between the ages of eighteen and

---

1. SS-Gruppenführer Fritz Katzmann, commander of the German SS and police in Galicia, wrote a report submitted on June 30, 1943, to the SS and police chief Friedrich Wilhelm Krüger on "The

sixty to register for work. The Judenrat was given the task of organizing the registration. The Jews registered, while the Jewish Order Police searched homes for any Jews who were hiding and then handed them over to either the Germans or Ukrainians for execution.

After registering, Joseph Łukawiecki and his two sons continued to evacuate bodies from streets such as Kazimierzowska, Gródecka, and Plac Głowackiego. Every night they returned home.

One day, Ukrainian police stormed the building next to Mundek's. The house on 45 Kazimierzowska Street was owned by the wealthy Shprecher family. It was used as a rental property for very wealthy Jewish families. The authorities ordered all the occupants to be out within the hour, as they were now confiscating it and establishing it as their new headquarters. Realizing that this would be quite tumultuous and upsetting to the occupants, they told the occupants that they would each be allowed to take one suitcase with twenty-five kilos (fifty-five pounds) of their most prized possessions.

The tenants ran down the stairs with their suitcases and gathered in front of the building. The Ukrainians ordered them to line up. At gunpoint, they then ordered them to hand over all of their jewelry, money, and any other valuables. A Ukrainian soldier then opened each suitcase and took what he wanted, discarding the rest of the contents. When this task was complete, the occupants were ordered to undress. All of their clothes were then loaded onto a truck.

During this humiliating ordeal, the occupants were further degraded by being kicked, beaten, and abused in every way imaginable. But just as quickly as they were ordered out of their apartments, the occupants were suddenly permitted to return home, because a better building for the new police headquarters had just been located around the block.

Between July 25 and 27, 1941, the Ukrainian Auxiliary Police, supported by the Ukrainian nationalist movement, conducted an anti-Jewish pogrom to commemorate Symon Vasylyovych Petliura, the antisemitic Ukrainian leader who was responsible for Ukrainian pogroms in 1919. On May 25, 1926, he was killed by a young Jew – Shalom (Samuel) Schwartzbard – in Paris, France. Schwartzbard was acquitted, however, because the assassination was determined to be a "crime of passion" during the trial. On July 25, 1941, Ukrainian peasants from

---

Solution of the Jewish Question in Galicia" ("Lösung der Judenfrage im Distrikt Galizien").

Lwów gathered at the Ukrainian police headquarters. Armed with axes, knives, and clubs, they were escorted by Ukrainian police to Jewish areas and brutally executed every Jew they encountered. They conducted house-to-house hunts. When they couldn't find an actual Jew, they demolished Jewish property instead. Other peasants joined in by looting and raping as best as they could. By the end of the day, two thousand Jews had been killed.

The Ukrainians justified this Jewish execution and other pogroms as avenging the memory of "the blood of Petliura." Later that day, they burned down a majestic synagogue on Żółkiewska Street. But they didn't just commit arson. First, they forced members of the congregation to assemble in the synagogue. Then they gunned them down and burned the synagogue simultaneously, so that both the living and the dead were cremated inside.

While all of this madness was going on around them, the Łukawiecki children hid in their apartment. At first, Mundek and a friend of his, Zigo Friedman, built a hiding place in the bathroom by camouflaging a corner with a double wall and putting some food rations there. Mundek's parents, however, refused to hide, saying that they were too old.[2]

The hiding place was small and did not have ventilation, an external water supply, or even electricity. The entrance was camouflaged and made to look like part of the bathroom wall. It was designed to provide shelter and refuge for two people. Sarah Łukawiecki gave them one twenty-liter water container, a few cans of corned beef, sausages, dry meat, potatoes, bread, strawberry jam, salt, sugar, pepper, biscuits, chocolates, towels, and some clothing for each of them. For light, they used candles and matches. To make the time go by more quickly, they equipped the hiding place with blankets and pillows so they could sleep. In one corner, Mundek placed his violin, as he was a very talented player and the music helped him to calm down. If it hadn't been for real, it might have looked like a scout tent.

Mundek and Zigo Friedman settled themselves in the hiding place. But after a few days they would pop out and then run back to it whenever there was potential danger. They developed a procedure for retreating to the hiding place, although it was fraught with complications. One of them would stand on guard day and night to see if any German or Ukrainian soldier was approaching the

---

2. Joseph Łukawiecki was fifty-seven years old.

front entrance of the house on Kazimierzowska Street. As soon as there was a sign of a potential home invasion, both of them ran to the hiding place. The problem was, with Brygidki Prison opposite their house, there were always German and Ukrainian soldiers present. Usually, they were just coming and going from the busy prison. It was difficult to discern their movements but it was important to minimize false alarms, because getting to the hiding place was time consuming and emotionally draining.

Mundek's siblings also built a hiding place, in the attic on top of the apartment. It had the same characteristics as Mundek's, so they all shared the guard duty, and on the alert, everybody ran to his hideout. The family did not expose their hiding places to anyone, not even neighbors or friends. It was not safe to trust anyone.

All family members who stood guard outside witnessed the torture, random murders, and organized executions that took place at Brygidki Prison. During the day, Jews were brought there by Ukrainian police and executed. Then the Jewish policemen cleared out the bodies, with the help of other Jewish prisoners. All day long, masses of people stood under heavy armed guard at the entrance. The Ukrainians watched over them to prevent any escape attempts. To justify the killings, Jews were accused of being Russian supporters. But after a while, just being a Jew was a good enough reason to be killed. Hundreds of Jews were murdered in Brygidki Prison.

The disturbing scenes at the prison witnessed by the Łukawieckis gave the family first-hand knowledge of what was going on in Lwów and the increasing hostility building toward the Jews. It also put them in grave danger. Their mobility in and out of their home was perilous. Since the house was opposite the prison, it could be confiscated at any time for German use.

The situation for the Jews of Lwów became worse and worse. Kidnappings and killings in the streets were common. Jewish collaborators helped by revealing hideouts to the authorities.

The Łukawiecki family was raided quite often. However, the fact that two members of the Jewish council lived in the building afforded the family some protection. Nonetheless, their daily lives were paralyzed. Everything was put on hold. No one dared to go outside, unless it was completely unavoidable. The economy, cultural activities, and education within the city stopped dead in their tracks.

Chapter 7
Sokolniki Death Camp

On July 29, 1941, a member of the Jewish Judenrat took Joseph Łukawiecki and his two sons Mundek and Zygmunt to clean Janowska military camp, which was to be converted into a Wehrmacht military camp. They worked there for several days, cleaning the camp together with other Jews, and were then transferred to clean other military camps in Lwów. There were many military camps to be cleaned before the Nazis took them over. The workers were starving, as they had nothing to eat. Mundek and Zygmunt went to look for bread or even for non-Jews with whom to swap some goods for flour or bread.

On August 2, 1941, German police caught Mundek and his brother Zygmunt walking along Szpitalna Street searching for food. The sun was just coming up as they were put on a military truck and driven to the synagogue on Zołkiego Street. The Germans and Ukrainians housed captured Jews at this synagogue. Ironically, it was the same synagogue that the Łukawiecki family had formerly attended, where all the ceremonies were conducted in German and there was no separation between men and women during prayers.[1]

After a couple of hours, all of the Jews at the synagogue were transferred to the Sokolniki estate, which had been converted into a concentration camp.[2] The

---

1. The synagogue was burned down a few days later, on August 14, 1941.
2. Mundek Łukawiecki was very upset during his lifetime that proper documentation and remembrance ceremonies were not devoted to the camp. It has never been given its due, except by Tadeusz Zaderecki, "Gdy swastyka Lwowem władała" [When the swastika ruled Lwów], Yad Vashem Archives, 06/28, in a footnote. During the research for this book I was informed about Dr. Filip Friedman's book *Zagłada Żydów lwowskich* [The extermination of the Jews of Lwów] (Łódź: Centralnej Żydowskiej Komisji Historycznej [Central Jewish Historical Commission], 1945). which mentioned the camp. The camp is also recorded by the International Tracing Service, *Verzeichnis der Haftstätten unter dem Reichsführer-SS (1933–1945): Konzentrationslager und deren Aussenkommandos sowie andere Haftstätten unter dem Reichsführer-SS in Deutschland und deutsch besetzten Gebieten* [List of places of detention under the

Church built on the site of the former Sokolniki death camp

The Earl of Sokolniki owned a huge plot of land about twenty-five kilometers (fifteen miles) southwest of Lwów, known as Folwark Hrabiego Gołuchowskiego (Earl Sokolniki's Farm), and he had an agricultural farm for cattle and cowsheds, as well as stables for horses. The farm had about fifteen large barns in total. These had now been converted into various specific workshops whose purpose it was to renovate confiscated Jewish furniture and repair clothing, electrical appliances, shoes, and items that required carpentry work.

One barn, however, had been converted into a prison. The prisoners were generally wealthy Jews, and they were ordered to hand over sums of money to the Judenrat. If the prisoner's family failed to pay the ransom, he or she was executed. There was also a barn where the Jews who worked in the Sokolniki factories slept, mainly on the floor, which was covered with hay (*siano* in Polish).

The camp was surrounded by swamps and barbed-wire fencing on three

---

Reichsführer-SS (1933–1945): Concentration camps and their branch camps and other places of detention under the Reichsführer-SS in Germany and German-occupied territories] (Bad Arolsen: International Tracing Service, 1979), p. 575. In that document it is stated that the camp was opened in August 1, 1941, and was active three months till November 1, 1941. There is also a short description in the book written by Jacob Gerstenfeld-Maltiel, *My Private War: One Man's Struggle to Survive the Soviets and the Nazis* (London: Vallentine Mitchell, 1993), p. 75.

sides. The Nazis put watchtowers on each side of the camp, which were manned by Ukrainians. Not surprisingly, nobody dared to try to escape. Yet the guards invented imaginary flights and escapes and executed Jews anyway.

When new Jews arrived at the Sokolniki death camp,[3] all of the Jews gathered in the *Appelplatz* (a sadistic "parade ground" in which attendance was taken and selections were made) and a new selection of professional Jews was conducted. Following this "rite of passage," they were made to line up and had their names, ages, and professions recorded. The groups were separated into three categories: (i) white-collar professionals, (ii) artisans or skilled workers, and (iii) those without any profession.

A German SS guard pronounced – "*Schumacher – rechts* [right], *Tischler – links* [left]," and so on. Those without a profession were sent to work in the swamps. Those who looked wealthy and intelligent were sent to the prison, and a ransom amount was determined. Mundek soon realized that some Jews being held at Sokolniki were hostages from wealthy Jewish families. They were being held in order to blackmail their families into paying a ransom for their release. If the families refused, they would never see their relatives again.

It was impossible to escape. During the Russian occupation, the estate was confiscated and became a kolkhoz (collective farm) or sovkhoz (state-owned farm). The Nazis eventually transformed it into a death camp, complete with watchtowers surrounded by a barbed-wire fence.[4]

The Sokolniki camp was staffed by only a handful of SS soldiers, who all wore green SS uniforms and caps with the skull insignia. The remainder of the guards were policemen from the Ukrainian Auxiliary Police, who wore their traditional blue uniforms.[5] The population of the camp was about five hundred Jews at any

---

3. The term "death camp" was used by Mundek Łukawiecki always when he mentioned that camp, as only very few survived it. He regarded the camp's intended purpose as the execution of Jews, and not only as a labor camp. I have respected Mundek's nomenclature.
4. Ironically, the Germans called these camps *Arbeitserziehungslager* (AEL), "educational labor camps." Dr. Filip Friedman in his book *Zagłada Żydów lwowskich* said that Sokolniki camp was one of the first to be known as an *Arbeitserziehungslager*. The Sokolniki camp was certainly the first of its kind in Lwów.
5. Gerstenfeld-Maltiel, in his book *My Private War*, p. 75, said that the commander of the camp was a Ukrainian named Tshubak (Czubak) and his deputy was also a Ukrainian, called Jaworski. He also said that the Germans did not pay much attention to the camp knowing that that could trust the Ukrainians in the matter of sadistic treatment Jews.

given time. New waves of Jews were brought in to replace those who had just been murdered. There was always a full complement of prisoners at the camp. They were subject to constant beatings and harassment. During the summer of 1941, hundreds of Jewish men from Lwów were brought in. All of them were killed within weeks. In fact, very few people came back from Skolniki.

For the SS guards at the Sokolniki camp, killing Jews was seen as a fun activity. One of the Gestapo soldiers – a young man armed with a Parabellum pistol – used to take walks among the Jews. Without warning, he would throw his hat near a Jew to shoot it, and also shoot the prisoner at the same time. When he managed to kill the Jew while the hat was still in the air, he beamed proudly and laughed out loud. By doing so, he proved that he was an "accomplished sniper."

Killing Jews was just part of the daily routine at Sokolniki. Jews who did not answer questions fast enough or did not run as quickly as was expected were shot down regularly. Dead bodies accumulated everywhere. The only Jewish voices heard were groans after blasts of gunfire. It was the closest thing to hell on earth that Mundek and Zygmunt could imagine.

When the Łukawiecki boys arrived at Sokolniki, the new prisoners were severely beaten by the Ukrainian Auxiliary Police. Mundek was categorized as having no profession and was sent to dry the swamps, while Zygmunt went to work at the stables with horses (*koniuszy* in Polish) because he mentioned that he was a veterinary student.

Sokolniki was surrounded by huge swamps that covered an extensive area. The heavy, black soil prevented most of its water from seeping. Instead, it caused that thick layer of black soil to turn into something like spongy mud. Once in the swamp, it was almost impossible to get out, as you would sink up to your knees in mud. Walking in the swamps was just as difficult; it felt like you were walking in one spot as you slowly sank.

Drying out the swamps was very hard labor, not least because many of the prisoners were standing waist-deep in the water. Sand was brought into the swamps by wheelbarrows, and from there it was carried in by Jews. If one of the Jews slowed down the chain of workers or if the Ukrainian guards felt that someone wasn't working hard enough, he was brutally beaten with a wooden club or just shot on the spot. The body was then left in the swamps. Countless numbers of Jews died in these swamps, which essentially became a mass Jewish graveyard.

Mundek got a wheelbarrow and was forced to run and bring sand from elsewhere to the swamp. The amount of sand was imposed; he could not choose how much to take. They made him fill up the wheelbarrow until the sand was spilling over. The Ukrainians kept a close eye on this and hit anyone who failed to obey their rules. You also had to run with the wheelbarrow, whether it was full of sand or empty. No walking. Back and forth. To and fro. Always on the run. Those who failed were beaten; death was a certainty for almost all wheelbarrow carriers. The only question was when.

Mundek worked with a wheelbarrow for three days. He realized that he would not survive long like this. On top of the hard labor, his hunger was killing him. The food that they were given had no nutritional value. It was a watery soup without any real substance. Mundek was completely exhausted. He could not muster any energy from this lukewarm water of unidentified content that was served twice a day.

To increase his chances for survival, Mundek went to work in the swamp itself. The advantage of working in the swamp was that the Ukrainians did not enter the swamps. The task in the swamps was to disperse the sand brought in the wheelbarrows, while standing waist-deep in the swamp water.

Work in the swamp was very difficult as well. With each step, Mundek sank further into the pulpy, sucking quicksand. He had to fight and save his energy just to be able to walk in the swamps. In the evenings when they were ordered to stop working, it was even difficult just to get out of the swamp. The prisoners helped each other by carrying each other out of the swamp. They would then wash themselves and were given the warm "soup." Because they worked in the swamp and were not allowed to leave their work to eat, it was the only food they were given.

After a couple of days of this, Mundek decided once again that he could not survive any longer unless he changed his workplace. The following morning at check-in, he claimed to be a carpenter and was sent to work at a carpentry workshop. He was very happy. He felt that this would give him a better chance of surviving because the soup at the workshops was much thicker and more nutritious.

His joy quickly dissipated.

Sokolniki operated various workshops to repair confiscated goods taken from Jews before they were handed over to the Germans or Ukrainians. The workshops renovated furniture, fixed holes in furs, and patched up tailored clothing and old shoes. All of the items were looted from wealthy Jews in Lwów under order of the Judenrat – who in turn received their directives from either the Ukrainian or German authorities.

When Mundek arrived at the workshop, the Jewish head of carpentry ordered him to do something using professional language that only a carpenter would understand. Mundek thought that he wanted him to dust the furniture, so he took a rag and began dusting. After a few moments, the head of carpentry came to observe what Mundek was doing and began beating him. He shouted that Mundek was not a carpenter and that he had cheated and lied his way into the workshop.

"You cheated the Germans, but you will not cheat me!" he screamed. "Go away, right now!"

"Please let me stay until nightfall," begged Mundek, crying and weeping. "If I go out now, they will kill me. Please let me stay."

Mundek tried to hug and kiss him, as if he were a small boy asking forgiveness from his father, but the chief carpenter knocked Mundek to the ground in anger.

"I don't care if they kill you like a dog!" he shouted. "Get out of here, right now! Get out of my sight and leave the workshop!"

Just like that, Mundek's life seemed to have ended. He believed these were his last moments. His throat felt choked and it was hard for him to breathe. He expected the Gestapo or the Ukrainians to show up at any moment and kill him because of his lie.

Just then, another Jew from a nearby workshop came in and approached Mundek.

"You're a varnish expert, right?" he said. "Aren't you?"

Mundek replied that he was and the man took him to the varnishing workshop, where Mundek worked for the next two months until September 1941, when he and his brother Zygmunt were suddenly released.

During this three-month period, Zygmunt worked in the stables with a non-Jewish veterinarian. They took care of German horses and other livestock. Since they slept in the same barracks, the brothers saw each other every night. They realized that the best chance they had of being released was through a ransom, which would be used to blackmail their families. The brothers talked it over and decided that Zygmunt would ask the veterinarian, who was a Polish resident of Lwów, to help them by telling their parents where they were being kept.

The veterinarian kept his promise. He went to Joseph Łukawiecki's apartment and brought a sign of life from the brothers. Cries of joy overcame them. The family had been certain that they would never see them again, assuming that they had been executed. Joseph went to his neighbor to consult with him as to what to do and how. Dr. Lostinger and Dr. Lobliner, two prominent members of the Judenrat, told him to pay a ransom of $100 USD for each of the boys. The ransom payments were made with the assistance of the two doctors.

In late September 1941[6] – after what seemed like a lifetime – the boys were suddenly told to go home. On a chilly morning, while all the Jews in Sokolniki were standing in the *Appellplatz*, the words "*Mundek Łukawiecki, raus*" and then "*Zygmunt Łukawiecki, raus*" were suddenly shouted. The brothers stepped out. They were then told that they were being released. They left the Sokolniki camp as fast as they could.

Mundek and Zygmunt went home through the countryside. On the way, they were beaten and harassed by Poles. Then a Polish peasant's wife invited them into her house and gave them soup. One of her neighbors protested the fact that she was feeding them, saying they were supposed to die. She rejected him and answered, "They are human beings too." The conversation made the two brothers anxious, as they were afraid that he would wait for them and try to kill them. So they hurriedly finished their soup and ran the rest of the twenty-four kilometers (fifteen miles) from Sokolniki to Lwów.

It took the brothers almost the entire morning to get home. When they finally opened the apartment door, the family gathered, hugging and crying from joy. The unbelievable had happened. It truly was a miracle. Even the neighbors popped in to see the Łukawiecki brothers' return.

---

6. Testimony of Edmund (Mundek) Łukawiecki (Moshe Lavee) to Yad Vashem, July 28, 1993, no. 03-6946, tape no. 033c/2757. In this testimony, Mundek Łukawiecki said that he was in Sokolniki death camp for about six months. In a supplemental biography given to the UB on May 23, 1945, he claimed he was there only three months.

Chapter 8
Return to the Underground Movement

In late September 1941, after being released from the Sokolniki death camp, Mundek Łukawiecki renewed his connections with the ZWZ underground movement. He thanked his lucky stars that he was no longer in the hands of the Germans. He now had to regain the trust and confidence of Kulpa and convince him that he had not given away any of the ZWZ's secrets or plans while in custody. In truth, he had not revealed anything about the underground movement during his incarceration. After a short debriefing, Mundek proved that he had not exposed the ZWZ while at Sokolniki and was quickly reintegrated into the ZWZ.[1] The ZWZ instructed him to return to the Dąbrowa woods (in the southern part of the Mazury forest)[2] after retrieving his weaponry and uniform that was hidden near his grandmother's farm in Ostrowiec.

Mundek passed his time just trying to survive – and help his family survive – each day. Meanwhile, life in Lwów became more and more unbearable for the Jews. In August 1941, movement restrictions were imposed. The harassment and killing of Jews was on the rise. Children started to be targeted as they were seen as non-productive. Food was restricted and hunger prevailed. The Yiddish radio station stopped broadcasting. Jewish collaborators and spies increased their activities, hoping that their cooperation with the Nazis and Ukrainians would help them to save themselves and their families. Nothing was sacred – not hiding places, not men, not women, not even children. It became impossible to trust

---

1. Seven months after Mundek's arrival, the ZWZ reconstituted itself as Armia Krajowa (AK), which was formed in February 1942. Consequently, he became an AK member.
2. From Mundek's biographical information form in his UB file, filled out by Mundek Łukawiecki on April 6, 1946. UB personal file of Mundek Łukawiecki, IPN/OBUiAd/Kraków, Sygn IPN 16 057/1028.

Aleksander Łukawiecki, the adopted son of Hersh and Dora Łukawiecki, Jarosław, Poland, 1938

anybody. It was every man for himself and his family. Terror dominated Lwów, and any semblance of humanity had died.³

Life in Lubaczów was no better. The Nazis, Ukrainians, and their collaborators (including Galiziendeutsche inhabitants⁴) abused Jews and openly conducted atrocities on a daily basis. Half the Jews of Lubaczów had already been executed.

Amidst this climate of fear, families left Lwów and went to Warsaw and other small towns and villages, hoping that the harassment of Jews in these places would be less severe. Jews bought false Polish or German passports to try to finesse their way through the roadblocks on the way. To counteract this emigration, the Nazis increased the number of checkpoints.

Mundek's uncle Aleksander Łukawiecki – the adopted son of Hersh and Dora Łukawiecki – decided to escape to Hungary, where the Łukawieckis owned a vineyard in the vicinity of the city of Kisvárda.⁵ Aleksander succeeded in making

---

3. For a comprehensive description see Yones, *Smoke in the Sand*, pp. 75–98.
4. Their ancestors had been resettled by the Austrian empire in Galicia. These ethnic Germans spoke a dialect of German called Volksdeutsch.
5. He was an agronomist by profession; in Kisvárda he found a job as a chief agronomist in a sovkhoz (a state-owned farm).

Aleksander Łukawiecki and his wife, Jarosław, Poland, 1938

his way there – leaving his Polish wife and daughter behind – and hid in Kisvárda for the duration of the war. He was the only Łukawiecki, apart from Mundek, to survive World War II.[6]

Joseph Łukawiecki felt that the family's chance of survival would be greater in the countryside than in Lwów. The possibility of moving to Żydaczów (the small

---

6. As this book was written, the author met his daughter, Zofia, and grandson Professor Grzegorz Bubak. Aleksander never spoke about his history. He told no one that he was the adopted son of a Jewish family. He kept it secret even from his wife – a Polish Christian woman who survived WWII in her birth town of Jarosław. A glimpse was revealed to them by the author. It seems Aleksander was under the impression that he was the only survivor of the family. He never returned to Poland. His wife and daughter and later his daughter's children used from time to time to travel to Hungary to visit him. He passed away in 1979. In 2011, DNA material provided by Aleksander Łukawiecki's daughter and Mundek's son were analyzed in order to establish their potential family relation. Results were negative. Robert M. Archer, MD, Chief Scientific Officer, Genetic Identity, Kinship Screening Report, case number ZG 201016142, dated June 10, 2010, stated, "The individuals tested are unlikely to be biologically related."

hometown of Joseph's wife Sarah) was dismissed.[7] Żydaczów is located twenty-nine kilometers (eighteen miles) northeast of Stryj on the banks of the Stryj River, seventy kilometers (around forty-five miles) south of Lwów. The town consisted of only Jews. The Jewish community at that time had already been annihilated; the Germans entered Żydaczów on July 3, 1941, and immediately, on July 4–5, 1941, hundreds of Jews from Żydaczów were deported to Bełżec, and the rest of the Jews were transferred on September 30, 1941, to Stryj.[8] From mid-1942 until the end of 1943, Austrian policemen in Stryj killed the area's Jews.[9] Twenty uniformed policemen established a precinct post. Most of them were members of the NSDAP[10] and the majority wore the honor chevron awarded to "old fighters." On September 3–6, 1942, five thousand Jews were deported to Bełżec. On October 17–18, an additional two thousand Jews were deported to Bełżec, and in November, a further fifteen hundred.[11]

Because of its remote location, isolation, and the German origin of its inhabitants, it seemed likely that life in Ostrowiec would be better and that there would be far less harassment of Jews than in Lwów or even in neighboring Lubaczów. The family therefore decided to try to leave for Ostrowiec once again.

Then one night, Zygmunt was wounded by a German patrol while seeking food at night. Mundek rescued him and brought him back home. The bullet had penetrated and exited his right shoulder, so there was no immediate threat to his life. Joseph Łukawiecki decided that Zygmunt should be transferred to Ostrowiec as quickly as possible so that he might get medical care. Staying in Lwów meant death because the Ukrainians executed the wounded and the ill. In Ostrowiec, Zygmunt's care and rehabilitation could be arranged for and looked after by his grandmother, with the assistance of the Kulpas.[12] In addition, Joseph

---

7. In retrospect this was the right decision. Żydaczów's Jews were annihilated in summer 1942 and Lubaczów's Jews by winter 1942–1943.
8. Shmuel Spector, ed. in chief, *The Encyclopedia of Jewish Life before and during the Holocaust* (New York: NYU Press, 2001), vol. 3, pp. 1522–23; Yitzhak Arad, *Belzec, Sobibor, Treblinka: The Operation Reinhard Death Camps* (Bloomington: Indiana University Press, 1987), p. 386.
9. Edward B. Westermann, *Hitler's Police Battalions: Enforcing Racial War in the East* (Lawrence: University Press of Kansas, 2005), pp. 213–16.
10. Nationalsozialistische Deutsche Arbeiterpartei, commonly known as the Nazi Party.
11. Arad, *Belzec, Sobibor, Treblinka*, p. 386.
12. See Kulpa family request to the embassy of Israel for Righteous Among the Nations status for Józef Kulpa and his wife, dated December 31, 1992.

Łukawiecki had another business associate in Lubaczów: Shimon Bern, whose wife, Gittel Katz Bern, was a distant relative of the Łukawieckis. Shimon Bern and Joseph Łukawiecki were very good friends and Joseph had assisted Shimon on numerous occasions. He knew therefore that Shimon would also help Zygmunt and make sure he received good medical care.

The situation presented the perfect opportunity to renew the family plan of relocating to Ostrowiec and for Mundek to report to the Dąbrowa woods at the same time. After all, Mundek was the perfect person to go to Ostrowiec and to take Zygmunt there; he had German papers, he knew the area, and his food and supplies were sufficient for the next few days.

Rafael, the youngest brother, asked to join as well. Mundek turned down the request and said that Rafael must remain with their parents and sister to assist them, since he was the only son left at home. Besides, it was too risky for the three of them to go together because the larger the group the greater the likelihood of them getting caught. In any event, Mundek could take care of Zygmunt on his own and Rafael's help wasn't needed for the journey. Mundek added that he was going to arrange the immediate transfer of the family to Ostrowiec with Kulpa. He also rejected Rafael's request to join the ZWZ, saying he was too young to survive in the woods.[13]

On September 19, 1941, Mundek and Zygmunt left the house for their two- to three-night walk. The seventy kilometers from Lwów to Ostrowiec were to be covered using countryside roads and only at night.

When they finally arrived in Ostrowiec at sunrise on September 21, 1941, their grandmother hugged her grandsons and kissed them fervently. Not a word was said. She quickly served them bread and hot soup. Mundek told his grandmother that he was going to arrange the immediate transfer of the family to Ostrowiec and after that would be heading back to Lwów. Her response surprised Mundek and Zygmunt. She said, "God is with us. Today it is the eve of the Jewish New Year. We are opening a new page in our lives with God's blessing." Dora Łukawiecki was not religious, but her words filled them with hope.

After dinner, Zygmunt went to sleep and Mundek went to see Kulpa. Kulpa responded promptly and positively. It was decided that Kulpa would arrive in

---

13. Mundek regretted this decision his entire life. Interview with Aliza Segal, February 5, 2012.

Lwów on Friday, October 3, 1941, at eight P.M. and would meet them at the corner of Kazimierzowska and Brajerowska Streets.

Mundek left Kulpa and went to look for his weaponry and uniform near his grandmother's farm. Unfortunately, all of it was useless. The weapons were covered with a thick layer of rust and were impossible to fix. His uniform had also become very much worse for the wear and looked more like a pile of rags. It had basically disintegrated due to water damage – and all this after only four months. Mundek feared that the same thing had happened to the weaponry that was hidden next to Kulpa's farm.

Mundek then went to the Dąbrowa woods to meet with ZWZ members. He requested and was granted permission to go to Lwów to attend to a family matter – the transfer to Ostrowiec.

Chapter 9
Relocation to Ostrowiec

Ostrowiec was a small suburb about two kilometers southeast of Lubaczów, seventy kilometers northwest of Lwów.[1] It was formed as a German-speaking settlement at the time of the Habsburg monarchy[2] in 1783,[3] and was populated by a minority of people of Austrian or German origin. On December 3, 1932, it was annexed to Lubaczów as a suburb and until 1939 was part of the Lwów district.[4]

The ethnic German population struck roots here and were devoted to Poland. They did not cooperate with the Nazi occupation and in 1941 formed a local militia to defend themselves. They were a very important source of information to the underground movement.[5]

The Łukawieckis' first attempt to move to Ostrowiec had failed when Mundek and Zygmunt were caught and detained in the Sokolniki camp. Now was the time to try to relocate again. After transferring the wounded Zygmunt to Ostrowiec, Mundek returned to his family in Lwów and told them of Kulpa's decision to move them from Lwów to Ostrowiec on Friday October 3, 1941, at eight P.M., two days after Yom Kippur.

The family prepared for their move very secretly. They decided not to take any luggage – only small personal bags – so that they would not draw any attention

---

1. According to the terms of the Molotov-Ribbentrop Pact, Lubaczów would be part of the USSR.
2. Filip Sulimierski, Bronislaw Chlebowski, and Władysław Walewski, *Slownik geograficzny królestwa polskiego i innych krajów slowianskich* [The geographical dictionary of the kingdom of Poland and other Slavic countries] (Warsaw, 1880–1902), vol. 7, p. 719.
3. Wiesław Zarzycki, "Kolonizacja józefińska w powiecie lubaczowskim" [Josephian colonization in Lubaczów county], master's thesis written under the direction of Professor Joseph Półćwiartek, Rzeszów, 1992, p. 57.
4. Ukrainian nationalists believed that the Germans would allow the establishment of an independent Ukrainian state that included Lubaczów. See Roman Ogryzło, "Wybrane Zagadnienia Demograficzne" [Selected demographic issues], in *Rocznik Lubaczowski* [Lubaczów yearbook], vol. 5 (Lubaczów: Towarzysto Miłośników Ziemi Lubaczowskiej, 1994), p. 96.
5. See Ogryzło, "Wybrane Zagadnienia Demograficzne," in *Rocznik Lubaczowski*, vol. 5, p. 98.

to themselves on the road and would be able to move easily. They decided to leave on a Friday night so that they would be less likely to be identified as Jews, since it was the beginning of the Sabbath, rather than leaving on Yom Kippur, as they were not sure that the Gentiles would reduce their road blocks on that day. Mundek had arranged with Kulpa that he would bring a two-wheeled, one-horse wagon on Friday night at eight o'clock and wait for them at the corner of Kazimierzowska (now Horodocka) and Brajerowska Streets.

On Friday night, October 3, 1941, Kulpa waited with a horse-drawn wagon for the Łukawiecki family, as agreed. Mina and Mundek arrived first. A few moments later Rafael and Judith appeared. They were soon followed by their mother Sarah. Lastly, Joseph showed up. All of them wore peasant-style clothing, without any Jewish signs or badges, carrying small, brown fabric bags. Although it was autumn, they were enveloped in heavy coats and hats.

They sat very quietly in the wagon and you could cut the tension with a knife. Kazimierzowska Street and the Brygidki Prison entrance were both quiet. There was little or no traffic on the street. The light train on Kazmierzowska had ceased operating already. There was also no movement on tiny Brajerowska Street. Electric lamps illuminated the entrance to Brygidki Prison, so any shadows could be seen clearly.

Mundek sat next to Kulpa. They steered the wagon toward Mickiewicza Street, next to the Stadpark, and then to the west, in and out of small streets and alleys to avoid encounters with checkpoints. After about half an hour, they had left Lwów. Looking back, they did not know if they would ever see it again.

Kulpa, Joseph, and Mundek knew the route by heart. They steered the wagon all seventy kilometers through the countryside, away from main roads, northwest to Ostrowiec. No words were spoken. They sat in complete silence.

Needless to say, it was not a happy journey. They moved only at night. During the day, the family hid and rested in the woods, making sure that strangers could not see them from the roads. They ate canned food warmed up over a fire.

The journey took a lot longer than usual – three nights – but it was much safer that way. Three nights of complete silence. When they had to talk, they whispered to one another. Absorbing the seriousness of the situation from the adults, even the boisterous and talkative eight-year-old Judith was quiet.

At the end of the third night, as dawn approached, they arrived at Józef Kulpa's farm. Kulpa immediately took them into his barn and hid them for the day.

The following day after their arrival, Kulpa made sure that the Łukawiecki farmhouse was still safe. He spoke to Dora, Joseph's mother, and at night he brought the Łukawiecki family to the farmhouse where Dora and some other family members were residing. The reunion was punctuated by intense hugging and quiet crying, but there was no real joy. Kulpa then laid out the rules of the safe house: "Do not leave this house. I will promise to take care of your needs."

Zygmunt and Rafael did not stay, however. Shortly after arriving in Ostrowiec, around October 6, 1941, the two brothers went to Rawa Ruska to see their grandmother Rebecca Nestel's widower husband, Jacob Gerstenfeld, with whom they were still in contact.[6] Jacob and Rebecca had previously lived in Narol,[7] but when the Lubaczów district (*powiat Lubaczów*) was divided in autumn 1939 between Germany and USSR, Narol became part of the German district of Lublin.[8] Upon entering Narol in September 1939, the Germans had expelled all the Jews to Rawa Ruska, which was under USSR control.[9]

Now tragedy struck the family: Zygmunt and Rafael were caught on their way to Rawa Ruska, brought to the town, and summarily executed.[10]

After Zygmunt and Rafael were killed, Mundek and his parents lost contact with Jacob Gerstenfeld. Only years later was it discovered that Jacob and his daughter from his first marriage, Rebecca,[11] had decided to flee to the Soviet Union in mid-1942 and ultimately ended up in a city named Biysk[12] in Siberia.[13]

---

6. Sarah kept her mother's maiden name, Nestel, and did not use her stepfather's name, Gerstenfeld.
7. Narol is a small town, located about twenty-five kilometers (fifteen miles) northeast of Lubaczów. See the Central Zionist Archives, file no. 79947, database S104DB.
8. The Lubaczów district was divided according to the Molotov-Ribbentrop Pact between the USSR and Germany. Narol was incorporated into the General Government formed by Germany, and became part of District Galizien, in the Lublin District.
9. Spector, *Encyclopedia of Jewish Life*, vol. 2, p. 875.
10. Moshe Lavee (Edmund/Mundek Łukawiecki), recorded interview by USC Shoah Foundation Institute, interview code 31895, May 27, 1997.
11. Mundek's grandmother – Jacob's second wife – was also named Rebecca. Jacob and his first wife Michal had ten children. All of them emigrated (most to the United States) except the youngest one, Rebecca, born in 1907.
12. Biysk is located 360 kilometers (about 225 miles) south of Novosibirsk. See the Central Zionist Archives, file no. 79947, database S104DB.
13. In the Central Zionist Archives, Jerusalem, files S104P/79947 and S6P/3405/G, is a letter written on June 6, 1946, by another child of Jacob Grestenfeld, Rebecca's brother Leo Gerstenfeld, to Palestine authorities requesting an entry permit for Rebecca to Palestine. In the letter, Leo states that Rebecca and her father left Rawa Ruska to travel to Siberia on May 11, 1942. In further letters he wrote that her address in Siberia was 5 Proletarskaya, Biysk (Leo Gerstenfeld, letter dated September 7, 1943). In Siberia Jacob died and Rebecca was married.

Chapter 10
Partisan Fighting Company

On October 6, 1941, Mundek reported back to the ZWZ. Upon his return, he was assigned to platoon no. 15 of Mariarmia in the Dąbrowa woods and was given the code name Łuk.[1] He was very proud and happy. The local commander was Jerzy Zagajski ("Lopek").[2] The unit was divided into small groups of eighteen to twenty ZWZ members. They were primarily Spaleni[3] who were under the command of Marian Warda ("Polakowski"), a high-ranking ZWZ commander. They practiced their shooting skills in the woods. After living and training together for several months, they became very close and felt like one big, extended family. ZWZ members who were known to the Nazis were subject to persecution and could therefore not stay in their homes any longer. They were constantly hunted down and wanted by the German Gestapo or the police. As a result, they too were forced to seek refuge in the woods.

Marian Warda became the commanding officer of the Spaleni and his group

---

1. Łuk means "violin bow" in English. Mundek indeed played the violin and this may have been the reason this code name was chosen for him. From Mundek's biographical information form in his UB file, filled out by Mundek Łukawiecki on April 6, 1946. UB personal file of Mundek Łukawiecki, IPN/OBUiAd/Kraków, Sygn IPN 16 057/1028. Mundek was not introduced to all of the members of the movement, but only to his cell. None of them knew he was a Jew until later, after he had brought Chana Bern to the forest.
2. Ireneusz Caban, *Oddziały partyzanckie i samoobrony obwodu AK Tomaszów Lubelski* [Partisan units and self-defense in the Tomaszów Lubelski district AK] (Warsaw: O.K. Tomasz Wiater, 2000), p. 65. The Caban family were well known in Tomaszów Lubelski. Israel Kelner, who was born there in 1921, told me in a personal interview on April 11, 2013, that every May one of the members of the Caban family used to climb up on top of the water tower every evening and play the trumpet for the pleasure of all the town's inhabitants.
3. Spaleni means "burned" in English. The so-called "burned" were underground members who had to hide in the woods because they were on the Gestapo's hit list. To avoid being recaptured, they ran away to the woods and hid there. Mundek himself was not one of the Spaleni, but was initially placed with them, perhaps as an indication that the AK did not fully trust him.

gradually became the largest gang of Spaleni. Most of them were around twenty-four years old. No women were allowed to join in the beginning. The group consisted of intelligent people like the four children of Professor Ostrovsky from Lwów, who had been caught by the Ukrainians.

As time passed and their numbers increased, the Spaleni were transferred to the Red Army Partisan Camp commanded by Miszka Tatar[4] for military training.[5] This was surprising considering the mutual distrust between the ZWZ and the Red Army Partisans.

The day after Mundek's arrival, he was called upon to swear an oath of allegiance to the ZWZ.[6] The ceremony was conducted by four members whom Mundek recognized as students from Lwów. After the ceremony, he officially became a soldier and was given a weapon, a Česká zbrojovka.[7] The main sources of weaponry were the peasants. In each farm, the peasants hid weapons and ammunition, and they gladly gave them to the partisans.

Aside from each having their own weapons, the unit had a machine gun and a nearly unlimited quantity of hand grenades. Mundek was equipped with a Mauser rifle, Parabellum pistol, and four grenades. Most of the unit wore military uniforms. The woods were divided into zones and each group had its own boundaries.

The Spaleni, the ZWZ members, and the Red Army had no contact with other partisan groups. They were afraid of being captured by partisans who cooperated with the Ukrainians and were affiliated with the national movement of Bandera. Since it was still fall, the Spaleni lived in the woods below the wide branches of pine trees. They covered the branches with tar paper (*papa* in Polish) to block the penetration of rain and moisture, and placed blankets on the

---

4. His real name was Michaił Atamanow. The troops he commanded were called the Miszki Tatara.
5. Caban, *Oddziały partyzanckie*, p 42.
6. The ZWZ was renamed Armia Krajowa (AK) on February 14, 1942. Probably this was the reason that prior to the forming of AK, Mundek adopted the name "*Czyn*," the name of the pamphlet he had distributed, as the name of the ZWZ, which itself had been a union of organizations.
7. The vz. (model) 24 rifles designed and produced in Czechoslovakia from 1924. (Česká Zbrojovka means "Czech Arms Factory.") It was developed from the Mauser Gewehr 98 line, featuring a 600 mm (23.6") barrel.

ground. Up to four Spaleni shared one tree each. To get through the winters, they built bunkers.

Food was not a problem. They collected potatoes and other types of vegetables from the fields. On occasion, they went to peasants and asked, "*Jesteśmy grupą partyzantów polskich, brakuje nam chleba, czy zechcecie podzielić się chlebem?*" (We are a group of Polish partisans. We don't have any bread – could you spare us some?). Mundek would approach peasants and, speaking in excellent Polish, would ask for food, explaining, "*Jesteśmy polskimi partyzantami, będziemy walczyć za Polskę*" (We are Polish partisans who will be fighting for Poland). They never used force and they rarely received a negative response. The peasants would ask how many partisans were in need and Mundek would always double the number. Willingly, they often gave twenty to thirty loaves of bread.[8] In some instances, the partisans asked the peasants to cook them soup. The response was normally a positive one.

This was not the case when they dealt with Ukrainian peasants. The attitude of the Ukrainians was completely different – and mostly cruel. They would fire at the partisans, trying to kill them.

The partisans cooked for themselves as well. For a stove, they dug a pit in the ground and covered it with a metal plate. To heat it, they used coal, which minimized the fire's smoke. On the heated metal plate they put cookware that was taken from peasants, since the peasants kept these outside their cabins.

Mundek was fastidious and had something of an obsession with cleanliness; he avoided eating the food cooked in the woods and did not drink the water collected from nearby streams. He would use a jerry can to collect water at the nearest village.

At night, they used paraffin lamps for light. They were very careful to turn them off when the slightest strange noise was heard, as the light could be seen from great distances. Most nights, when they were in their hideouts, they preferred not to light paraffin lamps as a precaution. They would just sit in darkness and go to sleep early, listening to the voices of the woods and the wolves howling. They ate most of their meals together. Spirits were high during the meals, out of satisfaction that they had food and were not starving.

The game in the woods provided them with food in times of distress. Kulpa's

---

8. They were large Polish peasant loaves, which were not easy to carry.

family, including his sons, Czesław – who was a personal friend of Mundek's as in better times they had shared the same hobby of photography – Jan, and Stanisław, also provided food, water, and clothes.[9]

During spring and summertime, the woods' flora supplied them with food such as various types of berries, wild cabbage, and potatoes from the fields, which they would harvest at night under cover of darkness. During winter when the snow covered everything, they went hunting. The fauna in the woods was very rich. There were many types of birds, such as cranes, bee-eaters, red-backed shrike, white storks, and mud buzzards, and at night there were bats.[10] They hunted any game that was edible, regardless of whether it was kosher or not. This included birds, deer, and even wild boar. Hunting was not an easy task. They had to use traps to avoid the noise of gunfire. When the traps did not work, the only solution was to hunt in the distant woods and return immediately after the killing to the bunker. Hunting with guns was very risky; the noise could draw enemies to the hunters' position, and they might subsequently be followed back to the hideout.[11]

Aside from the need to get food supplies, contact with peasants served two further purposes. The first was that it gave the peasants an umbrella of defense against Ukrainian harassment. The second was that it allowed the partisans to be updated on any outside news published by the press.

There was no serious problem of disease in the woods. Despite the fact that there were no medical supplies and no medical care, none of the partisans were sickly, although a common problem – due to lack of hygiene – was scabies (*świerzb* in Polish). This caused people to scratch themselves until they bled.

None of the partisan members had knowledge of medicine. Simple injuries were treated with bandages of salt water or woodruff leaves, which they believed had medicinal qualities. Serious injuries were treated by the *znachor* (quack; a pseudo doctor) in the village. He was not a physician. The *znachor* had little medical knowledge, but was able to help with basic problems. No one within the partisan group required hospitalization during their time in the woods. They

---

9. Kulpa family request to the embassy of Israel for Righteous Among the Nations status for Józef Kulpa and his wife, dated December 31, 1992.
10. Mundek used an owl call as his personal signal.
11. Personal interview with Dr. Isaac Weinberg, May 30, 2011, quoting conversations with Mundek Łukawiecki.

understood that in time, they would be treated by the *znachor*, who would provide instructions and perhaps consult a physician if required.

After a short time with the Spaleni, Mundek was transferred to a combat partisan company. There had been change within the partisan system since the days when he'd been delivering the *Czyn*. The changes, which must be connected to the forming of the Armia Krajowa (AK) on Febrary 14, 1942, primarily related to methods, orientation, and how the partisans organized themselves. Mundek also noticed that a new, more aggressive attitude prevailed. The AK's main operations involved sabotaging the Nazis' ability to fight by destroying crucial infrastructure, such as railroads, bridges, trains, and German farms.

In the early 1940s, the ZWZ was not really aware of the partisan movement, as it was too busy organizing the Polish underground movement, but eventually the ZWZ-AK became the largest and strongest underground resistance movement in Poland – and maybe all of Europe. Without a doubt, the group had the best military structure throughout Poland. This was because the AK's original goal was to prepare for a military uprising. Secondarily, they collected information for the Allies and conducted general sabotage.[12] The AK and other Polish underground movements did not form any partisan units until the end of 1942, and even then they were very insignificant.[13]

The company[14] to which Mundek was assigned was deployed in the Janowskie woods, Lubelski woods, Ruda Różaniecka, Huta Różaniecka, and Paary most of the time. They took part in fighting and sabotage activities in Ciechanów, Płazów, and Narol. The company consisted of forty-one soldiers. The impact of their activities was well beyond their size. On one occasion, the company went to Lisie Jamy – a village near Lubaczów – to get food from a local supporter. A few days later, the supporter informed the company that Lisie Jamy inhabitants had told the Germans that three hundred partisans had raided Lisie Jamy, some of them riding horses and others operating horse-drawn wagons to carry the

---

12. Władysław Pobóg-Malinowski, *Najnowsza historia polityczna Polski* [Recent Polish political history], vol. 3, *1939–1945* (London: Gryf, 1960), p. 379.
13. The relative unimportance of forest-dwelling partisan units to the AK is evident by its organizational structure. No one within the organization was responsible for the partisans; AK units were urban and there were no forest-dwelling units. Sabotage raids were executed by urban units. See Bór-Komorowski, *The Secret Army*, pp. 142–51.
14. This term was used by Mundek. In size its strength might be more that of a platoon.

things they had taken from the villagers. The Nazis began to believe that a large number of partisans were hiding in the forest.

Mundek's AK company was formed by Father Józef Sliwa, who had served in the Polish army under General Władysław Anders. After he was wounded he was evacuated back to his hometown, Narol, Poland. Upon returning to Narol, he formed an underground unit named Konsolidacja Obrony Narodowej (Union of National Defense) and adopted the codename "Kolon."[15] The direct commander of Company 1 was Marian Zuchowski ("Orlik"). Under him was Platoon Commander Józek Michalski. Mundek became a member of this platoon.

Józek Michalski was killed at the beginning of 1943 in a German ambush, while the platoon was on its way to raid a German target. In his stead, Marian Zuchowski appointed Mundek as commanding officer of the platoon.[16] Zuchowski promised that he would impose Mundek's leadership, despite his young age.[17] Mundek remained commanding officer of this platoon until he formed his own Jewish hit squad in May 1943.

Mundek had already known Marian Zuchowski, whose family was from Narol, before the war.[18] Zuchowski was the son of Andrzej Zuchowski,[19] a member of the Polish Sejm[20] and the person who had given Mundek his false identity papers when he had first joined the ZWZ-AK. Marian Zuchowski's identity was kept a secret, as part of the secrecy surrounding AK members. Only a few knew who he was. Zuchowski appreciated Mundek's fighting ability and combat experience. A special relationship developed between the two of them. He was

---

15. Ireneusz Caban, *Związek Walki Zbrojnej Armia Krajowa w Obwodzie Tomaszów Lubelski: relacje, wspomnienia, opracowania, dokumenty* [Armed Combat Union Army in the Tomaszów Lubelski district: Reports, memoirs, studies, documents] (Lublin: Czas, 1999), p. 96.
16. Mundek recalled his exact words: "*Od dzisiaj będziesz dowódcą*" (From today you are the commander). Moshe Lavee (Edmund/Mundek Łukawiecki), recorded interview by USC Shoah Foundation Institute, interview code 31895, May 27, 1997.
17. Mundek had replied to him, "*Jaki dawódca, ja jestem młody?*" (How can I be commander when I am so young?). Ibid.
18. Mundek's grandparents Jacob and Rebbeca Gerstenfeld lived in Narol.
19. Andrzej Zuchowski was born on November 18, 1883, in Narol, where he graduated elementary school. A farmer by profession, he became a prominent local official. In the 1920s he was mayor of Narol and a member of the district council in Lubaczów. In 1928 he was elected to the Polish Sejm from elector district number 51. He was also a member of BBWR (Bezpartyjny Blok Współpracy z Rządem – The National Bloc for Cooperation with the Government).
20. The lower chamber of the Polish Parliament.

the only one in the company who knew that Mundek was a Jew.[21] Zuchowski was killed in 1943.[22]

The partisans had no means of communication. Radios and other means of communication were only available at headquarters, and these were off limits to partisans. This radio dispatch station (*stacja nadawcza*) transmitted intelligence to England and was manned by young male and female operators.

At the ground level, orders were given to the commanding officer by a special courier. Upon arrival, the company officer huddled with the courier out of the company's sight. Identification with the courier was done by whistling. Another means of identification was through the use of a flashlight.[23] The signaling was done by illuminating the flashlight in a certain sequence that was decided in advance by the two parties.

The Germans repeatedly tried to trap Mundek's company, which was consequently always on the move. Not only did the Nazis operate against them, but Ukrainian partisan groups – affiliated with the Ukrainian nationalist movement of Bandera – did as well. They pretended to be friendly but they were in fact foes, as were the Russian partisans, who cooperated with the Nazis.

From the end of 1942 to the beginning of 1943, the company was heavily engaged in raids and operations against German and Ukrainian targets. In the beginning, they were not complicated operations, but rather hit-and-run activities like burning German fodder and grain storage for horses. Later they carried out raids on *Liegenschaften*[24] near Ciotusza,[25] in which Mundek was praised for his agility and his impressive ability to jump over fences.

The targets of these were intentionally pinpointed next to Ukrainian villages and away from Polish ones so as to avoid German revenge against the Poles. The

---

21. Zuchowski treated Mundek like a brother. Knowing that Mundek avoided eating food prepared in the woods, he used to always bring him food prepared at his home.
22. Caban, *Związek Walki Zbrojnej Armia Krajowa*, p. 101. Ireneusz Caban in his book *Na dwa fronty: Obwód AK Tomaszów Lubelski w walce z Niemcami i ukraińskimi nacjonalistami* [On two fronts: The Tomaszów Lubelski district AK against the Germans and Ukrainian nationalists] (Lublin: Czas, 1999), p. 345, wrote that Zuchowski was wounded in an ambush set by robbers, and he passed away in the hospital in Tomaszów Lubelski.
23. In Polish the technique was called *sygnalizacja świetlna*, signaling by illumination.
24. This was the word Mundek used. Probably he meant large farms or estates (in German *Gutshöfe*) taken over by the Germans.
25. About twelve to fifteen kilometers west of Tomaszów Lubelski.

raids were carried out at night. The commanding officer formed a team of eight to ten partisans. Eight AK partisans stood guard, while two others approached the storage houses with gasoline-soaked rags. The building was set on fire and the partisans fled.

On one occasion in March 1943, they had to break their policy of avoiding targets near Polish towns; they were sent along Majdan Nepryski, two kilometers northeast of Józefów (in the county of Biłgoraj). The company was ordered to attack a German train going to Bełżec.[26] The raid was very successful. The train was blown up and destroyed. Mundek prepared the explosives and set them up himself. The Poles paid dearly for it, however. The Germans took vengeance and executed all the men of the village.

The company were also tasked with capturing German officers and soldiers. They were told to force them into the woods and interrogate them. The aim was to gather and collect information such as battle orders, deployment, identity of commanding officers, plans, etc. The information they gathered was handed over to headquarters.

Because he spoke German fluently, Mundek was in charge of these operations and was assigned to conduct the interrogations of the captured Nazis. These operations were known as "capturing tongues"[27] and were done at night. The actual abductions were carried out by two Polish partisans, Funiak and Franek. They were ordered to ambush Nazi soldiers and bring them to the woods for interrogation, which in Polish was referred to as *"przyprowadzić nazistów"* (literally: bringing the Nazis). The partisans pretended to be Germans and ambushed the Nazis. Mundek, wearing a German uniform,[28] would then command them in German. When the Germans realized that they had been captured by partisans, they would start to cry and beg. They immediately lost all their bravado.

The Germans did not resist during the interrogation and revealed sensitive information relatively easily. They were scared. After the interrogation, the captured Nazis were killed. Franek used to roll a cigarette and than execute them. The Nazis' begging did not save their lives.

---

26. Research was unable to determine what type of load the train carried.
27. This is the terminology Mundek used in his interview.
28. Partisans captured by Germans wearing German uniforms were treated extremely and severely cruelly. See document 665-F(ii) from the International Military Tribunal at Nuremberg, p. 310.

These "capturing tongues" operations were counterinsurgency actions, with two major goals: reconnaissance and interrogation. The information collected was handed over to the radio dispatch station (*stacja nadawcza*), which served as headquarters. In addition, these operations served an indirect purpose as well; they terrorized the Nazis and prevented them from traveling freely.

Mundek was known for his bravery in the field and was not afraid of the Nazis. He was not even deterred by the whistle of bullets. He was also a demolition expert and was skilled in assembling mines and demolishing bridges, roads, and so on. He was a very good athlete and could walk thirty kilometers (eighteen and a half miles) very easily without any problems. He was also very agile and was able to overcome obstacles and fences. But at the same time, his fellow soldiers were afraid of him. He had a reputation for having a short temper. His tendency toward unexpected reactions meant that it was better not to mess with him. He was even known to kill people who argued with him.

Chapter 11
The Establishment of the Lubaczów Ghettos

The Third Reich left the responsibility of solving the Jewish question to SS "specialists" so they could clean up the Jews once and for all. Between 1939 and 1941, Nazi leaders discussed various possible solutions. Besides the forming of ghettos, deportation to Madagascar and various means of killing Jews were also considered. The decision to kill all Polish Jews in the General Government area completely and systematically was taken from autumn 1941. Task forces (*Einsatzgruppen*) in Russia had already been killing people, but it was only from August 1941 that they started to systematically kill all the Jews. Deportations of German Jews to Riga, Minsk, and other places in the East were organized in autumn 1941.

Most probably the basic decision to murder all Jews in the German domain was made by Hitler in December 1941, but Himmler did not wait for this decision before taking action. Two years earlier, in 1939, he had already ordered Reinhardt Heydrich to deal with the Jews in two phases. First, Jews who were living in Germany would be sent to Poland.[1] Second, those who were already living in Poland would be concentrated into ghettos.

Brigadeführer Dr. Otto Rasch,[2] a forty-nine-year-old SS man, was appointed as leader of the task force Einsatzgruppe C with one general order: to initiate pogroms against Jews. For some towns in Galicia, there are possible causes for these pogroms (i.e., as ostensible punishments for various events), but it is likely that most of the pogroms in June and July 1941 were simply random. The task

---

1. Herman Katz, the brother of Gittel Katz Bern (wife of Shimon Bern, Joseph Łukawiecki's business associate in Lubaczów), his second wife Selma, and their children were deported from Ludwigsburg, Germany (to where they had moved), back to the Katz family hometown of Lubaczów. Later they were exterminated there with the entire Katz-Bern family.
2. Rasch was succeeded by SS-Gruppenführer Dr. Max Thomas, a physician by profession.

force, which had four commandos,[3] followed behind the fast advance of the Wehrmacht through western Ukraine (Galicia), with the result that most Galician Jews survived the first wave of killing, and the majority of mass killings by Einsatzgruppe C took place in eastern Ukraine.

Paul Blobel[4] was commander of Sonderkommando 4a,[5] which was active in Galicia[6] and advanced from Zamość to Sokal via Hrubieszów. The first executions by 4a of seventeen Communists took place in Sokal on June 28, 1941, and the first executions of 183 Jewish Communists on June 30, also in Sokal. On the same day, around 300 Jewish men were shot by 4a in Luzk.[7] In June 1942, Blobel was ordered to hide and conceal all evidence of the atrocities and make the murdered bodies disappear as part of Operation 1005.[8] However, the Blobel commandos could not remove all the traces as there were too many and the Russian troops were advancing too fast.

During 1941–1942, SS-Obersturmführer Oswald Heyduk, the head of the security police in Sokal, organized actions against Jews in Lubaczów.[9] The Ukrainian chief of police, Vasyl Kułczycki, accepted the orders enthusiastically. He began arresting and prosecuting Jews and Poles suspected of cooperating with the NKVD.

During the summer of 1942, some Jewish families anticipated the

---

3. From north to south, Sonderkommando 4a, Sonderkommando 4b, Einsatzkommando 5, and Einsatzkommando 6.
4. An architect by profession, Blobel lost his job after becoming an alcoholic. He was known to be extremely brutal, violent, and efficient in organizing massacres.
5. At least sixty thousand people (mostly Jews) were Blobel's victims. He was sentenced to the death penalty in the military tribunal in Nuremberg and executed in 1951. See Ernst Klee, Willi Dressen, and Volker Riess, eds., *The Good Old Days: The Holocaust as Seen by Its Perpetrators and Bystanders* (New York: William S. Konecky Associates, 1996), p. 289.
6. See for example Leon Weliczker Wells, *Ein Sohn Hiobs* [A son of Job] (Munich: Hanser, 1963).
7. He used Jewish prisoners as slave workers of the commandos. All of them were executed in order not to leave witnesses.
8. Jens Hoffmann, *Das kann man nicht erzählen: Aktion 1005; Wie die Nazis die Spuren ihrer Massenmorde in Osteuropa beseitigten* [This cannot be told: Operation 1005; How the Nazis removed the traces of their mass murder in eastern Europe] (Hamburg: Konkret Verlag, 2008); Father Patrick Desbois, *The Holocaust by Bullets: A Priest's Journey to Uncover the Truth behind the Murder of 1.5 Million Jews* (Houndmills, UK: Palgrave Macmillan, 2008), p. 153. See also Klee et al., *The Good Old Days*, p. 273.
9. Dean, *Ghettos in German-Occupied Eastern Europe*, pp. 800–802.

German-Ukrainian atrocities that were about to occur. As a result, these families built hideouts, bunkers, and shelters. Unfortunately, they were easily discovered because they weren't well concealed. In addition, they were not well protected and lacked a basic infrastructure, such as a water supply, heating system, and facilities for hygiene, not to mention any food storage or supplies. Consequently, those who hid in these "secret shelters" had to leave quite often, thereby exposing themselves and their locations. And when they did come out of hiding, if the Gestapo didn't get them, the Ukrainian police did.

Hans Adolf Asbach,[10] the German *Kreishauptmann* in the Rawa Ruska area, developed the idea to concentrate the Jews in every community into one residential area. Asbach vigorously promoted this idea from August 1941.[11] In 1942 his concept evolved: the idea of concentrating the Jews was just a stepping stone that would pave the way for the Jews' annihilation. In light of this, concentration of the Jews served three main purposes. The first was to ease the capture of the Jews to be exterminated. The second was to prevent the Jews from escaping from their final fate. The third goal was to collect proper and comprehensive documentation and data on the Jews; concentrating them in a small area would enable the Nazis to calculate the exact size of the Jewish population. A further advantage would be that the Jews would be close to transportation facilities and therefore very easy to transport.

The residential areas – called ghettos[12] – would be under permanent central control and supervision, and were to be under centralized management.[13]

Thus began the concentration of all Jews from nearby villages and towns into one small area. In May 1942, Jews were evacuated from nearby villages and towns such as Rawa Ruska[14] and were transferred to Lubaczów[15] under the direction

---

10. Born in 1904 and educated in law, he joined the NASD in 1934 and in 1943 volunteered for the Wehrmacht. He was detained after WWII for a short time and later held ministerial positions in Schleswig-Holstein.
11. Pohl, *Nationalsozialistische Judenverfolgung*, p. 155.
12. The word has been in use since 1611, when the Venetian word *ghèto* (island) was first applied to an isolated living area for Jews.
13. Pohl, *Nationalsozialistische Judenverfolgung*, p. 193.
14. Archiwum Żydowskiego Instytutu Historycznego (AŻIH; Archives of the Jewish Historical Institute), Zydowska Samopomoc Społeczna (JSS)/333, B1. 9, Judisches Hilfs-Komitee Lubaczów, Judische Soziale Selbesthilfe (JSS) [Jewish Relief Committee of Lubaczów, Jewish Social Self-Help], May 22, 1942.
15. Pohl, *Nationalsozialistische Judenverfolgung*, p. 196.

of the Ukrainian chief of police, Vasyl Kułczycki, who, thanks to his enthusiasm and the success of his initial missions, was appointed commander in chief of the Ukrainian Auxiliary Police in Lubaczów, responsible for the two Jewish ghettos that were to be formed in Lubaczów.[16]

Hryhorij Czapacha, another Ukrainian from Borochow, was responsible for the entire Ukrainian police of the Landkommisariat Lubaczów. He was the deputy Landkommisar of the local civil administration of the district of Lubaczów and was subordinate to the so-called *Kreishauptmann* – the Chief of the Civil Administration of the District.[17] The *Kreishauptmann* in Rawa Ruska – who was also in charge of Lubaczów – was Hans-Walter Zinser from August 1941 to February 1942, and Gerhard Hager[18] from March 1942 to July 24, 1944.[19]

A post of German Gendarmerie and a squad of Ukrainian Auxiliary Police were based in the Lubaczów area, reporting to headquarters in Rawa Ruska. Vasyl Kułczycki drafted two hundred Ukrainian volunteers into the Ukrainian Auxiliary Police unit, whose headquarters were situated in the *rynek* (market square) of Rawa Ruska.

The Ukrainians formed a special court, the Ukrainian People's Court. Its judges were all Ukrainian nationalists, such as Hryhorij Czapacha, who was also the head of the local civil administration in Lubaczów,[20] and Teodor Kułczycki, Vasyl's brother. A lawyer by profession, Teodor was appointed as deputy to the Landkommissar but was accidentally shot by the German Gendarmerie in Lubaczów.[21] (Hyrhorij Czapacha was then appointed to replace Teodor as deputy Landkommisar.) Other members of the bench included Anatoli Kozak,

---

16. From Nowe Sioło.
17. Tomasz Róg, Polish historian from Cieszanów, e-mail dated March 11, 2010. See also Tomasz Róg, "...i zostanie tylko pustynia": Osobowy wykaz ofiar konfliktu ukraińsko-polskiego 1939–1948 ["...And there is only one desert": Personal list of the victims of the Ukrainian-Polish conflict, 1939–1948] (Rzeszów: Gmina Cieszanów, powiat Lubaczów, 2011), p. 53.
18. 1896–1961. He was the mayor of Potsdam. After the war he settled in Hamburg. See Pohl, *Nationalsozialistische Judenverfolgung*, p. 414.
19. Markus Roth, *Herrenmenschen: Die deutschen Kreishauptleute im besetzten Polen – Karrierewege, Herrschaftspraxis und Nachgeschichte* [Master race: the German district captains in occupied Poland – career paths, governing practice, and subsequent history] (Göttingen: Wallstein, 2009), p. 450.
20. Tomasz Róg, e-mail dated October 22, 2010.
21. His brother's death at the hands of a German policeman did not diminish Vasyl's sympathy with the German cause or his hatred of Jews, however.

Lubaczów ghettos

a priest in the Greek Catholic Church of Lubaczów, three teachers (Harasowski, Eliasz Symko, and Jan Lewicki), and Eugeniusz Bandyra, a veterinarian. The aim of the court was to enforce Ukrainian nationalist ideology.

The newly minted Sergeant Major Vasyl Kułczycki, commander of the Ukrainian squad in Lubaczów, was in charge of guarding the ghettos and executing Nazi orders. Vasyl enjoyed his new office and living quarters, where he ceremoniously started each morning with a shot of Horylka.[22] When it came to guarding and monitoring the ghettos, he was mercilessly cruel and thoroughly enjoyed beating and killing Jews. His bloodthirsty desire was seemingly never satisfied. He would personally chase down Jews who managed to escape. No one was granted compassion, including innocent babies, pregnant women, and the elderly. His favorite pastime was randomly shooting down Jews as a form of entertainment. Likewise, the Ukrainians in general developed a bloodthirsty desire to chase down Jews. They considered shooting down Jews a form of entertainment.

Vasyl – as commander in chief of the Ukrainian Auxiliary Police –enthusiastically took on the task of making sure that the ghettos were well guarded. His goal was to ensure that nobody would escape and go into hiding within the first forty-eight hours. The main part of the ghetto was on the eastern corner of Piłsudskiego and Kociuszki Streets. First, the non-Jews were evacuated. The ghetto

---

22. Pronounced "gorilka," a popular Ukrainian drink (GORILKA).

Site of Ghetto 2, the small ghetto of Lubaczów, September 24, 2010

was then surrounded by a fence and later with two-meter-high barbed wire. The Ukrainian policemen fulfilled their duties brutality and vigorously. No mercy was shown to anyone.

Two ghettos were formed in Lubaczów.[23] On October 8, 1942, the Germans announced the establishment of an open ghetto in the eastern part of the *rynek* (market square) and on Piłsudski Street,[24] in the center of town. The boundaries of this larger ghetto were Stanisława Konera Street to the north, Kopernika Street to the southeast, Tadeusza Kosciuszki Street to the south, and Anny Street to the west. In a short time, this area was enlarged and overlapped most of Piłsudskiego Street to the south. This meant that it included Joseph Łukawiecki's business associate Shimon and Gittel Bern's family home, on 2 Piłsudskiego Street, opposite the local prison and the court of law.[25]

The ghetto was very small relative to the number of Jews forced to live in

---

23. Adam Szajowski, Plan Lubaczowa e usytuowaniem Getta Lubaczów, styczeń 1943 [Map of Lubaczów with the location of the Lubaczów ghetto, January 1943].
24. Eugeniusz Szajowski, "Tylko ziemia została ta sama: Lubaczów 1942–1943" [Only the land was the same: Lubaczów 1942–1943], in *Rocznik Lubaczowski* [Lubaczów yearbook], vol. 9–10 (Lubaczów: Towarzysto Miłośników Ziemi Lubacozwskiej, 2000), pp. 276–90.
25. Dean, *Ghettos in German-Occupied Eastern Europe*, pp. 800–802.

this concentrated area. It held more than three thousand Jews heavily crowded and packed into a small number of houses. Five to six families (between forty and sixty people) were forced to live in one apartment, with up to ten people sleeping in one room. The conditions in the ghetto were inhumane and intolerable. Not surprisingly, disease and infections such as diarrhea and typhus spread quickly.[26]

Eventually, seven thousand Jews were crowded into the two ghettos within Lubaczów, some of them brought from nearby villages and towns by Ukrainian policemen.

A second, smaller ghetto – which was actually a work camp – was established in a one-story building in Lubaczów known as Kurierów, built by the Russians during the Soviet occupation. It was located behind Kościuszki Street, near what is today known as Kurierów Armii Krajowej Street. The director of the ghetto was a German named Kohlus.[27] This ghetto would end up being liquidated very quickly.[28]

If a person came down with any kind of illness in the ghetto, death was almost inevitable. Those who were sick did not get any kind of medical treatment. Instead, they were executed in the Jewish Cemetery. The winter of 1942 was one of the coldest winters in Lubaczów history. The temperature was routinely below minus twenty Celcius (-4 Fahrenheit). The snow never measured below half a meter (a foot and a half). The Jews were stripped of their warm clothing, furs, and shoes, and were left with tattered rags. Not surprisingly then, the winter also claimed many of their lives.

Few were lucky enough to gain refuge and support from Polish peasants. Children were begging their parents to leave them and rescue themselves. A mother and her three children were hiding in an empty hedge on a farm. They had been running from one farm to another for weeks. The mother, Feiga Kammer,[29] went

---

26. For a comprehensive eyewitness description, see Szajowski, "Tylko ziemia została ta sama."
27. "Związek Bojowników o Wolność i Demokrację Koło Miejsko – Gminne w Lubaczówie, 30 lat pracy i działalności organizacji Lubaczowskiej związku bojowników o wolność i demokrację 1949–1979" [Union of Fighters for Freedom and Democracy near the town of Lubaczów: Thirty years of work and activities of the Union of Fighters for Freedom and Democracy, 1949–1979] (Lubaczów, September 1979 [manuscript stored in Muzeum Kresów w Lubaczów]), p. 188.
28. Adam Szajowski, Plan Lubaczowa; Eugeniusz Szajowski, "Tylko ziemia została ta sama."
29. See testimony of Feiga Kammer to Yad Vashem M49/1174 LB.440. Feiga Kammer survived the Holocaust and emigrated to Canada. She was a relative by marriage of Chana Bern's. They

out every night to try to find bread for the children. Feiga Kammer was thirty years old, with black hair that she wore at the back of her head in a ribbon. She had beautiful, black, round eyes which had become very sunken.

One day, her ten-year-old daughter asked her, "Mama, why do you trouble and suffer because of us? Leave us alone and save yourself." Another time, she asked, "Mama, pray to Almighty God that our death will be fast and without any suffering."

One night, that daughter left the hideout to search for food and assist her mother. She was caught. Despite the fact that she was tortured, she did not expose her family's hiding spot, saying, "One soul is less valuable than three souls, and my life is about to end anyhow." Before she was executed, she begged for her life, saying, "I did not harm anybody." In the morning she was taken to the woods. On her knees, she begged once more in front of a Ukrainian policeman. When she realized that it would do her no good, she said to him, "If you kill me, my blood will haunt you for the rest of your life."[30]

But when it came to Jews, conscience played little role for the Ukrainian policemen. As Vasyl Kułczycki, commander of the Ukrainian squad in Lubaczów, became more bloodthirsty, he began a campaign of mass murder. Jews were brought to an anti-tank ditch two kilometers (just over a mile) north of Lubaczów (near Dachnów) and shot by a firing squad.[31]

Vasyl's policemen also forced Jews to dig mass graves in the Dachnów forest. They then oversaw the Jews on the way to their own executions, killing those who were not walking fast enough. But the real excitement and entertainment came when the unit enthusiastically murdered Jews by tossing them into the mass graves alive and then watching them die of suffocation or starvation. The accompanying screaming and weeping only strengthened their resolve and encouraged them to further purge the world of the "Jewish menace."

---

met after the war in Kraków and she convinced Mundek Łukawiecki to have a Jewish wedding with Chana. Personal interview with Chana Diner; Moshe Lavee (Edmund/Mundek Łukawiecki), recorded interview by USC Shoah Foundation Institute, interview code 31895, May 27, 1997.

30. It is unknown how Faiga Kammer could have witnessed this herself and survived, but this is the testimony she gave to the Jewish Historical Institute in Warsaw (ZIH Warsaw), which appears in Yad Vashem's records, 1174 M49E.

31. State archives of the Russian Federation, Documentation of the special committee for Nazi crimes in the USSR, in the area of Grodek, Rawa Ruska, p. 44.

Jewish massacres in Lubaczów during 1942–1943 were a daily occurrence. SS officers Adam Wach (or Wachet) and N. Walter, together with the SS commander of Sanok,[32] sat on four-wheeled carts holding shotguns and ordered Jews to start running. After the Jews had reached a fair distance, they fired at the silhouettes on the horizon. Accurate shots were applauded; misses were mocked.[33] The atrocities committed by the Ukrainian police were beyond imagination. Any sense of humanity was nonexistent.

Two Poles from Ostrowiec, Władysław Serdyński and his son Roman, were recognized as Volksliste (of German origin) and became Jewish blood hunters. They killed Jews for sport on a regular basis.[34] The Serdyńskis boasted that they could not have a proper night's rest if they had not killed Jews during the day.[35] They were assisted by another Lubaczów resident of German origin named Reisinger.[36]

The first sign that the Jews were going to be exterminated occurred in October 1942. It was at this point that all footwear and clothing produced in the ghetto went to the Nazis. People in the ghetto became restless. Those who knew Polish peasants begged them to shelter their families, or at least their children. In Zalz – a village five kilometers (three miles) from Lubaczów – the head of the village (Stefan Hołub) handed Jews over to the Nazis to be shot down in the nearby woods.

After his exemplary job of massacring the Jews of Rawa Ruska, the SS Gestapo commanding officer in Rawa Ruska, SS-Untersturmführer Helmut Späth, was transferred to Lubaczów to recreate those atrocities there.[37] He was tasked with overseeing the execution of the Jews in Lubaczów.

---

32. "Związek Bojowników o Wolność i Demokrację Koło Miejsko," p. 189.
33. Ibid.
34. After the war both of them were sentenced to death as war criminals and were executed.
35. Testimony of Edmund Katz to Yad Vashem, no. M49E/3300. Excerpt from the Polish newspaper *Słowo Polskie*, published in Wrocław on January 17, 1948. The exerpts are kept at the Żydowski Instytut Historyczny (ZIH; Jewish Historical institute), Warsaw.
36. Testimonies given at the Buro der Juristischen Abteilung beim Zentral Komitee der befreiten Juden Deutchlands [Office of the Legal Department of the Central Committee of Liberated Jews in Germany], Munich, by Leon Gar on February 17, 1948; Benjamin Kammer on February 18, 1948; Zanwet Weiner on February 18, 1948; Luba Weiner on February 18, 1948; Samuel Baecker on February 19, 1948; Max Schoegker on February 22, 1948; Pepi Feber on February 26, 1948; and Regina Post.
37. Pohl, *Nationalsozialistische Judenverfolgung*, p. 420; Tomasz Róg, e-mail dated November 3, 2010.

At the beginning of December 1942, in accordance with the order issued by SS-Obergruppenführer Friedrich Wilhelm Krüger (the highest-ranking SS and police leader of the General Government) on November 10, the Lubaczów ghetto was officially recognized as one of the few remaining places in Distrikt Galizien where Jews could reside, and it was then enclosed.

As a result, before the end of November 1942, nearly two thousand Jews from Oleszyce arrived in Lubaczów to beat the deadline. According to one source, about a thousand of these Jews were among two thousand deported to Bełżec from Lubaczów before the end of November.

On December 1, 1942, Späth restricted free movement into and out of the Lubaczów ghetto. The penalty for breaching this order was death. Death was also imposed on those who hid Jews.[38] This was the beginning of the liquidation of the ghetto.

A severe typhus epidemic spread in the ghetto, claiming a daily death toll of about twenty-five Jews. The rampant disease was then used by the Germans as a justification for their plans to annihilate the ghetto.

The AK was the first group to find out that the Nazis were going to annihilate Lubaczów's Jews at the beginning of 1943. The Armia Krajowa intelligence network indicated that the Jews of Lubaczów were going to be exterminated.

When he learned of this, Mundek requested and was given permission to go to Lubaczów. His main aim was to convince the Jews of Lubaczów to join him in the woods and through that, to rescue them. In particular, he wanted to try to save his family, and someone else special to him: his fiancée. Mundek had become engaged to the daughter of the Silberschmidt family.[39] Her family was hiding in the Bern bunker together with the Łukawieckis' friends Shimon and Gittel (Katz) Bern, as a result of the friendship between their two daughters – Chana and the Silberschmidt girl – who were best friends.

On December 27, 1942, at night, he left his AK friends for Lubaczów. He was not wearing a uniform, nor was he carrying a gun; he was armed only with his Leica camera.

---

38. Zygmunt Kubrak, *Ofiary Holokaustu* [Victims of the Holocaust] (Lubaczów: Towarzysto Miłośników Ziemi Lubacozwskiej), 2003, pp. 11–12.
39. Her name is unknown. Mundek never spoke of her in later years, nor did Chana.

Chapter 12
Rape

The very same night, events were unfolding in Lubaczów that would have a very significant impact on Mundek's life.

The story had begun some time before. The Ukrainian Auxiliary Police commander, Vasyl Kulczycki, had developed something of a fascination with the Bern family, and most especially with their twenty-one-year-old daughter Chana. The Berns were considered very good-looking, and, due to their white complexion and fair features, were even regarded as very Aryan-looking by some. Vasyl could not believe that such a phenomenon was possible, particularly in his jurisdiction. When the decision to liquidate the ghetto was made at the end of 1942, he decided to act.

Shimon Bern was taken out of the ghetto and brought to Vasyl's office, escorted by policemen from the auxiliary unit. When he arrived, Vasyl looked up from his mail and stared at the haggard blonde man in the wide-brimmed black hat and long black coat with the yellow star on it. Vasyl snapped in German: "I want to save your daughter Chana. Send her to be our cook." Chana knew nothing about cooking; she had studied in a trade high school for girls in Lubaczów[1] and after hours had attended the very religious Bais Yaakov[2] Jewish girl's school

---

1. Personal interview with Chana Diner, January 29, 2012.
2. In Hebrew "the house of Jacob," the name of a chain of girls' schools for the strictly Orthodox. The name is based upon a verse in Exodus 19:3 ("Thus shalt thou say to the house of Jacob, and tell the children of Israel"). The term "house of Jacob" is traditionally understood to refer to Jewish females. The chain of schools was established by Sara Schenirer in Krakow in 1883 to provide Jewish education to Jewish girls and young women. Schenirer received approval from all leading rabbis, including the Belzer Rebbe. She started the first school on her own, then trained her students to be teachers. More schools were established in Central Europe and then in the US, Europe, and Israel. The teaching philosophy was "For Thy mercy is before mine eyes" (Psalm 26:3), and instruction was given in Yiddish. Initially, there was not a dress code and schools operated in the afternoon, while in the morning students attended public

The Ukrainian Auxiliary Police HQ in Lubaczów, where Chana Bern was raped by Vasyl Kułczycki

in Cieszanów.[3] Shimon remained silent for a moment, thinking, "What can I say to this butcher? There is no way to argue with him. He could just decide to kill all of us." Vasyl continued in broken German: "Go and send for her now, immediately – fast, fast." Shimon was then savagely thrown out of the room. On his way to the apartment that he shared with two other families, Shimon wept bitterly. He felt like Abraham being asked to sacrifice Isaac – he was being forced to give up his daughter Chana for the sake of the rest of his family.

He stumbled into the family hiding place, which was below the staircase of the house,[4] and could barely speak. "They want her!" he cried out, pointing his finger at Chana. Shortly afterward, he fainted. Gittel, Hanoch, and Henye stared at Chana, who froze in shock. The silence of death paralyzed everyone in the

---

schools. See also Pearl Benish, *Carry Me in Your Heart: The Life and Legacy of Sarah Schenirer, Founder and Visionary of the Bais Yaakov Movement* (New York: Feldheim, 2004). For further background, see also Bais Yaakov Center Archive, Tuva Uskwitz list of Bais Yaakow school chains in Poland in 1927.

3. The Bais Yaakov school operated in the afternoons. In the morning, students went to public schools. There was no school in Lubaczów; the nearest one was in Cieszanów and was founded by Ben Zion Friedman, Binna Taicher, and Feiga Alter. See Kiddush Hashem Archives, Bnei Brak, at 15 Harav Meltzer Street.

4. Personal interview with Chana Diner, January 29, 2011.

hiding place – Gittel's brother Herman Katz and his second wife Selma,[5] Shimon Bern's aunt and her husband, and their friends the Silberschmidt family. Then from their paralyzed mouths, screams broke out.

The Ukrainian policemen followed Shimon in, grabbed Chana, and dragged her out of the hiding place. Her high-pitched cries could have cracked open the sky. Those who remained in the hiding place were certain they would never see her again.

Chana was taken to the Ukrainian Auxiliary Police headquarters in the *rynek* (market square) in Rawa Ruska. It was a typical two-story building, similar to many other *rynek* buildings. In the center of the first floor was the office of the chief of the Ukrainian Auxiliary Police, Vasyl Kułczycki. This large room featured a huge wooden desk, a sofa, and a coffee table. Heavy, red cotton curtains hid the entrance. His living quarters were adjacent to his office, connected by a double door that led to a large bedroom and a private bathroom. Three flags hung in those rooms: the Nazi swastika, Vasyl's battalion flag, and the gold-and-blue Ukrainian national flag.

At the side of the house, there was a door that led to the inner court, which was used as a foyer and waiting area. From the inner court, there was a second, rear door that opened outside, opposite the church at the back of the *rynek*.

Chana worked in the kitchen along with two other Jewish girls, Eidel Kresner,[6] who was the cook, and Deborah Schneider,[7] who was her assistant and a waitress for the policemen stationed at headquarters. Chana was the waitress for the officers, who ate separately in their own fancy dining room.

Kitchen staff were given uniforms and instructed to maintain their hygiene, as they would be working with food. They all shared one room in the basement. The entrance to the basement was from a lower passage partially below ground level, which was accessed from the inner court rather than from the main stairway that led to the first floor. They were only allowed in the kitchen and dining rooms and were forbidden to enter any other part of the headquarters. They worked from five A.M. to eleven P.M. every day. Since food was all around them,

---

5. Her maiden name was Friedland. She was born on March 29, 1886, in Darmstadt am Neckar.
6. Pseudonym.
7. Pseudonym.

it was a huge temptation to steal some for their families. This act was punishable by death, which is what had happened to the girl that Chana replaced.

Two nights after Chana's arrival, there was a Christmas party. At the end of her shift, Chana left the kitchen and headed down to the basement. Suddenly, Vasyl appeared out of nowhere, grabbed her by the hair, and pulled her up the stairs to his private room. There was no screaming or weeping; Chana quietly resisted, but nothing slowed Vasyl's monstrous and brutal behavior, and he reacted aggressively with punches to her face. Even after getting her into his room, he lost no momentum. Chana was thrown onto the bed, almost unconscious. Her face was bloodied and she lost her sense of balance. Vasyl tore at Chana's dress savagely and tossed it away. He bent down between her legs while she lay in front of him, too paralyzed to move. She knew he could try to kill her at any moment; his left hand was fixed tightly around her neck, causing her near suffocation, and his hatred and disgust of Jews seethed through him like a demonic spirit. Quickly, he pulled down his pants, and fully erect, shifted her underwear over with his right hand. His penis penetrated her fiercely. After a few thrusts, Vasyl discharged and left the evidence of his heinous act inside her.

A few seconds later, he stood up, with his trousers still rolled down, pulled Chana by her arm, picked up her dress, opened the door, and threw her and the dress out of the room. She heard the door lock behind her. With her last bit of strength, Chana picked up her dress, covered herself with it, and limped back downstairs.[8]

When she reached her room, Chana sat on the edge of her bed, barefoot, with her dress wrapped around her, legs glued one to another, bent over with her palms on her knees. She did not move. She did not cry. She did not say a thing. Eidel and Deborah were asleep or pretending to be asleep. Nothing and nobody moved. The silence spoke volumes. All the vitality had been extinguished out of her aching body.

She stayed on the edge of her bed all night. At five o'clock in the morning, she walked to the kitchen, poured a little water into a bucket, and washed herself. Then she put on a clean dress. That day, Eidel and Deborah didn't speak to her. They wanted to make it seem that they were unaware of the rape. They did

---

8. Hoffman, *Keep Yelling*, p. 174. Also see personal interview with Aliza Segal, February 5, 2012, in which Mundek told her about the rape but with slightly different details.

not want to be involved, afraid that it might happen to them as well. Not a single word of sympathy or comfort was spoken; they just simply ignored her all day.

Chana continued doing her job as usual in spite of the previous night's events. But she was in her own world. She wondered about her family – her younger brother and sister, her father and mother. She started to think about why she was being punished like this. What sin had she committed? Where was God and why was He hurting innocent people? She realized that everybody she knew and cared about was just struggling to survive. Even her fellow coworkers' silence was part of the struggle to try to overcome these apocalyptic days. "It is better to be a live mistress than a dead girl," she concluded.

That night, after Chana was already in the basement, Vasyl called for her. She froze for a moment in the grip of fear. She quickly regained control, stood up and walked out. When she entered his room, Vasyl was in his underwear. He ordered her to undress. He watched her, his eyes following her every movement. He ordered her to stand in front of him, so he could look at her more closely.

"Santa Maria, how beautiful you are!" he exclaimed. "Why are you a Jew? I would marry you if you weren't a Jew."[9]

He became quiet for a moment and then asked, "Maybe you can convert to Christianity?" After some more reflection, he continued, "But you are a Jew and should be killed like all the Jews. All of you are demons!"

Chana didn't utter a word in response. The conversation ended abruptly. Vasyl pointed her onto the bed and crawled in after her in his underwear.

"I was never with women. I was never married," he said as he pulled down his underwear, but this time he failed to penetrate her. Instantly his mood changed and he hit her, shouting, "You bloody Jew! You caused it!" After a few more attempts, Vasyl screamed at her to go back to her room and return the following night after eleven.

The following night, on December 27, 1942, Chana closed the kitchen at eleven and made her way to Vasyl's room. The door was open, but nobody was there. Chana sat on the bed and waited. Then she heard Vasyl in the adjoining room. He was drunk, sitting with one of the other officers and guffawing that he

---

9. Chana had an Aryan appearance – blonde hair, blue eyes, milky white complexion. Personal interview with Dr. Isaac Weinberg, May 30, 2010, recalling conversations he had with Mundek Łukawiecki.

had killed more than twenty Jews in the ghetto that day. Vasyl also mentioned that their task to destroy the ghetto was almost complete. In just a few days, all the remaining Jews in the ghetto would be executed, whereupon the Ukrainian Auxiliary Police unit under his command would be transferred to another town. Chana suddenly realized that her days were numbered, as were the lives of all the remaining Jews in Lubaczów.

Quietly, and without being detected, she made her way downstairs to the kitchen and grabbed a knife, returning after a few moments to Vasyl's lair. She waited there for quite some time before she heard his heavy footsteps on the stairs approaching the room. Vasyl stepped inside and closed the door behind him, so drunk he was hardly able to stand on his feet. Instinctually, Chana lunged at him and stabbed him over and over again. They both fell to the floor; he from stab wounds and she from exhaustion. The screams coming from his room did not arouse any suspicion, as they were a regular occurrence.

Chana sat quietly on the bed while Vasyl's bloody body lay on the floor. Nobody ever dared to enter Vasyl's room, so she was not scared of being found out. After some time, she stood up, left the room, locked it behind her, and took the key. She put on a clean dress and went to the kitchen. She found a gallon of gasoline, spilled it in the adjoining room, and set it on fire. Then she quickly fled the building through the back door.

Later the Ukrainians in Nowe Sioło would spread a cover story about the death of Vasyl Kułczycki that said he was killed by the NKVD, the Soviet secret police.[10]

When she reached the rear gate, the building was already on fire and people were rushing to extinguish it. Nobody paid any attention to her. She slipped through the rear gate, crossed the street to the church, and ran eastward toward Kościuszki Street, which was covered in white snow.

The entrances to the ghetto from both Anny Street and Krótka Street were blocked, so Chana made her way to Piłsudskiego Street, where she was able to enter the ghetto undetected. She did not stop once but ran as fast as she could to the room she had left only a few days earlier. She found it empty. Her family must be in the hideout below the staircase in their house.

Around midnight, Chana burst through the bunker entrance. The whole

---

10. Testimony of elderly Nowe Sioło resident Władek Sikum, March 12, 2011.

family were shocked. All of them had been certain that they would not see her alive again. Chana was out of breath, her face was very pale, and out of it two big, round blue eyes stared blindly. As she crashed into the bunker she tripped over something and collapsed in a dead faint. Nobody spoke. Nobody moved.

After a heavy frozen moment, Shimon knelt next to his daughter and patted her face. Gittel rushed to bring water following Shimon's terse whispered request. Shimon gently sprinkled water on Chana's face and into her mouth, and she woke up. She burst into tears, and the whole family wept with her. Shimon embraced Chana and everyone crawled to her and kissed and hugged her. Selma Katz had an extra dress and Gittel brought it to Chana. They threw the uniform dress into the stove.

No words were spoken. Chana fell asleep and the whole family was very quiet. Shimon consulted with Herman Katz. They tried to guess what had happened. They realized that it was only a matter of time until the Ukrainians would come to fetch Chana back, and they might search the house, exposing the hiding place and Chana inside. They decided that the family should move back into the house and leave Chana behind in the hiding place, to reduce suspicion, pretending that Chana had not returned home since she was taken to the Ukrainians.

No Ukrainians arrived that night. In the morning Chana woke up. No one dared to ask her what had happened, and she did not speak at all.

The first time she spoke was when Mundek Łukawiecki arrived at the home the next day.

Chapter 13
Vus Macht der Urel Du?

In the early morning of December 28, 1942, Mundek Łukawiecki arrived in Lubaczów. First, he went to the hideout where his fiancée the Silberschmidt girl was hiding with her family. In addition to Chana Bern, her parents, and her two siblings, a niece of the Bern family, Matel (Matilda), and her husband Meir, along with their three-year-old baby Shimon,[1] also found refuge there. Chana's uncle Herman Katz and his wife Selma, who had been deported from Ludwigsburg in 1938, were also living there, as was Chana's step-grandmother – who had married her grandfather Benjamin Cieszanówer after his first wife Chana passed away – along with her children from her first marriage and their families.

After seeing his fiancée, Mundek went with her to see his parents, sisters, and grandmother, who had been forced to move from the neighboring suburb of Ostrowiec to the ghetto two months earlier. His brothers Zygmunt and Rafael had already been killed in Rawa Ruska. This wasn't the first time that Mundek had entered the ghetto. In the two months since it had been established, he had entered it several times wearing a German Wehrmacht officer's uniform,[2] to try to convince his family to join him in the woods. Each time, they had turned him down.[3]

Now Mundek had come to try to convince them one last time to run away to the woods with him. This time, however, he came dressed in peasant clothing, as in addition to trying to convince his family, he planned to speak to the leaders

---

1. Personal interview with Chana's cousin Chana Diner, January 27, 2012.
2. Mundek disguised himself as a German officer very often, due to his proficiency in German. See Hoffman, *Keep Yelling*, pp. 187–88.
3. Roman Ogryzło, "Holocaust Żydow Lubaczowskich" [The Holocaust of the Jews of Lubaczów], *Pogranicze* 33 (August 1995): 6. In the article, the author mentions the name Zygmunt Łukawiecki by mistake. He was already dead at the time in question and was never a partisan. He is instead actually referring to Mundek.

Mundek Łukawiecki and an unidentified partisan praying before an operation, summer 1944

of the Jewish community. Mundek thought that a German Wehrmacht uniform would intimidate them. Since he didn't know Yiddish, he would need to address them in Polish, and therefore he wore Polish peasant's clothing.

Despite his entreaties, Mundek's parents refused once again, as they said that they would be a burden on him and lessen his chances of survival. The Silberschmidt girl pleaded that she couldn't survive in the woods in any case. Nevertheless, all of them urged Mundek to try to convince the members of the Lubaczów congregation.

Beyond the reasons stated by Mundek's family and fiancée, there were two additional reasons why Jews refused to flee to the woods. Firstly, they lived under the illusion that part of the Jewish world would survive, and they hoped to be among the fortunate ones. Secondly, they thought that fleeing the ghetto would only cause the Nazis to execute their relatives in retaliation, and consequently, their consciences prevented them from fleeing.[4]

---

4. Joseph M. Moskop, ed., *The Tomaszow-Lubelski Memorial Book*, trans. Jacob Solomon Berger (Mahwah, NJ: Jacob Solomon Berger, 2008), p. 474.

Following his conversation with his family, Mundek made his way to the temporary shul to talk to the rabbis and leaders of the Jewish congregation. Both of the regular synagogues of Lubaczów had been burned down by the Nazis during the first few days of occupation, and therefore the temporary *shul* had become the only gathering place for Jews.

It was late in the day on Monday, December 28, 1942. Mundek waited until Maariv, the evening prayer service, concluded. Then he entered the dimly lit *shul* and found it full of people. Despite it being the evening service, the men were wearing *talleisim* (prayer shawls), like on Yom Kippur. It was a surreal scene. Turning to the men assembled inside, he began to speak.

"My name is Mundek and I am a Jew who was born in Lwów. I am now a partisan," he began in Polish. "My family lived in Ostrowiec at my grandfather's and grandmother's house. Probably most of you met my grandmother – she worked at the local bank. We had a distillery."

His captive audience waited silently for him to continue. Then one of them asked in broken Polish, "What is your family name?"

"Łukawiecki," Mundek replied.

"Yes, I know that family," the man continued in his broken Polish. "What is it you want from us?"

"Nothing," replied Mundek. "I just wanted to warn you that the Nazis are going to kill all of you in a few days."

"How do you know this?" somebody without a beard, but with a big black yarmulke, shouted in a voice close to a hysterical shriek.

"As I told you, I am a partisan with the Armia Krajowa. They have very reliable intelligence information that this is the Nazi plan."

Mundek paused for a second and then continued, "This is the reason I am here in Lubaczów. I came to try to convince you to run away to the woods with me. I also came to convince my fiancée to run away with me to the woods as well."

"And what did she answer?" the same man asked.

"I do not know as I have not asked her yet," Mundek retorted.

"Let me understand," the man clarified, speaking a mixture of Yiddish and limited Polish. "You are asking us to run away to the woods. Is it possible to accommodate all of us? Lubaczów now has about a thousand Jews left.[5] How

---

5. This was an underestimate. There were at that point probably closer to four thousand.

safe is the journey? Do you have enough food for all of us? Do you have shelters for us; do you have medical support for sick people? Do you have a *shul*? Do you have a place for prayer, and do you have our holy books? How can we live there as Jews? We prefer to die here as Jews, than to die like *beheimes*[6] in the woods!"

Mundek was competely shocked by these questions and by the attitude he was encountering. "No," he replied, "we do not have most of the things you are asking about. But we have the desire to live, so as not to give the Nazis the pleasure of killing off the Jewish nation. What I am offering you is a chance to survive. Right now you are doomed to death. You are going to be executed within a week. Come with me, and some of you might be rescued!"

"You are talking nonsense," another voice called out in Yiddish. It was a very soft voice and hard to hear. There was complete silence in the *shul* as the voice spoke. "We have had a bad experience with an idea like this. And God punished us. We gave one hundred of our children money and weapons and sent them to the forest to save themselves. Then some of them returned after a few days. Many of them were killed. They did not know how to live in the forest. Or how to fight. They didn't know who was their enemy and who was a friend."

There was a pause, then the voice continued in a mixture of broken Polish and Yiddish, "God tried us. We failed. He deliberately tried us as He did at the Tower of Babylon. Almost all of our children died. The few who came back told us. We do not want to risk it a second time. We must trust our Almighty God."[7]

Mundek could not see who was speaking, but judging by the audience's hushed respect he grasped that it was the head of the congregation. Mundek tried to interject, but he was hissed down. The leader continued to speak.

"Maybe our destiny is doomed, but it is the will of God. Our God's will. The Almighty God is punishing us. We have to receive His sentence with love. We are not allowed to disobey the Almighty God. If we run away to the woods, we are disobeying His almighty judgment and sentence. You say here, the Nazis will kill us. That may be so. But if we stay, we save ourselves in Heaven. And if that is God's will, so be it."

The voice paused for a moment, and then continued, "Your offer is against our

---

6. In Yiddish, "beasts" (literally "cattle"). This is a derogatory term indicating one whose life resembles that of an animal, with the focus on eating, sleeping, and other bodily needs, rather than on the life of the soul.
7. Hoffman, *Keep Yelling*, pp. 88–94.

faith and is not the Jewish way." Then the speaker shifted from broken Polish and spoke in Yiddish for a few moments, probably repeating what he had said in broken Polish. At the end of his Yiddish address, he said, "*Vus macht der urel du?*"[8]

Mundek was frightened to death. They were committing mass suicide, and they had called him a Gentile who cannot be trusted. He had come to offer them a chance to save themselves and they had slapped him in the face. He could not believe it. He realized that the *shul* was completely full and that most of the remaining Jews of Lubaczów had heard the conversation.

Mundek was told to leave the *shul*. He left angrily. Nobody seemed to be listening to his apocalyptic prophecy – that their lives were over if they did not flee to the woods. Mundek went directly to the shelter that the Silberschmidt family shared with the Bern family. He tried again to convince his fiancée to flee with him to the woods one last time. She refused. By that time, the conversation from the *shul* had made its way back to her. Her parents ordered her to obey what was decided by the rabbis, so she did.

Frustrated and angry, Mundek turned to leave. Suddenly, Chana Bern, Mundek's fiancée's best friend, stepped out and stopped him on his way out. Chana had not spoken since her return to the bunker the previous night, but now, in front of all the families, she asked him, "Would you take me with you? Please take me to the woods."

Mundek was paralyzed. He had not expected such a request. After regaining his composure, Mundek tried to turn down Chana's request, describing the risks and how dangerous and difficult life in the woods is. Nevertheless she insisted. What choice did she have? After what she had done to Vasyl, the Ukrainians surely were looking for her. And all the Jews were soon to be murdered by the Germans in any event. Nothing but death awaited Chana here in Lubaczów. Chana's father, Shimon Bern, intervened. He offered Mundek some gold he still possessed. Mundek finally agreed. Hanoch, Chana's younger brother, stepped out and asked to be taken as well. Mundek refused.[9] The families were astonished,

---

8. The translation is "What is the Gentile doing here?" It was said as an indication of mistrust, indicating Mundek was not a part of "us," the Jewish community. The term *urel* means one who is not circumcised, and therefore Gentile.

9. Personal interviews with Aliza Segal, February 5, 2012, and April 17, 2012.

but they did not try to change either of their minds.[10] They burst into tears. They thought that their children were all doomed to death.

So Mundek agreed to take Chana with him. Not because of love, but because her father gave him gold.[11] Chana felt guilty and confided later, "I have been an assassin's mistress. I have stolen my best friend's fiancé. And I now live with a man who does not love me. I have placed my own interest above all; above brotherhood, justice, and honor."[12]

---

10. Even Chana Bern's father understood that the only chance to survive was in the woods.
11. Chana Bern and Mundek Łukawiecki told the same story about this. Chana said that Mundek agreed after her father offered Mundek money. In her words, "He took me not because he loved me, but because he was out of money and my father offered him some."
12. Hoffman, *Keep Yelling*, p. 174.

Chapter 14
Leica Camera No. 334164

Chana's mother, Gittel Katz Bern, hugged her and wept quietly. The shelter was pitch-dark, as it had no lights or windows. The black, fearful atmosphere was worsened by shadows – both real and imaginary. This was what hell looked like, and they were in the center of the inferno. Gittel's tears flowed like rain onto Chana's blonde hair and coat collar.

"Oh, Almighty God, help us, save us," she sobbed. "Yes, we committed sins and the rabbis are right. You punished us rightfully. But the punishment is too severe. We have learned our lesson. Please save us."

Chana's brother Hanoch and sister Henye pressed their heads against their mother and sister on both sides. Their tears created big, wet stains. They embraced their mother and older sister tightly, gripping her clothing, not letting go.

Shimon Bern stood next to them, his eyes closed as he prayed. "Almighty God, controlling the universe and humankind, we trust You and trust Your judgment brought to us by the rabbis. Save us as You saved the slaves in Egypt, for we are just simple Jews. We obeyed all of Your rules. If we committed sins, we did so innocently. Please save our family, as the rabbis promised."

In the corner of the shelter, the Katz and Cieszanówer families gathered together, staring blankly into the abyss. As they bade farewell to Chana, Mundek Łukawiecki went back to the room where his family was hiding. He was in complete shock as a result of the rabbis' responses. Mundek could not understand it. He sat on the floor crying openly, his unshaven face covered with tears. He cried like he had never in his life cried before. He hugged his little sister Judith in his arms so strongly that he almost crushed her, and buried his face in her curly black hair, soaking it with his tears.

The whole family crowded together on the edge of the only bed in the dark room, which now had sealed windows. Mina, who was thirteen, was dressed in her winter coat with a knitted brown wool hat. It was freezing cold in the room. Mina's shoulders slumped helplessly.

Joseph, Mundek's father, sat apart from his wife and children. His lips were sealed tight against any display of emotion. Years later Mundek would speculate on what his father must have been thinking in those moments.

"Why did we listen to the rabbis?" Mundek supposed Joseph thought. "Who said that theirs is the voice of God? Why should we not try to save our lives? Is it for Isaac's sacrifice that we are now sacrificing ourselves? Oh, God, where are You? Give us a sign!" And then, after a pause, Mundek imagined that his father concluded: "The rabbis are wrong. What sins did Judith or Mina commit?"

Joseph thought that his two daughters should go with Mundek, but was also worried that if he were wrong, he would be killing his own family.

Sarah sat with her head down, interlocking her fingers nervously. She waited for Joseph to do something, but he did nothing. Mundek imagined she must have felt paralyzed. Should she stand against the rabbis and their decision, or would it be better to be with them? Who was right? No doubt each cry from Mundek cut her heart to pieces. But what could she do?

Mundek's grandmother, Dora, was sitting next to her grandchildren and hugging them. No word was said. The silent tears spoke volumes. The entire family remained as quiet as possible. Their tough and strict education had taught them to be stoic at all times – no emotions were to be shown. When the time came to bid each other farewell, there were no hugs or kisses. Only handshakes. Dora whispered in German, *"Meine liebes Kind, weine um uns alle"* (My beloved child, cry for all of us).

At 4:00 A.M. on December 29, 1942, in the darkness of the night, Chana and Mundek left the Bern family shelter. That was the last time either of them were with their families.

They walked south along the alley to Konery Street and crossed it to Anny Street. They went to Tragowa Street until they once again reached Piłsudskiego, until it became Kościuszki Street. That junction featured one of the gates out of the ghetto. After a few moments, they walked alongside the building in the shadows and approached the gate. Only one Ukrainian Auxillary Police officer was standing guard. He was armed with a rifle, which was slung over his shoulder. He was standing next to the gate, not moving. It looked like he was literally asleep on his feet. They observed him for a few more moments. Mundek held Chana tightly against his back with his left hand, while he grabbed his Leica camera from around his neck with his right.

Very quickly, they approached the Ukrainian Auxillary Police officer from behind. He stiffened and froze as he felt the Leica camera on his back, thinking it was a gun. Mundek quietly whispered in fluent Ukrainian, "I am holding a pistol at your hip. You are coming with us and nothing will happen to you if we pass the gate. If you try to do anything I will kill you, you Ukrainian bastard!"

"What do you want me to do?" The policeman's voice cracked.

"Start walking!" Mundek replied. "Walk close to us, but in front of us. Do not turn around. Do not make noises or any signs or I will kill you."

Mundek pressed the Leica camera more firmly onto the policeman's hip and signaled to the policeman to start walking. They walked toward the cemetery on Kościuszki Street. When they arrived at the entrance to the cemetery, Mundek yelled out, "Run and do not look back behind you. If you stop for any reason I will kill you." The policeman did not need to hear another word and took off as fast as he could.

Mundek and Chana entered the cemetery and began to zigzag between the gravestones, which were covered in snow. It was difficult to run between them because they could hardly see the tombs. They ran quickly down the hill, to the other side of the cemetery toward the Lubaczów River. They had to make it there before the policeman could alert the garrison to start searching for them. They had the advantage of being able to run downhill, but the heavy snow slowed them down and left tracks.

They arrived at the bank of the river and Chana was exhausted and out of breath. She was not used to such physical effort. She felt weak, but her desire to live kept her going. Mundek ordered her to rest and they sat on the bank of the river for a few moments. They were very quiet. They listened for voices coming from the north, from the direction of Lubaczów. It was very quiet. There were no signs that they were being chased. Everything seemed normal. "Perhaps the Ukrainian policeman did not report the escape because he was embarrassed?" they thought.

After a few moments, Mundek stood up and decided it was time to continue. The Lubaczowka River had not frozen yet as the temperature had not reached minus twenty degrees Celsius; it was only minus ten (fourteen degrees

Fahrenheit). The water stream was relatively strong. They looked to the west, toward the bridge on the road from Lubaczów via Ostrowiec to Lwów.

There was no traffic on the bridge. This was a very good sign.

The bridge was guarded as well. The Ukrainian Auxiliary Police officers guarding the bridge demanded money from every Jew who escaped from the ghetto. If the Jew refused, they killed him. If the person gave them money, they killed him anyway after he had paid. They further looted the corpse for more valuables after death – since they were sure that those who tried to escape were carrying valuables.

The river was shallow. They crossed it at a narrow point, climbed the bank, and ran as fast as they could to the road. Mundek walked in front of Chana. To their left, they saw an old farmhouse that had been evacuated by the Germans. Mundek decided to walk beside the paved road so that they wouldn't leave any tracks in the snow.

At some point, Mundek turned to look behind him. There was no one in sight – Chana had disappeared! He turned back and saw that she had fallen into a hole in the ground. Mundek pulled her out. She was terrified. All her clothes were sopping wet and she said she had fallen because she had gone blind and lost her sight.[1] She was very scared.

They continued walking, with Mundek leading the way. As day broke, they arrived in Ostrowiec. Since it was already daylight, Mundek felt that going to Józef Kulpa's farm might be too dangerous. Instead, Mundek led Chana to a

---

1. Personal interviews with Aliza Segal, February 5, 2012, and April 17, 2012. Chana was never examined by a doctor for this condition, and the cause of her blindness cannot be determined with certainty. There is a condition called snow blindness, temporary damage to the cornea caused by excessive exposure to UV light. The technical name of the condition is photokeratitis. Snow reflects about 80 percent of the sun's ultraviolet rays, so walking for many hours in freshly fallen snow without protective eyewear can easily cause this problem. People with light-colored eyes are more susceptible. However, at this point in the journey, although they were walking in snow, Mundek and Chana had been hiking at night. Even bright moonlight would ordinarily not be enough to cause snow blindness. Another possibility is that she was suffering from central serous retinopathy, a buildup of fluid under the retina that can actually be stress induced. Chana certainly was suffering from severe trauma. In the space of a few days this religious girl had been repeatedly raped, learned that the ghetto was to be liquidated, killed her rapist and escaped from the police, separated from her family for what would prove to be the final time, and run away with her best friend's fiancé to the woods, where she had been walking without pause for many hours across rough terrain.

nearby barn. It belonged to the Burek family. Mundek knew that this family was trustworthy, as they were relatives of Józef Kulpa; Kulpa's wife and Burek's wife were sisters. Mundek therefore decided it would be best to hide there for the day.[2]

---

2. Personal interview with Władysław Burek in Lubaczów, February 24–25, 2010.

Chapter 15
Mother Maria

It was sunrise on Monday December 29, 1942, when Chana and Mundek arrived in Ostrowiec. They made themselves a hay bed in the barn of the Burek family and tried to get some sleep after their exhausting night. Yet Chana couldn't sleep. She had lost her sight and was very afraid. Her thoughts were with her family. Their faces kept appearing in her mind, over and over again. Tears warmed her frozen face. She could not know that indeed on this day, December 29, her younger sister, Henye, would be killed, but she found out later that her father, Shimon Bern, gave money to one of her step-grandmother's sons, Isaac, to take Henye to a small remote village and hand her over to a trusted family. Instead, Isaac deserted Henye and ran away with the money. Henye was captured and executed. Mundek coincidently met Isaac in Kraków after the war and intended to kill him for this act of cowardice, but Isaac fled to Canada before Mundek could catch him.[1]

As he lay in Burek's barn, Mundek couldn't sleep either. He was very agitated, replaying his conversation with the congregation and his fiancée's refusal to join him. Suddenly, he and Chana heard somebody come in. It was Władysław, the eight-year-old son of Burek. He recognized Mundek and Mundek recognized him. The boy stared at them, shocked and surprised. Not a word was said. After a few seconds, he turned and ran away.

At noon, when Burek arrived home for lunch, Władysław told his father who was hiding in the barn. His father cursed him for not coming to him immediately. This was a risk for the entire family. If Jews were discovered and caught on their premises, the whole family would be arrested. He told Mundek that he would not turn them over to the Nazis, but he ordered them to leave at sundown, telling

---

1. Personal interview with Chana Diner, January 27, 2012.

them, "You two can go to hell at night; otherwise I will call the Gestapo."[2] That night, Mundek and Chana were already on the move. Mundek left Burek a gold chain.[3]

After leaving Burek's barn, Mundek and Chana headed for Kulpa's farm. Mundek led the way. They went to the rear side of the farm on the edge of the Niwki woods, to the brown-gray agricultural building made of wooden logs and covered with mud. The building was long, with several partitions. The first one was the barn. They went to the barn, covered themselves with hay, and waited.

At dawn when Kulpa went to milk his cow, Mundek snuck out of the barn to speak to him. Kulpa then returned with Mundek to the barn, where he met Chana. In a quiet voice, Mundek told Kulpa of the events since their last meeting. After a while, Kulpa went to another part of the agricultural building and returned with food. He told them that he must go or his family might become suspicious, but he promised to return at night.

After supper, Kulpa came back with warm food. He told them that the Nazis were executing Jews in Lubaczów and beginning to liquidate the ghetto. The cemetery had become a site of mass murder.

Complete quiet set in and the world seemed to stop. Everything seemed to be happening in slow motion. Mundek and Chana turned their backs to each other. Chana moaned loudly and tears covered her face. Mundek sat on the ground, thinking about the meeting at the synagogue. He could have saved his family if only he had been more stubborn, he thought.

Kulpa did not give them much time to mourn and brought them back to reality. He told Mundek that he didn't think Chana was suitable and fit enough for partisan warfare with Mundek's company. Kulpa suggested that they return to the company, but that first, for a temporary period of a couple of months, they carry out a trial to see if Chana could adjust, staying in a bunker close by where he could support them. Kulpa added that they would still be AK partisans, but would reside temporarily at a different site from the other AK members – much like other partisans who lived at their residences and participated in operations only. He said that during Chana's adjustment period, Mundek should still join AK partisan operations on a regular basis. Mundek and Chana agreed.

---

2. Taped interview with Władysław Burek in Lubaczów, Poland, February 24–25, 2010.
3. Personal interviews with Aliza Segal, February 5, 2012, and April 17, 2012.

Mundek and Chana in the hideout, spring 1943

The following morning, Kulpa came and told them that Mother Mary had appeared to him in his dream and ordered him to save them. Therefore he would do his best to do so. He allowed them to stay on the farm for a couple more days as their physical condition was very bad. On January 1, 1943, they decided that it was too risky to stay at Kulpa's farm any longer. Kulpa was also worried that he might be evacuated from his farm.[4] Before they left, Kulpa supplied Chana with a Parabellum pistol, Mundek with an English Colt pistol[5] and munitions, as well as food and clothing for both of them.

Mundek and Chana journeyed two kilometers (just over a mile) south of Ostrowiec to a young pine forest in the northern part of the Bór woods, where they decided to dig a temporary bunker as a hideout for the adjustment period.[6] On the way to the woods, Chana's sight did not improve but rather deteriorated

---

4. Józef Kulpa's son Stanisław Kulpa answered on March 12, 1987, a questionnaire sent to him by the Żydowski Instytut Historyczny w Polsce (Jewish Historical Institute in Poland, AR-051/911-8/83), following his request to award Józef Kulpa as Righteous among the Nations. He was answered by the Żydowski Instytut Historyczny w Polsce (AR-051/1-275/87, dated June 26, 1987) that a survivor must also support the request. In that questionnaire it is mentioned that Józef Kulpa feared deportation in April 1944 by the Ukrainians.
5. Stanisław Kulpa, questionnaire, March 12, 1987, in which it is mentioned that Józef Kulpa equipped Mundek with a Colt pistol. Chana and Mundek said that he also equipped them with a Parabellum for Chana.
6. Personal interview with Isaac Helman, February 3, 2010; personal interview with Czesław Podporski and his mother Maria Szutka, September 24, 2010, in Ostrowiec.

so that she couldn't see at all, losing her sight completely. The deterioration was caused by the endless white snow. She did not have any sunglasses or other means of eye protection.

Mundek looked for a young pine tree with branches low to the ground. The formation looked like a cone, but short and wide like a ballerina's dress. He crawled below the lowest branch like a lizard, trying not to touch it. The soil below the branch was relatively dry as the branches above it kept the snow off. Mundek did not touch the tree so as to keep the snow from falling on him. He then prepared a bed out of blankets they had brought with them. As the woods were very humid, cold, and wet, he put the blankets on some greenery he collected nearby, as a preventive measure against catching pneumonia; straw, which he preferred, was unavailable.[7]

Chana crawled inside, took off her boots, put them below her head as a pillow, and covered herself with another blanket to get warm. She covered her eyes. The hideout was dark and it eased the pain in her eyes. There was no special medication for snow blindness, apart from covering the eyes with a rag. Mundek prepared another hideout not far from her for himself. He came to her hideout from time to time and fed her, and left her in the Bór woods while he returned to Józef Kulpa alone. Chana stayed in the hideout for three days and slowly recovered.

On January 5, 1943, Kulpa arrived at the hideout. He brought food and told Mundek and Chana that the Nazis were executing the remaining Jews of Lubaczów by firing squad at the anti-tank ditch in Dachnów, which had been dug by the USSR in 1940 as a defensive line against the Germans on the border of the General Government. It had been converted by the Germans into a mass grave, prepared by Jewish slave work for that purpose.

After Kulpa left, they decided to go there the following night to see for themselves. On the night of January 6, 1943, they went to the anti-tank ditch. It was a four-kilometer walk and they arrived at dawn on January 7. They hid themselves at the edge of the forest. Even from that distance, they could hear the screaming, crying, weeping, and yelling of Jews. Voices of children mixed with voices of elderly people; shouting women and men were using their last breaths to plead

---

7. At a later stage, when using such hideouts for longer periods, Mundek would cover the hideout with canvas and put pine branches on the top for camouflage.

Left to right: Simon Lavee and Or Lavee at the Dachnów memorial site, February 24, 2010

for mercy. Mingled with the cries, they heard the firing orders in German and the sound of bullets. It was the song of hell conducted by the Devil himself.

The previous day in the ghetto, on January 6, the Jews had been driven into the *rynek* (the market square), where many were shot down indiscriminately and then buried in a mass grave in the Jewish cemetery. The Security Police, assisted by Ukrainian policemen, then conducted an *Aktion* by searching the houses and shooting down hundreds of sick and elderly Jews who had not reported to the *rynek*.[8] About two thousand Jews were deported to the Sobibór extermination camp. An additional two thousand Jews were forced to walk to the Dachnów ditch, two kilometers north of Lubaczów, to be shot down by the Gestapo from Rawa Ruska.[9]

This massive operation was supervised by Odilo Globocnik, originally from Slovenia,[10] who was the SS and police chief of Lublin and responsible for the deportation and mass shootings of the Jews in the Lublin district. He supervised

---

8. Dean, *Ghettos in German-Occupied Eastern Europe*, pp. 800–802.
9. Ibid.
10. Born in Trieste in 1904 to a bureaucrat's family of Slovenian descent who considered themselves Germans, he was a member of the Austrian Freikorps and SA.

the three annihilation camps of Operation Reinhard (Bełżec, Sobibór, and Treblinka), whose purpose was to kill the Jews.

There already weren't many Jews left in Lubaczów. Following evacuation of Jews from nearby villages and towns, in October and November 1942 the Germans had conducted an *Aktion* in which about two thousand Jews from Lubaczów and the surrounding area were deported to the Bełżec extermination camp. Others had been sent to Sobibór. Several Jews managed to escape to the nearby forests and obtain weapons and organize themselves into partisan groups.[11]

Now a typhus epidemic was the excuse the Germans exploited to annihilate the remnant. On January 6, 1943, the final mass execution of the Jews in Lubaczów really began. At five o'clock in the morning the streets surrounding the ghetto were sealed by armed Ukrainian and Polish policemen. They were supported by Polish volunteers to the German Volksliste, such as Władysław Serdyński and his son Roman.[12] No one could escape the ghetto at this point. Jews who were caught trying were forced out of their houses and sent to Bełżec.

Bodies were strewn everywhere. The promise of rewards led many Poles and Ukrainians to expose hiding Jews. In return, they would be given the deceased's belongings.

Mundek and Chana watched the terrible scene at the anti-tank ditch at Dachnów. The Jews stood naked on a dirt rampart. The temperature was twenty degrees below zero Celsius (minus four Fahrenheit). The snow stood fifty centimeters (twenty inches) high. A firing squad of four Nazis fired at the back of the Jews' heads. One bullet was allocated to each Jew. As a result, not all of the victims died immediately. They were just left there to die in agony. Dying and wounded Jews shouted from the ditch. Then a second shift of naked Jews were forced onto the dirt rampart, and so on, and so on. Every few minutes, another layer of Jews toppled onto those already in the ditch like sediment. Long and endless convoys of Jews were forced to walk from Lubaczów to the anti-tank ditch, guarded by Ukrainians. Those who fell before they reached the ditch were shot immediately. There was no separation between men, women, children, or

---

11. Miron and Shulhani, eds., *The Yad Vashem Encyclopedia of the Ghettos during the Holocaust*, vol. 2, p. 419.
12. See testimony of Edmund Katz to Yad Vashem, no. M49E/3300.

the elderly. All of the Jews went to the ditch together. Shortly before reaching the ditch, they were forced to take off their clothes so they would be ready to be executed as soon as their turn came.[13]

Chana and Mundek were frozen in shock as they watched the execution scene from the woods. They could not take their eyes off this horrific exercise. It was that day they saw how their families were executed. From the moment that the massacre started until it ended at three in the afternoon, they remained in their hiding places in the woods, unable to move. Mundek saw one of his family members fall dead, and then they saw an SS policeman kicking the corpse because it had not rolled down into the ditch.[14] They were completely stunned and speechless.

Over the following nights Mundek went to Kulpa and told him what he and Chana had seen at Dachnów. Mundek knew that Kulpa and his father had been like brothers. Kulpa listened to Mundek and hugged him, proclaiming that God would punish those who had done this.

During the days of January 8–13, the killing in Lubaczów continued. The Gestapo went into the ghetto daily and simply fired at anyone who was alive in cold blood.[15] This "Jew-hunting" was a form of amusement and was conducted happily, as if they were hunting rabbits. It was a joyous occasion when a Jew was found. He was shot down immediately. Sometimes shots were fired at innocent Polish houses. The local Polish population were upset that they had to suffer because of the Jews.

On January 8, 1943, the Security Police, assisted by Ukrainian policemen, raided and shot hundreds of sick and elderly Jews in their homes in Lubaczów.[16] The rest were killed at the Jewish cemetery. The bodies were then transported on horse-drawn sleds from the Jewish cemetery to the Dachnów trench to be buried. Two hundred Jewish bodies were transported from the Jewish cemetery in this manner. However, the corpses were not buried immediately. This process took

---

13. Fairly early on in the Final Solution, the Nazis had come up with the efficient process of having victims remove their clothes before execution, so that the clothing could be reused, and any valuables that may have been hidden in them confiscated. At the Dachnów ditch, most likely the Ukrainians took the clothes.
14. Testimony of Edmund (Mundek) Łukawiecki (Moshe Lavee) to Yad Vashem, July 28, 1993, no. 03-6946, tape no. 033C/2757.
15. See testimony of Dr. Jakob Herzig to Yad Vashem, no. M49/E 1132.
16. Dean, *Ghettos in German-Occupied Eastern Europe*, p. 801.

a few days, and in spite of the frozen winter, the smell of rotting bodies spread to Lubaczów. It was indescribably awful. At night, peasants from nearby villages would come with axes and chop off body parts for loot.[17]

Hundreds of Gypsies had been brought to Lubaczów, and they too were sent into the woods to be killed, along with fifteen Jews who were sent to dig a mass grave. After they had completed this task, the Jews were executed themselves and buried with the gypsies. According to one source, Jews from France were also brought to the Dachnów trench and executed there.[18]

Those Jews who did manage to run into the woods rarely survived. Most of them had very limited knowledge of how to survive in a hostile, frozen environment, and therefore the majority of them died of hypothermia. Polish and Ukrainian peasants, armed with axes, went looking for these frozen Jews. They saw them as potential sources of money, gold, clothes, or boots. When a valuable item was found, the part of the body it was attached to was simply cut off.

One of the members of the Judenrat, a man named Diamond, who had been a corporal in the prewar Polish army, tried to save his family by putting them on a peasant cart and fleeing. He and his family were caught and Diamond was executed. However his wife, Esti, and their baby boy were not executed immediately. The Gestapo used them as operatives against Jewish partisans in the woods.

Mundek's fiancée, the Silberschmidt girl, was murdered on January 7, 1943, by Roman Serdyński, a Pole of German extraction who, with his father Władysław killed Jews for sport. He met her in Lubaczów and, seeing that she was wearing an engagement ring, cut her finger off to steal the ring. As she lay there losing blood, dying in agony, pedestrians urged Roman to spare her from pain and kill her. He shot her.[19]

---

17. See eyewitness testimony by Feiga Kammer, testimony of Feiga Kammer to Yad Vashem, no. M49/1174 LB.440, taken in Warasw by the Żydowski Instytut Historyczny. No date of the testimony is recorded. While writing this book I was informed by Chana's cousin Chana Diner that Feiga Kammer was a relative of Chana's.
18. Testimony of elderly Nowe Sioło resident Władek Sikum, March 12, 2011.
19. Testimony of Benjamin Kammer, taken on February 18, 1948, in Munich, Germany, by Juristische Abteilung des Zentralkomittees Juden in der US Zone (the legal department of the Central Committee of the Liberated Jews in the US Zone). Mundek never knew how his fiancée had died; the testimony was discovered during research for this book. In fact, his close friends the Weiner family knew about it, but despite the fact that Mundek continued to be in touch with them after the war, they simply never spoke of it. Perhaps it was too painful to say. While writing this book, I interviewed the late Mrs. Lula Weiner Baum. Her eyes widened

On January 7, 1943, the Łukawiecki family was captured and taken to the Dachnów anti-tank ditch, where they were executed by a Nazi firing squad, with the assistance of Ukrainian collaborators.[20] The Bern, Katz, and Cieczanower families were also captured on January 7. SS policemen raided the shelter of the Bern family and captured all who hid there. In his shock and confusion, Matel's husband Meir started to look for his coat. Matel told him that he would not need it anymore.[21] The entire family was shot down by the gunfire of Nazi soldiers, one after the other. All of them are buried in the Dachnów mass grave.[22]

It is likely that the use of the Dachnów ditch as mass graves was ordered by the local Security Police in collaboration with the German Ordungpolizei and the Ukrainian Auxiliary Police. Jewish slave laborers were brought from the Lubaczów ghetto to prepare the Red Army's defensive trenches for their new role as mass graves for Lubaczów's Jews. The slave laborers who did not survive the hard labor were buried on site, in the mass grave they had prepared.[23] The Ukrainian Auxiliary Police officers, who were guarding the workers, forced them cynically to sing the following in Polish in loud voices:[24]

Rydz Smigły nie nauczył nas nic
Hitler złoty nauczył nas roboty,
Uj, waj przez nas wojna.[25]

Two thousand Jews were executed at the massacre of Dachnów on January 9, 1943. No list of names exists. And after the winter of 1942–1943, the Jews never returned to Lubaczów.

---

when discussing the murder of the Silberschmidt girl by Roman Serdyński, which her parents Zanwet and Luba testified to.

20. Mundek Łukawiecki wrote in his Curriculum Vitae, given to the Kraków municipal UB, that his family was murdered on January 28, 1943. Based on other evidence, I believe this date to be mistaken. UB personal file of Mundek Łukawiecki – IPN/OBUiAd/Kraków, Sygn IPN 16 057/1028.

21. Personal interview with Chana's cousin Chana Diner, January 27, 2012. Chana Diner heard this from Feiga Kammer after the war.

22. Chana Lavee, pages of testimony to Yad Vashem, January 23, 1978.

23. "Związek Bojowników o Wolność i Demokrację Koło Miejsko, pp. 187–89.

24. Testimony of elderly Nowe Sioło resident Władek Sikum, March 12, 2011.

25. The translation is "Rydz Śmigły taught us nothing; dear Hitler taught us work. Oy vey, because of the war." Rydz Śmigły, a marshal of Poland, commander in chief of Poland's armed forces, was Poland's ruler prior to WWII and before the German occupation of Poland.

A few days after returning to the hideout in the Bór woods, Chana started to bleed. Mundek brought her back to Kulpa's farm one night after consulting with Kulpa. She concluded that she was pregnant after being raped by the Ukrainian policeman, Sergeant-Major Vasyl Kułczycki.[26] They all agreed that she should terminate the pregnancy, as it was impossible to survive that way in the woods. They decided to wait a few more days for Chana to regain her strength. Kulpa's second wife, Amana,[27] carried out the abortion at the end of January 1943. Both Józef Kulpa and Amana supported Chana intensively and made sure that she recovered. During this ordeal, Mundek and Chana hid at Kulpa's farm.

The night before Chana and Mundek left the farm, Kulpa and Amana came into the barn with bread, salt, and a bottle of vodka. Kulpa opened the vodka, poured it into four glasses, and said: "Mundek, your father was like my brother. When I took you into the underground, I promised him that I would protect you. And I have been doing it ever since. It is not easy for me as a Christian to help you. My own family is at risk. But a promise is a promise. I know that according to the Jewish faith, bread, salt, and wine are holy and are involved in prayers. It is also the case in our beliefs. So, let all of us swear to God that we will not betray each other and that we will continue to fight for the independence of our homeland, Poland, and be loyal to Armia Krajowa."

When he had finished speaking, each of them said "I swear" and then they drank the vodka and ate bread with salt. On the way out, Kulpa hugged Chana and told her that she should be proud of herself for being a member of the AK. Through this, she would fight the Nazis.

---

26. Hoffman, *Keep Yelling*, p. 174, quotes Chana describing the rape. See also the taped interview with Aliza Segal, February 5, 2012, in which she recounts what Mundek told her about the rape, with slightly different details.

27. Personal interview with Janusz Kulpa (grandson of Józef Kulpa) in Lubaczów, January 1, 2012. He related that his grandmother (Józef Kulpa's first wife Rosalie) and two of their children were killed in 1941 by German air bombardment.

Chapter 16
Partisan Land

In the two years following the start of the war, two retreating armed forces found themselves wedged into eastern Poland. The Polish army retreated before the Wehrmacht invasion of 1939 at the beginning of WWII, with those who did not manage to flee to Romania or Hungary being captured by the Red Army.[1] In 1941, the Red Army itself retreated from Eastern Poland as a result of Operation Barbarossa, the German invasion of the Soviet Union.

During the Wehrmacht offensive, Red Army soldiers who retreated found refuge in the Polish woods.[2] While few Polish soldiers hid in these woods, many Red Army soldiers did. Before Hitler broke his non-aggression pact with Stalin in June 1941 and attacked the USSR, the partisan movement in Poland did not really exist,[3] and it took more than half a year after this pivotal event before a substantial Polish partisan movement developed.

The area south of Lublin was covered by dense woods and was therefore a natural site for guerilla warfare, or in other words, partisan warfare, whose key features were mountain-type warfare, night fighting, street fighting, and generally the use of tactics that limited the Germans' ability to use armor. The forests had the best conditions for partisan warfare. The terrain was very rugged, with many trees and rocks making mobility very difficult.[4] It was therefore an ideal site for carrying out guerilla attacks against the Germans.

The area south of Lublin held less importance for the Germans, as it was in between two major support lines to the east – the Kraków-Lwów road and the

---

1. Bór-Komorowski, *The Secret Army*, p. 126.
2. Bór-Komorowski, *The Secret Army*, p. 118.
3. Shmuel Krakowski, *The War of the Doomed: Jewish Armed Resistance in Poland, 1942–1944* (New York: Holmes and Meier, 1984), p. 5.
4. Ibid., p. 75.

136 · CHAPTER 16

Mundek and Chana preparing food, spring 1943

Mundek in front of a bunker, March–April 1943

Chana prior to an operation, spring 1943

Mundek and Chana preparing food, spring 1943

Chana Bern preparing food, spring 1943

vWarsaw-Brest-Moscow line.[5] Since the primary routes to Moscow were located more to the north, the area south of Lublin was less strategically important to the Nazis. And as the main routes to Lwów were in the southern part of the country, that area was not very strategically important to the Nazis for their offensive on Stalingrad. These factors directly influenced the partisan fighting in the region where Mundek Łukawiecki's partisan group was based.

---

5. Ibid.

Polish soldiers and underground activists hiding in these woods were hunted intensely by the Russians[6] and the Nazis.[7] These were the Spaleni[8] with whom Mundek had spent his early days in the ZWZ/AK. In most cases the Spaleni hid near their families and just tried to survive, while gathering the odd snippets of information. They rarely conducted assaults or military actions against the Germans, as most had no weapons. For this reason, they were not considered aggressive or threatening. Their singular aim was to try to stay alive. During the German occupation, they rarely visited their families and were only seen in public once in a while when gathering food.

From the German point of view, in the General Government, the police were in charge of anti-partisan warfare. The field commands were responsible for military affairs in a narrow sense. The Wehrmacht had to operate together with the civil administration and several organizations of the police. The field command and supreme field command had to report to the Militärbefehlshaber in the General Government. The reports that have survived bear very valuable information regarding German anti-partisan activities.[9]

In section 8c of a report containing twenty-four pages, which covers the period from June 16, 1942, until July 15, 1942, under the general heading "Fighting gangs of bandits [*Bandenunwesen*]" and the subtitle "Nuisance of gangs of bandits," it was reported that the police and the Sicherheitsdienst (SD, the Nazi intelligence agency) acted in a sharp manner against bearers of epidemics and small vagabond groups composed of gangs of robbers who came from the districts of Lublin, Rawa Ruska, and Kaminka.[10] One hundred twenty people

---

6. In the territory under USSR rule.
7. In German-controlled territory.
8. Spaleni, "burned," refers to underground members who had to hide in the woods because they were on the Gestapo's hit list. Testimony of Edmund (Mundek) Łukawiecki (Moshe Lavee) to Yad Vashem, July 28, 1993, no. 03-6946, tape no. 033c/2757; UB personal file of Mundek Łukawiecki – IPN/OBUiAd/Kraków, Sygn IPN 16 057/1028.
9. These reports, known as the OFK or Oberfeldkommandantur reports to the Militärbefehlshaber in Lwów, are part of the war diary of the Supreme Field Command. The diary was captured by the Allies at the end of WWII. These files were microfilmed in the US. The German courts made extensive microfilm prints from these films. A serial of these prints became part of the collection of documents of the Zentrale Stelle. The original war diary has been restored to Germany and is now stored in the military archives in Freiburg.
10. Oberfeldkommandantur (OFK) 365 monthly report for the period June 16, 1942–July 15, July 19, 1942, p. 361, Bundesarchiv-Aussenstelle Ludwigsburg Abt. Ia.

were killed. The report also states that the view that these gangs of bandits are conducted in a military manner is not correct. Rather they were ordinary gangs of robbers who had operated in the area for generations.

The monthly report for the period May 16, 1942, until June 15, 1942, describes that, from the beginning of June 1942, in the area of Rawa Ruska, gangs whose composition and/or existence was previously unknown became noticeable.[11] These gangs were from Lublin. The report goes on to suggest that these gangs of robbers had always resided there, but that now they had been strengthened by escaped Russian POWs and political desperados. The report further states that these gangs were used by the Russians, who aided them with leaders and tactical support. The report then makes it clear that the police are in charge of fighting these robbers, and deploys four companies for that purpose.

Under the heading "Fighting gangs of bandits," the report specifically mentions raids carried out in the south of Lublin conducted by individual gangs numbering one to three men. These operations were conducted in a military manner. The report states that the police are responsible for fighting bandits and are already engaged in this task fully. The report orders that forces must defend their posts, and also describes the chain of command and the units to be involved.[12]

Under the heading "Present situation," the report expresses concern regarding the rectangle of Hrubieszow-Zamość-Doruhusza-Dorohusk. It says that a greater number of firefights occurred in which gangs were annihilated and smashed and their supporters among the civilian population were arrested. According to the report, during these fights five hundred people were shot and fourteen hundred civilians were arrested as supporters, of which 250 were active partisans. The German losses were twenty-one dead, twenty-four wounded, and three missing.[13]

From the partisans' point of view, life in the woods was extremely cruel.[14] However, the more time the Spaleni spent in the woods, the better their outdoor survival instincts became. The woods were generally very humid and wet, and in the winter time, they were cold and frozen over. The partisans learned how

---

11. OFK 365 monthly report for the period May 16, 1942–June 15, 1942, dated June 16, 1942, p. 211, Bundesarchiv-Aussenstelle Ludwigsburg Abt. Ia.
12. Ibid., pp. 251–52.
13. Ibid., pp. 302–3.
14. Lukas, *Forgotten Holocaust*, p. 81.

to build hideouts and bunkers and how to remain camouflaged for long periods of time. The hideouts were made out of pine tree branches, and sometimes out of canvas tent fabric with the tops covered with branches. Other times they dug into the ground and used straw or greenery to lie on so as to avoid catching pneumonia or developing arthritis. They learned how to expertly cover their tracks and travel secretly.

Their crash course on wilderness survival included observing how animals behaved during the day and at night, and picking up crucial skills such as how to start a fire from scratch, how to find and prepare food and store water, that fog meant they must stop cooking as the smoke would spread a very long distance, that wind meant their food could be smelled a very long way away, and that human waste had to be buried to avoid wild animals or wild dogs carrying it off and being noticed by peasants or soldiers. They also had to learn about a myriad of natural medical treatments, as well as ways to maintain their personal hygiene in the wild.[15]

Along with an understanding of the tactical advantages of fighting from the woods, it was important that the partisans become familiar with military doctrine and tactical behaviors – particularly involving the use and maintenance of firearms in extremely cold conditions. The harsh weather would often freeze the oil and the firing mechanisms of their guns. This would result in misfired weapons. To overcome this, the partisans needed to safeguard their weapons and ammunition, especially at night. One tactic was to sleep with their munitions to keep them warm. Along with their weapons, they also often slept wearing boots or shoes to keep frostbite at bay during the frigid winter nights.

The Armia Krajowa (AK) was formed on February 14, 1942, by General Władysław Sikorski with the explicit purpose of unifying the ZWZ underground movements. A few months later, on August 15, the independent underground movements were ordered to take command of the AK. The ZWZ was an organizational monstrosity. There were six regional centers, each with its own commander, and each with its own communication links to the Polish government-in-exile. This amalgamation just exacerbated the chaos that already existed

---

15. Testimony of Edmund (Mundek) Łukawiecki (Moshe Lavee) to Yad Vashem, July 28, 1993, no. 03-6946, tape no. 033c/2757; Moshe Lavee (Edmund/Mundek Łukawiecki), recorded interview by USC Shoah Foundation Institute, interview code 31895, May 27, 1997.

in the underground.¹⁶ This provincial formation was modeled on the prewar civil administration structure¹⁷ and was not very compatible with military command, because it had been designed to handle urban administrative matters.¹⁸

The ZWZ/AK was the military wing of the Polish underground movement, which operated under orders from the exiled government in London. The Allied forces implemented a policy of discouraging a premature uprising in Poland,¹⁹ and the Polish government in exile was completely responsive to the Allied agenda. The AK therefore decided to minimize military action against the Wehrmacht until such time as they would be ready to mount a major offensive.²⁰ The AK's main focus was to prepare and coordinate for this general military uprising against the Nazis.

Their secondary mission was to continue sabotage operations against the Germans.²¹ This policy was adopted, in part, to minimize Nazi atrocities against the civilian population.²² The Germans undertook very harsh and aggressive attacks against Polish civilians in rural areas,²³ and these terrorist tactics lessened the local support for the Polish underground and partisan activities.²⁴ Therefore

---

16. There were "four types of units: full conspiratorial platoons, cadre conspiratorial platoons, sabotage-diversionary units, and partisan groups. The sabotage-diversionary and partisan groups conducted most of the operations against the enemy while the bulk of the AK was immobile." Lukas, *Forgotten Holocaust*, p. 62.
17. Bór-Komorowski, *The Secret Army*, p. 148.
18. Argasiński, *Konspiracja w powiecie*.
19. Anthony Eden, "Secret Resistance in Poland," War Cabinet Report of the Foreign Office, October 5, 1943, The National Archives (TNA) WP (43) 439, CAB 66/41/39.
20. Pobóg-Malinowski, *Najnowsza historia polityczna Polski*, p. 381. See also Lukas, *Forgotten Holocaust*, p. 61.
21. Pobóg-Malinowski, *Najnowsza historia polityczna Polski*, p. 381. See also Lukas, *Forgotten Holocaust*, p. 61; Krakowski, *The War of the Doomed*, p. 5.
22. That is how the Germans confiscated the Łukawiecki family distillery in Ostrowiec, as it was Jewish property. This was the usual pattern of conduct all over German-dominated Europe.
23. For examples, see chapter 18, "Susiec," and also see War Cabinet Report of the Foreign Office, August 15, 1944, The National Archives (TNA) WP (44) 447, CAB/66/53/47. That report describes partisans in Poland, emphasizing the NSZ (Narodowe Siły Zbrojne – National Armed Forces) underground movement, which rescued a British RAF crew on April 23, 1944 southeast of Sandomierz.
24. United People's Party, Chief Committee, Department of History of the People's Movement, *Materiały źródłowe do historii polskiego ruchu ludowego* [Source materials on the history of the Polish peasant movement] (Warsaw: Ludowa Spółdzielnia Wydawnicza [People's Publishing Cooperative], 1966), vol. 4, pp. 143–44. See also Archiwum Zakładu Historii Partii (AZHP, Archives of the Institute for Communist Party History in Warsaw), 202/III-28, p. 132.

the ZWZ/AK decided not to initiate and conduct aggressive military operations for fear of reprisal against the people.[25] Nevertheless, German military authorities captured AK members contrary to the laws of war[26] and executed them after interrogation.

All the while, the ZWZ/AK was also not cooperating with the Soviets or the Soviet partisans. This was because of the Molotov-Ribbentrop Pact and the murder of a Polish officer captured as a POW in Katyń,[27] as well as the murder of a number of officers and Polish civilians in other places in spring 1940.[28] Trust was never restored between the Soviets and Poland, even after the renewal of diplomatic relations between the Polish government and the USSR on July 27, 1941. The Polish-Soviet difficulties did not establish a constructive basis for their relationship. The Molotov-Ribbentrop Pact and the division of Poland were sufficient grounds for mistrust.

Until the Germans revealed mass graves in April 1943, the AK feared the death of their POWs but had no intelligence about their fate. The Polish intention to request Red Cross investigation was not accepted by the Allies. The Soviets blamed the Poles as "Hitler's Polish collaborators," which eventually led to the rupture of their official relationship on April 25, 1943. The negative Polish-USSR relationship contributed to the Soviet rejection of proper Russian assistance to further development of Polish forces.[29] However, at the field level mutual relationships were developed due to the local commanders in the field.

A further factor that the partisans took advantage of was that the German administrative division of the area did not lend itself to fighting the partisans, and in fact probably led to command and control difficulties. Efficient fighting against the partisans required the Germans to coordinate between various districts, unlike the AK organization which was structured in line with the old

---

25. War Cabinet Report of the Foreign Office, February 17, 1943, The National Archives (TNA) WP (43) 69. That report quotes a representative of the Polish underground movement, who arrived specifically from Warsaw.
26. War Cabinet Report of the Foreign Office, August 23, 1944, The National Archives (TNA) WP (44) 462.
27. Lukas, *Forgotten Holocaust*, pp. 72–73.
28. George Sanford, "The Katyn Massacre and Polish-Soviet Relations, 1941–43," *Journal of Contemporary History* 41, no. 1 (2006): 95–111.
29. George Sanford, *Katyn and the Soviet Massacre of 1940: Truth, Justice and Memory*, BASEES/Routledge Series on Russian and East European Studies, no. 20 (London: Routledge, 2005).

Polish administrative structure and could carry out operations via one chain of command. For example, the Lubaczów district was divided by the Germans in autumn 1939 between Germany and the USSR. Zamość became part of the German district of Lublin while Lubaczów and the bigger part of the former district became part of the USSR. After German conquest of Galicia, Zamość remained in the district of Lublin, while the town of Lubaczów and the new rural municipality, together with several villages of the former Polish district of Lubaczów, became part of Kreishauptmannschaft Rawa Ruska, of the district Galicia.

The AK did not want to establish a military presence in woods that were essentially in a state of anarchy.[30] Despite the fact that it was heavily criticized, the truth was that there was better communication between Warsaw and London than between Warsaw and Lwów. The strategic policy of the AK was not to operate partisan units, so as to differentiate themselves from the partisans supported by the Red Army. While the "forest folks"[31] lived by the good graces of local peasants and received their support from them, this was regarded as looting and robbery by the AK. Another argument against forming a partisan group was that the AK considered Jews – who were not beloved by the AK – to be the main backbone of the Communist partisans.[32]

The German blitzkrieg captured hundreds of thousands of Red Army soldiers as prisoners of war in eastern Poland. A small band of them, maybe a thousand or so, managed to avoid arrest or escaped from POW camps. In the woods, they rapidly organized themselves into military units under Red Army command. As the front line between Germany and the USSR advanced to the east, the number of Russian soldiers who joined the Russian partisans increased. Conversely, when the Germans retreated to the west, the number of Russian partisans started to diminish. In the beginning, the Russian partisans limited their activities to surviving and procuring food. Later, they expanded to military action against the Wehrmacht.

The Red Army understood the military advantages of the partisans and their

---

30. Lukas, *Forgotten Holocaust*, p. 82.
31. This was the nickname given by Bór-Komorowski to the Russian partisans. Bór-Komorowski, *The Secret Army*, pp. 171–72. Mundek Łukawiecki actually used a similar word he invented in the Polish language – "Lasowcy" – to cover his whereabouts during WWII in his official UB biography.
32. Lukas, *Forgotten Holocaust*, pp. 78–79, 125, 128, 168.

deployment behind the German army. They were instructed to carry out sabotage missions against German facilities and infrastructure installations, as well as logistical supply lines and confinement forces, and to collect intelligence against the General Government.[33]

The Red Army supported the partisan units very generously. They trained the personnel, sent armament, logistics, supplies, food, and so on. They even opened a special training center for partisan commanders.[34] Surprisingly, even after being informed about the Russian partisan training center near Moscow, the AK did not give a second thought to Russian partisan movements.[35]

Contrary to the Russian partisans, the AK units were poorly equipped and poorly supported.[36] Justifiably, they felt inferior to the Soviet partisans.[37] Yet the AK itself inadvertently supported the growth of the Russian partisan movements; since the AK did not focus on partisan warfare and did not develop a partisan force, the territory was left wide open for the Russian partisan movement to flourish on Polish soil.

On September 29, 1941, just three months after Operation Barbarossa began, a Moscow conference attended by the US, UK, and Soviets, questioned why four Polish divisions (totaling about forty-four thousand troops) were not equipped to equal a single Soviet armed division. The Poles, in spite of this, never asked for Russian support for their underground movements. This may be because of the mutual distrust and dislike that had existed between the two countries for the previous twenty years.[38]

Then, two years later, in September–October 1943, the combined chiefs of staff in Washington turned down a Polish request to equip the Polish Secret

---

33. The part of occupied Poland that was not annexed by Germany was put under the General Gouvernment (in English, the General Government); its governor was in Kraków.
34. Bór-Komorowski, *The Secret Army*, p. 118.
35. Ibid., p. 120. Bór-Komorowski describes the local population's complaints caused by the Communist partisans' violence.
36. See for example the request denied to equip the Polish army. Chairman of the British Mission, Notes on the Moscow Conference, October 8, 1941, The National Archives (TNA) WP (41) 238. See also chapter 18, "Susiec."
37. War Cabinet Report of the Foreign Office, August 15, 1944, The National Archives (TNA) WP (44) 447, CAB/66/53/47.
38. Chairman of the British Mission, Notes on the Moscow Conference, October 8, 1941, The National Archives (TNA) WP (41) 238.

Army.[39] While the combined chiefs of staff declared support of sabotage and intelligence missions, their commitment never translated into practical support,[40] nor did they even officially recognize the Polish underground until 1944.[41]

The dramatic disparity in the logistical situation of the partisans supported by the USSR and those under the command of the Polish government in exile, especially in terms of weapons and military equipment, can't be explained only by the dislike between the Russians and the Allies[42] or the mistrust between the Poles and the Russians. Time after time, the Allies rejected requests to equip the Polish underground.[43]

It is fair to say that the military strategy of the Polish underground at that time was to prepare themselves for a final insurrection that would entail full-scale revolt.[44] But that policy can't be an excuse for withholding real support to the Polish underground, as any new equipment they would have received would have required a time-consuming training period, and delays were counterproductive. The Polish underground was both praised and valued for its intelligence work and achievements.[45] It is possible that the Allies were afraid that diverting the main activity of the Polish underground to military conflict and engagement would harm its intelligence collection, and that the Allies preferred to keep the Polish underground underequipped for that reason.

In any event, AK members had to arm themselves.[46] Their weaponry was an eclectic mix. The main sources were peasants and raids on Polish and Red

---

39. Anthony Eden, "Secret Resistance in Poland," War Cabinet Report of the Foreign Office, October 5, 1943, The National Archives (TNA) WP (43) 439, CAB 66/41/39.
40. War Cabinet Report of the Foreign Office, February 17, 1943, The National Archives (TNA) WP (43) 69. This report quotes a representative of the Polish underground movement, who arrived specifically from Warsaw.
41. War Cabinet Conclusions, August 21, 1944, 5:30 P.M., The National Archives (TNA) WM (44) 109.
42. Chairman of the British Mission, Notes on the Moscow Conference, October 8, 1941, The National Archives (TNA) WP (41) 238, Enclosure II, "Military Mission and Future Co-operation with Russia," p. 11.
43. See Anthony Eden, "Secret Resistance in Poland," War Cabinet Report of the Foreign Office, October 5, 1943, The National Archives (TNA) WP (43) 439, CAB 66/41/39; and see War Cabinet Conclusions, August 21, 1944, The National Archives (TNA) WM (44) 109.
44. Bór-Komorowski, *The Secret Army*, pp. 172–73.
45. Ibid., pp. 150–51; and War Cabinet Report of the Foreign Office, August 15, 1944, The National Archives (TNA) WP (44) 447, CAB/66/53/47.
46. Argasiński, *Konspiracja w powiecie*, p. 69.

Army camps. As a result, the AK was essentially a light infantry unit operating in "enemy territory." Armaments included handguns, light machine guns, and hand grenades. There was no heavy weaponry, nor was there, obviously, any air force or navy support.

Originally the new order of the General Government was planned within the framework of the so-called Generalplan Ost,[47] which consisted of several different colonization plans conceived during the years 1939–1942 to prepare for an eventual German takeover of all of central and eastern Europe.

In the summer of 1941, Odilo Globocnik,[48] SS and police leader for the Lublin district, propelled Heinrich Himmler to initiate a special project in the county of Zamość in the district of Lublin with German *Wehrbauern*, "soldier peasants" who were to help forcibly settle the lands that the Germans conquered. Although the city of Zamość was never actually renamed, the written plans referred to it as "Himmlerstadt" or Pflugstadt (Plow City).[49] The plan was that it should be an outpost and base for the newly occupied areas in the east and also form the cornerstone of a German bridge between the Baltic and Transylvania.

Himmler visited the area on July 21, 1941, and approved the plan, most likely because of the city's German heritage.[50] Only a small part of the plan was started. By the spring of 1942, this area had already been declared *judenfrei*, "free of Jews." The evacuation of Polish villages began in November 1941 and lasted until August 1943. Nearly three hundred villages were affected and 110,000 Poles were

---

47. Franz Wilhelm and Josef Kallbrunner, *Quellen zur deutschen Siedlungsgeschichte in Südosteuropa* [Sources of German settlement history in southeast Europe], Schriften der deutschen Akademie [Publications of the German Academy], no. 2 (Munich: Ernst Reinhardt, 1936).
48. Austrian Nazi (April 21, 1904–May 31, 1945) acquainted with Adolf Eichmann. Appointed on November 9, 1939, as SS and police chief of Lublin, he oversaw the liquidation of the Warsaw and Bialystok ghettos and was complicit in exterminating more than 1.5 million people. He was charged with implementing the Generalplan Ost.
49. Bór-Komorowski, *The Secret Army*, p. 111, states that the Germans did change the name of Zamość.
50. R. Unterschutz, Die Deutschen Siedlungen in Galizien, stand 1939 [(Map of) German settlements in Galicia as of 1939].

expelled.[51] Children below the age of eleven were taken from their parents and transferred to Berlin to be brought up as Germans.[52]

A considerable number fled before the screening started. Children, ill people, and elderly people over sixty were resettled in so-called *Rentendörfer* ("retirement villages"). Poles between the ages of sixteen and sixty who were able to work were sent to the armaments industry to replace the Jews, who had been deported to the extermination camps. Those who were not able to work were sent to concentration camps: sixteen thousand were deported to Lublin-Majdanek and two thousand to Auschwitz. Forty-five hundred children were kidnapped for Germanization in the German Reich. A certain number of Poles were allowed to stay temporarily as workers for the new German masters.

The settlement of the Germans began in summer 1942. Many were ethnic Germans from Bessarabia who had been resettled in Germany in 1940. Other ethnic Germans came from Romania, Serbia, Bulgaria, and Russia. From the very beginning they lived there in peril to their lives. The SS and police (gendarmerie, Polish police, and police battalions) as well as additional Wehrmacht units were not able to guard them. Massive retaliation against the remaining local population was ineffective in putting down resistance; the Russian partisans and the local AK continued to do all they could to fight the German intrusion.[53] The Zamość action was interrupted in spring 1943 and stopped in September 1943. Also in September Operation Reinhard was finished and Globocnik was sent back to Italy, where he was from.[54]

---

51. See Joseph Poprzeczny, *Odilo Globocnik, Hitler's Man in the East* (Jefferson, NC: McFarland, 2004). See also Bór-Komorowski, *The Secret Army*, p. 111, who mentions that 297 villages were evacuated and a hundred thousand inhabitants were transferred, among them thirty thousand children. This does not include Jews or Poles who were sent to concentration camps or murdered.
52. Bór-Komorowski, *The Secret Army*, p. 112.
53. In truth, the resistance was mostly driven by the Russian partisans. The local AK commander, Marian Warda, was actually disobeying his AK orders by sending men and arms to Zamość, but when he found out the Russian partisans were resisting the German incursion there, he wanted to make sure the Russians didn't take all the glory for themselves.
54. See Bruno Wasser, *Himmlers Raumplanung im Osten: Der Generalplan Ost in Polen, 1940–1944* [Himmler's spatial planning in the East: The General Plan for the East in Poland, 1940–1944], Stadt Planung Geschichte [City planning history series], no. 15 (Birkhäuser, 1993). See also Isabel Heinemann, *Rasse, Siedlung, deutsches Blut: Das Rasse- und Siedlungshauptamt der SS und die rassenpolitische Neuordnung* [Race, settlement, German blood: The Race and Settlement Main Office of the SS and the new racial political order] (Göttingen: Wallstein,

On the one hand, German activities in 1941–1942 made it difficult for the AK to establish a military presence. On the other hand, the AK needed to react. Outside the structure of the AK, armed resistance arose from farmers and other locals who fled to the woods. A group headed by Edward Misiarz from Zamość called on all villagers to join him in the fight against the Germans. The German policy of expulsion and settlement terrorized the Poles. They even feared deportation to Bełżec.[55]

By the end of November 1942,[56] the AK finally woke up[57] after "the inhabitants of the district reacted in spontaneous self-defence even before appropriate orders could be given."[58] The Generalplan Ost terrified the Poles.[59] Tomaszów Lubelski's AK members and other Polish underground movements – including Communist partisans – worked together to try to combat the horrific Nazi plans and actions.

The high commander of the AK in Tomaszów Lubelski was Marian Warda,[60] also known as "Polakowski."[61] Warda was responsible for the region of Tomaszów Lubelski, which included Lubaczów in the south (encompassing the Dąbrowa woods) and the Zamość area in the north. The AK unit in Lubaczów, which was given the codename "Lusia," was established at the end of 1942, under the command of Zdzisław Zathey ("Gładzicki").[62] The deputy was Michał Franuś ("Siciński"). The Lubaczów AK remained autonomous until the spring of 1943.

2003), chapter 5; Helga Hirsch, "Wir waren Besatzer in einem fremden Land: Warum Artur Singer sein Dorf in Bessarabien verlassen musste" ["We were occupiers in a foreign country: Why Arthur Singer was forced to leave his village in Bessarabia"], in *Entwurzelt: Vom Verlust der Heimat zwischen Oder und Bug* [Uprooted: On the loss of the homeland between the Oder and Bug] (Hamburg: Körber-Stiftung, 2007), pp. 93–126.
55. Zygmunt Klukowski, *Zamojszczyzny* [The Zamość region], vol. 1, *1918–1943* (Warsaw: Ośrodek Karta, 2007), pp. 315–18 (entries for December 8, 11, 14, 16, and 25, 1942); see the differing English edition: Zygmunt Klukowski, *Diary from the Years of Occupation, 1939–44* (Urbana: University of Illinois Press, 1993), pp. 230–32; inter alia Bełżec is missing.
56. Bór-Komorowski, *The Secret Army*, p. 112.
57. Pohl, *Nationalsozialistische Judenverfolgung*, p. 370.
58. Bór-Komorowski, *The Secret Army*, p. 111.
59. Even Józef Kulpa, who lived in Ostrowiec, eighty kilometers southeast of Zamość, was sure that he would be evacuated. As relayed to Mundek Łukawiecki.
60. The local commander was Jerzy Zagajski ("Lopek").
61. Caban, *Oddziały partyzanckie*, p. 65.
62. He was appointed after being sworn in on December 1942 by the commanding officer, codename "Bosak."

After that point, it was subordinated under the command of the Lwów AK (this unit was given the code name "Lira").

Marian Warda encouraged his members, including the Spaleni, to fight against the Nazis, even though this contradicted AK policy.[63] He established a combined camp of Spaleni and AK Spaleni together with Russian Spaleni partisans.[64] There he conducted military training for the Spaleni, including setting up a live shooting range. Warda also established the Soviet partisan training camp in the Dąbrowa woods. In September 1942, the unit was made up of small teams of eighteen to twenty members.

Under the command of Marian Warda, the Tomaszów Lubelski region pioneered the first AK partisan units – considerably earlier than any other area in Poland (there were Communist partisans, but the AK were the first nationalist Polish partisan groups). In fact, Warda established the first partisan group in the woods of Susiec in mid-1942.[65]

In addition to including the Spaleni in military operations, Warda set up a unique intelligence-gathering system. The formation of partisan units by the AK was a countermeasure by Warda to fight the expulsion of Poles and the settlement of Germans in the Zamość area, so he cooperated with other movements, including the Soviet partisans. Warda understood that partisan warfare must be conducted from the woods by warriors who lived there permanently. However, the main contingent of AK members who carried out operations continued to live in their own homes rather than in the woods.[66]

Warda's partisan units fought the German attempts to implement the Generalplan Ost by sabotaging and destroying facilities, as well as protecting the rural population. This resistance was locally organized[67] and they were commonly supported by the AK in the area.[68] The units ranged from as small as fifty to larger

---

63. Lukas, *Forgotten Holocaust*, p. 73.
64. Caban, *Oddziały partyzanckie*, p. 65.
65. Ibid., p. 6.
66. Lukas, *Forgotten Holocaust*, p. 62.
67. Archiwum Zakladu Historii Partii (AZHP, Archives of the Institute for Communist Party History in Warsaw), 202/III-28, p. 132.
68. Polish Military Historical Institute, *20 lat Ludowego Wojska Polskiego – II sesja naukowa poświęcona Wojnie Wyzwoleńcze Narodu Polskiego, 1939–1945* [Twenty years of the Polish army: Second scientific session devoted to the war of liberation of the Polish nation] (Warsaw:

groups of several hundred men.[69] But they were not well equipped or adequately armed. Consequently, German troops could easily retaliate against the civilian population for any actions the AK might take.[70]

The AK and another Polish underground movement conducted a bitter military operation at the end of 1942. On December 30, the first large engagement between partisan forces and a German army unit took place near Wojda.[71] On the Polish side,[72] members came from the Batalionów Chłopskich or BCh (Peasant Battalions)[73] and Soviet partisan groups.[74] The AK partisan movement, which was formed on the basis of fighting only in the Zamość area, also took part. By the winter of 1943, it totaled three thousand members in Radom, Kraków, and other areas.[75]

The increase of Soviet partisan involvement in the AK enabled them to deploy permanent units in the woods. This helped to tip the balance of power in their favor. After a short time, they held a majority over the other underground movements fighting the Germans. Even though the AK claimed that they were 268,000 members strong,[76] only 30 percent (realistically somewhere between two thousand and at most 3,160) operated on the east bank of the Bug River.[77] The Allies estimated the AK power to be around sixty-five thousand men.[78] Fol-

---

Wydawnictwo Ministerstwa Obrony Narodowej [Ministry of Defense Publishers], 1967), p. 845.
69. Bór-Komorowski, *The Secret Army*, pp. 112–13.
70. See for example the report concerning retaliations and executions of civilians by the SS in reprisal for partisan operations on January 5–6, 1943, in the Ruskie Piaski region. United People's Party, *Materiały źródłowe*, vol. 4, pp. 143–44.
71. Krakowski, *The War of the Doomed*, p. 5.
72. Lukas, *Forgotten Holocaust*, p. 74. Interestingly, the AK is not mentioned.
73. This was a separate underground movement.
74. Józef Niećko and Maria Szczawińska, eds., *Żelazne Kompanie Batalionów Chłopskich* (Warsaw: Chłopski Świat, 1948).
75. Lukas, *Forgotten Holocaust*, p. 74.
76. Jerzy Kirchmayer, *Powstanie Warszawskie* [The Warsaw uprising] (Warsaw: Książka i Wiedza, 1959), p. 27.
77. Ibid., and see also Tadeusz Rawski, Zdzisław Stapor, and Jan Zamojski, *Wojna wyzwoleńcza narodu polskiego w latach, 1939–1945: Węzłowe problemy* [The war of liberation of the Polish nation in the years 1939–1945: Key problems] (Warsaw: Ministerstwa Obrony Narodowej, 1963), p. 401.
78. Anthony Eden, "Secret Resistance in Poland," War Cabinet Report of the Foreign Office, October 5, 1943, The National Archives (TNA) WP (43) 439, CAB 66/41/39.

lowing the formation of a directorate of underground resistance in late 1942, the AK formally started to organize the entire partisan movement.[79]

The fierce fighting and resistance of the underground forced the Germans to reinforce their numbers in the Zamość area, and it was declared a "partisan fighting zone"[80] in the summer of 1943 by Himmler himself.[81] The anti-partisan warfare troops of the Germans in the Lublin district were a few small commandos of the security police (Gestapo) and order police consisting of police regiment twenty-five (three police battalions), the squadrons of the third SS and police cavalry detachment, gendarmerie platoons, Polish police, Ukrainian police, and Trawniki men. More and more Wehrmacht troops had to assist the police units.

Special partisan fighting units were also formed. In June 1942, in the district of Galicia, hunting (or raiding) commandos were formed by security battalions 543, 582, 887, and 888, and the motorized field gendarmerie platoon B 898. In Lwów and Ternopol, stand-by companies of security battalions 990 and 543 were trained for fighting partisans.[82]

Through June and July of 1942, the Germans claimed that in Galicia they killed 120 partisans and twenty escaped POWs.[83] A leaflet[84] issued by the commander of the order police in Galicia was the initial point for detailed orders for potential future partisan missions by the subordinated security battalions (Landeschützenbataillone).[85]

Despite all of this, by March 1943 only 14,300 Germans had been resettled in the whole Lublin district. The Germans stopped the resettlements in May. The project could be continued only after security in the General Government had

---

79. Lukas, *Forgotten Holocaust*, p. 74.
80. Kazimierz Radziwonczyk, "Niemieckie Siły Zbrojne w okupowanej Polsce" [The German armed forces in occupied Poland], *Wojskowy Przeglad Historyczny* [Military history review] 4 (1962): 60–61.
81. *Polska Partia Robotnicza Kronika, 1942–1945* [Polish Workers' Party Chronicle] (Warsaw, 1962), pp. 182–183.
82. OFK 365 report for the period May 16, 1942–June 15, 1942, dated June 16, 1942, pp. 201–24, Bundesarchiv-Aussenstelle Ludwigsburg, USA 314c.
83. OFK 365 report for the period June 16, 1942–July 15, 1942, dated July 19, 1942, pp. 359–382, Bundesarchiv-Aussenstelle Ludwigsburg, USA 314b.
84. OFK 365 report for the period June 16, 1942–July 15, 1942, dated July 19, 1942, pp. 359–382, Bundesarchiv-Aussenstelle Ludwigsburg, USA 314b.
85. Landesschützen were backup infantry units comprising a high percentage of elderly soldiers and normally hardly mobile. Their main task was guarding important installations and POWs.

been assured. At the same time, the Wehrmacht lost control of rural areas and stopped entering the woods in Wołyń. German garrisons only protected the railroads and administrative centers.[86]

In June 1944, the Germans attacked partisans in Biłgoraj in the district named Puszcza Solska in an operation called Sturmwind I. Sturmwind II then took place in Ruda Różaniecka, Huta Różaniecka, and Płazów. The Germans did not venture into Narol, Lipsko, and Bełżec. The partisans, however, anticipated that there was going to be an attack in the area of Narol and Bełżec, and therefore decided to avoid engagement by blending in among the peasants.

Even though the AK sent reinforcements into the fighting zone, the organization was not updated and was routinely kept in the dark about partisan movements. AK headquarters was isolated from the battlefield and did not have real-time familiarity with the situation on the ground. High command orders mainly revolved around the Burza Operation to attack German military trains and rear unit activities. Patrolling the Rawa Ruska–Oleszyce route as well as Płazów–Cieszanów–Oleszyce and Horyniec–Lubaczów–Oleszyce was also ordered after the Russians were already in control of the area.[87]

Along with military battles, the Nazis also fought the partisans in the gathering of intelligence. The Germans employed many spies, including women who pretended to be escaped Ukrainians from the east. The Germans also planted Ukrainians as partisans to fight against real partisans.[88]

It could be asked then, why didn't the Germans crush the partisans? They easily could have if they had fought the partisans more intensely, but decided not to do so. The German potential was limited. They had conflicting aims: to have as many troops as possible at the frontline and to keep the lines of supplies open. So

---

86. Czesław Madejczyk, "Deportations in the Zamość region 1942 and 1943 in the light of German documents," in *Acta Poloniae Historica I* (Warsaw: Państwowe Wydawictwo Naukowe, 1958), pp. 92, 98; Tadeusz Piotrowski, ed., *Genocide and Rescue in Wołyń: Recollections of the Ukrainian Nationalist Ethnic Cleansing Campaign against the Poles during World War II* (London: McFarland, 2000), p. 194.
87. Argasiński, *Konspiracja w powiecie*, p. 94. This contradicts accounts given by Gen. Bór-Komorowski, who says this only happened when the Germans retreated in May 1944. Bór-Komorowski, *The Secret Army*, p. 197.
88. War Cabinet Report of the Foreign Office, August 15, 1944, The National Archives (TNA) WP (44) 447, CAB/66/53/47.

the Germans avoided entering the woods that the partisans inhabited.[89] In turn, the partisans provided law and order to the civilian communities in the woods and protected them. This despite having Waffen-SS units, security police (which contained Gestapo, Kripo [criminal police] and SD) and order police, consisting of so-called "Truppenpolizei" (police battalions, police regiments, gendarmerie platoons, and other police troops, e.g., "Schutzmannschaftbataillone") and local order police (gendarmerie posts, Schutzpolizei [Schupo]) posts in the towns, including Polish and Ukrainian police.

Fighting partisans were referred to as *Banden* (gangs) by the Germans.[90] The nickname was more of a pejorative term, not acknowledging the partisans as a real military threat.[91] Hitler likened the war against the partisans to fighting lice. He believed that the gendarmeries should "take them by the root" and the bandits should be "finished individually."[92] The partisans were considered undesirables, to be annihilated like the Jews.[93] Early in the formation of the partisan movement, the Germans disregarded the partisans as a bona fide military force. They argued that these were bandits and criminals who found refuge in the forests.[94]

All the German Wehrmacht knew of the partisan movement in the area of Rawa Ruska (Galicia) in June 1942, and that it was made up of escaped Red Army

---

89. Bór-Komorowski, *The Secret Army*, p. 113.
90. *Banden* is the plural of *Bande* (gang). A member of a *Bande* is a *Bandit*. The term *Bandenkrieg* (gang war) wasn't used at first. Initially the Germans referred to *Bandenkampf* (gang fighting), which is belittling in comparison with *Bandenkrieg* or *Bandenbekämpfung* (gang control). In September 1942 Himmler ordered that the term *Partisanen* (partisans) had to be replaced by *Banden* (gangs) in the event reports. That was a reaction to a growing problem especially in Belorussia.
91. Himmler's Address to the SS Leibstandarte (originally the bodyguards of Adolf Hitler), September 7, 1940, in *Trial of the Major War Criminals before the International Military Tribunal, Nuremberg, 14 November 1945–1 October 1946*, vol. 29 (Nuremberg, 1948), pp. 98–110 (1918-PS), p. 103.
92. Roberts, *The Storm of War*, p. 160.
93. Himmler noted in his diary on December 18, 1941, in an entry headed "Judenfrage" (the Jewish Question) that Hitler's instruction was "*als Partisanen auszurotten*" (to eliminate [them] like the partisans). Peter Witte, ed., *Der Dienstkalender Heinrich Himmlers 1941–1942* [The dairy of Heinrich Himmler, 1941–1942] (Hamburg: Christians Verlag, 1999), p. 239. The comparison between the "Bandits" and Jews was also shared by some of the AK leadership, including Bór-Komorowski.
94. OFK 365 report for the period June 16, 1942–July 15, 1942, dated July 19, 1942, Bundesarchiv-Aussenstelle Ludwigsburg, USA 314b, p. 382.

prisoners of war, who originated from the Lublin area. They did not consider, however, that the USSR was supporting the partisans with a command structure from which they could organize attacks.[95] The reports cited just now indicate a certain amount of complacency among the Germans. They ignored suspected Soviet involvement and continued to put the onus of anti-partisan operations on the police. All these factors together limited the responsibility of the Wehrmacht to fight against the partisans.[96]

Despite the fact that the partisan movement grew in strength and organizational capability, in the General Government the responsibility of fighting them was nevertheless left to the police as it had been from the very beginning of the occupation. But the German police were simply not equipped to oversee the Generalplan Ost and this led to the creation of an area mostly controlled by the partisans, in other words, "Partisan Land."

A bonus of fighting the partisans, in German eyes, was the elimination of Jews, as they were regarded as the main backbone of the partisan movement.[97] Himmler, in his report to Hitler in the fall of 1942, claimed that anti-partisan warfare in Ukraine had resulted in the execution of 387,370 "gang helpers" and "suspected bandits," 363,211 of whom were Jews.[98]

From Germany's perspective, due to limited resources and the growing capabilities of the Russians, the main goal was to keep the lines of supplies to the east open, while the success of the Generalplan Ost was of lower priority. Hitler himself underlined the importance of this by ordering the combined task force operations of the Wehrmacht, the SS, and the police battalions to seek out partisans. This order promoted mass murder and gave free reign to troops to commit atrocities.[99]

---

95. Wehrmachtsbefehlshaber (Wehrmacht commander,) General Government, minutes of meeting, June 16, 1942, Bundesarchiv-Aussenstelle Ludwigsburg, USA 314c, p. 251.
96. Bundsarchiv-Aussenstelle, Ludwigsburg, USA 314c, pp. 251–52.
97. Wilhelm Kube, the commissioner general for Byelorussia, July 31, 1942. The secret report said the Jews were the main and major members of the partisan movement.
98. Report Commissioner General of Belorussia (Generalkommissar Weissruthenien) to Reichskommissar Ostland, July 31, 1942, in *Trial of the Major War Criminals before the International Military Tribunal, Nuremberg, 14 November 1945–1 October 1946*, vol. 29 (Nuremberg, 1948), pp. 279–82 (3428-PS). English translation in Office of United States Chief of Counsel for Prosecution of Axis Criminality, *Nazi Conspiracy and Aggression*, vol. 6 (Washington: US Government Printing Office, 1946), pp. 131–33.
99. Westermann, *Hitler's Police Battalions*, p. 329.

In the General Government the police were responsible for anti-partisan warfare from the very beginning. Inasmuch as the occupied areas of the Soviet Union – such as Reichskommissariat Ostland (consisting of District General of White Ruthenia, District General of Lithuania, District General of Latvia, and District General of Estonia) and Reichskommisariat Ukraine – were part of the German civil administration, the situation was similar. On August 18, 1942, Hitler issued his *Weisung* (directive) number 46, *"Richtlinien für die verstärkte Bekämpfung des Bandenunwesens im Osten"* (Rules for the enforced fighting of the nuisance of bandits in the East). According to this directive, Himmler was in charge of partisan fighting in the Reichskommissariat, the Wehrmacht was to assist him, and he had to keep meticulous records of everything that transpired.

In late summer 1942, the Chef der Bandenkampfverbände was installed by Himmler. It was an institution of the SS and police and not of the Wehrmacht, which was busy with the front line and the military government further to the east.

During the summer of 1943, Himmler's declaration of a "partisan fighting zone" proved that he was aware of the responsibility that lay on his shoulders, but he was simply unable to focus his energies on this task completely. This, in large part, was because of the Battle of Stalingrad. It is this significant event – more than anything else – that influenced the fighting against partisans and modified German policy. The German war machine was forced to invest all its resources, capabilities, and manpower into the battle for Stalingrad. As a result, it had to put the anti-partisan fighting on the back burner and conduct the life-or-death struggle on the Eastern Front.

Hitler appointed Himmler in charge of anti-partisan German warfare. The battle for Stalingrad and the fighting against the partisans were to be integrated. This integration resulted in Himmler being appointed to organize the fight against the partisans, and the Wehrmacht being tasked with battling the Russians.

Chapter 17
Jewish Partisans in Southeast Lublin

The area where the Łukawiecki partisans operated was a stretch of land bordered by the San River in the East and the Wieptz River in the West. These boundaries were essentially the geographical triangle of Lwów – Przemyśl – Zamość, with Lubaczów in the center. Much of this mainly rural area was wooded terrain, villages, and cultivated fields. Also typical of this area were a multitude of streams and swamps. Overall, in principal, mounted movements could be done only alongside roads. Yet there were only a few good roads, making the terrain a bastion for partisan activities due to the exceptional operational advantages it offered.

After the German attack on Poland on September 1, 1939, and the subsequent Soviet invasion into eastern Poland on September 17, 1939, the area was divided between Germany and the USSR according to a secret additional protocol of the German-Soviet Non-Aggression Pact of August 23, 1939. This division lasted until the Nazis attacked the Soviet Union on June 22, 1941.

Even Przemyśl (also divided by the San River) was split politically in 1939. The northern area became part of the German General Government and the southern part fell under Soviet rule. The borders between the German and Russian spheres of influence were along the San River from Jarosław (where the western bank was controlled by Germany) to Sieniawa (where the eastern bank was controlled by the Russians). From there it transformed into the Bug River (some fifteen kilometers [nine miles] north of Sokal). As a result, Oleszyce, Lubaczów, and Rawa Ruska came under Soviet control while Zamość and Tomaszów Lubelski were in German hands as part of the district of Lublin and the General Government. This division – combined with the aforementioned topographic characteristics – was an additional operational advantage; in case of emergency, one could cross the border to shake off pursuers.

When the Russians took over, they immediately imposed Communist rule and persecuted all who opposed them. At the same time, they initiated a compulsory draft into the Red Army. For these reasons – among others – many Polish peasants hated the Soviets more than the Nazis. In August 1944, a British report stated that if the Germans had given the Poles better treatment, the latter would have stood alongside their Nazi occupiers against the Russians.[1]

The strong Russian grip on the local populace enabled the arrest of most of the Polish underground resistance and essentially dismantled any underground organization in the area. This resulted in no active operational engagements by the Polish underground. It was decimated by arrests made between March and May 1940 in eastern Galicia. The remaining resistance was further infiltrated by the Soviets. Each group undertook more passive resistance, such as the distribution of no fewer than 168 underground pamphlets by the various underground groups and movements.[2] As a result, potential Jewish conspirators had scant chance of finding any active Polish partner.[3]

More than like-minded Gentile groups, the Jewish partisan movement was created out of necessity in the German-controlled area. It started as a means of survival and not as a tool to fight the Nazis. Hiding in the woods increased the chances of survival for Jews who found refuge there. An increase in the atrocities against Jews, including massacres and deportation to extermination camps, paved the way for the development and growth of the Jewish partisan movement. Thousands of Jews thought that the best way to escape the inferno engulfing their lives was to run away and seek refuge in the woods.

By the spring of 1943, after it was clear that all the ghettos were doomed for destruction, Jews began settling in the woods permanently. At the time, the

---

1. See War Cabinet Report of the Foreign Office, August 15, 1944, The National Archives (TNA) WP (44) 447, CAB/66/53/47. The report confirms that Polish enmity for the Russians exceeded their hostility toward the Nazis: "The Poles, indeed, actually admitted that had the German treatment of their country been better, they would have had no hesitation in siding with the occupational authorities against the Russians."
2. Bór-Komorowski, *The Secret Army*, p. 121.
3. Rafał Wnuk, "Resistance 1939–1941: The Polish Underground under Soviet Occupation and the Jews," in *Shared History, Divided Memory: Jews and Others in Soviet-Occupied Poland, 1939–1941*, ed. Elazar Barkan, Elizabeth A. Cole, and Kai Struve (Leipzig: Leipziger Universitätsverlag, 2007), p. 170.

Germans did not take these *Banditen*[4] very seriously. They regarded them as criminals or robber gangs who should be killed.[5] In addition, those who supported the Jews took huge risks[6] because if they were caught, they faced execution by the Germans.

It has been estimated that fifty thousand Jews escaped from surrounding cities and towns to live in the woods, of whom more than forty-eight thousand were killed following German raids.[7] Most of these "fugitives" were the last survivors of entire families, but tragically, very few of them actually survived. The overwhelming majority were executed either in the woods or while on the run. Assuming they could handle the harsh conditions of outdoor living, if the Germans didn't get them, the anti-Jewish partisans probably would.

In the minutes of a meeting held on January 25, 1943, referring to the security situation in the General Government, the hasty measures taken against Jews in the district of Lublin are given as the primary reason why Jews fled to the woods and joined partisan groups.[8]

In principle, Jewish partisans were interested in open military action as a countermeasure to the Nazis' mass murder of Jews.[9] Even Jewish women partisans took part in military operations. But in reality, the actions of Jewish partisan groups were essentially raids for looting. Their primary goal – like that of the Jews in the family camps – was simply to survive.[10]

Geographical advantages in the southern area of Lublin encouraged fleeing to these particular woods; the area was rocky and jagged, making vehicular mobility

---

4. This was the nickname given to the partisans by the Germans. "*Banditen*" were members of a "*Bande*" or of "*Banden*" (pl.).
5. Hans Frank, *Okupacja i ruch oporu w dzienniku Hansa Franka, 1943–1945* [Occupation and resistance in the diary of Hans Frank, 1939–1945] (Warsaw: Książka i Wiedza, 1972), vol. 2, 1943–1945, p. 119.
6. For a description of German measures against those who helped Jews, see Pohl, *Nationalsozialistische Judenverfolgung*, p. 367.
7. Krakowski, *The War of the Doomed*, p. 11.
8. Hans Frank, *Das Diensttagebuch des deutschen Generalgouverneurs in Polen, 1939–1945* [The service diary of the German Governor-General in Poland], ed. Werner Präg and Wolfgang Jacobmeyer (Stuttgart: Deutsche Verlags-Anstalt, 1975), p. 609.
9. Rafał Wnuk, *Lubelski Okręg AK, DSZ i WiN, 1944–1947* [Lublin District AK, DPS (Delegatura Sil Zbrojnych–Armed Forces Delegation for Poland) and WiN (Wolność i Niezawisłość–Freedom and Independence), 1944–1947] (Warsaw: Volumen, 2000), pp. 200–204.
10. See Pohl, *Nationalsozialistische Judenverfolgung*, pp. 370–71.

impossible and giving the partisans the upper hand. Most partisan units formed by Jews (or partisan units that allowed Jewish membership) were based in the Lublin area.

The Germans set up police posts, sent patrols into the woods, and worked hand in hand with numerous collaborators. Even the local population kept its eye out for Jews. Those who were caught were executed immediately. At one point, a German SS and police leader in Galicia distributed leaflets in Ukrainian promising to pardon partisans who turned themselves in. It also said that only Jews deserved to die and demanded that they be killed. But as part of the partisan threat, Jews were merely a peripheral annoyance for the Nazis.[11]

It is likely that their relevancy was significant only because of their great numbers in the district of Lublin. It was estimated that more than fifty thousand Jews within the General Government area (with the exception of the District of Galicia) escaped from surrounding cities and towns to live in the woods. Most of the time, they were the last survivors of their families who had all been exterminated. And nearly half – by some accounts, more than twenty-one thousand – came from the Lublin area.

But the Nazis weren't the direct cause of death for most Jews living in the woods. Starvation and freezing winters were responsible for claiming the majority of lives. Most had fled with only light clothes that were inappropriate for winter. Plus, their outdoor survival instincts were limited and a significant number of them simply died from hypothermia or exhaustion. Jewish fugitives who gathered together formed a family-style hideout because they lacked military knowledge, a commanding echelon and structure, and knowledge of armaments and weaponry.

The Jews who survived developed special skills – almost animal-like instincts – that enabled them to stay alive in the woods. Not only did they learn how to find and prepare food, but also how to live in freezing temperatures, develop various healing methods, find flora and fauna, maintain personal hygiene, undertake surveillance and reconnaissance, defend themselves against intruders or enemies, and create ways to identify friends from foes through early warning systems. This invaluable knowledge was only developed because these partisans lived in the woods day and night. The other groups who shared these survival instincts were

---

11. Pohl, *Nationalsozialistische Judenverfolgung*, p. 373.

the Russian partisans and the Spaleni. Newcomers often lacked this expertise and therefore found themselves thrown into the "battlefield" without proper preparation.

Nevertheless, these difficult circumstances did not prevent a steady stream of Jews from running to the woods. Self-imposed evacuation from surrounding cities grew as atrocities and deportations to death camps continued. Bunkers were designed for residential camps and not for fighting. Fighting camps that were more suitable for military operations were dug in separate locations.[12]

Survival in the woods depended heavily on assistance from Polish peasants. However, peasants often took part in raids against Jewish fugitives, either by participating in Nazi-led raids or organizing roundups themselves. It was common for Polish peasants either to loot the spoils of Jewish belongings or to round up Jews in exchange for German rewards, such as sugar, salt,[13] or vodka.[14] On the flip side, the death penalty normally awaited those peasants who dared to actually help Jews.[15]

Only a minority of partisans adopted an offensive strategy. One of those groups was led by Mundek Łukawiecki, who operated a special small task force consisting mainly of Jews, as well as a few non-Jews. Another such group, in a family camp in the Tomaszów Lubelski area, comprised Mendel Heler, Shimon Goldstein, and Meir Kalichmacher. They operated in the Rogozno woods, northwest of Tomaszów Lubelski, and were eventually exposed by local Poles.[16] Both groups were aggressive and belligerent toward the Nazis, all the while trying to rescue Jews. They both operated under the AK umbrella.

The AK, following its predecessor organization ZWZ (Związek Walki Zbrojnej – League for Armed Struggle), was the armed branch of the institutions of the Polish exile government in Poland. It was based on different political groups, and the AK itself tried to integrate other armed groups. Ultimately the strong

---

12. See Krakowski, *The War of the Doomed*, pp. 10–11, figures on p. 11.
13. See Israel Gutman and Shmuel Krakowski, *Unequal Victims: Poles and Jews during World War Two* (New York: Holocaust Library, 1986), pp. 208–12.
14. Maurie Hoffman, e-mail to the author dated May 22, 2009.
15. See Pohl, *Nationalsozialistische Judenverfolgung*, pp. 366–68.
16. See Tomashover Relief Committee, *TomashoverLubelski Yizkor Bukh* [Memorial book of Tomaszów Lubelski] (New York: Tomashover Relief Committee, 1965), p. 773 [Yiddish]; Moskop, *The Tomaszow Lubelski Memorial Book*, p. 474; "Tomaszow Lubelski," Jewish Virtual Library. And see Krakowski, *The War of the Doomed*, pp. 81–82.

Batalionów Chłopskich (BCh, i.e., Peasant Battalions) were integrated completely. The armed part of the National Party, the NOW (Narodowa Organizacja Wojskowa – National Military Organization), split twice in 1942. Approximately sixty thousand out of one hundred thousand members joined the AK. The rest of the NOW merged with the right-wing ZJ (Związek Jaszczurczy – Band of Lizards) and formed the NSZ (Narodowe Siły Zbrojne – National Armed Forces), a nationalist (and antisemitic) Polish underground movement focused on resisting both the Nazis and the Communists. The year 1944 saw a failed merger with the AK. Later that year, the former NSZ and NOW formed the NZW (Narodowe Zjednoczenie – National Military Association), which fought the new Communist authorities. The left-wing partisans of the Polish Workers' Party, the AL (Armia Ludowa – the People's Army) and the Communist people's guard, GL (Gwardia Ludowa – the People's Guard), never joined with the AK.[17]

From the very beginning, AK strategy was to organize a national military uprising in advance of forthcoming Allied troops. In order to do so, it had to avoid military confrontations with the occupational forces. So in 1940, the ZWZ/AK was not undertaking any offensive actions; only retaliatory activities to protect the ZWZ were allowed. Consequently, the AK was originally not interested in developing tactical methods and operational tools for partisan fighting. The woods were only used for weapon caches and as a place to start assault operations. In connection with the broad reaction of the AK to the German resettlement and pacification in the Zamość area, January 1943 saw the exile government advise the AK to limit its activities to those of diversion and sabotage only. Obviously the Jews' survival did not concern the AK very much – they were more preoccupied with the fate of the Christian Poles.[18]

During World War II, AK's principal strategy was to prepare a full military uprising, and until then to avoid any direct military full-scale confrontations with the Wehrmacht as much as possible,[19] but at the same time inflict as great

---

17. Grzegorz Mazur, "Der Bund für den bewaffneten Kampf-Heimatarmee und seine Gliederung" [The Federation for armed struggle-Home Army and its structure], in *Die polnische Heimatarmee: Geschichte und Mythos der Armia Krajowa seit dem Zweiten Weltkrieg* [The Polish Home Army: The history and the legend of the Armia Krajowa since the Second World War], ed. Bernhard Chiari (Munich: Oldenbourg Verlag, 2003), pp. 114–17.
18. See Marek Ney-Krawicz, "Die Führung der Republik Polen im Exil" [The leadership of the Republic of Poland in exile], in *Die polnische Heimatarmee*, ed. Bernhard Chiari, pp. 154–60.
19. Pobóg-Malinowski, *Najnowsza historia polityczna Polski*, p. 381.

a loss as possible through sabotage activities.[20] This meant that the AK did not encourage the forming of partisan units. Many AK members, including those who carried out sabotage raids, had homes very close to the forest, which allowed for immediate and relatively easy hiding.

The AK did not develop tactical methods and operational tools for partisan fighting against the Germans. Instead, they just used the woods as killing zones or a place to start assault operations against the Nazis. Jews were mainly accepted by Russian partisans.

The AK colored the Jews as Communist sympathizers or as Communist partisans outright. The AK mistrusted the Russian partisans, regarding them as Communist. The cooperation in the woods between the Red Army partisans and the Jewish groups illustrated to the AK that many of the Red Army partisans were Jews. That coincided with the image that Jews played a leading role in the Bolshevik Revolution. As a school of thought, the Russian partisan movement was considered a Jewish movement in the eyes of the AK. Because of this, the AK preferred not to be identified with the partisan movement at all. That argument gave the AK another reason not to allow Jews to join, as well as to keep any Communist influences away.[21] It was in the interests of the Communist Polish and Ukrainian partisan groups – the Kolpak group, the PPR, and the *Vyzvolennja vitičzny* – to adopt young and strong Jews, mostly men.[22] It is probable that the AK, on the rare occasion that a particularly strong or valuable Jew approached them, would agree to let him join.

One way or another, however, the survival of Jews was not an AK goal.[23] The existence and survival of Jews in the woods, either independent of partisans or belonging to the underground movement, did not concern the AK. Yet the

---

20. Bór-Komorowski, *The Secret Army*, p. 109.
21. Lukas, *Forgotten Holocaust*, p. 79.
22. Pohl, *Nationalsozialistische Judenverfolgung*, p. 371.
23. See the letter written by the president of the Polish Republic in Exile to his Holiness the Pope, in April 1941. In the letter, the president urges the Pope to declare that German atrocities not receive the Holy Seal of approval, as Germany requested. In this letter, which contains a very revealing picture of German oppression against the Poles in Poland, there is not one word about the atrocities against the Jews. Anthony Eden, "Conditions in Poland," War Cabinet Report of the Foreign Office, April 23, 1941, The National Archives (TNA) WP (41) 91, CAB 66/16/14.

possibility of survival for those Jews who were connected to the underground movement was greater than for those who were isolated.

In truth, due to the AK's strategy – and the fact that Jews who wanted to join AK partisans were later turned down outright by AK groups – Jews had little alternative to joining Communist partisan detachments to save their lives, quite apart from sympathizing with Communist ideology.

It has been asserted that antisemitism played only a minor role in keeping Jews out of the AK.[24] A study based on interviews with Jews who served in the Home Army concluded, "Although antisemitism existed within the ranks of the Home Army, it was not an official policy. Additionally, antisemitism occurred on an individual basis; while some Jews experienced it, others did not."[25]

Insight into the official policy of the AK toward the Jews can be determined by an order issued by General Stefan Rowecki ("Grot"), commander in chief of the AK until June 1943. The document was issued on February 1943, most probably in reaction to the Jewish ghetto uprising in Warsaw and the activities of ZOB (the abbreviation of the Polish name of the Jewish organization Żydowska Organizacja Bojowa) to acquire weapons and assistance from the AK. The order was issued to all AK units and not limited to the Warsaw Jewish uprising led by ZOB. It stated:

> The participation of the Jews in the resistance is to be as follows:
> 1. My order of February 1943 regarding giving assistance to Jews wishing to fight still stands.
> 2. I allow the formation of Jewish fighting groups only from certain groups (Bund, Zionists). These groups are not to be used in sabotage or partisan actions, but to be prepared for uprising.
> 3. I allocate money for that purpose, i.e., upkeep of Jewish groups under the control of the central commission.

---

24. See Lukas, *Forgotten Holocaust*, pp. 78–79.
25. Amy Sara Davis Cores, "Jews in the Armia Krajowa," M.A. thesis, Florida State University, 2000, pp. 23–24. In addition to the three Home Army members the author interviewed (Stanisław Aronson, Seweryn Tyteleman-Pilipski, and Ada Rackoz), her study lists eighteen Jews who joined the Home Army in Warsaw (p. 67).

4. Arms purchased for the Jewish units are to be safeguarded in secured places and to be provided only in emergencies.[26]

General Stefan Rowecki's order reflected the attitude toward the Jew: mistrust. The formation of Jewish groups separate from the non-Jewish units and the fact that Jews were not allowed to be integrated in combat missions such as sabotage or partisan actions all indicate mistrust as reflected by Rowecki's policy of close supervision. That mistrust was also reflected in the other rules of the order: inspection by a special entity such as the central commission (unlike the other AK units) and no regular policy of providing arms, with weapons only provided to Jewish fighters in emergencies.

It was the general mistrust of Jews, as expressed in Rowecki's order, that explained the AK's refusal to integrate Jewish warriors in the AK ranks.[27]

After Rowecki's capture by the Nazis, Tadeusz Bór-Komorowski ("Bór") became his successor. This meant a shift in policy. Bór-Komorowski's order 116, dated September 15, 1943, dealt with the "assurance of local security" for the population that was "subject to theft, threats, violence, and quite frequently, loss of life at the hands of gangs of various origin." All regional and district commanders should "take action against plundering or subversive-bandit elements where necessary," but "only against especially troublesome groups above all against those who murder and rob." The aim should be to liquidate "gang leaders and agitators" and not the entire gang. Finally, it was stressed that supplies for the AK itself should never be provided via robbery. The order had no direct reference to Jews.[28]

Another key document, Bór-Komorowski's Organizational Report no. 220 of

---

26. The Polish original document was not found, but a copy of the order is in the archive of the ŻIH. Ber Mark, *Powstanie w getcie warszawskim: Nowe uzupełnione wydanie i zbiór dokumentów* (Warsaw: Idisz Buch, 1963), pp. 347–48n15. See also Dariusz Libionka, "ZWZ-AK i delegatura rządu RP wobec eksterminacji Żydów polskich" [ZWZ-AK and the Polish government delegation of the extermination of Polish Jews], in *Polacy i Żydzi pod okupacją niemiecką, 1939–1945* [Poles and Jews under German occupation, 1939–1945], ed. Andrzej Żbikowski (Warsaw: Instytut Pamięci Narodowej, 2006), p. 74.
27. Mark, *Powstanie w getcie warszawskim*, p. 347.
28. John L. Armstrong, "The Polish Underground and the Jews: A Reassessment of Home Army Commander Tadeusz Bór-Komorowski's Order 116 against Banditry," *Slavonic and East European Review* 72 (1994): 266–67. Armstrong presents the correct text of the order, but fails to contextualize his finding with a balanced and convincing interpretation.

August 31, 1943, was sent to the government-in-exile in London. Under one subtitle, "*Bandytyzm*," it speaks of well-armed gangs constantly prowling in urban and rural areas and attacking estates, banks, commercial and industrial companies, houses, apartments, and larger peasant farms. The report continues:

> The plunder is often accompanied by acts of murder, which are carried out by Soviet partisan units hiding in the forests or by ordinary gangs of robbers. The latter recruit all kinds of criminal subversive elements. *Men and women, especially Jewish women, participate in the assaults....* [*W napadach biorą udział mężczyźni i kobiety szczególnie Żydówki*. Emphasis mine.] In order to provide help and shelter the defenseless population... I have issued instructions regarding local security to district and regional commanders, in which I ordered district and regional commanders to take armed action against plundering and/or subversive-bandit elements where necessary. I emphasize the need to liquidate the gang leaders, and not efforts to destroy entire gangs....[29]

This can be seen as a draft of order 116. It shows more clearly that AK units were permitted to fight and kill Jews who were hiding from the Nazis in the forests. The strange logic of the AK leadership seems to have been that the Jews had the right to hide, but they could not resort to "bandit" methods of survival. That people could have helped the hiding Jews of their own free will is not mentioned. Nothing in these or other documents indicates that help for fugitive Jews was considered.[30]

In the field, however, the AK attitude was different with regard to accepting Jews into its ranks and turning them over to the Nazis.[31] The commander of the

---

29. *Armia Krajowa w Dokumentach, 1939–1945*, tom 3: kwiecień 1943–lipiec 1944 [AK documents, 1939–1945, vol. 3, April 1943–July 1944] (1976; repr., Wroclaw: Osssolineum, 1990), pp. 63–95, document 482, p. 92; translated in John L. Armstrong, "The Polish Underground and the Jews," 267–68.
30. See Adam Puławski, "Postrzeganie żydowskich oddziałów partyzanckich przez Armię Krajową i Delegaturę Rządu RP na Kraj" [Perceptions of Jewish partisan units of the Home Army and the Delegation of the Polish Government in Exile], *Pamięć i Sprawiedliwość* [Memory and justice] 2, no. 4 (2003): 295.
31. See for example the order issued in April 1944 by AK regional commander of the Wilno (Vilnius) district Aleksander Krzyżanowski ("Wilk"), forbidding mistreatment of the civilian population, which included Jews. The Kraków region's commander of Batalionów Chłopskich (Peasant Battalions), which was part of the AK, issued directives to the field to assist Jews,

AK in Tomaszów Lubelski issued an order on December 10, 1942, that punished those who captured Jews and handed them over to the Nazis.[32]

Jews were accepted into AK units in Lwów.[33] At least a dozen Jews, led by Abram Baum, joined a Home Army unit based in Hanaczów (about forty kilometers [twenty-five miles] east of Lwów), under the command of Sergeant Major Kazimierz Wojtowicz ("Głóg") and, later, Lieutenant Paweł Jastrzębski ("Strzała").[34] Several Jews joined a partisan group led by Zbigniew Morawski from Dolina near Stryj.[35] Four members of the Igiel (Igel) family joined a Home Army unit operating near Bircza, southwest of Przemyśl.[36]

Most Jews who joined the AK, like Mundek Łukawiecki, concealed their Jewish origin. Those few Jews who were taken into the AK's ranks refused to accept other Jews who wanted to join, claiming that the AK did not draft Jews into their underground movement. Mundek Łukawiecki's Jewish origin was only known to his fellow Polish partisans at a later stage when he started rescuing Jews,

---

and such help was forthcoming; see Elżbieta Rączy, "Stosunki polsko-żydowskie w latach drugiej wojny światowej na Rzeszowszczyźnie" [Polish-Jewish relations during the Second World War in Rzeszów], in *Polacy i Żydzi pod okupacją niemiecką, 1939–1945* [Poles and Jews under German occupation, 1939–1945], ed. Andrzej Żbikowski (Warsaw: Instytut Pamięci Narodowej, 2006), pp. 905–7.

32. Puławski, "Postrzeganie żydowskich oddziałów partyzanckich," p. 294.

33. Eliyahu Jones, *Żydzi Lwówa w okresie okupacji, 1939–1945* [The Jews of Lwów during the occupation, 1939–1945] (Łódź: Oficyna Bibliofilów, 1999), p. 203; Jolanta Chodorska, ed., *Godni synowie naszej Ojczyzny: Świadectwa nadesłane na apel Radia Maryja* [Worthy sons of our country: Testimonies contributed to Radio Maria], vol.2 (Warsaw: Wydawnictwo Sióstr Loretanek 2002), pp. 204–7; Henryk Komański, Szczepan Siekierka, et al., *Ludobójstwo dokonane przez nacjonalistów ukraińskich na Polakach w województwie tarnopolskim, 1939–1946* [The genocide committed by the Ukrainian nationalists against the Poles in Ternopil province, 1939–1946] (Wroclaw: Nortom, 2004), pp 286–90, 774–78, 789–91, 798–99; Libionka, "ZWZ-AK i delegatura rządu RP wobec eksterminacji Żydów polskich," pp. 112–13.

34. Jerzy Węgierski, *W lwowskiej Armii Krajowej* [In the Lwów AK] (Warsaw: Pax, 1989), pp. 77–78, 147–48, 151–52, 201.

35. "Ludobójstwo – Grabieże – Zniszczenia – Powiat Stryj" [Genocide – Looting – Destruction – district of Stryj], *Na Rubieży: Czasopismo historyczno-publicystyczne* [On the rim: Historical and current affairs magazine] 35 (1999): 44.

36. John J. Hartman and Jacek Krochmal, eds., *I Remember Every Day… The Fates of the Jews of Przemyśl during World War II* (Przemyśl: Towarzystwo Przyjaciół Nauk w Przemyślu, 2002), p. 63.

although Józef Kulpa knew of Mundek's ethnicity and religious affiliation from the very beginning.[37]

As mentioned earlier, two Jewish partisan units were formed alongside the AK, one in Lubaczów, commanded by Mundek Łukawiecki, and the other in the Tomaszów Lubelski area, commanded by Mendel Heler, Shimon Goldstein, and Meir Kalichmacher.

At the field level, AK units cooperated with Jewish partisan units. The commanders of the Jewish unit (such as Captain Fryderyk "Proch" Staub and Isaac Braun) were decorated for their valor by the AK commander of the Lwów district.

Rescuing Jews was also accepted at the field level. As previously stated, the AK commander in Tomaszów Lubelski ordered his subordinates to punish those assisting the Germans in hunting down Jews.[38] Yad Vashem awarded the Wojtowicz brothers – AK members at the outpost in Hanaczów – as "Righteous among the Nations."[39] Richard Kalinowicz, a Jew who led an AK unit near Sambor, assisted in saving Jews with Polish rescuers.[40]

Partisan efforts to rescue Jews, however, were sporadic and individual, and for the most part Jews were on their own to overcome Nazi forces in every situation imaginable. A large number of Wehrmacht soldiers were deployed in the General Government, many of them on march for training or for recreation: approximately 300,000 were deployed in February 1942, about 450,000–550,000 in 1943, and nearly 550,000 in April 1944.[41] But their role in the Jewish annihilation was limited. That task was handed over to police units commanded by the SS and

---

37. Testimony of Edmund (Mundek) Łukawiecki (Moshe Lavee) to Yad Vashem, July 28, 1993, no. 03-6946, tape no. 033c/2757. Moshe Lavee (Edmund/Mundek Łukawiecki), recorded interview by USC Shoah Foundation Institute, interview code 31895, May 27, 1997.
38. Puławski, "Postrzeganie żydowskich oddziałów partyzanckich," p. 294.
39. Shmuel Krakowski, "The Polish Underground and the Jews in the Years of the Second World War," in *Nazi Europe and the Final Solution*, ed. David Bankier and Israel Gutman (Jerusalem: Yad Vashem 2003), p. 226.
40. Irene Tomaszewski and Tecia Werbowski, *Code Name: Żegota; Rescuing Jews in Occupied Poland, 1942–1945; The Most Dangerous Conspiracy in Wartime Europe* (Santa Barbara, CA: Praeger, 1999), pp. 144–50.
41. Leon Herzog, "Die verbrecherische Tätigkeit der Wehrmacht im Generalgouvernement in den Jahren 1939 bis 1945" [The criminal activities of the Wehrmacht in the General Government in the years 1939 to 1945], *Zeitschrift für Militärgeschichte* [Journal of military history] 6 (1967): 449.

police leaders of the respective districts. They organized the mass deportations to the extermination camps, in collaboration with the civil administration.

Most of the time in the General Government, the police were in charge of anti-partisan warfare including the hunt for Jewish fugitives. At the beginning of May 1943, 11,400 men of the German Order Police and 15,000 Polish and Ukrainian policemen were deployed by the General Government.[42] The Wehrmacht had a field commander for the respective districts to assist the police on a case-by-case basis. As the partisan movement grew, the role of the Wehrmacht became more important.

In the Lublin district, a number of German police and auxiliary forces' primary directive was to deport Jews to death camps and eliminate Jewish fugitives and partisans. It was an order for Police Regiment 25 to eradicate Jews by employing its Police Battalions 65, 67, and 101, Police Battalion 41 (the first motorized Gendarmerie Battalion), the Police Cavalry Detachment 3, and the Police cavalry platoons in Zamość, Lublin, and others. They worked hand-in-hand with other parts of the Order Police like local gendarmerie, as well as the Polish and Ukrainian police. The Security Police and detachments of Trawniki men also took part,[43] and special squads of gendarmerie – consisting of two gendarmes and fifteen to twenty policemen of the Polish police – were created to intensify the hunt for surviving Jews.[44] This group was also known as the "Blue Police" because of their blue uniforms. The Polish police was a collaborative entity,[45]

---

42. Wolfgang Curilla, *Der Judenmord in Polen und die deutsche Ordnungspolizei, 1939–1945* [The murder of the Jews in Poland and the German Order Police, 1939–1945] (Paderborn, Germany: Ferdinand Schöningh, 2011), p. 55. Additionally, one must take into account the members of the Security Police.
43. Dieter Pohl, *Von der "Judenpolitik" zum Judenmord: Der Distrikt Lublin des Generalgouvernements, 1939–1944* [From "Judenpolitik" {policy on the Jews} to the murder of the Jews: The Lublin district of the General Government, 1939–1944] (Frankfurt am Main: Peter Lang, 1993), pp. 143–45.
44. Curilla, *Der Judenmord in Polen*, p. 773; see pp. 683–832, with numerous details regarding the role of the Order Police in the Lublin district.
45. Lukas, *Forgotten Holocaust*, p. 118; Zygmunt Klukowski, *Dziennik z lat okupacji Zamojszczyzny* [Diary of the occupation of the Zamość region] (Lublin: Lubelska Spółdzielnia Wydawnicza, 1959), p. 290.

although some of those who joined were sent there by the AK as infiltrators and a few officers of the Blue Police even helped Jews.[46]

In Galicia, the German policing structure was similar to that of the Lublin area. According to the composition of the population, the Ukrainian police played a major role. In his report "Lösung der Judenfrage in Galizien" (Solution of the Jewish Question in Galicia) dated June 30, 1943, Friedrich Katzmann, the SS and police commander in the district of Galicia, declared that Galicia was *judenfrei* (free of Jews) with the exception of 21,156 Jews still left in the camps, and that individual fugitive Jews would get *Sonderbehandlung* (special treatment), the Nazi code word for killing, by the respective Order Police or Gendarmerie posts, when caught.[47]

By the beginning of 1944, northeast of eastern Galicia, and especially the south, was no longer considered a manageable area for the Nazis. The German police did not dare to enter the woods willingly. Instead, they instructed auxiliary units like the Polish criminal police or the Ukrainian Auxiliary Police to search for Jews and kill them. In any case, gendarmerie and detachments of police battalions continued their raids. Their actions were often based on denunciations by locals and members of the forest administration. Sometimes villagers and forest rangers were invited to chase and hunt Jews as well.[48]

There was also the threat of ethnic Germans who resettled in former Polish villages. Each village was required to appoint a headman (*soltys*), as well as a night watchman and fire brigade chief to fend off intruders. Once these people assumed a position, often voluntarily, they were then required to follow German orders. So headmen, night watchmen, and fire brigade members were

---

46. Israel Gutman, ed., *The Encyclopedia of the Righteous Among the Nations: Rescuers of Jews during the Holocaust*, vols. 4 and 5, *Poland*, edited by Sara Bender and Shmuel Krakowski (Jerusalem: Yad Vashem, 2004), part 1, Kraków – Franciszek Banaś, p. 69; Rzeszów, p. 71; Siedlce, p. 88; Jarocin, p. 149; Tomaszów Lubelski – Piotr Czechoński, p. 157; Aarocin, p. 200; Warsaw – Jan Fakler, p. 210; Sokołów Podlaski, p. 371, Międzylesie – Jan Kubicki, p. 413; Łaskarzew. p. 477; part 2, Warsaw – Wacław Nowiński, p. 556; Kraków – Władysław Szalek, p. 777.

47. *Der Nürnberger Prozess gegen die Hauptkriegsverbrecher vor dem Internationalen Militärgerichtshof, Nürnberg, 14 November 1945–1 Oktober 1946* [The Nuremberg Trial of the Major War Criminals before the International Military Tribunal, Nuremberg, November 14, 1945–October 1, 1946], vol. 37 (Nuremberg, 1949), document 018-L, p. 401.

48. Pohl, *Nationalsozialistische Judenverfolgung*, p. 372.

often involved in anti-Jewish actions as well, and in some situations they did so eagerly for rewards.

Outside the settlements, Jewish partisans had to face other dangers, like independent Polish armed groups who did not answer to any underground movement. Some of them cooperated with the Nazis. Others were Ukrainian partisans from the Ukrainian Insurgent Army (Ukrainska Povstanska Armiia, UPA), and the military branch of the Organization of Ukrainian Nationalists (OUN).[49] Their members, who were mostly antisemitic, fought for an independent Ukrainian national state. Their focus was ethnic cleansing against bandits, particularly Poles and Jews. In every instance, they were hostile to Jewish partisan groups and Jews in Communist partisan groups.[50]

Finally, there was the Polish radical right-wing underground movement Narodowe Siły Zbrojne (NSZ; National Armed Forces). Their official strategy (according to an order) was "to cleanse the area of the revolutionary and criminal gangs of minority units." This obviously meant Communist partisans of the People's Guard and Jews who had fled to the forests. Secondarily, they also initiated counterattacks against the Germans as a self-defense mechanism in cases of dreadful injustices, as part of the agenda of the NSZ.[51] Members of the NSZ killed Jews or extradited them to the Nazis.[52] The NSZ was the primary enemy of Jewish partisans. Numerous killings that were charged to the AK were most likely conducted by the antisemitic NSZ.[53] To make matters even worse, the local populace would also hand over Jews to whoever was interested in killing them.[54]

In the summer of 1943, about ten thousand Wehrmacht soldiers reinforced the order police for Operation Werewolf, a large-scale, anti-partisan operation in the Zamość area.[55] It was a resumption of the Nazi resettlement policy under the pretext of combating partisans. The operation continued right until the end of the year and resulted in many family camps being discovered and their members

---

49. Testimony of Edmund (Mundek) Łukawiecki (Moshe Lavee) to Yad Vashem, July 28, 1993, no. 03-6946, tape no. 033c/2757.
50. See Pohl, *Nationalsozialistische Judenverfolgung*, pp. 374–77.
51. Krakowski, *The War of the Doomed*, pp. 7, 13, 14.
52. Tadeusz Szymański, *My ze Spalonych Wsi* [We of the burned village] (Warsaw: Ministerstwa Obrony Narodowej, 1965), p. 198.
53. Lukas, *Forgotten Holocaust*, p. 81.
54. Klukowski, *Dziennik z lat okupacji Zamojszczyzny*, p. 299.
55. Herzog, "Die verbrecherische Tätigkeit der Wehrmacht im Generalgouvernement," p. 453.

murdered. In fact, most family camps in the southern part of the Lublin district were annihilated by the Nazis.[56]

In 1944, the Lublin area partisans were strengthened by a few Jewish fugitives from forced labor camps, in addition to well-armed Soviet partisans. Shortly prior to the arrival of the Red Army in June 1944, the Germans began the biggest anti-partisan operation ever in Poland. Sturmwind I focused on the forests of Janów and Lipskie, west of Zamość, and later Sturmwind II on the forests of Puszcza Solska, southwest of Zamość. The commander in chief was the military commander of the General Government.

Twenty-five thousand men, consisting of Wehrmacht (three divisions and its Kalmuk Cavalry Corps) and units of the Order Police, took part in the mission. A German Air Force bomber squad was also deployed. Three thousand Soviet partisans were involved: 560 from the People's Guard (GL) of the Polish Worker's Party, 570 from the AK, and 700 from the Peasant Battalions (BCh). Among them at least one hundred Jewish partisans in the GL – half of whom were from the Adolf Unit – as well as a number of Soviet partisan units participated. The Polish partisans suffered heavy losses, as did the Jewish partisans. The Adolf Unit failed to defend the area of Knieja, comprised mainly of family camps. Almost all of them were eventually killed.[57]

---

56. Pohl, *Von der "Judenpolitik" zum Judenmord*, p. 168.
57. Krakowski, *The War of the Doomed*, pp. 96–98.

Chapter 18
Susiec

Susiec is situated on the northern slopes of the Puszcza Solska –Paary[1] forest, in eastern Galicia – about one hundred kilometers (sixty miles) southeast of the regional capital of Lublin. Primarily an agricultural town, it was tranquil enough to earn the nickname "the holiday village." It was developed along a tarred, winding road, as most Polish villages were in those days. This tar road was actually the boundary between a shaggy and dense natural forest covering a vast area to the south, and cultivated land to the north. Since the land was very fertile, Susiec was included in the German resettlement plans in the Zamość area as part of the pilot project of the master plans for Germanization and exploitation of the occupied East (the Generalplan Ost).[2]

Just north of Susiec was a railroad connecting the west to the death camp of Bełżec. The distance between Susiec and Bełżec was only sixteen kilometers (ten miles). As one approached Susiec from the west, the railroad wove its way through heavy pine and thick oak woods. Once out of the woods, it passed through the very small village of Długi Kąt.

Susiec was under the responsibility of the Tomaszów Lubelski AK. The woods of the Puszcza Solska forest, as well as the Huta Różaniecka and Paary woods, became a sanctuary for AK units. These woods hosted large numbers of AK partisans, who helped combat the Nazi resettlement plan in the Zamość area. It is from here that the AK fought the resettlement plan, eventually leading to its collapse; once the Nazis lost control of these woods and the neighboring rural area, they stopped entering the woods altogether.

Susiec was also a prime target of AK missions because the town cooperated with the Nazis. During the second half of 1942, the AK arrested Susiec mayor

---

1. Northwest of Narol.
2. See the discussion of the Generalplan Ost in chapter 16, "Partisan Land."

Władysław Skroban for collaborating with the Germans and betraying AK members. The AK interrogated him and he admitted his guilt. He also revealed and exposed other collaborators, including the head of the Polish Blue Police, as well as two others (Stanisław Gontaze and Bialot). He was executed after the interrogations.[3]

Mundek Łukawiecki on the way to an operation in full combat gear, 1944

Mundek Łukawiecki checking a pistol, summer 1944

---

3. Caban, *Na dwa fronty*, pp. 46–47.

Mundek on the way to an operation in full combat gear, summer 1944

Mundek on the way to an operation in full military gear, summer 1944. Notice the short trees, the Łukawiecki partisans' chosen perfect hiding place.

Since Susiec was such an important strategic location, the Tomaszów Lubelski AK launched several attacks on facilities near the town. On January 1, 1943, the railway bridge was blown up. And on April 26, 1943, an armored train was destroyed (with the assistance of Soviet partisans). One year later, in April or early May 1944, another train – reported as containing Polish prisoners on the way to a concentration camp – was stormed, probably not successfully.[4]

The AK decided to attack the fuel train between Susiec and Długi Kąt (running from Zamość to Zawada to Bełżec, to the east) and sabotage the rail itself. Needless to say, the railroad near Susiec was under repeated raids, as it was a good tactical killing zone on the one hand, and easy to retreat from into the woods on the other. This made it a very logical and effective target. The attacks unfortunately did not affect the extermination of Jews in Bełżec,[5] but only impacted

---

4. War Cabinet Report of the Foreign Office, August 15, 1944, The National Archives (TNA) WP (44) 447, CAB/66/53/47. See also Hoffman, *Keep Yelling*, p. 163. The Bundesarchiv in Ludwigsburg, Germany, has an index card referring to a report of the SS and police leader of Lublin dated April 10, 1944, stating that the station building of Susiec was blown up by bandits.
5. Bełżec death camp was closed in December 1942 as the last transport arrived. From November 1942 till spring 1943 the Nazis tried to remove the traces of the mass murder by forcing

the supplies to the Eastern Front of the German war machine, which was at that time fighting the Red Army in the east.

AK scouts provided intelligence that the fuel train ran daily and carried about fifteen fuel cars. The train ran slowly, since it carried a heavy load. They also learned that it was guarded by a squad of soldiers who were situated in the car behind the locomotive. The ten or so soldiers were only equipped with personal guns.

"Adam," the commanding officer of the area, decided that the operation would be organized by the AK commanding unit "Horseshoe." The assault unit was chosen from the small town of Zwierzyniec, in the Lublin area, under the command of Konrad Bartoszewski ("Wit"). Twenty AK members were mobilized with three submachine guns, rifles, pistols, hand grenades, and one demolition explosive to set off on the railroad itself. Along with the assault unit, a platoon commander with the codename "Osa" was dispatched. Osa brought one package of hay with him. Another unit, "Bip," were assigned as reconnaissance scouting and backup. Mundek Łukawiecki was in the Bip unit.

It was decided that the killing zone would be where the railroad curved, near the Długi Kąt area, where there were thick, heavy woods. The advantages of this chosen killing zone were numerous: the curve helped slow the train down even more; there was a lot of time to see the train approaching; the area allowed a relatively small number of partisans to take control of the train easily; it provided a well-concealed hiding place to prepare the ambush; it gave the partisans the ability to approach the killing zone without being detected; and the location gave them a safe way to retreat after the ambush.

The plan was to set the explosive on the railroad and activate it when the locomotive passed over it so the train would derail. The assault partisans would then spread out over the train and blow up the fuel cars with hand grenades and gunfire. The Bip unit was to continue its reconnaissance and patrol, as well as reinforce the attack if necessary. Bip was also ordered to block both sides of the railroad against any German or Ukrainian intervention. It was decided that the

---

Jewish slave laborers to exhume and burn the corpses. After their horrible work was done, they were transported to Sobibór and killed there at once. On the grounds of the former camp a farm was established to complete the camouflage. See Arad, *Belzec, Sobibor, Treblinka*, pp. 370–72.

operational unit would arrive at the killing zone at night on either April 21 or 22, 1943. The operation would be executed the following day at noon.

There had been a few prior operations by an AK unit under the command of Wit against the trains and this railroad. The first involved a railway bridge over a stream called Potok Łosiniecki on December 5–6, 1942, and then on January 6, 1943, the unit destroyed a bridge and the railway station in Susiec. Therefore this operation, in which Mundek was involved in April 1943, was the third strike of its kind in this particular location.

Zwierzyniec – the small town from which the units were deployed – was located about nineteen kilometers (twelve miles) northwest of Długi Kąt. Wit left from Kolejowa Street at seven P.M. and walked into the woods to avoid any contact with local peasants and Ukrainian or German units. He navigated his unit southeast, passing Majdan Kaszelański and crossing Samsonówka.

Wit and his unit of twenty partisans arrived wet and cold at 3 A.M. They had chosen light clothing for flexibility rather than warmer gear to protect them from the cool dampness outside. As a result, they had absorbed the moisture from the trees above them when walking through the woods. The temperature that night was about minus five degrees Celsius (twenty-three Fahrenheit). This did not bother them while they were walking, but once they arrived at the killing zone and sat on the frozen ground, their body temperatures dropped immediately. To combat this, Wit ordered them to start campfires to warm themselves up. It worked, and gradually the men warmed up. This was only possible because of the excellent location of the killing zone, which allowed them to light campfires without being detected.

At 10 A.M., Wit ordered the assault commanding officer Podkowa to deploy the partisans. Podkowa divided the unit into three squads. The assault squad consisted of the platoon commander "Osa"[6] and an additional three partisans equipped with submachine guns. Before taking their positions, Osa and the three partisans gathered hay from the area, dividing it into small sheaves so they could set it on fire after the raid. This would further flame the fuel cars. The second squad was equipped with one submachine gun. Its mission was to act as a backup. The third squad was ordered to block the railroad against approaching reinforcements and prevent any enemy support from reaching the train from Susiec.

---

6. *Osa* in Polish means "wasp."

It was important that the entire train make its way into the killing zone before being blown up. They readied the explosive, a 155 mm canon shell. A small demolition fuse was attached to it, as well as a delay fuse of ten centimeters, allowing the partisans ten seconds to retreat after activating the fuse. The charge was placed between two railroad ties, under the track, and was covered with gravel.

At 12:00 noon, the fuel train approached. All the units were fully alert and prepared. The partisans dispersed along the railroad. The train was only about 120 meters from reaching the explosive. Podkowa ran to the demolition charge and activated it. Ten seconds passed as the train slowly made its way up the track. As if in slow motion, the charge blew up and created a huge crater in the railroad itself. The only problem was that the train was still a hundred meters away from the spot where the explosive had blown up!

After the loud, violent explosion, the train conductor slammed on the emergency braking system and managed to stop it just short of the crater. As the train came to a halt, the assault squad opened fire. Within a few moments, Bip partisans also joined in on the firing. It wasn't long before all units were simultaneously firing on the train, with the second and third squads leaving their original missions to assist.

Within a matter of minutes, the train's military escort and staff had run to the woods from the opposite side of the train. The partisans continued to fire on the fuel car with armor-piercing bullets, causing it to leak. Osa and his three partisans set the hay on fire and threw it on the leaking fuel from the fuel cars. Shortly thereafter, the operation was complete and Wit and his partisans retreated, as did the Bip partisans. Mundek Łukawiecki took pictures of the burning train. The flames and smoke could be seen a long distance away.

The operation was completed successfully without any casualties. In total, the partisans destroyed fourteen fuel tanks. After the raid, another German armor train arrived to help the fight, but it was already too late. The German casualties were minimal; only one guard was killed. There were very few wounded as well – mostly Polish railroad workers.

The following morning at 5 A.M., a Nazi battalion launched a retaliatory siege on Susiec and set the village on fire. It was burned to ashes. The attack killed approximately half of Susiec's inhabitants – including women and children.[7]

---

7. A slightly different version is recounted in Hoffman, *Keep Yelling*, pp. 161–62.

Chapter 19
Forming the Jewish Hit Squad

Life in the woods was extremely cruel.[1] However, the more time Mundek spent there, the better his group's outdoor survival instincts became. He improved the technique to build hideouts and bunkers and to remain camouflaged for long periods of time. He insisted that they carefully follow various methods for covering their tracks in order to travel secretly.

Edmund (Mundek) Łukawiecki, January 1943

Mundek, January 1943

Mundek defined himself as a "forest beast." Like a beast, he could smell from a distance if something or somebody entered the woods. He could survive in the woods by hunting game and eating forest fruits such as blueberries and strawberries, as well as vegetables, such as wild cabbage. The partisans hunted everything

---

1. Lukas, *Forgotten Holocaust*, p. 81.

that was available, including wild pigs, deer, rabbits, and birds.[2] Mundek was able to predict how animals would behave during the day and at night in particular situations, and used this to alert him of any danger or change in circumstances. Mundek instructed the partisans on how to start a fire,[3] on finding and preparing food, and on storing water.

Mundek's biggest advantage as a "forest beast" was his ability to convert his knowledge into tools that could be used against the Germans in military warfare – that is, clandestine warfare against the Nazis. His survival skills thus went well beyond mere survival; Mundek understood the tactical advantages of fighting from the woods.

Chana Bern had also become an excellent soldier. She was courageous and tough, and developed a sense of vengeance for the massacre of her family. She felt that she had a moral obligation to avenge her family's murder. The atrocities she had witnessed steeled her character.

Chana took part in daily operations and safeguarded the campsite.[4] Mundek tried not to take her on highly risky operations. Some partisans objected to her membership in the group, but Mundek was firm in his support. Chana was therefore grudgingly accepted, but as the only female in the company, she received a lot of unwanted attention.

Mundek had been in the company four months when he was appointed commanding officer and was tasked with the combat mission to blow up the train near Susiec,[5] in which Mundek's company acted as both a reconnaissance and scouting force. He decided that Chana should not participate in the mission, but should stay behind to guard the hideout with another two soldiers.

The assault group, consisting of the rest of the company, left on April 20, 1943, as their mission required advance deployment prior to the attack. While Mundek and the others were gone, the two remaining guards tried to rape Chana. While she was resting in her and Mundek's bunker, the two guards entered and tried to force themselves on her.

It had only been four months since she was raped by the Ukrainian chief of

---

2. Personal interview with Dr. Isaac Weinberg, May 30, 2011.
3. Testimony of Edmund (Mundek) Łukawiecki (Moshe Lavee) to Yad Vashem, July 28, 1993, no. 03-6946, tape no. 033c/2757.
4. They used to exchange night bird whistling to communicate their safe return.
5. Described in the previous chapter, "Susiec."

police, and now her fellow soldiers and comrades were attempting to rape her. She pulled out her Parabellum pistol, cocked it, and while struggling with them, fired a bullet. They were shocked and froze. After a few seconds that seemed to take an eternity, they left – walking backwards and staring at her the entire time.

Chana remained in the bunker and did not leave until the company returned. She eventually told Mundek what had happened and he became furious. Like a raging, wounded bull, he shouted and cursed. He went directly to the guards and dragged them outside. The entire company watched as he screamed at them, telling them that they deserved to be executed – not just for the attempted rape, but also because they had rebelled against him as their commander. Then he grabbed his pistol.

As the two guards stood speechless, one of the company's soldiers spoke up loudly. "You are not allowed to kill them. Detain them and send them to headquarters for court marshal."

Mundek turned toward the speaker with lightning speed and aimed his pistol at him. There was absolute silence and you could hear a pin drop. Nobody dared to move. Mundek was shocked that the speaker would challenge him. Mundek stared him down. All the time his pistol was aimed at the speaker. After a minute or so, Mundek's hand lowered very slowly. Then, in a sharp move, with rage and uncontrolled fury, he turned toward the two guards and in a barrage of fire he killed them after all.[6]

The rejection of Chana and the rape attempt were some of the reasons why Mundek decided to depart from the company and form his own group of Jewish partisans in May 1943, which became the Jewish hit squad.

In addition, as time passed, Mundek had rescued a number of Jews and integrated them into the AK company. This came about in various ways. For example, the company often encountered Jews in the woods who were either hiding with peasants or who were simply on the run. Whatever the situation, they were brought to the hideout by Mundek. He forbade them from speaking Yiddish, however, instructing them to speak only Polish or German so that nobody in the camp would know they were Jews. In other instances, Józef Kulpa would tell Mundek about Jews who were in danger of being handed over. Most of them

---

6. Personal interview with Aliza Segal, Febraury 5, 2012; personal interview with Dr. Isaac Weinberg, June 5, 2012.

had just run out of money to pay off those who were hiding them and were now being threatened with being denounced to the Nazis. When he received this kind of information, Mundek reacted quickly and brought these Jews to the company hideout.

As time passed, Mundek had rescued a total of thirteen Jews.[7] The soldiers in the company preferred that the company be homogenized, which prompted Mundek to form his own Jewish AK partisan unit, although the Jewish hit squad consisted of Poles as well, most of whom Józef Kulpa had introduced to Mundek for various reasons.

In May 1943, Mundek and the Jewish partisans in the company returned to the Bór woods, where he and Chana had first hidden when they escaped from the ghetto. He told Kulpa about his decision in advance and he confirmed the move. The Jewish hit squad, known as the Łukawiecki partisans, was born as its own independent AK unit. Following are profiles of some of Mundek's men.

Berish Brand

In February 1943, while the company was enduring a very cold winter, they were in a village asking for food. Mundek missed potato soup. He approached one of the residents and asked if the woman of the house could cook him some. While he waited for the soup, a man stumbled out of the attic. This was Berish Brand. He assumed that the partisans were Polish and could be trusted. He did not know that Mundek was a Jew. Berish asked Mundek if he could take him to the woods. He said that he was Jewish and he would like to go with the partisans. Mundek agreed.

On his way out of the house, Mundek noticed a *mezuzah*[8] in the doorway that had been placed there by its previous Jewish inhabitants. He ripped it from the doorframe and took it with him.[9]

Berish Brand was the third Jewish partisan in the company and became one

---

7. Apart from those who are profiled in this chapter, Mundek also rescued a man named Weiner (not related to Zanwet and Luba Weiner). Weiner became a member of the Łukawiecki partisans as well.
8. A *mezuzah* is a piece of parchment inscribed with specific verses from the Bible, rolled up and affixed to each doorframe in a Jewish home in fulfillment of the biblical injunction in Deuteronomy 6:9, "And you shall write [these words] upon the doorposts of your house, and upon your gates."
9. Aliza Segal notes.

Berish Brand, Germany, 1960

Berish Brand and Mundek in Cracow, 1946

Berish Brand and his wife and child, Cracow, 1946

Berish Brand, Haifa, Israel, 1952

of its best soldiers. Berish Brand was born in 1907 in Lwów. His family owned a fur store. When the Germans took over Lwów, Berish Brand and his sister fled to the woods, but their time there was disastrous; they starved and swelled up, as they had very little knowledge of how to survive.

The Nazi atrocities did not change Berish's character. He was kind, good-tempered, always smiling, and devoted to his family. After the war, Mundek and Berish spent time together in Kraków, while Berish reestablished himself as a fur dealer. In 1948, the Brand family moved to Israel, residing in Haifa, where Berish got a job in the harbor. He made use of the tax-free stores and always bought his two daughters plenty of candies and chocolate.

Twenty years after the war, he became very sick. His sister – who had also survived the Holocaust – transferred him to Germany for medical treatment. He passed away there in 1965, at the age of fifty-eight.

Isaac Helman

Lisie Jamy – meaning "foxhole" in Polish – was a pre–World War II Polish community of about fifty families. It acquired its name during the seventeenth century, after it became the preferred fox-hunting grounds of King Jan III Sobieski (1620–1696) due to its large number of foxholes. This quiet hamlet was approximately three kilometers (just under two miles) southeast of Lubaczów. The only time that the tranquility of life was interrupted was when the noise of traffic from the main road between Lubaczów and Lwów was overheard.

Only two Jewish families lived in Lisie Jamy – the majority of its inhabitants were Poles and Ukrainians. All the families in Lisie Jamy were poor and fought daily to make ends meet. The houses were simple country huts made from wood from the nearby forest. They generally comprised two sleeping rooms, a multipurpose space used for storage, as well as a barn, cowshed, and henhouse.

Originally from Hamburg, Germany, the Helman family had eight members. The great-grandfather, Bernard, had emigrated to Lemberg (Lwów) during the Austro-Hungarian monarchy. His son, Moses Helman, was born there. When

Isaac Helman

Moses was old enough, he enlisted in the Austro-Hungarian army. Upon completing his service, he was allowed to settle in Lisie Jamy and build a small farm.

Success, however, did not come easily, a plight that was shared by the majority of the townsfolk. Every member did their part in contributing to the family's basic necessities. In other words, there was no clear breadwinner. The reality of living in poverty resulted in the loss of a baby daughter because there was not enough money for medication to treat an illness.

Still, Moses cultivated his tiny family land and grew wheat and vegetables, mainly for the family's consumption, but never quite enough to sustain them entirely. The matriarch, Tili Schtelzer from Mełchów, looked after the production of dairy and cheese. The two older brothers, Bernard and Leon, worked from home as tailors, while the three smallest boys – Motel, Isaac (born August 20, 1924), and Paweł – studied Torah in the nearby village of Kórnik, as the Helman family were very religious.

One of Isaac's chores was to sell his mother's dairy products after school, primarily to Jewish families in nearby towns and villages. One of his regular customers was the Łukawiecki family from Ostrowiec. He would usually deal with Mundek's aunt, who worked at the local bank branch in Lubaczów. Mundek and his brother Zygmunt visited their aunt there while on holiday. During those visits, Isaac met Mundek and Zygmunt.

Lubaczów and Lisie Jamy were occupied by the Germans in autumn 1939 for just a few days before they were handed over to the Soviets in line with the secret protocol of the Molotov-Ribbentrop Non-Aggression Pact between Germany and Russia. A few weeks after Germany invaded the USSR, Lubaczów and Lisie Jamy were occupied for the second time by the Nazis, and all the Jewish families of Lisie Jamy were evacuated and transferred to Lubaczów.

In Lubaczów, Isaac was subjected to forced labor as a woodcutter in the nearby woods. Upon hearing rumors that the Nazis were going to eliminate the Jews, Isaac and his younger brother Paweł fled to the woods. Most of the Jews who tried to escape were caught and executed at the Dachnów anti-tank ditch, but the Helman brothers managed to escape and survive in the woods despite the harsh, freezing-cold winter of 1942–1943. However, as winter thawed and became spring, the brothers were caught while searching for food and were turned over to the Gestapo. Isaac managed to escape while being transported to Lubaczów, but his brother Paweł was killed at Dachnów.

Meanwhile Bernard, the oldest brother, had also managed to escape the ghetto and had hidden himself in a bunker with other families. This bunker was eventually discovered, and Bernard was sent to Bełżec extermination camp, but during transport, he escaped yet again by jumping off the train. Even though he was wounded, he managed to make the twenty-kilometer (twelve-mile) trek to meet Isaac, who was hiding in the woods.

Bernard worked as a tailor in the woods, making alterations for the local population. One day, a Nazi informant followed him into the woods and later pinpointed the hiding spot to the Nazis. Bernard was eventually brought to Dachnów and executed there.

Isaac Helman met Mundek and Chana in the forest by coincidence. He would end up fighting with the Łukawiecki partisans until they were liberated. After their liberation by the Red Army, Isaac joined the Soviet military and fought with them until the end of the war. In 1947, he went to Lwów and married a woman named Gołda. They had two daughters – Tili and Hedva. Isaac later became a grandfather to five grandchildren from his two daughters. He emigrated to Israel in 1961 and raised his family in upper Nazareth, working as a weaver in a local textile factory until his retirement.

Life wasn't easy for the Helman family in Israel. The children's clothes were normally in a state of disrepair. When shoes were too small, holes were cut in the front to give growing toes more space. Furniture and household appliances were rarely replaced, just repaired again and again. The family members learned not to ask for much. Yet despite the privation at home, Isaac made sure his family never wanted for food; they were always given complete freedom to buy groceries without any price restrictions.

The dreadful horrors and difficult times he experienced during the Holocaust as a partisan molded Isaac into a rigid and inflexible man. Consequently, living with him was not easy, and his family suffered under his brittleness. He educated his children harshly "for the future life." The family rarely heard any kind, warm words of encouragement, never mind receiving a kiss or a hug. On the contrary, they were always in fear of the family patriarch.

Isaac passed away March 18, 2012.

Anshel Bogner

Anshel Bogner was born in Lisie Jamy on December 21, 1902. His father Zalman and mother Pearl Singer were peasants and traders of livestock. In addition, they also operated the only pub in Lisie Jamy, located on the main road between Lubaczów and Lwów. The family had five children. The eldest was Neshel, then Gittel, Anshel, Bella (Pearl or Penina), and the youngest, Isaac (Isadore).

Anshel was a man in his early forties when Mundek and Chana met him. He was tall, standing just over six feet, athletic and well built. He was very strong and used his strength to intimidate his countrymen as well as to maintain horses. His handshake meant everything to him and God forbid if the other party didn't keep his promise.

A very young Anshel left Lisie Jamy to go to Lubaczów to open a trade business on his own. Anshel was a very righteous man and often loaned money to

Anshel Bogner, Canada, 1960

Anshel Bogner with his niece and granddaughter in Israel, 1981

locals before their crops were harvested. Because the majority of men in town were poor, they always ran out of money before they could bring their crops to market. Yet while he was generous, he was also very principled. There were consequences if a loan wasn't repaid on time. On one occasion, he was sentenced to three years' imprisonment, which he served in a Lubaczów jail, because he fatally beat a peasant who refused to honor his loan agreement (the man also made antisemitic remarks).

While in his thirties, he met and married his wife Rebecca in Lubaczów. The newly married couple bought a house in Lubaczów. They had two children, a son and a daughter. Anshel continued his business during the Russian rule of Lubaczów, as well as at the beginning of the German occupation. Not long after the Nazi invasion, Anshel's generous ways came to an end. He could no longer advance money to others, not knowing what situation Jews would find themselves in, himself included.

It was at this point that Anshel sent his wife, mother-in-law, and their children to Lisie Jamy, hoping that they would be safer there. They hid among friends, while he stayed in Lubaczów.

During the liquidation of the Lubaczów ghetto, Anshel joined his family in Lisie Jamy. In late 1943, two Polish collaborators from Lubaczów (Milue Frank and Becholek) found out where the Bogner family was hiding in Lisie Jamy.[10] They went there to capture them and hand them over to the Gestapo in Lubaczów – in return for one kilogram of sugar and one bottle of vodka for each family member.

Tragically, Anshel's entire family was killed. Only Anshel survived, escaping into the night. He made his way to a Ukrainian friend named Hayddok in Lisie Jamy and continued to hide in his home. The night his family was murdered, Anshel and Hayddok went back and buried the four bodies of his wife, mother-in-law, and two children.

The fact that Hayddok was hiding a Jew became well known in Lisie Jamy and therefore it became necessary to rescue Anshel. Józef Kulpa told Mundek Łukawiecki of the entire ordeal. Together they decided that Mundek would go to Lisie Jamy and offer Anshel an opportunity to join the Łukawiecki partisans, as a way of saving his life. As a result, Anshel joined the Łukawiecki partisans – but only on the condition that they would avenge his family.

A few days later, the Łukawiecki partisans returned to Lubaczów at night with the task of killing Milue Frank and Becholek in their homes. Since it was urban terrain and very close to German and Ukrainian troops, the mission had to be carried out very quickly to avoid any resistance and potential capture.

---

10. See a partial description of the events in Hoffman, *Keep Yelling*, p. 166. The whole situation was told to the writer by Isaac Helman, personal interview, May 1, 2010. He added that after the war, Anshel went to Lisie Jamy, recovered the bodies from where they where buried, and transferred them to the Lubaczów cemetery.

The AK provided them with very accurate and precise information about the exact addresses, the layout of the homes, and the number of family members, etc. The partisans were divided in half, one group for each target. They were ordered to get in and out of the houses as fast as possible and to avoid any prolonged fighting at all costs. The aim was to execute the targets as quickly as possible.

Each assault team consisted of three partisans. The Milue Frank team included Mundek, Chana, and a Polish partisan. The Becholek team was made up of Berish Brand, Anshel Bogner, and another Polish partisan.

The assault teams approached Lubaczów on Kosciuszki Street and spread out at the junction with Tartaczna Street. Each team went to its target. The mission was carried out very quickly, without any resistance by the collaborators or their families. Milue Frank was dragged into the street and shot by Chana. Becholek was executed in his bed by Anshel, after his wife was forced to leave the room. The success of this mission calmed some of Anshel's anger and ended his obsession with avenging the murder of his family.

After being liberated by the Red Army, Anshel took a horse and buggy and went to his family's burial site, which he had succeeded in locating. He dug them up and loaded them onto his buggy. He then transported them back to the city of Lubaczów and buried them in the old Jewish cemetery.

In 1946, he met his second wife, Sylvia, who was born in Lubaczów on March 23, 1912. They left for Vancouver, Canada, in 1947 because Anshel's brother Isaac and sister Gittel were living there. In Canada, Anshel owned and managed a drugstore. He passed away on July 1, 1985. Sylvia passed away five years later. Throughout his life, motivated by grief over his losses, he donated generously to Magen David Adom and to the Laniado Hospital in Netanya, Israel.

He rarely spoke about his activities as partisan. His sister's daughter, Perl Fishman, quoted him saying that while he was a partisan he killed twenty-two Germans.[11]

Maurie Hoffman and His Brother Tobias

During one operation of the Jewish hit squad near Lisie Jamy, Mundek and Berish Brand heard branches breaking and realized that they were being followed by an unknown person. Berish Brand shouted in the Ukrainian language, "*Stoi!*

---

11. Perl Fishman, personal interview, April 16, 2010.

Maurie Hoffman, Australia, 2014

Ruki virch!" (Stop! Hands up!). They were afraid that a Ukrainian peasant had detected them in the woods and was following them to hand them over to the Nazis. Either that, or it was a Ukrainian Auxiliary Police officer or an opponent partisan who wanted to expose them. The squad immediately became vigilant, assuming battle positions and aiming their firearms toward the direction from which they had heard the follower.

At the sound of the harsh Ukrainian command, the follower, Maurie Hoffman, froze in fear and literally could not move. Born in 1929, he was at that time just fourteen years old. A cold sweat covered him despite the fact that it was the particularly harsh winter of 1943 and the weather was bitterly cold. He thought that his life had come to an end. He was sure that he had encountered Ukrainian partisans and that they would kill him.

All of a sudden, with the impulse of caught game, he started to run away as fast as he could from the scene. This seemed proof to Mundek that he was an opponent who must be killed in order to keep him quiet so he could not expose the squad. Otherwise in a very short time the woods would be crawling with Ukrainians and Nazis. Mundek knew that they had to kill him despite the fact that the sound of the shots would alert the entire zone. But this was better than to be chased by Nazis and Ukrainians.

Mundek and Berish Brand, acting as rearguards, opened fire into the darkness, in the direction where they thought the person was running away. The bullets grazed Maurie's ear. Maurie shouted (in Ashkenazi pronunciation), "*Shema Yisroel*"[12] and fell to the ground. When the squad heard the words "*Shema Yisroel*," they realized that the figure they had been shooting at was a Jew. Mundek immediately shouted, "Cease fire," and he and Berish jumped out of the bushes and ran to the person.

Berish Brand sat on his chest, completely immobilizing him. He had a big lighter, and with it he illuminated the captive. The face was that of a young boy. He had very pale blue eyes, which gave him a typical Aryan country-boy look. He was wearing an oversized khaki jacket and a Polish military hat. His young age, combined with his stature – he was only about 5'6" – made him a rather unimposing figure. The boy was not wounded; the gunfire had missed him.

"Who are you?" Mundek asked him in Ukrainian.

"I am Maurie Hoffman from Lubaczów," he answered.

"Are you a Jew?"

Even though Maurie felt sure these would be the last words he would ever utter, he answered, "Yes."

"Why you are following us?"

"I want to join the partisans," he replied.[13] And suddenly, Maurie recognized the voice of the man who had been talking to him in Ukrainian. Maurie opened his eyes and cried out in surprise, "Mundek!" The large man who sat on his chest slowly got up and let Maurie go.

"Maurie! You're alive...!" was all Maurie remembered hearing – this time in Polish – from the person who had been questioning him, before he fainted.

Members of the Jewish squad were acquainted with the Hoffman family from Lisie Jamy, of which Maurie was the youngest of six siblings; Anshel Bogner and six or seven other members were themselves from Lubaczów.

Mundek looked at Maurie happily, with tears in his eyes, relieved that he had not accidentally killed him. Suddenly, the encounter with Maurie was interrupted by a burst of machine-gun fire. The partisans returned fire to their unseen

---

12. "Hear, O Israel," the beginning of an important Jewish prayer said twice daily and also traditionally said if possible when facing death.

13. Mundek and Maurie Hoffman told the same story. Personal interview with Maurie Hoffman, February 3, 2009.

enemy and retreated further into the woods. Mundek ordered the partisans to leave the area quickly to avoid a full-scale attack against them.

Maurie was not only one of the youngest members of the Łukawiecki partisans, he was also the only member to write a book. Entitled *Keep Yelling: A Survivor's Testimony*, it was published in 1995 by Spectrum Publications in Richmond, Australia. The book outlines Maurie's experiences as a partisan after joining the Jewish hit squad at the end of 1943 at the age of fourteen.

Maurie had already endured many difficult years by the time he joined the Łukawiecki partisans. In addition, by this time the fighting between the Poles and Ukrainians had become a lot fiercer. One of the areas where the fighting was most deadly was Młodów, about three and a half kilometers (two miles) west of Lubaczów. As a result of this intense fighting, the Polish inhabitants of Młodów had evacuated their village and moved west, fleeing quickly with their horses, cows, and other livestock in tow in order to escape the wrath of the Ukrainians, who enjoyed looting and then burning down Polish homes. Flames would eventually engulf most of Młodów.

Among the Poles who fled was the Polish landlord who had been hiding Maurie and his brother Tobias. Once he left town, the boys found themselves all alone in an abandoned house. This was an incredibly fearful and anxious time for both of them. But Maurie was dealing with an additional, serious issue: Tobias was not in his right mind and could not be left on his own.

However, Maurie was worried that someone would discover that he and his brother – two Jews – were hiding in an abandoned house. In spite of his brother's condition, therefore, Maurie decided to leave Młodów one night and make his way to Borowa Góra, three and a half kilometers (two miles) west, to see if he could find a safer hideout. He told Tobias to stay in hiding and promised to come back for him.

Maurie left Młodów in the dead of night and made his way very slowly, walking with trepidation along the edge of the forest and picking green vegetables from the fields along the way. As he approached what he thought was an uninhabited cottage, he heard voices from behind him, coming out of the forest. Since all the Polish farmers had been driven out of the area, Maurie assumed that they were Ukrainians. He quietly and quickly approached the cottage, but the door was locked.

He looked back in the direction of the voices and saw a group of armed partisans approaching. Maurie panicked, and instead of remaining motionless, he tried to hide. His movements attracted the partisans' attention and while he was bending down, shots whistled by his head.

Fortunately he had escaped injury then as now.

Once Mundek's group were out of harm's way, Maurie told Mundek that he had a brother still hiding in Młodów.

"Let's go and get him!" Mundek immediately responded.

When they arrived at the Hoffman brothers' hideout, Mundek and the other partisans noticed how strangely Tobias was behaving. He sat in complete darkness, wrapped in a tallith, with tefillin on his left arm. He was praying. He did not pay any attention to the arrivals. It looked like he had lost his mind from starvation.

Even so, Mundek asked Maurie if both he and Tobias would like to join the partisans. Maurie agreed but Tobias protested and refused to join. He fell to the ground and could not move, paralyzed with fear.

"I'm not moving. I won't be able to walk more than ten meters because of my feet," he said.

"Come on," Mundek encouraged. "You'll see that you'll feel better once you start walking."

But traveling with Tobias was difficult. He cried out in pain after each step and the partisans had to stop frequently to help him. He urgently needed to be fed, but to do so they first had to get him to the company hideout. Despite the difficulties, the partisans did not give up. Berish Brand held him and kept his hand over Tobias's mouth all the way to the hideout, as Tobias was screaming incoherent sentences and prayers. Eventually, Mundek took him on his shoulders and carried him the rest of the way.

When they finally arrived back at the partisan hideout, Tobias said that he was hungry. Chana, who was waiting for them to return, served him boiled potatoes. Tobias swallowed the potatoes whole, without even chewing! It was an astonishing sight to behold – Tobias collecting boiled potatoes from the pot, shoving them into his mouth, and immediately swallowing them intact. Tobias ate about ten pounds of potatoes that night and then fell asleep. After a couple of days – during which time he ate potatoes endlessly – he began to behave normally and returned to his senses.

From that day forward – until the end of the war in 1944 – the Hoffman brothers would no longer go hungry.

Chapter 20
Bunker 1

The year Mundek spent as a *Czyn* dispatcher and then at the Spaleni camp – as well as his military training during his high school years at the VIII Gimnazjum im. Kazimierza Wielkiego for boys in Lwów – gave him knowledge of how to construct hideouts in the woods.

The site of Bunker 1 in the Bór woods

As the winter of 1942–1943 was about to end, the cold was no longer a major problem. It was more a matter of how to stay out of the enemy's sights. And there were many enemies in the woods eager to betray the partisans. Ukrainians and antisemitic partisans and collaborators in particular had entered the woods to find and catch partisans, especially Jews.[1] The Germans also gave Jewish collaborators one kilogram of sugar and a bottle of vodka for every Jew extradited by them.[2] Another threat was posed by Polish shepherds and other passersby, who in collecting mushrooms or picking blueberries, cherries, and raspberries might come close to the hideout.

Mundek's group selected a young pine forest in which to hide. It was in fact a tree nursery (*kultura leśna*). Mundek's opinion was that nobody would search a tree nursery. The trees were young and averaged only about two meters, or human height. Moreover, the forest was not dense and the branches trailed on the ground, forming a cone shape around the trees much like a dancing dress, short but wide. Because of this, nobody would imagine that a tree nursery was hiding partisans and this therefore gave them perfect camouflage.

Known as the Dąbrowa woods, it was located two kilometers (just over a mile) south of Ostrowiec. Beyond the obvious fact that no one would suspect such a short forest, there were additional advantages to this seemingly unlikely hiding place. People usually didn't enter these woods, as it was inconvenient to traverse through the trees. The ground vegetation also grew wild and created an additional barrier. The challenge of such a hideout, however, was to avoid leaving signs of life. This was achieved by not traveling the same path twice and not leaving broken branches or trampled vegetation.

At first, the hideout in the Dąbrowa woods with the Spaleni was not a bunker. It was a shelter. The hideout was below the lowest branches of the pine trees. Mundek, Chana, and the others crawled into the shelter like lizards, slithering in below the lowest branch, trying not to touch the branches. The soil below the branches was relatively dry as the branches prevented the snow from falling in. At a later stage, the partisans built a kind of a tent from the branches, next to the pine trees. The top was covered with canvas which was in turn covered with pine branches. As the woods were very humid, cold and wet, they covered the ground with straw or greenery to reduce the risk of pneumonia or arthritis. The entrance was concealed by pine branches attached to a plank.

It was impossible to stay in the same hideout for a long time. The need to

---

1. See for example Roth, *Herrenmenschen*, p. 225. He indicates that within the first quarter of 1943, German gendarmes and Ukrainian policemen killed 172 Jews who escaped from Lubaczów ghetto. (The ghetto was annihilated December 1942–January 1943.)
2. See Maurie Hoffman, e-mail to the author, dated May 22, 2009.

Chana Bern digging a bunker, January 1943

Mundek digging a bunker, January 1943

be cautious was most important. Although they had to continue with daily life – walking to and from the hideout, preparing food, cooking, and attending to personal hygiene needs – everything was done with extreme care to keep their existence a secret. In addition, every few days they moved to another hideout.

Gradually, they learned the forest. The sound of the trees during the day and the night was completely different, as they had a different song for daytime and for nighttime. The partisans' ears became very sensitive to the orchestra of the woods, and any musical mistake caused alarm. They became experts in the types of flora and fauna in the woods, such as trees, vegetation, shrubs, and roots. Changes in the flora and fauna had meaning. They learned which vegetation and mushrooms were edible and which were dangerous. They discerned the linkage between the type of soil and what grew on it. They came to understand the noise of the wind blowing in the trees and how the different sounds depended on the trees, their age, and their leaves. Even the noise and pattern of the snow was different according to the trees and the places where they grew. The woods and everything that grew and lived within them spoke constantly to Mundek. Their language was very frank without any deception. Very valuable information and intelligence could be collected freely. Careful listening was therefore a key part of survival in the woods.

Nothing was left to chance. The woods had their own language and the partisans had to master it. Mundek called himself a "wild animal" and claimed he could find any foreigner who entered the woods by smell.[3] Mundek said that he used nature's warning indications. For example, when he noticed that the hen the partisans had been raising had escaped, he used the warning call of the chickadee. At night, they used the warning call of the robin, a sharp "*sey*."

Good indications of predators were the destruction of liverwort creeping on the surfaces, or the evergreen shrub of Daphne. Because of its young trees and wild nature, no transports went to these woods. There were also no large animals in the Dąbrowa woods, such as deer, for there was insufficient space for them to move freely. Rabbits were occasionally seen running between the trees.

As time went on the partisans improved their methods and survival skills for shelter living, and their comfort in hiding increased. They learned how to cook with minimal smoke by using very dry wood, as otherwise smoke would spread a very long distance. Water for drinking and cooking was carried from long distances. The streams nearby were used only for bathing. Mundek loved wild garlic soup, made from the plant's leaves. The problem was the smell of the cooking, which carried very far. Toilets did not exist. Human waste and other waste had to be buried far away to avoid animals and wild dogs who would carry it off and could be noticed by the peasants and forest people.

Those who approached the hideout were eliminated as suspected collaborators with the Nazis or the Ukrainians. On one occasion, while Mundek went to meet Kulpa, Chana was preparing supper near the hideout. A man dressed in civilian clothes came right up to where Chana was. She heard him at the last minute, as he was walking carelessly and breaking branches. As soon as she realized that the sounds were made by a hostile person, she took the Parabellum

---

3. Personal interview with Dr. Isaac Weinberg, May 30, 2011, quoting conversations with Mundek Łukawiecki.

pistol she had nearby and cocked it quietly. In one fast move she turned on the man. At the same time, the man raised his rifle to shoot her in the back. He was surprised by her rapid movements and she fired first. Two bullets hit his chest from seven meters away. He collapsed immediately.

The soldiers in the company immediately ran to see why shots had been fired. When they saw the body, they stared at her in admiration. This fragile Jewish girl without any previous experience did not lose her cool and reacted perfectly. It was then that she was accepted as the forty-second soldier of the company. But the incident proved that there was a breach of security at the hideout.

Chana promptly extinguished the fire and the entire company relocated several meters away where they could see the clearing. They wanted to make sure the man had been alone. They were also afraid that the shots might have been heard by others who would come to see what had happened. Chana would have to warn Mundek upon his return. For now, she hid in the observation point until nightfall.

Chana began to hallucinate. She imagined that her soul left her body and began to fly. She recreated the shooting in full color, but in slow motion. She saw the intruder's face looking at her with hatred and contempt. As her soul went up, she saw her school and herself wearing the Bais Yaakov uniform. She saw pictures of her family. They were happy, smiling, and joyful, but now it was in black and white. She saw her father, mother, brother, and sister. She saw her father's family and her mother's family. Her soul lingered on every picture – especially on her beloved aunt, Selma Katz, to whom she had been very attached.

Then Chana heard the voice of her teacher from the Bais Yaakov school. "Chana, what you did is exactly the Law of Moses," his voice said. "Our holy Talmud tells us that if someone comes to kill us, we should arise and kill him first."[4] The teacher continued to talk to her, reminding her that the Bible commands, "Remember what Amalek did unto thee."[5]

"Chana," he said, "you've seen the Nazis – they are Amalek, killing your family. You were sent by Almighty God to avenge them. Always remember your father, your mother, your sister, your brother. Remember your family, remember them and us; we died as martyrs."

---

4. *Sanhedrin* 72a.
5. Deuteronomy 25:17.

Chana didn't know long she had been hallucinating when she heard Mundek's password – the call of an owl. It brought her back to reality. She replied to the call, and after a few minutes, Mundek arrived in the clearing.

He brought with him a tarpaulin fabric to prevent water penetration, cooking equipment such as pots, pans, and matches, and bread, potatoes, and beef.

The soldiers of the company also appeared in the clearing. Chana told Mundek the whole story of the shooting in a quiet and calm voice. She did not miss a single detail. Mundek listened carefully. At the end he said to her, "Now that you've killed your first enemy, you have become a real partisan, a real warrior. You fulfilled our goal – survival and revenge against the Nazis. This is what we stand for."

The guards were debriefed as well. There had not been a mistake, but the lesson was that the number of guards should increase in order to keep a more vigilant eye on the hideout.

They decided not to stay at the clearing, but to move to another spot. The following morning, a company team returned to the body in the clearing in order to bury it. First, Mundek and Chana observed the clearing for a while. A pine marten was staring at them from a Carpathian beech tree, which proved to them that the area was safe. They approached the body and searched it, also taking the dead man's rifle and ammunition. The man was a Ukrainian from Lubaczów. Mundek had met him in the past. They decided to bury him in the clearing, as it was impossible to carry the corpse elsewhere because it would leave signs. It was easy to dig a grave in the wet soil. After the grave was deep enough that the body would not be smelled by wolves, they put the corpse in and covered the grave with soil, camouflaging it with loose pine needles and vegetation.

A few days later, two German policemen approached the clearing area where Chana had killed the Ukrainian, probably searching for their friend. The two wandered in the woods, looking around. They came dangerously close to the new hideout. Mundek shot them down after following them.[6] As was standard procedure, the partisans then stripped them of their German police uniforms and boots, and took their weapons and documentation.

With the new tarpaulin, they constructed tent-like shelters that could

---

6. Personal interview with Dr. Isaac Weinberg, May 30, 2011, quoting conversations with Mundek Łukawiecki.

accommodate two people. The tent was set up between two trees. The branches of the trees were so interconnected that it was impossible to distinguish the tent in the center of the branches. In addition, they made sure that the tents were covered on top by branches. Scattered pine branches on the ground and the wild vegetation above all helped to conceal the hideout. Then it was all covered with a blanket. They felt confident. They had a mule to carry heavy things, a chicken hen, and a bunker full of food.

Most of the fall of 1943 was spent in this type of hideout. During the day, they avoided being seen and didn't carry out any operations. At night, the company was very active. They executed operations against German targets, Ukrainians, supporters, and collaborators, always at a great distance from the hideout – and preferably close to Ukrainian villages.

At the same time, they also rescued Jews. The rescue of Jews was one of Mundek's fundamental goals. He would get information from Kulpa and others about Jews in hiding with Polish families. In order to deter the Polish family from handing over the Jews, Mundek and a team of partisans would visit the family and warn them against betraying their Jewish dependents. Not complying would result in severe punishment and even death. This deterrence policy worked very well; to the best of Mundek's knowledge, no Jew was ever handed over to the Germans. And if Mundek was convinced that a Jew faced real danger, he would take him to the hideout – as he did with Anshel Bogner.

During this period, the company was performing AK operations and the AK therefore knew the location of the company. Although the company also increased its number of Jews at this time, the AK appreciated Mundek and his company and, because of their stellar work, no one informed the Germans of their position.

Chapter 21
If I Am Not for Myself, Then Who Will Be for Me? And if Not Now, When?

Despite his young age (twenty-three), Mundek was an inspiring leader who worked hard to elevate the morale of his group. One night, he gave a speech to his fellow partisans. He did not speak loudly. The rule was to remain as quiet as possible in the woods. The men sat around him in a clearing, staring right at him. He focused on the importance of freedom.

"We have been fighting for our lives for years," Mundek began. "We fight the Nazis who killed our families, avenging them. We attack like lightning. We move fast, attacking hard, and then return to our hideout. Yes, the places we attack are long distances from our hideout. We do not attack in our 'neighbourhood.' This is a thieves' rule. A thief never steals at home, but only in distant places. We want to stay in these woods until liberation."

Mundek suddenly paused after repeating the word a few times, as if he had just suddenly grasped the meaning of the word *liberation*. He enjoyed and savored its meaning. His black eyes lit up and vaguely fixed on an imaginary spot. Mundek continued excitedly: "Our freedom is at hand. Every day that passes brings us closer to freedom, to liberation."

He paused and repeated the word *freedom* as he reflected upon the meaning of the word. His thoughts soared. His eyes shone and he imagined that he was in Heaven. After a few moments of complete silence, he came to and continued: "We must all hold out hope, for us, for our families who were destroyed. We have to make their voices heard. Can you imagine what freedom is? We would be able to go anywhere we want. We would be able to speak out loud and even sing as much as we wanted. We could walk freely and not care about leaving tracks and broken branches. We could cook for ourselves, all we want, when we want.

"Right now, here in the forest, we are somewhat free. But we have no real freedom. We live as slaves and savages. We have to always be on guard. At any second we might be attacked by Germans or Ukrainians or Russian partisans or even by local peasants. This is not freedom and liberation. Freedom is going back to normal life, where everyone does as they please.

"We are dead men. But our souls are alive. Freedom is rebirth. The fact that we are alive is a miracle. We saw with our own eyes how they killed our families. They were innocent. They slaughtered them like animals. What did my little sister Judith ever do to deserve to die?"

Mundek's voice choked up and broke off for a few seconds. There were tears in his eyes. "We have to avenge our beloved," he continued. "The Germans must pay for the murder of our families. Everyone keeps his family in his heart. The biggest revenge is our survival, our freedom. The last thing my grandmother said to me was to cry for her. To cry is freedom.

"We must be strong today and hope for tomorrow. Every day that passes brings us closer to freedom. All we did until now – all the operations, all the attacks and raids – were only to pave the way so that the sun will shine over our heads tomorrow. Our families rely on us for the hope that we will not forget them and the atrocities we all faced. We must survive today for the promise of tomorrow. Tomorrow we can freely cry for yesterday. This is freedom."

Mundek's optimistic attitude is illustrated well in a story told by Maurie Hoffman. A hen had escaped from its small poultry pen. One of the partisans noticed it and began to chase the bird. The faster he ran, the faster the hen fled. It ran to the edge of the forest, where it fell into the hands of a group of Ukrainians.

"A hen doesn't go into the forest by itself," one of them said. "If a hen comes out of the forest, it means there are partisans in there."

A siege took place the following day. It terrified the entire partisan unit. But Mundek continually lifted up their spirits by reminding them, "Why are you worried? Nothing has happened. We have enough food, we must remain optimistic. We mustn't despair while we are still alive and well." Hoffman did not describe how the story ended and how in fact they had managed to have chickens in the woods, but it is revealing that already at that time, neither the Germans nor the Ukrainians dared to enter the forests.

On the flip side, Mundek was also prone to uncontrollable outbursts of rage, as if he were possessed by a demon. In these moments, he could not control himself and had the potential to kill everyone around him. His face would become completely distorted. His already dark complexion would become even darker.

Alternating moods were a hallmark of Mundek's personality. He could be in euphoria one minute and then enraged within a few seconds. Nobody could ever predict his mood and when or why it would change.

One day, a short while before sunset, when Mundek's group of partisans were not operating and were settled in their bunkers following a heavy snowstorm the previous night, Mundek emerged from his bunker wearing full military dress, including his boots, as if he were going on a military operation. Yet the only weaponry he held was a violin in his left hand and a bow in his right. He centered himself in a nearby clearing. His footsteps left deep marks in the virgin soft snow. Wordlessly, with a sharp move, he hoisted the violin and mounted it on his left shoulder, resting his chin heavily on the base. His eyes closed. Very gently and softly, he moved the bow across the strings and started to play the music of his favorite composer, Fritz Kreisler,[1] choosing the cheerful and happy tune of Fritz Kreisler's Viennese waltzes "Liebesleid" and "Schön Rosmarin." The fingers of Mundek's left hand floated magically, touching and not touching the violin's strings, moving nimbly as if they were bewitched. The right hand led the bow up and down, traveling on the strings in coordinated moves without any hesitation.

Mundek's fellow partisans peeped out of their bunkers, wondering what was going on. Stillness prevailed as they gazed at Mundek in astonishment. The melody had a paralyzing impact. The usual quietness of the wood was interrupted by the extraordinary music, which seemed to spread all over; even the soft, white blanket of snow covering the pine trees and the soil and dirt could not muffle it.

Although Mundek had an emotional side, he was not soft: far from it. As commander of the partisan company, Mundek expected total obedience and loyalty, without any argument. He did not tolerate any form of insubordination whatsoever. He always expected his orders to be carried out immediately.

Chana Bern was a quiet and obedient woman who didn't express her emotions or feelings. She was an expert at internalizing everything. She never raised her voice and never argued with or confronted any of the men. As the eldest

---

1. A world-famous Austrian violinist and composer who emigrated to the United States in his later years, Kreisler was a Jew who converted to Christianity. His father was from Kraków and his mother from a small town near Lwów.

daughter of an observant Jewish family, Chana had been taught to accept God's judgments without any hesitation. Her deep faith in God was inherited from home and at the strictly religious Bais Yaakov school she attended as a girl.

Chana accepted Mundek's leadership and believed in it. Her personality was almost opposite to Mundek's. She never showed her feelings through tears, compassion, tenderness, or warmth. She was a woman seemingly made of iron and ice. In military operations, she was always cool. Because of these characteristics, she was involved in all partisan activities, including killing collaborators. The urge for revenge ran deep in her veins and this sense of ensuring that justice was served gave her the ability to execute any collaborator, without mercy. This was God's justice, in her eyes, and she was just carrying out His will.

Her rape actually made her stronger and enabled her to withstand the suffering and difficulties faced during her years in the woods. She was consequently able to execute orders and obey instructions very stoically, as well as reason with Mundek when necessary. She was the only one who could order Mundek to stop playing with his weapons when he would demonstrate how he would kill any and all Nazi collaborators. And he obeyed.

While she was cold and businesslike in the battlefield, she was warm toward her partisan comrades. She made sure that all their needs were met. She spoke to Mundek on their behalves and intervened in their favor. She made sure that all of them got enough food and heat in the winter. She was very kind and good-natured toward them. She always put extra food aside to give them all she could. She was really two different people – one in combat, and one in daily life.

While Mundek saw the fight against the Germans as a means of improving their own chances of survival, Chana saw the fighting as part of the agony of redemption. Each of their points of view was valid and had to be fulfilled in full force, without compromise and concessions. For Mundek, the goal was freedom and survival; for Chana, it was divine order. Both of them were motivated by a desire for revenge. Mundek's was uncontrollable and unforgiving. Chana struggled to put her feelings behind her. This internal struggle engaged them for the rest of their lives. Mundek externalized it at times – even weeping. Chana's struggle was more internalized.

The difference between their beliefs led Mundek to continue his pursuit of collaborators after he was liberated, while Chana tried as best she could to return to a normal life.

Chapter 22
Operations of the Jewish Hit Squad

The Jewish hit squad had four operational goals. The first was to simply survive. The second was to sabotage German war efforts in the area where they operated; that included sabotaging German train transports to the Eastern Front and derailing trains heading to the liquidation camp Bełżec. The third mission was to rescue Jews who were hiding with peasants or in the woods. The fourth goal, which developed due to circumstances, was to avenge collaboration with the Nazis.

One of the key characteristics of the Łukawiecki partisans was that they were a small group. Because of their size, they developed their military knowledge for clandestine warfare and were flexible in military maneuvers. And as a smaller group, they were able to improvise and camouflage more easily than a larger would. They had the ability and determination to carry out tasks precisely and efficiently. Their ability to carry out successful "hit and run" operations was remarkable. Since they lived in the woods, they grasped the tactical advantages that the forest provided better than interlopers. On top of this, they were all loyal, disciplined, obedient, and anti-Communist. What is more, their physical condition was excellent and allowed them to travel long distances from one night to the next.[1]

Mundek conducted his group with very harsh military discipline. A timetable was strictly kept. Orders, briefings, and debriefings were routinely done before and after any assault. No mistake was permitted. Duties were to be performed perfectly. No argument or hesitation was allowed. Every partisan knew exactly what his role was. Situations and responses were drilled and redrilled. Mundek

---

1. In his testimony, Mundek Łukawiecki said that they used to walk fifteen to twenty kilometers (about nine to twelve miles) in one night. Testimony of Edmund (Mundek) Łukawiecki (Moshe Lavee) to Yad Vashem, July 28, 1993, no. 03-6946, tape no. 033c/2757, p. 18.

Left to right: Anshel Bogner, Maurie Hoffman, and Isaac Helman on the way to an operation, summer 1944

trained the partisans in how to use their weapons and ammunition effectively. In order to maintain secrecy, everything was done on a need-to-know basis. For example, all the partisans knew the name Kulpa, but none of them met him or had any information about him.

In the same way as Mundek was very strict regarding military matters, he was also very strict about maintaining a high level of personal hygiene to prevent serious diseases. The partisans were forced to shave and wash themselves. As a result, not even one single partisan fell severely ill. When Chana bathed, Mundek ordered everyone into their bunkers and then she washed herself outside the bunker with a tub while Mundek concealed it behind a blanket that he held up like a curtain.[2]

Mundek planed the operations very carefully. He took every detail into consideration: when, where, and how to approach the collaborator, what was the best method and weapon for eliminating the target, what was the best route for

---

2. Personal interview with Dr. Isaac Weinberg, May 30, 2011, quoting conversations with Mundek Łukawiecki.

retreating afterwards, and so on. Mundek deployed his group according to a plan, which always included backup personnel. Nothing was left to chance. The group was split into two teams. With Mundek were five experienced warriors – Anshel Bogner, Berish Brand, Władi, Ludwik, and Chana Bern. The rest of the group was assigned as a backup team, blocking and isolating the operation theater and acting as decoys.[3]

One common tactical method they often employed was the use of the German Wehrmacht uniform, as members of the group could speak German fluently. Coupled with their knowledge of the terrain and the population, they were able to carry out commando-style "kill and vanish" operations easily.

The AK commander of Tomaszów Lubelski, Marian Warda ("Polakowski"), saw this advantage and decided to operate and engage the Jewish hit squad in operations that were suited to their abilities.

Marian Warda was adamant that the AK be tough on collaborators. Warda believed in being harsh when it came to exacting revenge against collaborators, whether they were Poles or Ukrainians. In 1942, two Polish collaborators were executed. By 1943, twenty-three more had been eliminated. Another four were killed in 1944. Ukrainian collaborators were treated no less severely. In 1943, the AK killed twenty-seven Ukrainian collaborators and in 1944, nineteen more were executed.

Warda's harsh policy suited Mundek perfectly. It corresponded exactly to his and his partisans' desire for vengeance. Mundek's partisans became Warda's "hit squad." He ordered them to execute several death penalties upon collaborators. For example, he gave the order to kill a Ukrainian collaborator from Ruda Różaniecka. In addition, the mayor Majdan Sopocki[4] (who turned in thirteen additional collaborators, all of whom were executed as well)[5] and others[6] were executed by Mundek's squad.

Operational orders were given by Warda or Kulpa. The squad operated in

---

3. Maurie Hoffman, for example, was a member of the backup team. He was fourteen years old, and his main duty was to assist in preparing food. He was equipped with a wooden mockup of a gun and two bottles painted black to look like hand grenades.
4. Caban, *Na dwa fronty*, p. 103.
5. Caban, *Oddziały partyzanckie*, pp. 41–42.
6. Ibid., p. 117.

towns such as Susiec, Jaworów, Józefów, Narol, Lipsko, Bełżec, Płazów, Cieszanów, Biłgoraj, and Tomaszów Lubelski.

Apart from hit-and-run operations, the Jewish hit squad was involved in regular combat activities and engagements, mainly armed resistance against the resettlement of Germans in the Zamość area in large farms, and burning down large farms taken over by the Germans in nearby Koniuszka and Kowalówka.

Mundek and Anshel Bogner were the experts in the handling of explosives, knowing best how to store them and how to activate them.[7] This meant that in operations where explosives were engaged, either Mundek or Bogner always took part. However, not all the operations they conducted were fire operations; they also conducted clandestine sabotage operations, such as dismantling railroads.[8]

Once, the Jewish hit squad was ordered to destroy a German officers' whorehouse club, which was located in a palace formerly owned by a baron. The plan was to storm the palace and kill all of its inhabitants with hand grenades. The operation had three stages: first, capture the palace; second, kill the German officers and prostitutes; lastly, destroy the palace.

Mundek led the assault group in overcoming the Nazi guards. The guards were taken by surprise, as they were sure that the new arrivals in Wehrmacht uniforms were customers looking for sex. The guards were executed quietly. Mundek and his team then stormed the palace, throwing hand grenades into all the rooms, instantly killing those inside.

In one room, they captured a couple: a Nazi officer and a girl. The girl grasped Mundek's hand and in Polish exclaimed, "I am Jewish!" He was shocked. She begged for her life and the life of her German lover. Tears welled up in his eyes and he eventually released them.[9]

While Mundek and his team stormed the palace, Anshel Bogner and his team prepared the demolition charges and explosives. After Mundek's team evacuated the palace, Bogner activated the explosives and demolished it.

---

7. Personal interviews with Aliza Segal, February 5, 2012, and April 17, 2012.
8. Personal interview with Dr. Isaac Weinberg, May 30, 2011.
9. Personal interviews with Aliza Segal, February 5, 2012, and April 17, 2012.

Chapter 23
Bunker 2

One of the worst-kept secrets in Ostrowiec was that Józef Kulpa was in contact with a group of Jewish partisans in the Dąbrowa woods. Shortly after Mundek Łukawiecki formed the Jewish hit squad, its numbers swelled to fifteen members, including Isaac Helman, Anshel Bogner, and two AK Spaleni members, Władi and Ludwik Żegowski from Lubaczów.

Many residents of Ostrowiec knew about a Jewish partisan group hiding in the forest. This endangered the partisans, as well as Józef Kulpa and his family. All someone had to do was decide to collect the Nazi reward being offered for turning over Jews and those who were helping them, and all their lives would be in jeopardy.

This was one of the reasons why Mundek moved his Jewish hit squad from the Dąbrowa woods (south of Lubaczów) to Ruda Różaniecka, part of the Puszcza Solska forest (north of Lubaczów). Another reason was to keep the fact that they were mainly a Jewish partisan group from the AK itself. They were able to do this because the name Łukawiecki did not reveal any links to Judaism. However, within Ostrowiec, everyone knew that they were primarily a Jewish group.

The third and most important reason for the change of location was the need to concentrate partisan forces in the Tomaszów Lubelski area.

It was therefore decided that the group would build two new hideouts outside of the Dąbrowa woods. One would be a logistical hideout manned by the seven non-fighting members; the second would house the eight "combat-ready" partisans. The logistical hideout was built not far from Ostrowiec, in the woods.

To ease the struggle with the cold as winter 1943–1944 arrived, Mundek decided to dig bunkers in the woods of Ruda Różaniecka.[1] Once again he found a young pine forest. He chose nearby pine trees with thick branches. They dug a

---

1. Personal interviews with Aliza Segal, February 5, 2012, and April 17, 2012.

square hole at a depth of nearly two meters, which was also two meters wide and two meters long. The hole was covered with wood beams brought from nearby woods that surrounded them, thereby creating a roof. The roof was covered with papa paper, which sealed it against water, and this in turn was covered entirely in soil. To further camouflage the bunker, it was covered with pine branches and vegetation. The entrance to the bunker was accessed by crawling under pine tree branches. They built three bunkers in this fashion.

The main problem was getting rid of the soil from digging the bunkers. They piled the remaining soil in five mounds, beneath thick pine trees to create the illusion of bunkers. The mounds were covered with pine branches and vegetation. The mounds were higher than the real bunkers, which were almost flat. The mounds were concentrated in one location, far away from the real hideouts. Mundek thought that the five false bunkers might exhaust searchers and discourage them from continuing searching for other bunkers in that region.

The intensive preparations for the winter paid off; none of Mundek's group got sick in spite of the severe weather.

The Janowskie wood was part of the Ruda Różaniecka series of woods. Janowskie was a young pine wood in the Puszcza Solska forest with trees over two

Left to right: Mundek Łukawiecki, Chana Bern, and Berish Brand consulting, summer 1944

meters tall, about forty kilometers (twenty-five miles) northwest of Lubaczów. Kulpa and Mundek decided to move the partisan operations to the Janowskie woods and build new bunkers for an assault force there. The bunkers they had constructed in the Dąbrowa woods in the Mazury forest (south of Lubaczów) would also remain intact and serve as a "rear bunker" for storing non-essential items, as well as extra food and clothing. They also decided to leave food supplies, such as chickens, rabbits, and potatoes, in the Dąbrowa bunkers. It was decided that the three youngest members of the partisan group would remain at the Dąbrowa campsite to guard it. They were told that if Nazis or Ukrainians appeared, they should not fight. Instead, they were instructed to run and hide until the other partisans returned.

Mundek Łukawiecki in the woods, spring 1944

The decision to move to the Janowskie woods also symbolized the transformation from passive partisan activities to an active participation in fighting the Germans for the Jewish hit squad. This was crystallized in the summer of 1943, when Mundek returned from a meeting with Kulpa. His eyes flashed with sparks of enthusiasm and joy. He seemed to be in a state of transcendence – full of vigor and energy.

"Friends," he began, "we are moving to other woods. We are not going to sit here like lame ducks and be caught by the Germans. We will not sit idly by and merely pray for our survival. Our families are watching us from above and calling on us to fight. We must prove to them that we can fight!"

Chana was quiet during Mundek's speech, but afterwards she softly murmured in Hebrew, "The voice of thy brother's blood crieth unto Me from the ground."[2] Tears streamed down all their faces. They were suddenly consumed with thoughts of their families, and with the knowledge that their struggle was analogous to that of David against Goliath.

The original Bór bunkers would actually remain their main campsite for the rest of the war. The new Janowskie site was meant to allow the armed unit of the Jewish hit squad to be based close to the fighting and military engagement theaters of Zamość. Being closer would give them flexibility to get in and out quickly for "hit and run" operations. The new site was to be an assault bunker, and as such it was a very spartan structure – they brought to that bunker only what was need for fighting. By contrast the Dąbrowa bunker was well appointed. It even had a library for the quieter, more leisurely times, as well as a synagogue. It was also close to Ostrowiec – a mere two kilometers' distance (just over a mile) – allowing them to return there easily for additional equipment or food, and when they needed to get in touch with Kulpa.

Kulpa was well acquainted with the commander of the AK in Tomaszów Lubelski and told him about a group of partisans that he supported in the Bór woods. The AK determined that communications with the group would continue to go only through Kulpa.

Mundek Łukawiecki and his partisans were expert bunker builders by the time they moved to the Janowskie woods. Their experience in the Dąbrowa woods had taught them how to build functional bunkers for fighting off the enemy. They dug three bunkers, hidden by pine tree branches. The bunkers were completely enveloped – ceiling, floor, and walls were all covered with wooden beams brought from nearby forests.

The bunkers were two meters deep and their roofs were parallel with the ground. The entrance to the bunkers was through a hatch, requiring the partisans to bend down and go through a narrow one-and-a-half-meter corridor that was

---

2. Genesis 4:10.

Mundek and an unidentified partisan conducting combat training in the field with hand grenades, summer 1944

built in an L-shape. Each bunker housed six beds, which were raised up off the ground. The beds were covered with vegetation to soften them. At the far side of the bunker, they built several shelves for storing food and water. There was no cooking inside for safety reasons; all food preparation was done outside. And there was no power supply or electricity – all light was supplied by oil lamps. The entrances to the bunkers' corridors were camouflaged and hidden behind dense vegetation that seemed impenetrable.

Lookout posts secured the bunkers and all group members used passwords, which were set up by Mundek. He also initiated daily weapons maintenance to ensure that the partisans cleaned and oiled their guns and other weaponry.

Another procedure created by Mundek was military and survival training. As the partisan group increased to fifteen members, it became essential to guide them through a basic training in survival in the woods and weaponry knowledge, as none of them had the slightest idea what they could or could not eat, and how to move without being detected in the forest. There were basic parameters for both day and night navigation in the woods and how to hike in inclement weather. It was essential to learn what is and isn't edible, how to prepare food in

Mundek and an unidentified partisan conducting combat training in the field, summer 1944. Mundek is in his full military gear and military backpack. The unidentified trainee is wearing a military uniform with backpack, and apparently is armed with a pistol (see holster).

the woods, how to build a fire without smoke, where to find a water supply – not to mention how to look after their own personal hygiene and waste – as these skills were all vital to surviving in the woods.

Basic military maneuvers and an understanding of field craft and weaponry were also essential knowledge for every partisan. Even the AK members who joined the Jewish hit squad needed this training. The four AK members (as well as the two former AK members) who joined the partisan group in the Janowskie woods were familiar with weaponry, but they still needed training in forest field craft and survival. In the past, these AK members would have returned home after carrying out their missions. Now that their homes had been burned down, they had to learn to be woodsmen.

Mundek instructed each member of the partisan group personally, according to the specific needs of the individual. He was very tough, strict, and demanding when it came to following his orders accurately. He was not patient when it came to mistakes and would not compromise when it came to training. There were many occasions when those on guard had to ask him to lower his voice for fear that the Nazis or Ukrainians might hear him yelling. Yet he continued training his

Part of the Jewish hit squad eating in the hideout, summer 1944. Left to right: unidentified, Anshel Bogner, unidentified, unidentified, Chana Bern, unidentified, Maurie Hoffman.

partisans until they did exactly what he instructed them to do. He would often yell at the partisans, "Our goal is to kill Germans and Ukrainians – not to eat potatoes!" Consequently, the other partisans feared and obeyed him completely. There were never any arguments, for they knew that only he could rescue them – he had the most in-depth knowledge of the woods and how to survive them.

Most of the partisans' operation orders were given to Mundek when he visited Kulpa. But sometimes they were also initiated by Mundek himself. It was Mundek's feeling that the group must be belligerent and proactive against the Nazis and Ukrainians. Not only to avenge the murders of their families as the Law of Moses ordered, "an eye for an eye and a tooth for a tooth,"[3] but also because they had to be an active force in helping to defeat the Nazis. Mundek often encouraged his partisans to think of themselves as an offensive force for the salvation of humankind itself.

It took them about one month to build the new campsite. Once it was finished, they began training in the Janowskie woods in order to conduct the raids

---

3. Exodus 21:24.

they were ordered to undertake. During the day they rested and at night they went back to the main campsite in the Dąbrowa woods.

This changed in early 1943, when the AK began concentrating large forces in the forests of Puszcza Solska to combat the Nazi plan to resettle Germans in the Zamość area. From that point forward, most of the Jewish hit squad spent their time in the Janowskie woods, until the Red Army liberated them in June 1944.

Chapter 24
Jaworów

Mundek Łukawiecki's eyes were fixated on the ground. He was completely lost in thought. Without even looking up, he muttered to his partisan group robotically: "Go get ready. It's time to collect payment." While the rest of the group stirred, Mundek remained motionless, his eyes still fixated on the ground.

Ludwik Żegowski from Ostrowiec was one of the non-Jewish members of the Jewish hit squad. He had just returned from an AK military court session in which he had testified. He relayed to the group that he had witnessed the execution of a Polish family – a father, mother, grandmother, and five children – by Nazi and Ukrainian military policemen in Jaworów. The family was executed because two young Jewish girls were caught hiding on their farm. The Jaworów police chief turned the family over to the Nazis for the "crime" of sheltering Jews. The Poles in the town were themselves a minority, whose numbers had been further reduced as a result of Ukrainian attacks. The remaining Poles were ordered to move from the region within a period of days and had to look for hiding places as well.

Before the Polish family's farm was set on fire, the Nazis invited the Ukrainian police chief who had incriminated them, together with his family, to loot the premises and take whatever they wanted as a reward. All the family members swooped in on the farm and picked it apart like vultures. This was a very generous reward, as usually only one-third of a property was given to be looted.[1] The two Jewish girls were shot on the spot. The following day, Jaworów was surrounded by members of the German order police and their auxiliaries. The rest of the Polish family was brought to the *rynek* – the marketplace – and executed by machine gun by a firing squad.

The echoes of the gunfire were heard all over Jaworów. Polish families shut

---

1. Roth, *Herrenmenschen*, pp. 224–25.

themselves in their homes and did not venture out. Ukrainian families, on the other hand, went out and watched the execution. No pleas helped the Polish family, not even the children crying and weeping. Nothing softened up the Nazi or Ukrainian police – they made sure that everybody in Jaworów knew that this was what happened to "Jewish sympathizers," in accordance with the law introduced by Hans Frank, governor of the General Government, on November 10, 1941, which stated that the death penalty was to apply to Poles who helped Jews "in any way."

Ludwik Żegowski was trembling as he told the story. After the execution, he went to the AK military court immediately and recounted the events. The military court had the authority to sentence those involved to capital punishment in absentia, and had done so in past cases like this. The court would convene and give its judgement after collecting more evidence and hearing more testimony. Ludwik was ordered to return the next day.

The next morning when Ludwik returned to court, he was told that the death penalty had been imposed on the Ukrainian police chief and all of his family, and that Łukawiecki's hit squad was to execute it.

Jaworów was about the same size as Lubaczów, a small town forty-five kilometers (twenty-eight miles) west-northwest of Lwów. After a brief, initial occupation by German forces in 1939, it was occupied for the second time when units of the German Seventeenth Army entered on June 25, 1941. The Germans were greeted with flowers and great enthusiasm by most Ukrainians.[2] Fifty percent of Jaworów's population was Ukrainian, and the headquarters for Bandera units (the OUN) was located two kilometers (just over a mile) from the town. The rest of the population was made up equally of Poles and Jews. All of the town's residents were peasants, who worked on and cultivated farms.

Since the Poles and Jews had a common enemy, their relationship was generally pretty good. They assisted and supported each other. In fact, most Jews had very close Polish friends. Some of these Jews found refuge at their Polish friends' homes. Such "collaboration" was unacceptable to the Ukrainians, and they did their utmost to expose and turn in any Poles who helped to hide Jews. This was a particular obsession of the Ukrainian chief of police in Jaworów, who lived on the outskirts of the town in a farmhouse with his family.

---

2. Dean, *Ghettos in German-Occupied Eastern Europe*, p. 784.

This was not the first time that the partisans had been ordered to execute collaborators guilty of turning in both Jews and those who dared help them. At the end of October 1942 – while he was in training with the Spaleni in the Dąbrowa woods – Mundek was instructed to execute a Ukrainian farmer in the Zwierzyniec-Zamość area for handing over Janina Sedlakowska to the Nazis because she hid Jews.

The second time, Józef Kulpa told Mundek to execute the gendarmerie commander of Nowy Majdan near Księżpol (nine kilometers or six miles south of Biłgoraj). The gendarmerie officer had murdered an entire Polish family on December 29, 1942, also because they were hiding Jews. Mundek carried out the execution wearing a Wehrmacht officer's uniform. He entered the gendarmerie office speaking fluent German, asking them for their help in capturing fugitives he had just seen nearby. A few moments after he entered the room, Mundek pulled out his pistol and fired two bullets from a short distance into the gendarmerie officer's chest.[3] Mundek quickly evacuated the room. The two AK members who accompanied him were waiting outside. In a matter of seconds, the three had disappeared into the nearby woods.

This would therefore be the third time that Mundek was involved in a "hit." He accepted the mission because the sentence seemed fair to him. Killing the police chief alone would not properly reflect the fact that the entire family had participated in the crime, therefore it was determined that the entire family would be liquidated and their farm set on fire in retaliation for what the Nazis had done. It would also send a strong message to anyone who was thinking of turning over Jews and Poles who helped them.

Before leaving for Jaworów, Mundek delivered instructions and a motivational speech to the group:

"We are a small group. We cannot and we should not try to kill all of Jaworów. We have to be as fast as lightning and as accurate as a surgeon. All of Jaworów

---

3. See Chaim Chefer, "Registry of over 700 Polish citizens killed while helping Jews during the Holocaust," http://www.holocaustforgotten.com/list.htm. In this registry the following persons from Majdan Nowy are mentioned as being executed December 29, 1942, for having helped Jews: no. 147, Józef Gniduła, age 70; no. 262, Katarzyna Kowal and no. 263, her son Józef Kowal; no. 344, Anastazja Łubiarz, age 43, and no. 345, and her mother-in-law Maria Łubiarz, age 76; no. 370, Anna Margol, age 50, cousin of Józef Gniduła. No. 592, Kazimierz Szabata, approximately age 40, was shot the previous day, mistakenly identified as the son of Anastazja Łubiarz.

and its surroundings should know that we killed this family as revenge for the Polish family and the Jewish girls.

"We also need to leave them with the impression that we are a big group of partisans. Therefore, all of us are going on this mission. We have three tasks: the first is to kill the whole family; then we need to confiscate all the food and other things that could be useful; lastly we have to set the farm on fire. This will ensure that everybody in Jaworów thinks twice about betraying Poles and Jews.

"The setup will be as follows: Chana and Berish, your task is to take care of the family. Anshel, you will go with me to take care of the chief. Weiner, Ludwik, and Władi, you will back up and block the entrance of the farm. The rest of you will assist us, if necessary. We are wearing Polish partisan uniforms so that they will think we are Polish partisans."

He stopped for a moment and continued: "The chief's house is close to the railway line near Jaworów. When we arrive there, everybody must immediately get into position. The raid will start when I give the owl call signal. When you hear that signal at the farm, make a lot of noise to make it seem that we are a very large military unit.

"After that, Anshel, Ludwik, and Władi will fire into the air and I will start shouting orders in Polish. The orders are not aimed at you. Do not pay attention to that. Now, let's go fight the devil!"

The group lined up in formation. Mundek Łukawiecki was at the front, followed by Anshel Bogner, who carried the machine gun. Those who had weapons stayed at the back. To create the illusion that they were armed and well equipped, Mundek had had the group design and make mock wooden rifles, pistols, and hand grenades – all painted black. This gave the impression that they were heavily armed.

When the group reached the railroad, they moved to their positions. Mundek gave the signal. They ran to and fro, making loud, stampeding noises, while Mundek shouted orders in Polish: "Władi, storm the farm with your company! Zygmunt, bring your company with me to the farmhouse! Marek, deploy your company and horses to block the farm entrance!"

All the while, Anshel, Ludwik, and Władi continued firing into the air.

The gate of the farmhouse was forced shut with a beam they found nearby. When Mundek, Chana, and their teams reached the residence door, Mundek kicked it open. There was no light on in the house, but because their eyesight was so acclimatized to darkness from living outside, they saw the family clearly anyway. The chief was in his underwear on one side of the room, while his wife and three children were huddled on the floor against the wall.

"I don't have to tell you that I will shoot you down if you move!" Mundek said in Polish.

The chief looked relieved that he was not killed instantaneously.

He asked Mundek in broken Polish, "What do you want from us? You know that I am the chief of police. I enforce the law. I never did anything wrong to a Pole."

After a short pause he continued, "On the contrary, I am the Poles' protector in Jaworów. You can ask every Polish family who lives here." He took a deep breath, sighed and continued, "We only cooperate with the Nazis so we can get arms and supplies – for no other reason!"

Mundek, Chana, and their teams remained quiet. Then Mundek spoke in fluent Ukrainian.

"Give us all of your arms and weapons, as well as all of your food."

Suddenly, his wife cried out and screamed that they didn't have anything to hand over. Her crying inspired the children to begin sobbing as well. Mundek quickly lost his temper and slapped her face.

"Quiet down and get it quickly or we'll kill all of you on the spot!"

Suddenly the room went silent. The chief of police stood up and told Mundek to follow him. Mundek was led to another room inside the house. The chief lifted up a few logs and revealed his weapons, consisting of two German guns, three German revolvers, a cache of bullets and ammunition, fifteen German hand grenades, a few smoke grenades, and a gas mask. Mundek ordered the Hoffman brothers and Isaac Helman to carry it all out. Then Mundek ordered the chief to show him his food storage. There they took potatoes, beef, eggs, sugar, flour, and oil – as much as they could possibly carry.

They brought the chief back to his family and Chana and her team executed them as they were ordered. On the way out, Mundek set the house on fire with hay and matches that they had brought with them. The entire operation took less than ten minutes. None of the Ukrainian neighbors tried to intervene in the raid. On the contrary, they stayed barricaded in their own homes.

As they were leaving Jaworów, three Ukrainian policemen from the local militia started dashing toward them. The partisans hid momentarily, ambushing them. At the same time, church bells began ringing in alarm. This helped to camouflage the sounds of the gunfight that was taking place.

The Ukrainian policemen were stripped of their clothes and weapons. Mundek ordered one of them to return to Jaworów and stop the firing. He pointed his Parabellum pistol at his head and said: "The Ukrainians are not our enemies. We were just retaliating against the murder of a Polish family, so we killed your chief of police and his family. They betrayed their Polish neighbors, as well as Jews. Consider this as a warning to all of you. As you can see, we are a very big formation. We can take Jaworów right now. But we aren't interested in that. As I already mentioned, we do not have any quarrel with Ukrainians. So go tell the people of Jaworów to stop firing immediately. You have five minutes. Otherwise we will storm Jaworów and kill your two friends. Tell everyone in town that if we have to come into Jaworów, we will kill all of you and set your houses ablaze. You can see that we have enough partisans eager to do the job!"

The policeman ran as fast as he could into town and shortly thereafter, the firing stopped. Then the partisans lived up to their word and freed the other two policemen.

Chapter 25
Chana's Pledge

On the morning of Friday, October 8, 1943, Chana Bern woke up restless. She and five other partisans had just returned to the Janowskie woods. The previous night, they had raided and burned the farmhouse of some ethnic Germans (Volksdeutsche) in Rapy Dylańskie, north of Biłgoraj. Despite their exhaustion, the partisans completed the fifty-kilometer (thirty-mile) trek back to the forest in two nights. When they arrived back at the bunker, Chana went to bed immediately – but she didn't sleep well.

She had an unusual vision that night. In it, her father Shimon and younger brother Hanoch were wearing white gowns. They stood silently, staring at her and smiling. Standing behind them were her mother Gittel Katz Bern and her younger sister Henye. Both of them were wearing special outfits reserved only for Sabbath and Jewish holidays. They all seemed so lifelike and real – and they appeared to be waiting for her.

Since her escape from the Lubaczów ghetto, Chana had had nightmares every night. Even if a dream started out pleasantly, it always ended up as a nightmare. She constantly dreamed about her family and their faith – and their execution at Dachnów. The dreams were always in black and white, but she could hear them as if they were in vibrant color. Their conversations seemed so genuine: the soft, gentle voice of her father, who spoke almost in a whisper; her mother's giggling and singing while doing the housework; the play fights with her siblings; the naughtiness of Hanoch, who often played instead of studying the holy books.

Important events, such as holidays and family gatherings, were often recreated in her dreams, as were her school and classmates. It was twenty-one years of living that seemed like a lifetime ago – if it had ever really existed at all. Right now, it all seemed imaginary. She was so far removed from that life that it seemed like it had never actually happened. Chana's nights were like a pendulum, constantly swinging between hallucinations and reality.

These nightmares repeated themselves over and over again in slow motion. Chana often woke up screaming. She could hear, even feel, her family's screams, weeping, and shouting. She rarely slept soundly. Quiet nights without the typical nightmares were few and far between. Yet she never spoke about these terrible specters. Only her moans, groans, and disturbed sleep attested to her agonized soul.

However, this last vision was unusual. It was neither a nightmare nor a dream. When she woke up at sunrise, she washed her hands and face with water from her canteen and started to prepare breakfast. All the while, she searched her soul.

It was only later that afternoon that Chana recalled and remembered her family's Sabbath evening customs. Her mother lit and prayed by the Sabbath candles, while she and Henye stood beside her. All three women covered their heads with white scarves. Her father and brother stood behind them, wearing the special Shabbat garb of the Hasidic dynasty of Belz.

After the candles were lit, the men went to the synagogue, which was on the other side of Mickiewicza Street. The girls waited with excitement for their return, which would mean the start of the evening Sabbath meal. While they waited, some of the girls from Chana's class in the Bais Yaakov school, such as Chana Strasberg, would come over. All the girls would inaugurate the Sabbath together by singing the mystical hymn by Shlomo Halevy Alkabetz, written in 1579: "My Beloved, let's greet the bride, let's welcome the Sabbath."

Suddenly, a cold sweat fell upon her.

"Today is Friday. And maybe it's even the eve of Yom Kippur or the eve of the Jewish New Year. This is what the dream meant! The family came to me in the dream to remind me of the holiness and sanctity of the day."[1]

Chana stood up and went to the bunker to get a prayer book, but it wasn't there. They had left it in the bunker in the Dąbrowa woods, the non-combat bunker. As evening approached, Chana emerged from the bunker carrying two oil lamps and a white silk slip. She placed the lamps at the entrance of the bunker on the soil and put the slip around her head, as if it were a headscarf. She lit

---

1. Chana was gifted with some sort of telepathy. In her later years in Israel, she had visions that proved to be true. In this case she was also correct: the night of Friday, October 8, 1943, was in fact Yom Kippur.

the lamps and stood in front of them with her eyes closed in silence for several minutes.

In low, hushed tones, Chana Bern began singing in Hebrew, trying to remember whatever she could from the liturgy that had once formed the rhythm of her days, a lifetime ago. She kept her eyes closed the entire time:

> My Beloved, let's greet the bride, let's welcome the Sabbath!
> "Observe" and "recall" in a single utterance
> We were made to hear by the One and only God.
> God is One and God's Name is One,
> In fame and splendor and praiseful song.
> My Beloved, let's greet the bride, let's welcome the Sabbath!
> Let us go to welcome the Sabbath,
> For she is the wellspring of blessing;
> From the start, from ancient times she was chosen,
> Last made, but first planned...

The Lukawiecki partisans were sitting in a small clearing among the pine trees, talking animatedly and eating. Mundek sat on a large wooden chair at the head of a small square table, while the other members of the group sat next to him near the table or on the ground. As Chana began to sing, the rest of the partisans fell silent. They were very moved and began to gather around Chana. After a short break, Chana continued singing in Hebrew from memory, as if a divine spirit had entered into her. Sporadically, fellow partisans joined her in singing:

> Peace upon you, ministering angels, angels of the divine,
> From the King of kings, the Holy One, blessed is He.
> Enter in peace, angels of peace, angels of the divine,
> From the King of kings, the Holy One, blessed is He.
> Bless me for peace, angels of peace, angels of the divine,
> From the King of kings, the Holy One, blessed is He.
> Depart in peace, angels of peace, angels of the divine,
> From the King of kings, the Holy One, blessed is He.

Without a pause, she started to sing the Aramaic text of the *Kol Nidrei* prayer, chanted on the evening of Yom Kippur. The rest of the Jewish partisans sang along or hummed the melody:

All vows and prohibitions and boycotts and anathemas and pledges of all names, which we have vowed, sworn, devoted, or bound on our souls – from this Day of Atonement, until the next Day of Atonement next year, may it arrive upon us in happiness – all of them will be void, deemed not to exist, invalid and not binding. The vows shall not be reckoned as vows, the prohibitions would not prohibit, nor would the oaths be considered as oaths.

The group was transfixed on Chana. All partisans gazed intently at her in awe and astonishment. She remained quiet again for several seconds, continuing to stand in the same place, without moving. The white slip still covered her head and shoulders. She did not open her eyes. Even the wren that normally prepared them for their night's sleep was calm. Then she spoke again, praying in her own words:

> In the valley of tears and darkness of night
> In the dead parade, I see you bright
> No shepherd gives light, shadows of death are tight
> The time is neither day nor night.
> Oh, family, I see you marching in the lane of death
> Ears and eyes are sealed, nobody stood in your path
> Each clod of ground soaked with blood, blood of the family crieth
> My soul cannot rest, I cannot have growth.
> Blot out their memories, was the fiat –
> No man to know their sepulcher, as a place to lament.
> No ash will remain, nor memory left;
> From the world of God, they should be wiped out.
> Voice of family's blood, howl unto me
> Day and night, as I sleep or am awake,
> I do not have a day or night
> The sun is burning me, the stares stabbing, I am in the pit.
> The voices are not going away, nor are they fading;
> They talk to me, they cry, they wail.
> Their language is understood, but sometimes is mumbling.
> They slice into my head, cut my soul, scratch my body.
> God turned His back on His people

In wrath He eagerly sent demons
To annihilate the Chosen One.
No remorse, no forgiveness, from infants to old men.
What sin of Judith?
Humanity is lost.
Demons are ruling.
Where is Almighty God?
We survived the valley of death, but we are in the wild.
We were left alive to walk out from the abyss.
We redeem ourselves from the plagues;
We must heal our minds and souls.
We are in the valley of darkness;
Let's not be afraid.
In remoteness, it seems already light.
Our souls have been forged.
Deadly foes were put to death for their own sins.
Fathers were not put to death for their children
Nor the children for their fathers;
Every man for his own transgressions.
Predators were beaten mercilessly –
A bloody price was charged, spirit was claimed.
Bravely we hurtle and strike our wrath
As manure beneath our feet becomes beasts of prey.
Families rest upon the Divine Presence's wings, forever kept.
Our remembrance is stronger than any rock, preserving faith.
Journeys of destruction will not break our faith to stand up,
Love righteousness, hate wickedness.
As today it is darkness, tomorrow will be bright.
We were left alone, but in our hands are our faith and hopes;
This will protect our ancestors and ourselves.
We must not become beasts, as our enemies.
Today and tomorrow, until the end of the war
We will continue to struggle.
Our fight for survival is not over;
Every moment and every day, danger is lurking.

After the war is over, we start our life from the beginning.
We will walk from darkness to brightness;
We will have families, raise children and grandchildren.
We must do that, not with hate, but with love and remembrance.
We should not forget, we should not forgive
But for our survival, we must also open our hearts
To include love and not just the rancorous.
Otherwise we will become as our foes.
Today we are masters of death.
We judge and implement extinction or redemption.
Tomorrow we must be masters of life.
We are not divine, but human with a lust for existence.
We are people walking in darkness, but we have seen great light.
We dwelt in the land of death, but grace shined upon us.
Those who want to live must be ready to die.
We are bound in affliction with an iron.
We break our bonds asunder;
We will close the gate of death.
This is our real strength, the secret of our existence,
Wallowing in the ashes of our forefathers and families:
The hope is the blood in our veins and the faith is our hearts.
No one can ever be beaten or destroyed.
And as it might be the eve of our Yom Kippur,
Pureness in our hearts gives proper spirit in me,
And with us, the survivors of our generation
Will dwell the revival of our nation.

The moment she finished, Chana collapsed on the ground and burst into tears. Her entire body was trembling. The partisans were hypnotized and paralyzed at the same time. None of them dared to say a word or move a muscle. They just continued staring at her intently. A few minutes later, Chana got up and without looking at the other partisans, she returned to the bunker to her bed – without removing the garment from her head.

Even after she went to bed, silence prevailed among the partisans. They did not know if it was the eve of the Sabbath or the eve of one of the Jewish High Holidays.

Mundek followed Chana into the bunker and returned after a few moments. In one hand he held Chana's hand and in the other he had a bottle of wine. Since the war began, they had not touched a drop of wine.

"Chana taught us an important lesson today," he said. "No matter what day it is, Chana emphasized the most important thing – the belief that we will overcome this and we will rehabilitate ourselves. Let's toast to this!"

He opened the bottle and poured out the wine into the partisans' cups. Mundek raised his glass and hugged Chana. They raised their cups and toasted, "To life!" Mundek would recall that this was the sweetest wine he ever tasted in his life.[2]

---

2. Personal interview with Dr. Isaac Weinberg, May 30, 2011, quoting conversations with Mundek Łukawiecki.

Chapter 26
The Bridge

The western boundary of the vast Ruda Różaniecka woods crossed near Osuchy, a deep ravine whose stream flowed into the San River, falling from a height of 250 meters down to 190 meters. The San River was a key waterway for the village of Łukowa. One of the village's main roads crossed the Osuchy Ravine via a bridge, which headed toward Wola Obszańska. The bridge was crucial, because it was the only way that vehicles could cross the ravine. This made the bridge tactically significant. The road overlapped the Puszcza Solska forest to the west, another factor that made it important for controlling vehicle movement in the area.

During World War II, the road became even more important as the Nazis started to use it to attack the partisans, who were fighting the German resettlement plan in the Zamość area. The Ruda Różaniecka woods were a key strategic site for the Jewish hit squad. The group often initiated raids from this area and would then return to it after fighting the Nazis.

Then came the day when the Jewish hit squad were ordered to demolish the bridge. They were told that an armored Nazi convoy crossed the bridge regularly, and it was therefore of vital importance that they take out the bridge – ideally while the convoy was still on it.

Mundek sent his deputy, Anshel Bogner, and four other partisans to blow up the bridge. The five-man assault team was to use a German mine that they had recovered from a Nazi military installation. Hand grenades would be used to detonate the mine. The assault team left the partisan bunker at night, after words of advice and a motivational speech had been delivered by Mundek. The rest of the group would pray for their safe return.

After an overnight excursion, the team arrived at daybreak. This made finding the bridge fairly easy, and also gave them ample time to set up the ambush. Anshel put two partisans on lookout. The first one situated himself on the bridge to see if it was being monitored by guards. To their surprise, the bridge had been left completely unguarded! Another of his tasks was to warn the team if any vehicle approached. Meanwhile, the second lookout situated himself about three hundred meters from the bridge. His job was to alert the group as the armored convoy approached. Anshel positioned the lookouts in such a way that they would be able to retreat from the area easily and make their way back to the bunker after blowing up the bridge.

Once the two lookouts were in position, the other three partisans assembled the demolition charge. Anshel picked a central part of the bridge to explode the mine. This was where the bridge supported the most weight and the point that had the least amount of engineering support. He felt that detonating the charge there would most certainly cause the bridge to collapse. He also decided that he would activate the delay fuse. So he mounted the charge and attached a two-meter delay fuse, calculating that this would give him about three and a half seconds to clear the area after the convoy approached the bridge. In their attempts to mount the charge, the men were interrupted several times as vehicles crossed the bridge. Eventually, however, everything was set up and ready. Now they had only to wait for the convoy.

At approximately two in the afternoon, the alert was sounded. Anshel quickly made his way to the demolition charge, activated it, and scurried to the spot where the other members had gathered. The armored convoy arrived and crossed the bridge without incident. Nothing happened! No explosion – nothing.

The group remained for two hours in hiding waiting for it to explode. After they were sure the charge was dead, Anshel went over to the explosive to see why it hadn't gone off as planned. He discovered that the delay fuse was defective; it had burned out before reaching the explosive.[1]

After the sun went down, they returned to the bunker. A few days later, they were sent back to try to blow up the bridge again. This time, however, they were equipped with an electric explosive, which they received from Władi, a demolitions expert. The same group – along with Władi – made their way back to the bridge. Once there, Anshel assigned the group members the same roles as on the first attempt. Then he and Władi mounted the charge at the center of the bridge, placing the electrical wire below it.

They waited in hiding for two hours. Suddenly, the alert was sounded. The

---

1. See also the description of Maurie Hoffman, in his book *Keep Yelling*, p. 163.

convoy approached, consisting of a tank in the front, then five trucks filled with soldiers, and then another tank bringing up the rear. When the lead tank reached the far side of the bridge, Władi ignited the charge. A deafening sound accompanied the bridge's collapse, as the tanks and trucks fell into the ravine below.

Anshel and his team did not stick around to count casualties. They were worried that some of the soldiers might have survived and would start a firefight, attracting attention. This time, they did not wait for nightfall to return to their bunker.

Chapter 27
Hitlerjugend

The partisan bunkers had been strategically dug out of a flat area of the woods. The only access to these bunkers was by crossing a bridge that arched over a canal. This made the bunkers easier to defend. An explosive device was located below the bunkers, enabling the partisans to blow up the bridge if the enemy tried to storm the site.

It was April 1944 when the Jewish hit squad spotted German soldiers marching on the road directly in front of their hideout. Fortunately, they were not in combat formation or readying for an assault. In fact, they were walking rather informally for a military unit. No one appeared to be in command, and although they wore their full military uniforms, their rifles were slung carelessly over their shoulders.

Nevertheless, the eight young Wehrmacht soldiers posed a serious threat to the partisans as they made their way toward the bridge. Mundek ordered the group to take their predetermined battle positions and wait. He thought that the Nazis might be lulling them into complacency – that this was perhaps some new tactical maneuver designed to minimize their attention and readiness. Ludwik, who was responsible for blowing up the bridge in emergency situations, was told to get ready.

Mundek moved very quickly and quietly. He managed to get behind the soldiers before they reached the bridge. "Drop to the ground right now! You are surrounded by partisans!" he shouted in German.

The young soldiers did as they were told. All of them were quickly on their stomachs, face down with their hands clasped behind their necks. As soon as the partisans saw them surrender, they streamed out of the bunkers and disarmed them.

One of the soldiers asked to speak to Mundek and told him that they were from the Hitlerjugend battalions.[1] He said that the Hitlerjugend battalions were now fighting alongside the Wehrmacht in Stalingrad. This was taken as a sign of Hitler's despair and desperation. The Nazis were being defeated in Russia. Indeed, the Wehrmacht were actually retreating as the Red Army advanced.

This story didn't seem to make sense. How could the Hitlerjugend be fighting in Stalingrad? There had been a sports club for Hitlerjugend in Lubaczów: Towarzystwo Gimnastyczne "Sokół" (school) in Mickiewicza Street. Mundek knew that the Hitlerjugend were not fighters or army combatants.

The young soldier continued and told Mundek that German soldiers felt betrayed by Hitler, as the Third Reich was exposing retreating soldiers and condemning them to death. This was why he and his fellow soldiers were fleeing their unit and defecting. He stated that he would be willing to join the partisans and fight with them – shoulder to shoulder against the Nazis.

He then made the mistake of comparing his group to the partisans. He felt that they both spoke a common language, as fighters, and that each should understand the other.

At this, Mundek flew into a fit of rage that the soldier had the audacity to compare himself to the partisans. He jumped on him and in a moment of uncontrollable anger, beat him senseless.

"How dare you compare yourself to me? You murdered our families. You massacred them like animals – and now you try to convince me that you are like us?! You are a bunch of bloody dogs. I am going to kill all of you!"

The soldiers began to cry and beg for their lives.

"Please forgive us. We are not real Nazis. We are just simple Germans who became mixed up in the war. We are not on the side of the Nazis – we are against

---

1. The Hitlerjugend originally was the youth organization of the Nazi Party (NSDAP). After the Nazis came to power, the Hitlerjugend became a state youth organization. Part of the duty was a paramilitary training. But they were not combatants. Younger members became combatants only as part of other units, especially the Volkssturm 1944/45 or as Luftwaffenhelfer. The older ones were regularly drafted to the Wehrmacht or Waffen-SS, or served as volunteers. If they volunteered under the age of eighteen (it was allowed from the age of sixteen), they remained members of the Hitlerjugend as well, until they reached age eighteen. In the General Government areas, there were also Hitlerjugend, but only in places with a significant number of German families.

them! We did not harm anybody. All we want is to return home safely. Our mothers and fathers are waiting for us, as yours are waiting for your return."

When he heard this comparison, Mundek became enraged. His face turned beet red. He jumped on top of the soldier who had spoken and beat him with his fists and kicked him with incredible fury.

When he caught his breath, he shouted: "You bastards! Nobody is waiting for us! We do not have mothers and fathers anymore. We have no siblings. We do not have aunts and uncles. We do not have anywhere to go. You killed them. You murdered them. You destroyed our homes and destroyed our lives. You expect us to have compassion for you. You did not have any mercy on us, no pity, no clemency. You killed us like animals!"

Mundek whipped out his Parabellum pistol from his belt, cocked it and fired all of the bullets into the soldier's head. He then replaced the magazine and continued firing until all the German soldiers were dead. The other partisans joined in and also began shooting the soldiers from very close range. It was all over in a couple of minutes. When they had finished discharging their weapons, the partisans collapsed on the ground, very close to the bodies that now lay dead.

Before sunset, Chana instructed her compatriots to strip the dead soldiers of their uniforms, boots, and any other documents they could find. They discovered that each soldier had a swastika tattooed under his armpit.

They did not want to leave the bodies near their bunker, for sanitary reasons and because it might also give away their hiding spot. Once they had taken what they needed, therefore, the partisans lifted the dead bodies – one body between every two partisans – and began to head out to the main road leading to Zamość. It was a long, difficult, and arduous journey, as they had to stop and rest every few kilometers. It was not easy for two partisans together to carry a dead soldier between them, as Mundek had instructed.

After dumping the bodies, the partisans reviewed the papers they had found on the soldiers. These proved that they were regular Wehrmacht soldiers and not part of the Hitlerjugend, as they had claimed to be.

Chapter 28
Air and Canon Bombardment

For a good part of 1943, neither Nazi soldiers nor Ukrainian policemen dared to enter the partisans' woods. In fact, the Germans had lost control of the woods entirely by late summer of that year. This loss of control – especially in the forests – meant the reduction and then the cessation of enemy activities against the partisans. German military activity was limited solely to towns and villages. Fearing for their safety, Nazi troops no longer roamed freely, but only in secure convoys.

The partisans noticed the changes in enemy behavior immediately. All of a sudden, they were able to move relatively freely through the woods and surrounding areas, without the constant threat of attack. Partisan commanders began acting as if they controlled a sovereign state. They relished their newfound power and found it easier to recruit more volunteers, as well as to acquire more food, weapons, and ammunition.

The partisans, especially the AK, felt that large parts of the area in the south of Lublin – particularly the areas around Zamość, Hrubieszów, and Biłgoraj – were under the complete and absolute rule of the partisans, and as a result it was dubbed "Partisan Land."[1] The partisans were now the protectors of the towns and villages, and resolved conflicts and disputes within the area. In fact, the partisans began overseeing law and order in the villages and towns – with the full consent of the area's residents.

However, the AK overestimated its power. The German police was still able to arrest and kill people in the villages. Within the framework of the big German anti-partisan operations, which reached their peak in 1943–1944, there were

---

1. In Polish, "Partyzancki kraj." See for example Jerzy Markiewicz's book, *Partyzancki kraj: Zamojszczyzna 1 i 1944–15 vi 1944* [Partisan Land: The Zamość Region January 1, 1944–June 15, 1944] (Lublin: Wydawnictwo Lubelskie, 1980).

assaults against partisans in this area, and especially in June 1944 when the German troops were cleansing the area in preparation for the advancing frontline. There were heavy fights,[2] and from June 15, 1944, the Germans started a massive assault using tanks against AK partisans in the surrounding areas.[3]

The Nazis did find one strategically sound way to fight the partisans. They used air bombardments, together with canon and mortar shelling. The air force played a minor role. When the Germans discovered partisan camps or hideouts, they targeted them with both canons and mortars or through air raids. Fortunately, the aerial and ground bombardments were never followed by an assault force, such as infantry soldiers.

The typical air raid was done by either one aircraft or a formation of planes, which dropped its bombs and then flew away. Sometimes after the bombardment, the planes would make another sortie and attack using machine-gun fire. This was more effective than the canon and mortar shelling, which had minimal impact on the partisan camps.

The Nazis' loss of their grip on the forest areas south of Lublin and the consequent threat posed to them in entering the woods known as "Partisan Land" was caused in part due to a lack of reliable intelligence. Field intelligence supplied from Ukrainian sources aimed to escalate the Polish-Russian threat and danger, and was a tool used by the Ukrainians to manipulate the Germans to support the Ukrainian national struggle. Polish sources exaggerated their information, as this then allowed them to claim that they had been forced to assist the partisans and were unable to refuse due to their large numbers. This provided them with an excuse for giving assistance and therefore the hope of gaining a pardon.

For example, the arrival of a partisan company to Lisie Jamy to get support was falsely described to the Germans; the Germans were told that three hundred partisans had raided the towm, some of them riding horses and operating horse wagons to carry away the things they took from the villagers. Actually, there were about forty partisans, without any horses or wagons.

The impact of this kind of false information was that the Germans totally

---

2. See mentions of Sturmwind I and II above in chapters 16 and 17. And see also the example of Kotlice in the Zamość area, in Waldemar Bednarski, "Das Gesicht des Krieges in der Gemeinde Kotlice (Kreis Zamość)" [The face of war in the municipality of Kotlice (Zamość county), 1939–1945], in Die polnische Heimatarmee, ed. Bernhard Chiari, pp. 412–29.
3. Bednarski, "Das Gesicht des Krieges in der Gemeinde Kotlice," p. 427.

overestimated the size of the partisan forces. The Nazis began to believe that a large number of partisans must be hiding in the forest, and reacted by heavily barraging and shelling a large forest where they believed three hundred partisans would hide – while in fact, the small company was hiding in a small forest that was used as a tree nursery.

In addition, the Nazis' reliance on unreliable sources that magnified the partisans' strength and activities resulted in the Nazis adopting extreme precautionary measures that were disproportionate to the actual number of partisans, such as restrictions on the free movement of Nazi vehicles.

Chapter 29
Scorched Earth

A Ukrainian state was not formed after World War I. Poland was the national winner, receiving a tremendous part of the areas where Ukrainians lived as either a majority or minority. Radical Ukrainian nationalists wanted not only their own Ukrainian state, but also a national homogeny. Since Poles constituted about one third of the population of East Galicia, Wołyń, and the eastern areas of Lublin – all of which were part of Poland between World War I and II – the Poles were seen as a major threat to Ukrainian ethnic homogeneity,[1] as the Ukrainians wanted to transform those areas where Ukrainians made up a significant part of the population into national homogenous areas as part of a new Ukrainian state.

Politically the only potential ally was Germany. However, the Ukrainian dream of a state wasn't fulfilled in the summer of 1941, and was in fact destroyed by the brutal persecution of the Nazis, following which the Ukrainian nationalist party Organizacja Nacjonalistów Ukrainskich (OUN), along with its military wing the UPA, fought against the German occupiers.

Then, in March 1943, the murder and expulsion of Polish residents in Wołyń began as the German security system partly collapsed. Thousands of the Ukrainian Auxiliary Police and other units subordinated to the Germans now deserted and strengthened the Ukrainian nationalist underground. A situation of civil war developed, including genocidal cleansing and killings. The OUN was burning crops and destroying infrastructure such as shelters, transportation, bridges, and communications lines. More than one third of all dwellings in the area were demolished. The Nazis supported the Ukrainians by issuing false

---

1. Timothy Snyder, "'To Resolve the Ukrainian Problem Once and for All': The Ethnic Cleansing of Ukrainians in Poland, 1943–1947," *Journal of Cold War Studies* 1, no. 2 (spring 1999): 86–120.

reports stating that AK members had burned down dozens of Ukrainian villages, killing fifteen hundred Ukrainians.²

The situation in East Galicia resurrected the desire to form an independent Ukrainian state that extended from Jarosław and Przemyśl to the San River, following the establishment of control over a substantial rural area.³ The OUN called on all Poles to leave "Ukrainian lands" and relocate to the other side of the Bug River. Later this declared boundary was changed to the San River, which was even further east.

In the spring and summer of 1943, at least forty thousand Poles were killed by Ukrainian partisans, UPA combatants, and local Ukrainian peasants. This terror made many Poles flee to the west. The UPA tried to create a fait accompli. Needless to say, it wasn't necessary to get rid of the Jews, as by that point they had already been murdered by the Nazis and their domestic collaborators.⁴

The AK tried desperately to defend the Polish minority – which had already been weakened by Soviet deportations to Siberia and Kazakhstan in 1939–1941 – against the UPA. By this point the Germans were in retreat, but remaining German forces did not try to stop the UPA's rampage and even cooperated for tactical reasons.⁵

Due to the weakening of German control in East Galicia and in parts of the Lublin District during 1943, Ukrainian nationalists tried to force Polish peasants to evacuate their land so they could take over their farms. For example, in the Wołyń area, Polish villages were attacked and the inhabitants were killed. Farms

---

2. Bernhard Chiari, "Grenzen deutscher Herrschaft: Voraussetzungen und Folgen der Besatzung in der Sowjetunion" [The boundaries of German rule: Conditions and consequences of the occupation in the Soviet Union], in *Das Deutsche Reich und der Zweite Weltkrieg* [The German Reich and the Second World War], ed. Jörg Echternkamp, vol. 9, bk. 2, *Ausbeutung, Deutungen, Ausgrenzung* [Exploitation, interpretations, exclusion] (Stuttgart: Deutsche Verlags-Anstalt, 2005), pp. 951–52.
3. The slogan was "Poles behind the San."
4. Galicia had already been cleansed of Jews.
5. See Snyder, "'To Resolve the Ukrainian Problem Once and for All,'" 86–100; Tadeusz Piotrowski, *Poland's Holocaust: Ethnic Strife, Collaboration with Occupying Forces and Genocide in the Second Republic, 1918–1947* (London: McFarland, 1998), p. 248; Bernhard Chiari, "Die Ukraine im Spannungsfeld von Nationsbildung und deutscher Herrschaft" [The Ukraine in conflict between nation-building and German domination], in *Das Deutsche Reich und der Zweite Weltkrieg* [The German Reich and the Second World War], ed. Jörg Echternkamp, vol. 9, bk. 2, *Ausbeutung, Deutungen, Ausgrenzung* [Exploitation, interpretations, exclusion] (Stuttgart: Deutsche Verlags-Anstalt, 2005), pp. 942–54.

and homes were burned. The AK and their allies tried to protect the Polish population in these locations, where Poles weren't even a minority. The situation worsened in 1944 as Soviet troops advanced and the UPA swept in and strengthened the local Ukrainian nationalists. In many places there was a two-front war for the AK – on the one hand against the Germans, and on the other hand against the UPA. In 1944 in the counties of Lubaczów, Hrubieszów, and Tomaszów Lubelski, the AK took revenge for the UPA's depredations and burned dozens of Ukrainian villages and probably killed fifteen hundred Ukrainians.

The UPA terrorized Polish villages and farms, annihilating all who resisted. Thousands of Poles were murdered. Hundreds of farms and villages were burned or destroyed. Polish assets and goods were looted and confiscated. This initiative was taken by organized UPA units[6] and local Ukrainian peasants armed with axes, pitchforks, and scythes. The UPA was reinforced and armed by the Germans via the Ukrainian volunteer Fourteenth Waffen-SS Galicia Division (Galicia is "Halychyna" in Ukrainian; the unit in German was called the SS-Freiwilligen Division "Galizien") as well as the Ukrainian partisans and the Kovpak First Ukrainian Partisan Division, known as "Sidor Kovpak."[7]

The retreating Wehrmacht followed the Nazi scorched earth policy. They aimed to destroy anything that might be of help or useful to the advancing Red Army. With great determination, local peasants organized their self-defense as the Nazis attempted to destroy everything in their path as they retreated back to Germany. Primarily, the self-defense units were made up of AK members and Batalionów Chłopskich,[8] as well as units of Soviet partisans.

At first, the AK established a regional self-defense command.[9] They initiated the evacuation of towns, villages, and farms such as Cieszanów and Lubaczów, since they were impossible to protect.[10] Lubaczów, for example, was evacuated

---

6. Piotrowski, *Genocide and Rescue in Wołyń*, p. 195.
7. Markiewicz, *Partyzancki kraj*, pp. 51–73n48, p. 76, quoting Mieczyslaw Juchniewicz, "Kowpakowcy w Polsce," in *Wojskowy Przegląd Historyczny* [Military history review] 3, no. 4 (1958): 156n9. See also Caban, *Związek Walki Zbrojnej Armia Krajowa*, p. 93.
8. The Peasant Battalions, an underground movement affiliated with the AK.
9. Snyder, "'To Resolve the Ukrainian Problem Once and for All,'" pp. 86–120.
10. Markiewicz, *Partyzancki kraj*, p. 264; and see August Fenczak, Zdzisław Konieczny, and Elżbieta Forbot, *Źródła do dziejów regionu przemyskiego w latach 1944–1949* [Sources for the history of the Przemyśl region in the years 1944–1949] (Przemyśl: Wojewódzkie Archiwum Państwowe w Przemyślu, 1979), p. 67.

in April 1944. Cieszanów was burned down in May 1944, after which the Ukrainians took control of it.

Fighting the UPA was the top priority of the Tomaszów Lubelski AK in 1944. AK units in Tomaszów Lubelski – under the command of Marian Warda – undertook operations against Ukrainian units, disobeying the explicit instructions of AK headquarters.[11] The AK in Tomaszów Lubelski conducted 246 operations in Zamość, which made up just 29 percent of all its actions against the UPA.[12] As a result of this intense fighting, Tomaszów Lubelski AK casualties were very heavy and considerably higher than in any other units; between 1940 and 1945, approximately 368 AK members of Tomaszów Lubelski were killed in battle.[13] The warfare conducted by the Tomaszów Lubelski AK was a two-front fight. One front took on the Nazis and the second battled the Ukrainian UPA.

The Ukrainians were particularly cruel to the civilian population in East Galicia, but they were even harder on AK members when they got hold of them; most were murdered immediately or handed over to the Gestapo, where their fate was sealed.[14]

The AK assigned the Łukawiecki partisans to partake in various activities against Nazi and Ukrainian targets. On one occasion, the Łukawiecki partisans were given the task of ambushing and assaulting a truck full of gendarmes on the road to Ruda Żurawiecka, a village situated about fifteen kilometers (nine miles) east of Bełżec. The gendarmes were rushing to rescue a Ukrainian police station in Ruda Żurawiecka that was supposedly under attack.

Two partisans fired on the police station to make it seem like it was the precursor to a major raid. The goal was to draw the gendarmerie reinforcement into the ambush, after which they would encounter a killing zone a couple of kilometers before Ruda Żurawiecka, set up by the partisans.

Less than half an hour after they arrived, a Tatra T27 police truck approached, carrying twenty gendarmes. Mundek used a hand grenade to stop the truck. This was the signal to start the operation. A couple of machine guns from the flanks

---

11. Caban, *Na dwa fronty*, p. 288.
12. Ibid., p. 10.
13. Ibid., p. 12.
14. For example, on January 4, 1944, twenty AK members were captured in Mircze and handed over to the Gestapo. They were then imprisoned in Majdanek and killed. Also on January 15, 1944, eleven AK members were killed in Paniow.

killed the gendarmes in just a few minutes. It all happened so quickly that the gendarmes did not even have time to return fire or escape from the truck. When the mission was complete, the partisans looted the truck and took weapons, ammunition, and any armaments they could find. They also stripped a few of the gendarmes of their uniforms and boots. The two partisans who had conducted the diversion at the beginning of the operation, Ludwik and Weiner, then met up with the main strike group back at the bunker.

Another operation targeted a permanent roadblock that had been deployed as a garrison on the road and for the railroad, about nine kilometers (six miles) along the highway west from Zamość – not far from the junction to Kąty Pierwsze. The road was blocked by German policemen and Ukrainian Auxiliary Police, including members of the Schupo. This roadblock was a perfect target for a retaliatory raid against both the Nazis and Ukrainians.

For this operation, all partisans were instructed to wear either a German Wehrmacht uniform or a German police uniform.[15] The operational plan was to approach the roadblock from the south, while the decoy, Kąty Drugie, would be walking in the woods. The assault was set up so that Maurie Hoffman and Berger would block the road to Wielącza, while Weiner and Berish Brand would block the road to Zamość. The rest of the group would then assault the roadblock garrison.

The assault plan required Mundek and Ludwik to approach the garrison wearing a German Wehrmacht uniform and a Ukrainian Auxiliary Police uniform, respectively. Then from a very close distance, they were to shoot the guards at the road block. At that exact moment, the rest of the partisan assault force would regroup south of the building occupied by the garrison. Commanded by Anshel Bogner, they were to attack and storm the garrison with hand grenades. Once the enemy was overcome, the building would be blown up by Władi. The partisans would then move back into the woods. The raid was set for sunrise, as traffic on the road was scarce and the garrison would be less prepared, making it the best time for a surprise attack.

After the two blocking teams had deployed themselves and were settled and

---

15. Bór-Komorowski, *The Secret Army*, p. 152, says that "The best method was to have our men dressed up in either Wehrmacht or SS uniforms." These methods were very popular and were used by various underground units, including the Łukawiecki partisans. See Hoffman, *Keep Yelling*, pp. 122, 187.

ready, Mundek and Ludwik approached the two policemen in charge of the roadblock. They were Ukrainian and did not speak German. In fluent German, Mundek asked them about the commander in chief of the roadblock. Before they could answer, Mundek and Ludwik gunned them down at very close range.

The garrison never had a chance to dig in and fight back. In a matter of seconds, Anshel threw a hand grenade into the garrison room. It exploded immediately. Those who survived did not shoot back; they weren't able to figure out who was friend or foe amidst all the commotion. By the time the Ukrainians came to their senses thirty minutes later, the delay cord had already been activated and the building exploded. The entire operation took less than ten minutes, giving the partisans plenty of time to retreat deep into the woods before the explosion went off.

As outlined earlier, there were also a few occasions when the Łukawiecki partisans were ordered to execute Polish collaborators who had handed over Jews to the Nazis in the Zamość area. In a few cases, they were ethnic Germans (Volksdeutsche) or Ukrainians. These missions gave the partisans the feeling of payback, so there was little doubt that these targeted killings would be accomplished successfully.

Targets were normally local Polish peasants who were being rewarded by the Nazis for their assistance by being allowed to stay on their farms. The Ukrainians were also ordered not to harm them. These Nazi rewards meant that there were incentives for collaboration. Nevertheless, the AK could not accept or ignore such collaboration.

The execution of collaborators was performed simply. A hit team of five partisans was ordered to execute the mission. The hit squad – wearing the German Wehrmacht uniform – went to the preselected execution site. This was normally deep in the woods, surrounded by plenty of trees. The site was also close to the collaborator's farm. The hit squad always operated at night. They would wait at the execution site while Mundek went to the residence building of the farm and asked the collaborator to step outside for a short talk. As Mundek led the collaborator outside, the hit squad would jump on the collaborator and tie his hands and legs.

When they reached the execution site, the collaborator would be ordered to get down on his knees. One of the partisans would inform the collaborator that a court of the Polish people had found him guilty of treason for handing over

Poles and Jews to the enemies of Poland.[16] As a result, the court had sentenced the collaborator to death by firing squad. Without any further delay, the collaborator was then shot by three partisan group members at close range. The hit squad would then evacuate the site as quickly as possible.[17]

Retaliatory raids against resettlements in the Zamość area, as dictated by the Nazis' Generalplan Ost (master plan for the east), were relatively easy to perform since they were executed against the civilian or semi-civilian population – those who had settled in the area. The main purpose of this kind of activity was to terrorize the settlers and cause them to leave or abandon the idea of resettling there. Since these operations were aimed at the civilian population, causing personal and physical injury was prohibited – unless it was absolutely necessary or if a partisan's life was in danger.

The most common type of action and most acceptable method of getting settlers to leave was to raid a farm that had been taken over by a German family. After the entire family was outside, the farm was burned down with all of its contents and possessions in it. The livestock, including cows and horses, were released before the fire was set. Again, the best time to execute these raids was sunrise, since the family would not be fully awake and this made it relatively easy to capture them.

These raids were carried out against isolated farms in particular, located in relatively remote sites where they could not call for German or Ukrainian military assistance very easily. Settler resistance was relatively minimal and rare, although some of them who were former military personnel put up a fight. The impact of the fires on the farms was seen by other settlers and sent out a clear warning message.

East Galicia and the areas south and east of Lublin were the AK's main theater of sabotage against the Nazis, although the AK carried out thousands of operations all over Poland, performed "by a small number of hand-picked men and women."[18] The AK was expert in tying down German and Ukrainian forces.

---

16. Handing over Jews was added by the partisans and was not part of the AK formal announcement.
17. See Markiewicz, *Partyzancki kraj*, p. 251, where he mentions these hits only in general terms.
18. War Cabinet Report of the Foreign Office, February 17, 1943, The National Archives (TNA) WP (43) 69. As this report was written in February 1943, it indicates knowledge of the Jewish extermination.

Its members engaged in sabotaging railroads, as well as clashing with Nazi units and their Ukrainian collaborators.

Operations against Nazi and Ukrainian targets continued well into the spring of 1944. The AK blew up ammunition and weapon depots near Tomaszów Lubelski. They burned down German stables after the horses were released. Another common tactic was dismantling railroads, which caused trains to derail. In addition, they also undermined railroad tracks while trains were crossing, as well as carrying out numerous attacks on trains near Susiec.

On March 16, 1944, on the road from Tomaszów Lubelski to Łaszczów to Dołchobyczów, next to the village of Nowosiółki, the Jewish hit squad carried out an ambush of German soldiers, and a second ambush the following day, next to Wirkowice in the Zamość area.[19]

Nazis reacted to such operations publicly by executing AK members and Poles. For example, on February 1, 1944, thirty AK members were publicly executed in the village of Potoczek. All Polish residents were forced to attend the execution as spectators. The German officer in charge told the Poles in attendance that Polish civilians had been executed earlier. Later that month, as collective punishment, the Gestapo publicly murdered a group of Poles in order to intimidate and deter the activities of any and all Polish underground movements.

In the action near Zamość, which was a combined operation of the Jewish hit squad and AK members from Lubaczów, Mundek was wounded very severely in both his legs and could not walk. The son of Józef Kulpa, Stanisław Kulpa, who had participated in the assault as an AK warrior, carried Mundek on his shoulders all the way to the *znachor* in Lipsko. The *znachor* operated on Mundek, pulling out a bullet and bandaging the wounds. Immediately after the medical treatment was over, Mundek and Stanisław left. In spite of his loss of blood and the bandages on his wounds, Mundek refused to be carried but insisted on walking back to the bunker.[20]

---

19. Markiewicz, *Partyzancki kraj*, pp. 124, 209, 210.
20. Personal interview with Janusz Kulpa, January 2012. Part of the story was told to Janusz Kulpa by Mundek in a telephone conversation on July 19, 1997.

Chapter 30
Caught with Trousers Down

Although Jews were never considered important by the Nazis, from time to time certain groups or individual Jews would receive a special status when their work was deemed critical for the Nazi war effort. Such was the case of the Borysław oil workers. Borysław had been in the hands of the USSR following the 1939 Molotov-Ribbentrop Non-Aggression Pact,[1] but the Germans retook it in June 1941.[2]

Borysław, nicknamed "Polish Baku," was the home of a burgeoning oil industry. In fact, one of the world's first oil rigs was built there. It was the center of Polish oil refining and one of the most important industrial zones in all of Poland. At the beginning of the twentieth century, oil production was at approximately two million tons – about 5 percent of world production. In 1925, about 80 percent of Polish oil (812,000 tons) was produced in Borysław.

It's no wonder then that the Nazis saw Borysław as one of the most important strategic cities for its war machine.

When the Red Army retreated during the 1941 Nazi invasion of Borysław, it set fire to oil wells, destroyed the power station, and executed Ukrainian prisoners. That led to a pogrom against Jews by Ukrainian nationalists that became known as "Bandera Day,"[3] since the Jews were blamed for the Russian crimes. It was on "Bandera Day" that the annihilation of Borysław's Jews began. On November 27, 1941, a systematic, three-day liquidation began, as German and Ukrainian soldiers executed fifteen hundred Jews. The atrocities and horrors continued without stop and a ghetto was soon formed. About 75 percent of Borysław's Jews were ultimately wiped out.

---

1. The events described in this chapter are taken from an interview with Joseph Rand, the son of Isaac Rand.
2. Borysław today falls within Ukrainian borders.
3. See the pogrom in Lwów (also named after Bandera) in chapter 6, "The Death of Humanity."

The Jews who worked in the petroleum industry, however, were relatively well protected. With the permission of the Nazis, the Beskidian Oil Company[4] selected the workers it needed for its oil refining process, which was now part of the German war effort. The one thousand selected Jewish workers received a certificate called "R" (for *Ruestungsindustrie,* meaning "armaments industry") attached to their chests.

The "R" certificate came with ID and promised immunity from persecutions and, thus, a chance of survival. These Jews were subsequently sent to a *Zwangsarbeitslager* (forced labor camp), which was surrounded by barbed wire and guarded by the Ukrainian Police. The labor camp became known as the *koszary* ("barracks" in Polish). Two of Mundek's relatives from his mother's side received the "R" certificate. The first was engineer Mauritius Ringler,[5] a world-renowned expert in oil drilling and mining, who patented hundreds of innovations in the oil industry. The second was Isaac Rand.

Not all the "R" workers were permitted to bring their wives and families to the "barracks." Even those who were allowed to bring their families did not do so, as they mistrusted the Nazis and preferred to keep them hidden in separate sites.

All the "R" workers knew that they and their families were doomed to death, sooner or later; the "R" certificate merely postponed the inevitable. One way of surviving in the long term, though, was to build a bunker in the woods for hiding when the time came.

Isaac Rand and his wife Regina did just that. They started to dig a hideout after they survived the largest Aktion in August 1942, in which five thousand Jews were deported to Bełżec. Since it was summertime, it made it easier to construct the hideout. They had to carry away the extra soil and disperse it in the woods where it would not look suspicious. The wooden hideout was hidden by pine branches. Isaac brought in sleeping bunks and a small stove from one of the huts

---

4. Renamed later the Carpathian Oil Company. During WWII, the company operated the oil fields in Borysław. The director-general of the company, Berthold Beitz, together with his wife Else, saved Jews and placed themselves at considerable risk. They were awarded as Righteous Among the Nations by Yad Vashem.
5. After several immigration requests were rejected due to security concerns relayed by the Communist Poles, he left Poland for Israel in 1958 and settled in the city of Ashkelon. He owned a factory there that produced drilling systems for the oil industry.

next to the oil rig. In addition, some pots, spoons, forks, and knives were kept there, as well as heating materials, food, and containers of water.

It took the Rand couple almost a month to build their bunker in the woods, as they only worked in the cover of night. During this time, they consulted with Mundek Łukawiecki, who visited them on occasion, although Borysław was 120 kilometers away from Lubaczów and seventy kilometers (about forty-five miles) south of Lwów.

Isaac visited his wife in the bunker often, whenever it was possible for him to sneak away from the "barracks," usually at night. Weekends were easier, as the Ukrainian guards imbibed alcoholic drinks on Saturdays and Sundays. What's more, the outdoor activities of the local peasants more or less ceased, as they rested in their homes and prepared themselves for Sunday mass. In this way, Isaac supplied his wife with all the necessities of life such as food, water, and essential supplies. In the beginning, only Regina hid there permanently; the plan was for Isaac to join Regina as soon as his "R" certificate expired.

Regina was not the only Jew hiding in the woods. There were many Jewish hideouts, most of which were family bunkers. However the Jews here did not take any preventative measures to conceal their presence in the woods. Jews went to farms and villages to purchase food and supplies, and they often left traces of their activities so it was easy to discover where they were hiding. Some were caught by the Ukrainians, who handed them over to the Nazis for a reward.

Consequently, the situation became more and more dangerous. In order to establish rules of survival in the woods, a committee headed by Mundek Schwartz from Borysław was formed. The committee was responsible for finding hideouts for Jews, supplying food and water, and determining procedures to minimize the risk of exposure in the woods. Members of the committee were assigned to implement the policies. There was very little weaponry for the committee members, as they did not regard themselves as partisans or warriors. Only Mundek Schwartz had a pistol.

The retreating Wehrmacht and the progress of the Red Army led to the deportation of the "R" workers to the Kraków-Płaszów and Mauthausen-Gusen concentration camps in April 1944. That was the sign Isaac Rand had been waiting for, and he fled to the woods permanently to hide with his wife.

The Rand couple lived on dwindling supplies and prayed that the approaching Red Army would liberate them as soon as possible. A couple of months after

Isaac's arrival, he heard the sound of somebody walking near the hideout. Suddenly the passerby shouted in Ukrainian, "Jews, get out!" Isaac realized that a Ukrainian had followed him and discovered their hideout.

Isaac ordered Regina to stay behind and went outside with his hands up. The Ukrainian aimed his rifle at Isaac and asked if there were any other people inside the hideout. He also demanded any gold and money that they had. Isaac answered that he had no money or gold, but he did have new clothes that he had brought from the "barracks."

Isaac went back inside the hideout and told Regina to get ready to run away as the Ukrainian tried on the trousers. Isaac took the clothes with him, went back outside, and handed them all to the Ukrainian. Isaac suggested he check if the trousers fit him. The Ukrainian agreed and put the rifle on the ground next to him. He then took off his shoes and started to put the trousers on.

Suddenly two rapid shots pierced the air and the Ukrainian fell dead, with the pants around his ankles.

Isaac was shocked. Regina had not even begun to run away yet, as the barrage of bullets came so quickly.

All of a sudden, Mundek Łukawiecki emerged out of the woods with three well-armed partisans. Isaac breathed a sigh of relief and started to weep, all the while hugging Mundek fervently. Still inside the hideout, Regina was sure that the bullets had killed her husband and that her fate would soon be the same. Listening intently, she was shocked to hear her husband weeping. After a few seconds, she mustered up some courage and peered out from the hideout entrance.

She did not fully grasp what she saw right away. Isaac was hugging Mundek Łukawiecki and crying like a baby on his shoulder. Beside them were another three partisans who were unfamiliar to her.

As she was peering out, Mundek pushed Isaac away and ordered them to leave the area as fast as possible. He knew the sound of the bullets would have traveled far and soon the area would be crawling with Nazis, Ukrainians, and dogs.

Regina and Isaac were still in a daze and could not figure out if what had just happened was real or a dream. They acted mechanically, taking a few things from the hideout and following Mundek and his group in moving quickly away from the site.

A few days later, Mundek told Isaac that his partisan unit – the Jewish hit squad – had been ordered in June to link up with the advancing Red Army. On the way, Mundek had decided to visit the Rand family in their hideout. Just by coincidence, the advance group of the Jewish hit squad had arrived at Rand's hideout in July 1944 and were scouting the site to see if the area was safe and the hideout secure when they saw the entire event with the Ukrainian. Mundek immediately assigned Anshel Bogner and himself to shoot down the Ukrainian. He also ordered that if the Ukrainian did not die after the first barrage, Berish Brand and Władi would coordinate a second attack. As it turned out, there was no need for a second barrage.

The Jewish hit squad took the Rand couple with them about 140 kilometers (a little over eighty-five miles), to Czerkasy, where they planned to wait for the Red Army.

Chapter 31
Qualms

By the summer of 1944, the Jewish hit squad had been enjoying a lengthy cease-fire of warfare from the Nazis and Ukrainians. They were living in relative tranquility, with enough food and water to last them a while. Their living area was quiet and there was no German military activity in the woods. Therefore the partisans started to move military and combat gear that was not needed at the combat bunker to their administrative hideout.

In mid-June 1944, Mundek was ordered to take his partisan unit and head east to link up with the advancing Red Army. He and his partisan group were to welcome Stalin's troops and ease their way westward, assisting them with their advance into Germany, while the AK prepared to defend against UPA atrocities.

Part of the Jewish hit squad, summer 1944. Left to right: Ludwik Żegowski (one of the non-Jewish members of the squad), Wladi, Berish Brand, Anshel Bogner, unidentified, Mundek Łukawiecki, Isaac Helman, Maurie Hoffman.

Liberation, June 1944. Top, left to right: unidentified, Tobias Hoffman, Berish Brand; middle, left to right: Mundek Łukawiecki, Chana Bern, Anshel Bogner; bottom, left to right: unidentified, Maurie Hoffman. The plaque was written in Yiddish by Chana Bern and it says: "די פערבליבינע איינצלי אידן נאך דעם גרויסן היטלער מארד" (*Di ferbliebene aintzli Yidden nach dem groysen Hitler mord*, the only remaining surviving Jews after Hitler's great murder).

Liberation with Red Army soldiers, June 1944. Left to right: Red Army soldier, unidentified, Red Army soldier, Red Army soldier, Mundek Łukawiecki, Red Army soldier, Red Army soldier, unidentified (this may be Ludwik Żegowski), Maurie Hoffman, Berish Brand, Red Army soldier, Anshel Bogner.

Left to right: Mundek Łukawiecki, Chana Bern, and Tobias Hoffman emerging from the woods, July 1944

Left to right: Tobias Hoffman, Chana Bern, and Mundek Łukawiecki emerging from the woods, July 1944

Left to right: Mundek Łukawiecki, Chana Bern, and Anshel Bogner upon liberation, July 1944

The Russian advance did cause the AK some anxiety. The Red Army expected strong support as well as aggressive combat assistance against the retreating Wehrmacht. This, however, was not AK policy, nor was it the policy of the exiled government in London or their British hosts. The Poles were concerned that supporting the Red Army might encourage them to form a Communist regime in Poland,[1] while the British were afraid that if the Red Army advanced to Berlin too quickly, it would overshadow the war efforts of the other Allies.

As a result, an agreement was signed in April 1944 between the Red Army and the Polish underground. This agreement recognized the Polish underground, but subordinated it to the Red Army. It was followed by another formal agreement, reached in July 1944, between the Polish government-in-exile and the Soviet Union. The agreements did not, however, help to alleviate the suspicions on both sides.[2] Nevertheless, cooperation between AK partisans and their Russian counterparts continued, as both had a common enemy – the Nazis.[3] Moreover, the AK did attack German troops, overcoming their disdain for the USSR in light of their mutual interest.[4]

On July 21, 1944, the Jewish hit squad was positioned in the woods, three kilometers or a little under two miles east of Czerkasy between Lwów and Stryj. Their aim was to demolish the bridge on the Dniester. When they awoke, they found that the paved road on the outskirts of the woods was occupied with large military convoys. Military cars, tanks, and trucks stretched down the road from one edge of the horizon to the other.

Their military instincts overtook them and they decided to try to sabotage the convoy. Immediately they began preparing to demolish the bridge with explosives. They understood that it was very complicated and dangerous. The density of the traffic on the bridge was so high that they could not get close to it to set up the explosives and then withdraw.

As a result, the plan to blow up the bridge immediately was aborted. Instead,

---

1. War Cabinet Report of the Foreign Office, February 17, 1943, The National Archives (TNA) WP (43) 69; Anthony Eden, "Secret Resistance in Poland," War Cabinet Report of the Foreign Office, October 5, 1943, The National Archives (TNA) WP (43) 439, CAB 66/41/39.
2. War Cabinet Report of the Foreign Office, April 11, 1944, The National Archives (TNA) WP (44) 47th conclusions, minute 2 (6:00 P.M.), confidential annex.
3. Argasiński, *Konspiracja w powiecie*, pp. 93–94.
4. Agreement between the Polish government-in-exile and the Soviet Union on July 30, 1944, to resume diplomatic relationship. See Bór-Komorowski, *The Secret Army*, pp. 210–11.

Mundek decided to wait until nightfall, hoping that the movement would stop and allow them time to set up the explosives under the bridge. They also decided that they should spread out along the road near the bridge. This would create a killing zone after the blast that would enable them to open fire against soldiers fleeing from the scene, just as they had done in Susiec.

At midnight, the traffic ceased and they set the demolition charge. This time it was an artillery shell, and the detonator was once again a hand grenade connected to an electrical accelerator. Władi set the charge himself and pulled the electrical cord to the ambush area.

The ambush area was ideal. There was a deep ditch that separated it from the road. This would enable the partisans to control the bridge, as well as the road, after the explosion. Mundek deployed two light machine guns at the wings of the ambush; one would be operated by Anshel and the other by Berish.

Since the ambush was very close to the road – and to increase the odds of successfully retreating after the ambush – Mundek ordered all partisans to wear Wehrmacht uniforms. This was a move designed to deceive any Nazis who might survive the explosion.

At sunrise, traffic started up again. At first it was light, but as time passed, it became heavier and heavier. By ten in the morning, the flow of traffic was constant and steady. However the movement of this traffic seemed odd to the partisans. Mundek felt that it was not the regular and typical mode of German military transportation. In addition, the color of the cars, trucks, and tanks was considerably darker than the usual Nazi gray. Something wasn't quite right.

Then suddenly, while observing the convoys with his binoculars, Mundek spotted a Red Star. With a start, he jumped out of his hiding spot, shouted "Red Army!" in Polish, and ran out of the woods toward the convoys. A burst of bullets forced him back into the woods. Then he remembered that he was wearing the Wehrmacht uniform. For a few moments he remained still. He shook nervously and his eyes sparkled. He looked like he had just had a frightening epiphany. His breathing became rapid. Finally Mundek relaxed and said to his group, "Boys, they are Russians. This is the Red Army!"[5]

The partisans ran toward the convoy but a burst of fire stopped them. Some of them were still wearing German uniforms.

---

5. Hoffman, *Keep Yelling*, p. 187.

It took the partisans a few moments to strip off their Nazi disguises. In the meantime, Mundek emerged from the woods and stood at the edge of the ditch, waving his hands at the Russians. A military car sped over to him and two armed soldiers jumped out with their weapons aimed at him. Mundek began to speak to them in Russian.

"Comrades, we welcome you. We have been waiting for this moment for years!"

"Put your hands up and walk over to us slowly!" one of the Russians answered him.

Mundek motioned to the other partisans to stay in the woods until he returned. Then he crossed the ditch to meet the two Russian soldiers, keeping his hands up the entire time. When he was about five meters from the soldiers, they told him to freeze and asked, "Who are you?" All the while, their guns were aimed directly at him.

"I am Mundek Łukawiecki, the commander of a partisan group of the Armia Krajowa," he answered.

"Where are your men and how many are you?"

"There are about fifteen of us. They are in the woods watching us. The fact that you have not noticed them is a sign that they are very good soldiers."

"Are they armed?" the Russians inquired.

"Of course we are armed. We're partisans!" Mundek answered.

"So why were you wearing the Wehrmacht uniform?"

Mundek roared with laughter.

"In the beginning, we thought you were the Wehrmacht as well. So we were going to blow up the bridge," he explained. "I suggest that you dismantle the charges. Or if you permit us, my men will do it."

One of the soldiers returned back to their car and used the communication system. He returned and told Mundek, "Our commanding officer has ordered us to bring you to him."

"I am not going anywhere without my men," Mundek replied.

The soldier went back to the car again. When he returned he said, "Instruct all of your men to come out of the woods with their hands up. They should approach us as you did, one by one."

While they were talking, another vehicle filled with soldiers approached. They got out and aimed their guns at Mundek.

"What guarantee do I have that you will not kill all of us?" Mundek asked.

"Simple," the soldier answered. "You have the word of the Red Army."

"That is not enough!" Mundek pleaded. "I want word from an officer of the Red Army to an officer of the Armia Krajowa!"

"You already have it," said the soldier. "I am Lieutenant Kagan of Armored Division No. 17 of the Red Army, and I give you my word that no harm will come to your partisans."

"Are you a Jew?" asked Mundek.

The soldier gave a quotation by way of an answer.

"Why, are you a Jew as well?" the Russian queried.

"Yes, I am," answered Mundek.

"Can you prove it to me?"

"Yes, just one minute."

Mundek turned to the woods and shouted in Russian, "Isaac, come here!"

As soon as Lieutenant Kagan heard the name Isaac, he began to relax. Sixteen-year-old Isaac Helman emerged from the woods dressed in a Polish army partisan uniform. When he arrived, Mundek told him to recite the Kaddish.[6] Isaac began praying the Kaddish. After a few sentences, Lieutenant Kagan stopped him and said, "I am convinced. Call all your people, disarm the demolition charge, and let's get out of here!"

Mundek did as he was told and sent Władi to disarm the charge. Lieutenant Kagan took them to his superior officer. Mundek debriefed them both about the group's activities as partisans. It was decided that the partisans would go with the Red Army and stay in the Red Army camp that night.

Mundek and his partisans went back to their hideout first. They washed themselves in a nearby stream, as they always did. Then each of them changed his uniform and put on a clean Polish army uniform. When they were ready – and before leaving their hideout in the Ruda Różaniecka woods forever – Mundek gathered all the partisans and delivered his last and final speech in a strong voice:

"Today our life has changed. We are liberated and free. To reach this day, we fought the Nazis and their collaborators and we survived. We were strong and

---

6. Kaddish is a Jewish prayer in praise of God. The central line is "May His great name be blessed forever and for all eternity."

tough. We did not give in to despair, hunger, and cold. We always believed that one day the sun would rise again. With that belief, and with the assistance of good Polish people, we are now free.

"Our relatives are watching over us and directing us. Let's not disappoint them. We have to behave as proud Jews. From here, we will go to our hometowns. Most likely, they are in ruins. But there is one thing nobody can take from us, and that is our memories of our beloved.

"Our journey of vengeance is just beginning. Remember that we never gave up hoping. Chana has prepared a small plaque in Yiddish that says the following: 'The only remaining surviving Jews after Hitler's great murder.'[7] Let's all take some final pictures with that plaque." The partisans took pictures of themselves leaving the woods, holding Chana's plaque.[8]

The Łukawiecki partisans were freed by the Red Army on July 22, 1944. That night, they stayed at the Red Army camp. When the partisans became hungry, Mundek approached an officer who seemed to him to be a Jew and asked, "Amchu?"[9]

The officer, who was standing with his soldiers, responded in anger. "Speak to me in Russian! What do you want?"

Mundek explained that the partisans were hungry and asked for food. Orders were given and food was brought for the partisans. After a few moments, the officer took Mundek aside and said to him, "Yes, I am a Jew – how did you identify me? I was afraid to answer you. Tomorrow we are going to fight the Germans. I am hiding from my soldiers that I am a Jew because I am afraid that one of them will shoot me in the back. The rate of antisemitism in the Red Army is unbelievable."

---

7. "די פארבליבענע איינצלי אידן נאך דעם גרויסן היטלער מארד," "Di ferbliebene aintzli Yidden nach dem groysen Hitler mord." In German: "Die verbliebenen überlebende Juden nach dem großen Hitler Mord."

8. Mieczysław Argasiński, in his book *Armia Krajowa: Wolność i Niezawisłość, Lubaczów* [The Home Army (AK): Freedom and independence, Lubaczów] (Lubaczów: Komisja Historyczna przy Zarządzie Koła Światowego Związku Żołnierzy Armii Krajowej [Historical Commission for the Management Board of the World Association of AK Soldiers], 2002), p. 120, quotes a written testimony given by Andrzej Drzewicki, Lubaczów, October 10, 1978, stating that they had been hiding in the Susiec woods. He claims that the group consisted of eight members. This number probably is based on the picture taken with Chana's plaque at the liberation, which does not include the entire thirteen members.

9. The literal meaning of this Yiddish word is "Your people?" meaning, "Are you Jewish?"

The next morning, the superior officer asked to see the partisans and told them that he had to confiscate their arms. He told them that nobody – other than Red Army soldiers – was permitted to carry guns. He added that if they wanted to have guns, they could enlist with the Red Army. In fact, he encouraged them to do so. If they refused to enlist, they would be sent to Russia to working battalions.[10] In other words, they would be sent to the gulags of Siberia.

Mundek and the partisans were shocked. Only a few moments earlier, they had taken pictures with their Red Army liberators. Now they were effectively under arrest by the Soviet NKVD organization. The NKVD, precursor to the KGB, helped to enforce the mandatory Red Army draft as a form of punishment to Jewish, Ukrainian, and Bandera supporters,[11] while all Poles were expelled to the west.

Mundek argued that although they were Jewish partisans, they were also Polish. To prove his point, he showed the Russians his false Polish identification papers. He emphasized that the group were both Jewish and Polish, and that they would want to volunteer with the Polish army. In fact, he pledged that they would all serve in the Polish army.

"We are Polish people. We are already soldiers of the Armia Krajowa. We cannot join the Red Army to fight the Nazis. But we will join our Polish army. And, of course, in good faith between you and us, we will hand over our weapons."

Mundek's arguments may have been what convinced the superior officer to release them. Although he did not react immediately, ultimately he agreed that the group could enlist in the Polish army instead of the Russian army.[12]

And so it was that the partisans handed over their weapons – though not

---

10. Penal battalions were used in the German Wehrmacht as a punishment for soldiers who required disciplinary action and as a way to put convicts or prisoners to work doing dangerous or laborious jobs that other soldiers did not want to do. Sometimes offered as the only alternative to execution, service in a penal unit often meant having to go out on suicidally dangerous missions. Soldiers in such units who exhibited bravery in battle were "promoted" to having the rights of a regular soldier, so the motivation to perform was high even though the conditions were bad. The German penal units were called *Strafbataillone*. The Germans also had *Bewährungsbataillone* (battalions for parole) and similar units like *Feldstrafabteilungen* (units for punishment in the field). Stalin admired the German system and thus the Red Army's penal units, called *shtrafbats*, were created in imitation. It was to these Red Army penal units that the officer was threatening to send Mundek and his men.
11. In Polish: Ukraińscy Banderowcy.
12. Isaac Helman joined the Red Army.

before taking some more pictures with the soldiers of the Red Army. Mundek, however, managed to hide his Parabellum pistol in his belt. Then they started the long walk back to life under the shadows of the Holocaust's horrors. Their first stop was the ruins of their families' homes in Lubaczów.

After a few days in Lubaczów, Mundek left by himself to Lwów. He was wearing the Polish army uniform. He went to his parents' flat, his childhood home. A woman holding a baby opened the door.

"I lived here with my family, before the war." Mundek said to her. "Please let me see the flat. I will look and leave. I will not cause you any harm."

The woman let Mundek in. He walked through each of the three rooms, his eyes streaming with tears. Then he left and returned back to Lubaczów.

Chana, by contrast, could not bring herself to go near her parents' residence. She never went to see the house; she turned away from it. She avoided walking near it and preferred to take routes that were far away from the house.

While in Lubaczów, Chana met a distant relative of her mother, Feiga Kammer,[13] who was very religious. Following this meeting, Feiga approached Mundek and said to him, "Chana is my family. I do not want you to live with her like that; I want you to get married."

Mundek agreed and a wedding ceremony was performed, at which some modest, home-made kosher refreshments were served. Needless to say, it was a sad wedding. Bride and groom, as well as everyone present, cried as they were reminded of the memories of their families.

---

13. See testimony of Feiga Kammer to Yad Vashem, no. M49/1174 LB.440 M49/1174.

Chapter 32
From AK to UB

The Red Army continued its push toward Berlin, defeating the German Heeresgruppe Nordukraine (Army Group Northern Ukraine). Subordinated to it was, among others, the 4. Panzerarmee (Fourth Tank Army), which operated roughly between Lublin and Rawa Ruska.[1] Lubaczów was liberated on July 22, 1944,[2] by the First Guards Tank Army, commanded by Marshal Mikhail Efimovich Katukov.[3] Some AK members welcomed the Red Army as they advanced onto Polish soil. Others moved west. At this point, most AK members had returned to their farms and homes.

At first, the Red Army had treated AK members well. But that changed very quickly. The Red Army sprung its military police – the NKVD – into action. Their primary task was to seek out "subversive elements," such as Nazi supporters or AK members, and arrest them. This sprang from an official Soviet decision that had been made already in 1943 to turn Poland into a Communist country.[4]

As the Red Army swept west, so did Communism: the Soviet-backed provisional government of Poland, the Polish Committee of National Liberation (Polski Komitet Wyzwolenia Narodowego, PKWN), established in July 1944,

---

1. See Earl F. Ziemke, *Stalingrad to Berlin: The German Defeat in the East*, United States Army Historical Series (Washington, DC: United States Department of Defense, 2002), pp. 331–32. See also the AK report on German military strength in *Armia Krajowa w Dokumentach, 1939–1945*, tom 4: lipiec 1944–październik 1944 [AK documents, 1939–1945, vol. 4, July 1944–October 1944] (London, 1977; repr., Wroclaw: Osssolineum, 1990), document no. 1194 dated September 30, 1944, p. 419.
2. Argasiński, *Armia Krajowa*, p. 120, and Hoffman, *Keep Yelling*, p. 187.
3. Zygmunt Kubrak, *Rok 44* [Year 44] (Lubaczów: Muzeum Kresow w Lubaczowie, 2004), p. 4.
4. Waldemar W. Bednarski, "Z dziejów okupacji Ziemi Tomaszowskiej przez Armię Czerwoną oraz terroru UB-NKWD" [The history of the occupation of the lands of Tomaszow by the Red Army and UB-NKVD terror], *Radzynski Rocznik Humanistyczny* [The Humanities Yearbook of Radzyn Podlaski] 5 (2007): 149.

Mundek Łukawiecki in the UB in Krakow, 1946

Mundek Łukawiecki's UB enlistment photo, Krakow, 1946

Mundek in the UB in Krakow, 1946

Mundek with UB colleagues

Mundek Łukawiecki (right) with unidentified friend from the UB, autumn 1946. Both of them wear the UB uniform. Mundek's military rank can't be identified in the picture. In his testimony to the Shoah Foundation he said he was a captain.

Mundek during his UB days in Krakow

made sure that as the Nazis retreated, Communism advanced. One of the new provisional government's main goals was to dismantle anti-Communist resistance groups such as the AK.

The Ministerstwo Bezpieczeństwa Publicznego (Department of Public Security) was formed in the USSR and became part of the Polski Komitet Wyzwolenia Narodowego (Polish Committee of National Liberation), which came into existence in Moscow on July 21, 1944. The Polish Committee of National Liberation was installed in Chelm on July 27, 1944, and soon after moved to Lublin. The Wojewódzki Urząd Bezpieczeństwa Publicznego (Department of Public Security district office) was set up in Lublin in August. By year's end, the Department of Public Security employed 21,000 people, including 13,000 functionaries of the Milicja Obywatelska (Citizens' Militia), 4,000 soldiers of the Wojska Wewnetrzne (Interior Army), and 3,000 members of the security apparatus.[5]

In August 1944, the Polish Urząd Bezpieczeństwa (UB; Department of Security) was formally established by the USSR in the Polish areas occupied by the Red Army. The UB was designed to be the Polish arm of the NKVD and functioned as a Polish secret police force. As a result, non-Poles (that is to say, Jews) were not normally recruited.[6] Initially, the UB was also dominated by Russians and was under the control of the Polski Komitet Wyzwolenia (Committee for National Liberation).[7] Following the formation of the temporary Polish government by the USSR, UB activities included safeguarding the Communist regime, of which a crucial part was operating and dealing with political and military underground movements.

Also in August 1944, AK headquarters in Lwów ordered the AK in Lubaczów – under the leadership of Michał Franus ("Siciński") – to form a civil militia (*milicja obywatelska*) in Lubaczów.[8] This became the standard procedure in all municipalities liberated by the Red Army.[9] Following the dismantling of the AK unit in Lubaczów, its members voluntarily mobilized and joined local administrative

---

5. Wnuk, *Lubelski Okręg*, pp. 87–123.
6. See the article by Marian Kulik, "Tragiczny epilog," in Caban, *Związek Walki Zbrojnej Armia Krajowa*, p. 244.
7. This committee was responsible for the Public Security Division, under the control of the UB.
8. Caban, *Oddziały partyzanckie*, pp. 100–102.
9. Argasiński, *Armia Krajowa*, p. 120.

First HQ of the secret police in Lubaczów, which would later become the UB

entities,[10] such as police units.[11] This enabled them to man police stations and the civil administration under the Communist regime. Consequently, the local police and administration in Lubaczów were made up of former AK members who had fought against the UPA,[12] the Polish Peasants' Party (Polskie Stronnictwo Ludowe, PSL), and the Labor Party (Stronnictwo Pracy, SP).

On November 14, 1944, Major Stanisław Szot, a senior officer of the Polish secret police, the Wojewódzki Urząd Bezpieczeństwa Publicznego (WUBP),[13] which was affiliated with the NKVD, issued Order Number 40, to the effect that

---

10. Argasiński, *Konspiracja w powiecie*, p. 19.
11. Caban, *Związek Walki Zbrojnej Armia Krajowa*, pp. 243–51.
12. Ukraińska Powstańcza Armia, the Ukrainian Insurgent Army, which fought to establish an independent Ukrainian state.
13. This organization, the WUBP (Provincial Office of Public Security), had been established by the USSR in July 1944 in Chelm as a department of the Polish provisional government, in order to assume control over land in Poland freed from German occupation.

all AK members be handed over to the Red Army.[14] As a result, 3,375 AK members were subsequently captured.[15]

The Red Army gave the Łukawiecki partisans two options – to be drafted into the Red Army or to go to Siberian punishment battalions. Agreeing to go to punishment battalions meant certain death. But fighting with the Red Army was against AK principles.

It didn't help that Mundek Łukawiecki had made it known that his group was made up of Jewish partisans. The Łukawiecki partisans were forced to join the Polish army, which was certainly better than being sent to Siberia or enlisting in the Red Army. In fact, because of their Jewish faith, most of the Łukawiecki partisans were enlisted into the Lubaczów Militia.[16] They weren't given any arms, but each of them was marked with an armband to identify their membership in the group. Their task was to find fifth columnists (Polish and Ukrainian collaborators, as well as Volksdeutsche)[17] and hand them over to the NKVD.[18] They took very seriously the mission to get rid of Ukrainians and Poles who had collaborated with the Nazis. They soon realized however that any fifth columnists they exposed were released a few days after they were "arrested."[19] The soldiers of the Red Army did not contribute to law and order in Lubaczów. On the contrary, they were looking to enrich themselves through thievery and bribe-taking.

Working for the secret police was not something Mundek did of his own volition. Rather, enlisting in the UB in Lubaczów was essentially forced upon him shortly after being liberated by Red Army soldiers in Płazów[20] on July 22, 1944.[21]

---

14. Slawomir Poleszak, ed., *Rok pierwszy: Powstanie i działalność aparatu bezpieczeństwa publicznego na Lubelszczyźnie, lipiec 1944–czerwiec 1945* [Year one: Establishment and operation of public security apparatus in the Lublin region, July 1944–June 1945] (Warsaw: Instytut Pamięci Narodowej, 2004), p. 139.
15. Wnuk, *Lubelski Okręg*, pp. 35–36.
16. Hoffman, *Keep Yelling*, p. 196.
17. Ethnic Germans – persons who lived outside Germany, but were regarded as German.
18. Part of the Ministry of the Interior in the USSR. The name stands for the People's Commissariat for Internal Affairs (Народный комиссариат внутренних дел, *Narodnyy Komissariat Vnutrennikh Del*), abbreviated NKVD. Formally it was a law enforcement agency of the USSR. In actuality it was the most powerful Soviet secret service.
19. Hoffman, *Keep Yelling*, p. 196.
20. Today this town is located on Route 865 between Żuków and Narol, about seventeen kilometers (ten and a half miles) southwest of the notorious Bełzec.
21. Lubaczów was liberated on July 22, 1944, after the Germans finally withdrew and the Soviet Red Army reoccupied the area. At that time the area was still largely under the control of

Ironically, the UB was formed by the Communists to persecute AK members, the group that Mundek had previously belonged to. However, although he joined the UB, he made sure that he did not betray his former allies.

Membership in the UB would have its benefits. Mundek was obsessed with taking revenge against collaborators – Poles, Ukrainians, Germans, and Volksdeutsche. It was an impulse he could not fight.[22] The UB, Mundek thought, would allow him to pursue his obsession in something of an official capacity. This preoccupation did not diminish once the war was over, and in fact stayed with him until years later, possessing him day and night. He thought constantly about prosecuting those who had collaborated with the Germans, particularly for their atrocities against the Polish and Jewish populations. The burning in his soul was constantly inflamed by the memories of the murder of his family at the Dachnów ditch.

Part of Mundek's drive to be a partisan was to ensure that justice was served during the war. When the war was over, Mundek naively believed that the justice system in Poland would bring Nazi collaborators and war criminals to justice. He truly believed that a sovereign Polish entity such as the UB would execute such a policy. To help with this cause, he joined law enforcement. He knew that he would be forced to enlist anyway, and he saw service in the UB as a way to get even with collaborators. His uncontrolled desire for justice combined with his drive for capturing collaborators was insatiable.[23] But he soon realized that this was not a top priority of the Polish authorities.

Mundek therefore decided to take matters into his own hands. He was a rebellious person by nature, and his sense of injustice only increased his anger, causing him fits of fury. He felt it was his personal obligation to seek revenge against collaborators and Nazi supporters, and being part of a law enforcement agency gave him the ability to act on his inner sense of justice. The gun that the

---

the Ukrainian Insurgent Army (UPA). Maurie Hoffman, in his book *Keep Yelling*, pp. 187–88, states that the partisans were liberated on July 22, 1943, more than a hundred kilometers from Lubaczów. Mieczysław Argasiński, on p. 120 of his book *Armia Krajowa*, quotes a written testimony given by Andrzej Drzewicki, Lubaczów, October 10, 1978, that Mundek's group arrived after July 22, 1943. Therefore it seems that the partisans were liberated a few days prior to July 22, 1943.
22. Personal interview with Lula Weiner Baum, February 24, 2010.
23. Ibid.

UB provided him with, and the powers they granted him, enlarged his scope of anti-collaborator activity. Needless to say, he did not hesitate to use his gun.

Mundek maintained his contact with the AK leadership in Lubaczów-Ostrowiec (whose head man was known by the pseudonym "Lusia"). Moreover, as a UB man, he could inform former AK members about activities being plotted against them and warn them in advance. For example, in August 1944, Mundek warned Franciszek Franuś ("Oszczepski")[24] and Jan Kopciuch that the Ukrainians – who were very cooperative with the NKVD – had informed the Soviet secret police agency that they were spies. The NKVD was planning to arrest them the following morning. Mundek warned the two AK members and advised them to escape to the other side of the San River in order to avoid imprisonment. They followed his advice and were thereby saved.[25]

In autumn 1944, Mundek had secret discussions with AK commander Zdzisław Zathey ("Gładzicki")[26] about a mutual cooperation plan. During this time, AK members were being persecuted by the UB. In spite of this, Zathey and other AK members were never exposed by Mundek.

Mundek joined the uniform wing known as the Korpus Bezpieczeństwa Wewnetrznego (KBW, Internal Security Corps).[27] Wearing the Polish KBW uniform and having the rank of captain[28] gave Mundek the freedom to exact the justice he was seeking so badly.[29]

---

24. Franuś was commander of AK Lubaczów in mid-1944. See also Caban, *Oddziały partyzanckie*, p. 102.
25. Argasiński, *Armia Krajowa*, p. 120; Argasiński, *Konspiracja w powiecie*, p. 109; Hoffman, *Keep Yelling*, p. 185.
26. Zathey was appointed by Warda to be the commander in autumn 1944. See Caban, *Oddziały partyzanckie*, p. 103.
27. Testimony of Edmund (Mundek) Łukawiecki (Moshe Lavee) to Yad Vashem, July 28, 1993, no. 03-6946, tape no. 033c/2757, p. 20. The KBW was a military unit formed by the Communist government of Poland on May 24, 1945, to protect infrastructure and to put down anti-Communist resistance from groups like Wolność i Niezawisłość (WiN, Freedom and Independence), Narodowe Siły Zbrojne (NSZ, National Armed Forces), and former AK members.
28. Moshe Lavee (Edmund/Mundek Łukawiecki), recorded interview by USC Shoah Foundation Institute, interview code 31895, May 27, 1997. Personal interview with Mr. Adam Bauman, January 18, 2012.
29. Whether other Jews were also taking advantage of the possibility for revenge in the UB is unknown; however, Jews were definitely a significant minority in the agency. According to research, in the years 1944–1954, 167 out of 450 top positions in the Polish secret services, or 37.1 percent, were held by Jews. See Krzysztof Szwagrzyk, "Żydzi w kierownictwie UB: Stereotyp

In 1945, Mundek was transferred to UB Kraków. He was formally transferred on May 23, 1945, but in actual fact, he was brought to Kraków at the beginning of the year, a short while after the unit was established in January 1945. This was around the same time that the AK was formally dismantled – in January of 1945 – since most of Poland had been "liberated" by the Red Army.

In Kraków, Mundek and Chana were provided with a residence at 5 Stanisława Konarskego Street, not far from UB headquarters, which were located in the former Gestapo headquarters in Pomorska Street. At this time, Chana was expecting. Before she gave birth, they moved to a larger apartment at 62 Karmelicka Street, and on June 20, 1945, their first son Joseph was born.

Mundek established contact with the head of the Jewish community, Dr. Blich, at his office on 30 Długa Street.[30] Thereafter, he assisted him with various matters in favor of the Jewish community, including intimidating Polish non-Jewish residents who harassed Jews. For example, Mundek did not hesitate to testify in court on behalf of a Jew in order to prevent him and his family from being evicted from their residence, pretending the Jew was his relative. The judge did not want to mess with the KBW or UB, and gave a judgment that was in favor of the Jew. Mundek also smuggled weaponry to Dr. Blich, which was then handed over to Jewish organizations. Mundek registered himself and Chana in the community books established for searching for relatives, but no family member was found.

Mundek wore a uniform but was also entitled to perform his duties in civilian clothes. In the military wing of KBW, Mundek was a demolition instructor. He was appointed as an agent-operator in the "Sek II" unit of the UB, dealing with political and military underground movements. A few months later, in August 1945, he was transferred to another department, "Sek III," which dealt with foreign enemies.

While serving in the KBW/UB, Mundek concealed crucial facts about himself and provided the authorities with as few details as possible. Some of the

---

czy rzeczywistość" [Jews in the leadership of the UB: Stereotype or reality], *Biuletyn Instytutu Pamięci Narodowej* 11 (2005): 37–42; Krzysztof Szwagrzyk, ed., *Aparat bezpieczeństwa w Polsce: Kadra kierownicza* [Security apparatus in Poland: The leadership], vol. 1, *1944–1956* (Warsaw: Instytut Pamięci Narodowej, 2005).

30. Moshe Lavee (Edmund/Mundek Łukawiecki), recorded interview by USC Shoah Foundation Institute, interview code 31895, May 27, 1997.

details he omitted were essential to understand his background. For example, he couldn't reveal to the KBW/UB that he had been an AK partisan during the war. In his UB application, he didn't reveal his connections to the AK whatsoever. He told them that during the war he was an independent, armed "forest man."[31] He claimed that he had led an armed group of forest men who were persecuted by the Nazis in the woods of Dąbrowa and Mariarmia. He recorded that it was Unit No. 15, nicknamed "Łuk."

Mundek also fabricated some other facts about himself for the UB. He told the UB that he was born earlier than he actually was, in order to convince them that he could enroll. He was actually born on December 20, 1921, yet claimed to have been born six years earlier on October 20, 1915. Another fact he changed was his mother's maiden name. Her real name was Sarah Nestel, while he wrote "Helena Sobol."[32]

It appears that all of these changes and discrepancies were designed to deliberately make it harder to detect and verify Mundek's personal information Mundek wanted to prevent anyone from digging into his past and discovering his true identity.

The same applies to his transfer to UB Kraków. Browsing Mundek Łukawiecki's personal file from the UB, there is no explanation as to why, despite documents proving that he was enlisted earlier, it states that he was enlisted in May 1945. Mundek himself a year later wrote in his UB résumé dated April 6, 1946, that he was appointed to the UB Kraków on April 14, 1945, a full month earlier than the UB files state.

It is also unusual that he received a recommendation from the Communist party Polska Partia Robotnicza (PPR, Polish Workers Party) that he be accepted

---

31. The word in Polish is *lasowcy*. It's possible that Mundek Łukawiecki was inspired to use this word, as it reminded him of "Kompania Leśna," the name of Company 3 from Tomaszów Lubelski at the end of 1943, after the former units were disintegrated because of German raids. See Caban, *Oddziały partyzanckie*, p. 43. Also Mieczysław Berezecki, in his article "Grupa Bojowa z Lasu Dąbrowa," uses the term "*leśni*" and not "partisans." See Caban, *Związek Walki Zbrojnej Armia Krajowa*, p. 117.

32. From Mundek's biographical information forms in his UB file, filled out by Mundek Łukawiecki on May 23, 1945, and April 6, 1946. UB personal file of Mundek Łukawiecki, IPN/OBUiAd/Kraków, Sygn IPN 16 057/1028.

into the UB, despite the fact that he was never a member of that party.[33] The PPR believed that Mundek was a partisan during the war and that he was an honest democrat. Therefore, they trusted him.

The most surprising aspect of Mundek's personal file, however, is that it states that he had active tuberculosis. On December 24, 1945, the medical board diagnosed that Mundek was suffering from active tuberculosis, which granted him fourteen days' sick leave, followed by a stay in a sanitarium. A document in the file from an earlier date also proves that he requested two weeks' sick leave. Another sick leave was approved on June 2, 1946. Moreover, during the investigation that the UB conducted after he disappeared on August 8, 1946, a medical certificate was found instructing that he was to stay in a sanitarium in Otwock for two weeks due to active tuberculosis.

This illness was in fact fictitious. The fact of the matter is that Mundek Łukawiecki never suffered from TB. However, it appears that claiming to have active TB enabled Mundek to be absent from work and to even leave Kraków on occasion.

During his time in the UB, Mundek was thought of as a talented, hard-working, and intelligent person who worked well independently and was politically dedicated. He was highly regarded even though he had not signed the Oath of Allegiance, as was requested of him on July 22, 1946. In addition, although the UB did not fully accept Mundek's version of his involvement in the partisan movement, they put their suspicions aside because he was a valuable asset to their organization. True, the UB repeatedly asked for explanations and questioned Mundek about his resume on a number of occasions, but in the end they were satisfied that Mundek was a partisan member of the forest men as he had stated.

In August 1946, Mundek deserted the UB. This happened a few days after he was transferred from the foreign enemies section back to the political and military underground movement division.[34] That day, he presented his superior

---

33. For the sake of honesty, it should be underlined that the recommendation did not say that he was a member of the party. Only Mr. Roman Janczyc, who was the referral in the UB, checked the Mundek Łukawiecki file in May 1945 and recommended he be enrolled. One of the claims Janczyc made in his June 22, 1945, recommendation letter was that Mundek was a member in the PPR party, after he was a "forest man" during the period of occupation.
34. The approval of the transfer was written by Eugeniusz Pająk on July 26, 1946.

Mundek, wearing the uniform of the military wing of the UB, in Zakopane, looking out over Mount Giewont, spring 1946

officer with a medical certificate verifying that he had active TB and that his physician had ordered him to go to the sanitarium in Otwock.[35]

Following his disappearance, the UB sent people to his dwelling several times, but Mundek and his family could not be found. There is no indication whether they looked for him in Otwock as well. On January 7, 1947, Mundek was declared a deserter by the head of the Manpower Division of the UB[36] and his name was removed from the UB employee list.

Three events, which occurred around the same time, caused Mundek Łukawiecki to desert from the UB. The final and most crucial one took place the evening before the desertion. That night, a friend of Mundek's – a non-Jewish officer who was Mundek's subordinate in the UB – stopped at the Łukawiecki apartment unexpectedly. He warned him that he would be arrested if he went in to work the next day.[37]

---

35. Otwock is a small resort town south of Warsaw.
36. UB document dated January 7, 1947, written by Eugeniusz Pajak and approved by Major Jan Olkowski, head of the WUBP of Cracow.
37. See also Joe Warner's e-mail to the author, on May 22, 2011.

This friend told the Łukawiecki couple that Mundek was suspected of anti-Communist subversive activities. Primarily, they suspected that he was executing Nazi collaborators whom the UB refused to punish and who had been released by them, because they had now converted to Communism or were assisting the Communist regime. This hypocritical attitude had only further stirred up Mundek's already hot blood. Indeed, Mundek had vowed to personally get rid of the collaborators that the UB released, and he used to enjoy rotating his finger between the trigger and the trigger guard. Chana would shout at him out of fear to stop, but he refused and threatened to kill her if she got in his way.[38]

The second alleged activity was that he was recruiting, arming, and shipping Jews to fight in Palestine for the Jewish underground movement the National Military Organization. As a former member of the youth movement Brith Hachayal[39] in Lwów, he sympathized with their cause. Mundek would later proudly confirm these allegations after arriving in Israel.

The warning from his UB colleague had been triggered by something that had occurred a week earlier, at the beginning of August 1946. Although Mundek had been on the surface a model employee, he had fallen under suspicion when Józef Kulpa had shown up unexpectedly at his office. Kulpa was visiting Kraków with a group of scouts from Lubaczów. He had found out where the secret UB headquarters in Kraków were and went to see Mundek without any advance warning. Upon arrival at the UB headquarters, Kulpa was immediately detained by a high-ranking UB officer and declared a security risk. When Mundek found out that Kulpa was being held, he immediately ordered his release and had him brought to his office.

Mundek welcomed Kulpa as a son would welcome his father; they hugged and kissed each other, to the astonishment of Mundek's staff. Mundek had all his appointments cancelled and told his staff not to disturb him that day. He assured Kulpa that no harm would come to him or any other AK member. Food and drinks were ordered and at the end of the five-hour meeting, Mundek gave Kulpa money and cans of food. He made Kulpa promise that if he were ever in need or in any kind of trouble, he and other AK members would come to Mundek

---

38. Lula Weiner Baum, oral testimony, April 17, 2011.
39. Union of Soldiers, a Jewish Revisionist organization (Ze'ev Jabotinsky's movement) founded in Poland in 1932 for the purpose of providing military training to Jewish youth.

without any hesitation. Kulpa was then escorted back to his scout camp. This was the last time they ever saw each other.[40]

The warning that he was about to be arrested brought matters to a head, but in truth, Mundek had already been considering desertion due to yet another event that had occurred around that same time. Ironically, it was an award that Mundek and another UB officer received. They were decorated with the Bronze Cross of Merit,[41] the highest civilian award in Poland. It was awarded to citizens who went beyond the call of duty in their work for the country and for society as a whole. The UB considered Mundek a devoted employee who fulfilled his obligations and had no addictions.[42]

The second awardee was known for his antisemitic views, which he frequently expressed openly and publicly. Mundek could not stand the fact that this man was given an award. In his view, the awardee deserved to be executed, not decorated. Mundek was greatly disturbed that the UB had chosen to award the medal to an antisemitic officer. He was forced to confront the reality of Poland and his role in it. Nothing had changed in Poland since the war had ended. In a storm of emotions, Mundek realized that the only place for him was among Jews. If he must fight, he would fight for his own state, not for the Communist regime in Poland. His land was Palestine.

Mundek's resolve was sealed with the knowledge that he was about to be arrested. The jig was up. He could no longer continue his service in the UB; the only option was desertion. Mundek was concerned that the UB would look for him, especially at the German borders. He therefore decided to deceive them so he could gain more time before the UB would start to look for him. He obtained a medical certificate that claimed he needed to be in the sanitarium in Otwock, as he suffered from TB.[43]

---

40. Personal interview with Mieczysław Argasiński, September 25, 2010, at Muzeum Kresów (the Borderlands Museum), Lubaczów. Mieczysław Argasiński is the author of the book *Armia Krajowa: Wolność i Niezawisłość, Lubaczów* [The Home Army (AK): Freedom and independence, Lubaczów] and former head of Muzeum Kresów.
41. The Brązowy Krzyż Zasługi, established on June 23, 1923, to recognize service to the state.
42. UB personal file of Mundek Łukawiecki – IPN/OBUiAd/Kraków, Sygn IPN 16 057/1028, and specifically the evaluation of Mundek Łukawiecki therein, dated October 12, 1945.
43. Precisely how he obtained this certificate is not known, but it is likely that any doctor he approached would have given him what he wanted due to his position in the UB, as UB members had the power to have citizens arrested at will.

On August 8, 1946, after taking the medical certificate to the UB office in Kraków, the whole family – consisting of Mundek, Chana, and fourteen-month-old Joseph – heeded the warning and left Kraków without hesitation that very night, making their way to Otwock, a resort and recuperation town south of Warsaw. Once in Otwock, still wearing his Polish uniform, Mundek asked to be taken to a Jewish organization. He was directed to the Jewish kibbutz of Gordonia.[44]

Mundek met with the head of Gordonia and told him that he wanted to escape Poland. The man agreed to help and gave him some civilian clothes, which hung limply on Mundek's undernourished frame. He also took from Mundek his pistol, military papers, and uniform; this would conceal Mundek's connection to the UB, and Gordonia could use the items for their own clandestine activities. The decision was made that they would flee to Czechoslovakia, where the border patrol was less vigilant.[45] That very night, a driver took the family by car from Otwock directly to the Czechoslovakian border (a distance of over 400 kilometers [250 miles]) and they crossed over near Frýdek-Místek. They used fake names on genuine Polish passports that Mundek had prepared in advance in Kraków using the name Friedman. After a night's rest near the border and another day of traveling, they arrived in Prague, where the passports were taken from them and they were placed in the Rothschild Hospital. During their two nights there, they met members of Brith Hachayal.

After a couple of days,[46] they were transferred by train to Ebensee[47] in Austria, where they would spend the whole winter. This time they traveled as Greeks, since they no longer had any identification papers and claiming Greek nationality was a relatively low-risk cover story because so few people spoke Greek. They

---

44. Like many socialist Jewish movements of the time, its ideology was that the salvation of Israel would come about through self-determination, hard work, and vocational training to meet the needs of a labor force.
45. Czechoslovakia, and particularly its capital, Prague, was the main center of the illegal immigration activities of Jews from Europe to Israel (then Mandatory Palestine). See for example Col. Yisrael Carmy, *B'derech lochamim* [In the way of warriors] (Tel Aviv: Maarachot–IDF Publishing House, 1960), pp. 249–82.
46. Personal interview with Dr. Isaac Weinberg, May 30, 2011, quoting conversations with Mundek Łukawiecki.
47. During WWII Ebensee housed a notoriously cruel concentration camp built by the SS to use slave labor to dig tunnels in a mountainside for the purpose of armament storage. This was part of the project to develop the V2 missile, which Germany hoped to be able to launch against the United States.

spent the entire winter in Ebensee, living in a DP camp in the former barracks of a notorious SS concentration camp. All their needs were taken care of, including nourishment and clothing. From Ebensee, the family moved to Ansbach, Germany,[48] a small town about sixty kilometers (thirty-seven miles) from Nuremberg. They received a room in the former barracks of the German army and lived there for two years, unable to get a certificate from the British Mandate for emigration to Palestine. It was in Ansbach that their second son, Simon (author of this book), was born in 1947.

While in Ansbach, Mundek established the ORT[49] Photography College and acted as its principal, despite the fact that he knew very little about photography. He hired German teachers and sat in with the other students during lectures, later studying by himself at night. This was how he learned to be a professional photographer. He also continued to enlist Jews into the Irgun Ha-Tzvai Ha-Leumi be-Eretz Yisrael (Etzel, the National Military Organization in the Land of Israel, a radical nationalist group that fought the British for control of Palestine and later fought in Israel's War of Independence), together with Yehuda Bornstein, whom he met in Ansbach. The newly drafted Jews waited in a former forced labor camp on Lohengrin Street[50] in Munich.

On August 14, 1948, Mundek had a motorcycle accident in which a pedestrian was killed. This was bad enough in and of itself, but the fact that Mundek did not have a driver's license turned the accident into a very complicated situation.

Zanwet Weiner and his son-in-law Anshel Baum – both very close acquaintances from Lubaczów – lived nearby in Munich at the time. They drove to Ansbach that night and silently evacuated the Łukawiecki family from Ansbach to Munich, using another set of forged passports under the family name Wolf. The Jewish youngsters that Mundek had enlisted awaited their emigration to Palestine in the former POW camp on Lohengrin Street in Munich, and now the Łukawiecki family joined them and found refuge there.

Keeping a low profile in Munich, the family managed to hide for a few days

---

48. This was the site of a former Wehrmacht camp where POWs were interned.
49. The Obshestvo Remeslenofo zemledelcheskofo Truda (Society for Trades and Agricultural Labor) is a Jewish organization established in 1880 in Russia to provide job skills training. ORT still operates today, all over the world.
50. Zwangsarbeitslager an der Lohengrinstraße was a DP camp not for Jews but for Baltic DPs. Nevertheless it was used for a short time as a collecting center for Jews.

until the necessary arrangements could be made and the papers created to get them out of Germany. They traveled to Marseille, France, where they boarded a boat for Israel. On October 6, 1948, they arrived along with hundreds of other refugees looking for a safer life in the newly formed state.[51]

The Łukawiecki family had finally completed the last stage of their journey to the Promised Land. Finally, they had a place where they could stop running away and start to feel a real sense of belonging, a feeling that had eluded them all their lives.

The newly arrived Łukawieckis were housed in barracks in an immigrant camp in Atlit, a small village on the Mediterranean seashore just south of Haifa. Chana Łukawiecki remembered that her mother's brother Isaac Katz and his family had emigrated from Germany to Palestine in 1937. She recalled that when Chana's uncle Herman Katz, her mother's brother, had come to live with the Katz-Bern family after being expelled from Germany, he had updated them that Isaac at first lived in Nahariya,[52] but had moved to 15 Balfour Street in Haifa soon after.

Chana succeeded in locating them, and a couple of days after the Łukawieckis' arrival, the two families shared an evening of agony, pain, crying, and tears as Chana told her relatives of the family's destruction. Isaac Katz, his wife, and their three children Henny, Leo, and Lucy – who were around Chana's age – wrapped the new arrivals in love, warmth, care, and support.

Shortly thereafter, the Katz family – following Mundek's request – found his uncle Leo Gerstenfeld, his mother's brother. Mundek knew that Leo had an upholstery business in Haifa, and it was therefore easy for the Katz family to locate him. The following night, the Katzes, the Gerstenfelds, and the Łukawieckis spent another heartwrenching evening together reliving the destruction of their families.

Chana and Mundek moved nearby to another newcomers' center in a small town called Pardes Chana near Caesarea. In November 1948, they moved to Acre,[53] where Mundek opened a photography studio, but unfortunately it did not

---

51. Central Zionist Archives, file number S104/607.
52. A northern city of Israel, near the border with Lebanon. Most Jews who immigrated to Palestine resided there.
53. The address was "house number 260."

succeed. After a short time, the family moved again, this time to Jaffa,[54] which had recently been liberated by Etzel, the organization Mundek had supported and recruited for while he was still in Europe. Mundek was hoping to search for his relatives who had settled in Tel Aviv before the war.

On October 11, 1948, Mundek was enlisted in the newly formed Israeli Defense Force (IDF), despite the fact that he was underweight, weighing just fifty-eight kilos (128 pounds). Mundek received the serial number of a reserve soldier, number 145296, and served in the Mapping and Photography Service of the Intelligence Corps. His acceptance into an Israeli military intelligence was rather remarkable considering the fact that he had served in the Polish UB, a Communist secret service agency, but apparently the IDF was willing to overlook this facet of Mundek's history, as the IDF was in real need of people with his skills. On June 5, 1949, he was released from compulsory service to reserves.

When he was off duty, Mundek spent most of his time searching for his father's cousin Joseph Łukawiecki.[55] He knew that he was supposed to live in Tel Aviv and that he owned a metal bed factory there, but other than that he had no information with which to locate him. He was also unaware of the fact that his cousin had changed his name back to the original family name of Cohen.

Mundek made countless trips to southern Tel Aviv to look for Joseph Łukawiecki. He focused on the southern part of the city where furniture stores and factories were located, looking for the metal bed factory owned by his cousin.[56] But no one had heard of a man by the name of Łukawiecki.

Mundek's hope to make a living as a photographer in Acre failed. Few customers entered the photography studio he opened in a large, deserted Arabic house, which was located outside the walls of Acre. Its owners had run away during the War of Independence together with many of the Arab inhabitants of Acre who had fled to Lebanon, bringing the economy in the area to a halt.[57]

---

54. The address in Jaffa was Givat Aliya (a former Arabic suburb named Jabelia), Street 114, house 27. Mundek opened his photography studio next to Gan Tamer, a very famous restaurant at that time and named it "Zion Studio."
55. Mundek's father was also named Joseph. Both of them were named after the same grandfather, Joseph Cohen. Two of Joseph's sons, Hersh (the grandfather of Mundek) and Shmuel David, named their sons after the same grandfather.
56. Later on he learned that the factory was located at 34 HaShuk Street in Tel Aviv (HaShuk means "the market" in Hebrew).
57. Personal interview with Motti Genosar, a cousin of Mundek Łukawiecki's, June 3, 2009.

The few Jews who resided in Acre rarely took pictures. The recurring trips to Tel Aviv became a big financial burden. Despite this, Mundek decided to take one last stab to try to locate his cousin. His time in the wilderness and his military service had taught him to be determined and persistent – and never to give up.

And so with the diligence and perseverance ingrained in him, Mundek decided to travel to Tel Aviv one last time. He spent the day in the same area of the city searching once more for a man no one seemed to know. By late afternoon, Mundek was thirsty and hungry. He finally gave up his seemingly futile search and returned to the central station to take the bus back to his family. He was tired and dejected, and walked up Herzl Street completely demoralized.

Then, just when he had given up all hope, Mundek suddenly noticed something unusual: the man ahead of him was walking very strangely. He walked in the same unique way that Mundek's cousin Joseph Łukawiecki had walked during his visit to Poland! It was at that moment that Mundek realized he was walking behind the very same cousin that he had escorted to the train station eleven years before. Mustering all of his energy, Mundek sprinted and caught up with the man walking ahead of him. He stopped him in his tracks and asked him in German, "*Heißen Sie Joseph Łukawiecki?*" (Is your name Joseph Łukawiecki?). The man turned to Mundek and answered without thinking, "*Ja, das ist mein Name*" (Yes, that is my name).

Those five words changed Mundek's life. It was as if he had literally found the proverbial needle in a haystack. Even though Mundek had not seen his cousin for more than a decade, he was still able to recognize Joseph Łukawiecki by his unusual gait. Joseph likewise immediately recognized Mundek and took him to his home, giving him food and money – and a lifeline. It was truly a case of truth being stranger than fiction. Or it was simply manifest destiny.

Shortly after their miraculous family reunion, Chana and Mundek Łukawiecki gathered together at the Cohens' home at 23 Chen Avenue in Tel Aviv. Joseph informed them that his father, Shmuel David (Mundek's grandfather's brother), had passed away a few months earlier on November 27, 1947, and was buried at the Mount of Olives. He also told them about his brother Zvi's family, as well as his sister Leiba's – the Zilbermans – and promised them all a big reunion dinner at his apartment as soon as possible.

Epilogue

Mundek and Chana seldom spoke about their experiences during the Holocaust. They were unable to tell their story coherently, yet referred to it from time to time, nonetheless. A few words here. A sentence there. But it was always very painful and accompanied with a flood of tears. Both of their consciences were wracked with guilt and this made their lives even more difficult – as they blamed themselves for not having rescued the rest of their families. Mundek often wept uncontrollably. He constantly wondered why his baby sister Judith had been killed. She was only three-years old.[1] What sin had she committed to deserve this fate? Why had he not saved her? And why had he not saved his entire family, for that matter? These questions tortured him for the rest of his life as he struggled to overcome the horrors of World War II.

Mundek and Chana were recognized by the State of Israel for their activities during World War II. Specifically, they were awarded for military services toward the establishment of the State of Israel – an award which commemorates their involvement through underground organizations and military units in engagements relating to the fighting and struggle for the establishment of the State of Israel – as well as the Fighters against Nazism Medal, which is a decoration that was awarded to World War II veterans.

Chana passed away on November 12, 1990. The inscription on her gravestone, in the Kiryat Shaul Cemetery, near Tel Aviv, dedicated by Mundek himself, reads as follows: "Ghetto and partisan warrior."

Only after writing this book do I understand the deep comprehension hidden behind those short and synoptic words, and appreciate how they tell of her brave

---

1. Mundek referred to Judith as his baby sister and constantly remembered her as she had been at age three. When she was murdered she was actually ten years old, but "she was only three" was his constant lament.

struggle against her rapist in the ghetto, whom she killed with her own hands. It was David versus Goliath: a fragile, innocent Jewish girl educated in the sheltered environment of the Beth Jacob school stood up and killed her foe, knowing that through that she had signed her own death warrant. Yet miraculously, she found her way to becoming a partisan warrior, and fought like a lioness.

Mundek passed away fourteen years later in Israel on July 24, 2004, at the age of eighty-two. In his lifetime, he had requested to be buried beside Chana, and his wish was honored. The following words are engraved on his gravestone in the Kiryat Shaul Cemetery, near Tel Aviv:

> He rose and stood alone, fearlessly
> Against the Nazi Ashmedai[2] and defeated him like a lion.
> He terrified the German brutal trooper and drove him away;
> From the pits of hell he saved Jewish lives.
> With his bare hands and courageous spirit
> Twelve times he rescued the whole world.
> May many be like him, a proud warrior in his devotion.

---

2. Asmodeus, king of the demons.

Bibliography

Primary Sources

German passport of Szmul (Shmuel David) Łukawiecki, no. 94527/6, dated June 16, 1916.

Szmul (Shmuel David) Łukawiecki, German passport application, dated May 18, 1922.

Palestine passport of Joseph Cohen, no 81472, dated March 3, 1937.

Pictures taken during WWII mainly by Edmund (Mundek) Łukawiecki.

UB personal file of Edmund (Mundek) Łukawiecki – IPN/OBUiAd/Krakow, Sygn. IPN 16 057/1028, 1945.

Shmuel Cohen, burial records, Mount of Olives, 1948.

Israel Defense Forces (IDF) personal file of Private 145296, Moshe Łukawiecki. Draft date October 11, 1948; discharge date June 5, 1949.

Lavee, Chana. Pages of testimony to Yad Vashem. January 23, 1978.

Lavee, Moshe. Pages of testimony to Yad Vashem. January 23, 1978.

Zvi Cohn (Łukawiecki), written memories, August 24, 1987, and two additional undated written memories.

Testimony of Edmund (Mundek) Łukawiecki (Moshe Lavee) to Yad Vashem, July 28, 1993. Testimony no. 03-6946, tape no. 033c/2757.

Testimony to USC Shoah Foundation Institute by Moshe Lavi. Interview code 31895, May 27, 1997. [The Hebrew family name was misspelled – it should be Lavee. This is Edmund (Mundek) Łukawiecki's recorded interview.]

Aliza Segal, undated written diary, dictated to her by Mundek Łukawiecki. Only four pages were found.

Robert M. Archer, M.D., Chief Scientific Officer, Genetic Identity, Kinship Screening Report, case number ZG 201016142, dated June 10, 2010.

Documents

BRITISH DOCUMENTS

War Cabinet Report of the Foreign Office, April 23, 1941. Anthony Eden, "Conditions in Poland." The National Archives (TNA) WP (41) 91, CAB 66/16/14.

Chairman of the British Mission, Notes on the Moscow Conference, October 8, 1941, The National Archives (TNA) WP (41) 238.

War Cabinet Report of the Foreign Office, February 17, 1943. The National Archives (TNA) WP (43) 69.

War Cabinet Report of the Foreign Office, October 5, 1943. Anthony Eden, "Secret Resistance in Poland." The National Archives (TNA) WP (43) 439, CAB 66/41/39.

War Cabinet Report of the Foreign Office, April 11, 1944. The National Archives (TNA) WP (44) 47th conclusions, minute 2, confidential annex.

War Cabinet Report of the Foreign Office, August 15, 1944. The National Archives (TNA) WP (44) 447, CAB/66/53/47.

War Cabinet Conclusions, August 21, 1944, 5:30 P.M. The National Archives (TNA) WM (44) 109.

War Cabinet Report of the Foreign Office, August 23, 1944. The National Archives (TNA) WP (44) 462.

GERMAN DOCUMENTS

Municipal records – Stuttgart. FR-Bd. 25 B-52; FR-Bd. 27-198, 1896; Bd. 232 S. 304, 1896; FR-Bd. 27-200, 1880.

Statistisches Gemeindeverzeichnis des bisherigen polnischen Staates, mit Berücksichtigung der am 28. September 1939 festgelegten Grenze der deutschen und sowjetrussischen Reichsinteressen [Statistical community directory of the current Polish state, with consideration of the September 28, 1939, border set by the interests of the German and Soviet Russian states]. Berlin, 1939.

Report by Oberfeldkommandantur (OFK) 365 (local Wehrmacht commander of district Galicia), for the period May 16, 1942–June 15, dated June 16, 1942, in Bundesarchiv-Aussenstelle Ludwigsburg, USA 314c.

Minutes of meeting of Wehrmachtsbefehlshaber (Wehrmacht commander), General Government, June 16, 1942. Bundesarchiv-Aussenstelle Ludwigsburg, USA 314c.

OFK 365 report for the period June 16, 1942–July 15, 1942, dated July 19, 1942, Bundesarchiv-Aussenstelle Ludwigsburg, USA 314b.

Report of Wilhelm Kube, commissioner general for Byelorussia, July 31, 1942.

Adolf Hitler, *Weisung* [direction] no. 46, "Richtlinien für die verstärkte Bekämpfung des Bandenunwesens im Osten" [Rules for the enforced fighting of the nuisance of bandits in the East], August 18, 1942.

Amtliches Gemeinde- und Dorfverzeichnis für das Generalgouvernement auf Grund der summarischen Bevölkerungsbestandsaufnahme am 1. März 1943, herausgegeben vom statistischen Amt des Generalgouvernement [Township and village directory for the General Government on the basis of the March 1, 1943, census, published by the Statistical Office of the General Government]. Krakow: Burgverlag Krakau, 1943.

Das Gedenkbuch des Bundesarchivs für die Opfer der nationalsozialistischen Judenverfolgung in Deutschland (1933–1945) [The Memorial Book of the Federal Archives for the victims of the Nazi persecution of the Jews in Germany (1933–1945)], 2nd ed. Das Bundesarchiv [Federal Archives], Ludwigsburg.

"Befreiten Juden in der US Zone" [Liberated Jews in the US Zone]. Testimony at Buro der Juristischen Abteilung beim Zentral Komitee der befreiten Juden Deutchlands [Office of the Legal Department of the Central Committee of Liberated Jews of Germany].

INTERNATIONAL DOCUMENTS

International Tracing Service (ITS), file T/D – 633 026.

International Tracing Service. *Verzeichnis der Haftstätten unter dem Reichsführer-SS (1933–1945): Konzentrationslager und deren Aussenkommandos sowie andere Haftstätten unter dem Reichsführer-SS in Deutschland und deutsch besetzten Gebieten* [List of places of detention under the Reichsführer-SS (1933–1945): Concentration camps and their branch camps and other places of detention under the Reichsführer-SS in Germany and German-occupied territories]. Bad Arolsen: International Tracing Service, 1979.

International Military Tribunal, *Der Nürnberger Prozess gegen die Hauptkriegsverbrecher vor dem Internationalen Militärgerichtshof, Nürnberg, 14 November 1945–1 Oktober 1946* [The Nuremberg Trial of the Major War Criminals before the International Military Tribunal, Nuremberg, November 14,

1945–October 1, 1946]. Vol. 29, Nuremberg, 1948; Vol. 37, document 018-L, pp. 391–431. Nuremberg, 1949.

The International Military Tribunal document 665-F(ii).

ISRAELI DOCUMENTS

Kulpa family request to the embassy of Israel for Righteous Among the Nations status for Józef Kulpa and his wife, dated December 31, 1992.

The Central Zionist Archives file number S104/607.

The State of Israel, Ministry of Interior records.

The Central Zionist Archive, Jerusalem, S6P/1707/1938 ל.

The Central Zionist Archives file number S104/607.

POLISH DOCUMENTS

Municipal records – Lubaczów. Death records, entry no. 57, 1920; no. 37, 1921; no. 26, 1918. Birth records, no. 37, December 1, 1920; no. 64, 1921; no. 19, 1923; no. 58, 1926. Marriage records, no. 1, 1920.

List of Bais Yaakow school chains in Poland in 1927. Bais Yaakov Center Archive, Jerusalem.

Księga Adresowa Małopolski, Lwów, Stanisławów, Tarnopol, z informatorem M. stoł. Warszawy, województwa Krakowskiego, Łódzkiego, Pomorskiego, Poznańskiego I Śląskiego, Rocznik 1935/1936, Krakow [Phone book for Malopolska, Lwów, Stanislaviv, Ternopil; table of information for Warsaw and the region of Krakow, Lodz, Pomeranian, Poznań and the Silesian, Year 1935/1936, Krakow].

Armia Krajowa w dokumentach 1939–1945 [The AK in documents, 1939–1945]. Studium Polski Podziemnej [Studies of the Polish Underground]. London: Zakład Narodowy imienia Ossolińskich, 1990.

Judisches Hilfs-Komitee Lubaczów, Judische Soziale Selbesthilfe (JSS) [Jewish Relief Committee of Lubaczów, Jewish Social Self-Help], May 22, 1942. Archiwum Żydowskiego Instytutu Historycznego (AŻIH; Archives of the Jewish Historical Institute), Zydowska Samopomoc Społeczna (JSS)/333, Bl. 9.

Polska Partia Robotnicza Kronika, 1942–1945 [Polish Workers' Party Chronicle]. Warsaw, 1962.

Biuletyn informacyjny. A weekly underground news bulletin published during the

German occupation in 1939–1944 in Warsaw (during the Warsaw Uprising as a diary) and 1944–1945 in Krakow.

Wielka Polska, pamphlet published October 10, 1943.

Sądu Powiatowego w Lubaczowie [District Court of Lubaczow], Powód Łukawiecki Aleksander Pozwany Szutko Michal [Plaintiff Aleksander Łukawiecki; defendant Michal Szutko], 1956.

"Związek Bojowników o Wolność i Demokrację Koło Miejsko – Gminne w Lubaczowie, 30 lat pracy i działalności organizacji Lubaczowskiej związku bojowników o wolność i demokrację 1949–1979" [Union of Fighters for Freedom and Democracy near the town of Lubaczów: Thirty years of work and activities of the Union of Fighters for Freedom and Democracy, 1949 to 1979]. Lubaczów, September 1979. Manuscript stored in Muzeum Kresów in Lubaczów.

Questionnaire filled out by Stanisław Kulpa dated March 12, 1987, addressed to the Żydowski Instytut Historyczny w Polsce (Jewish Historical Institute in Poland), AR-051/911-8/83.

Reply to Stanisław Kulpa dated June 26, 1987, Żydowski Instytut Historyczny w Polsce (Jewish Historical Institute in Poland), AR–051/1-275/87.

Chaim Chefer, "Registry of over 700 Polish citizens killed while helping Jews during the Holocaust," http://www.holocaustforgotten.com/list.htm.

RUSSIAN DOCUMENTS

Documentation of the special committee for Nazi crimes in the USSR, in the area of Grodek, Rawa Ruska. State Archive of the Russian Federation, Moscow.

Maps

Szajowski, Adam. Plan Lubaczowa e usytuowaniem Getta Lubaczów, styczeń 1943 [Map of Lubaczów with the location of the Lubaczów ghetto, January 1943].

Unterschutz, R. Die Deutschen Siedlungen in Galizien, stand 1939 [(Map of) German settlements in Galicia as of 1939]. An updated 2003 version of this map is credited to R. Unterschutz and Philip Semanchuk.

Testimonies

Baecker, Samuel. February 18, 1948, at Buro der Juristischen Abteilung beim

Zentral Komitee der befreiten Juden Deutchlands [Legal Department of the Central Committee of Liberated Jews of Germany], US Zone, Munich.

Feber, Pepi. February 26, 1948, at Buro der Juristischen Abteilung beim Zentral Komitee der befreiten Juden Deutchlands, US Zone, Munich.

Gar, Leon. February 17, 1948, at Buro der Juristischen Abteilung beim Zentral Komitee der befreiten Juden Deutchlands, US Zone, Munich.

Herzig, Dr. Jakob. Testimony to Yad Vashem, no. M49/E1132. No date recorded.

Kammer, Benjamin. February 18, 1948, at Buro der Juristischen Abteilung beim Zentral Komitee der befreiten Juden Deutchlands, US Zone, Munich.

Kammer, Feiga. Warsaw, Żydowski Instytut Historyczny. No date recorded. Yad Vashem no. M49/1174 LB.440.

Katz, Edmund. Excerpt from Polish newspaper *Slowo Polskie*, published in Wroclaw, January 1, 1948. Yad Vashem no. M49E/3300. Żydowski Instytut Historyczny [Jewish Historical Institute], Warsaw.

Post, Regina. February 18, 1948, at Buro der Juristischen Abteilung beim Zentral Komitee der befreiten Juden Deutchlands, US Zone, Munich.

Schoegker [sic], Max. February 22, 1948, at Buro der Juristischen Abteilung beim Zentral Komitee der befreiten Juden Deutchlands, US Zone, Munich.

Weiner, Luba. February 19, 1948, at Buro der Juristischen Abteilung beim Zentral Komitee der befreiten Juden Deutchlands, US Zone, Munich,

Weiner, Zanwet. February 18, 1948, at Buro der Juristischen Abteilung beim Zentral Komitee der befreiten Juden Deutchlands, US Zone, Munich,

Personal Interviews

Argasiński, Mieczysław. Lubaczów, Poland. September 24–25, 2010; March 11–12, 2011.

Baum, Lula Weiner Tel Aviv, Israel. February 24, 2010; April 17, 2011; January 18, 2012.

Bauman, Adam. Lubaczów, Poland. January 18, 2012.

Burek, Władysław. Lubaczów, Poland. February 24–25, 2010; September 24, 2010.

Diner, Chana. Tel Aviv, Israel. January 29, 2011; January 27, 2012; February 22, 2012.

Fishman, Perl. Haifa, Israel. April 16, 2010.

Genosar, Motti. Haifa, Israel. June 3, 2009.

Grzegorz, Prof. Bubek. See Łukawiecki, Zofia.

Helman, Isaac. Nazareth, Israel. May 1, 2010; June 2, 2011.

Kolodziej, Josefa. Nowe Sioło, Poland. March 12, 2011.

Kulpa, Janusz. Lubaczów, Poland. January 19, 2012.

Levin, Dahlia. Ramat Gan, Israel. June 6, 2011.

Łukawiecki, Zofia, and her son Prof. Bubek Grzegorz. Cracow, Poland. September 22, 2010; October 8, 2012.

Marcus, Miriam. Ramat Gan, Israel. February 27, 2012.

Podporski, Czesław, and his mother Maria Szutka. Ostrowiec, Poland. January 18, 2010; February 25, 2010; September 24–25, 2010; September 27, 2010; March 11–12, 2011; March 27, 2012.

Ran (Rand), Joseph. Tel Aviv, Israel. March 5, 2013.

Róg, Tomasz. Lubaczów, Poland. November 3, 2010.

Segal, Aliza. Ramat Gan, Israel. May 30, 2011; February 5, 2012; April 17, 2012.

Szutka, Maria. See Podporski, Czesław.

Weinberg, Isaac. Herzliya, Israel. May 30, 2011; June 5, 2012.

Władek, Sikum. Nowe Sioło, Poland. March 3, 2011.

Personal Correspondence

Hoffman, Maurie. May 21, 2009, e-mail.

Róg, Tomasz. October 22, 2010; November 3, 2010, e-mails.

Warner, Joe. May 22, 2011, e-mail.

Archives and Museums

Archiwum Zakladu Historii Partii (AZHP, Archives of the Polish Communist Party), Warsaw.

Archiwum Żydowskiego Instytutu Historycznego (AŻIH; Archives of the Jewish Historical Institute), Warsaw.

Bais Yaakov Center Archive, Jerusalem.

Bundesarchiv-Aussenstelle, Ludwigsburg, Germany.

Muzeum Kresów, Lubaczów.

State Archive of the Russian Federation, Moscow.

Sources in English

Arad, Yitzhak. *Belzec, Sobibor, Treblinka: The Operation Reinhard Death Camps.* Bloomington: Indiana University Press, 1987.

Armstrong, John L. "The Polish Underground and the Jews: A Reassessment of Home Army Commander Tadeusz Bór-Komorowski's Order 116 against Banditry." *Slavonic and East European Review* 72 (1994): 259–76.

Benish, Pearl. *Carry Me in Your Heart: The Life and Legacy of Sarah Schenirer, Founder and Visionary of the Bais Yaakov Movement.* New York: Feldheim, 2004.

Bór-Komorowski, Tadeusz. *The Secret Army.* Nashville, TN: Battery Press, 1984.

Browning, Christopher R. *The Origins of the Final Solution Policy: The Evolution of the Nazi Jewish Policy, September 1939–March 1942.* Lincoln: University of Nebraska Press, 2004.

Campbell, Stephen. *Police Battalions of the Third Reich.* Schiffer Military History. Atglen, PA: Schiffer, 2007.

Cores, Amy Sara Davis. "Jews in the Armia Krajowa." M.A. thesis, Florida State University, 2000.

Dean, Martin, ed. *Ghettos in German-Occupied Eastern Europe.* Vol. 2 in *Encyclopedia of Camps and Ghettos, 1933–1945*, edited by Geoffrey P. Megargee. Bloomington: Indiana University Press in association with the United States Holocaust Memorial Museum, 2012.

Desbois, Father Patrick. *The Holocaust by Bullets: A Priest's Journey to Uncover the Truth behind the Murder of 1.5 Million Jews.* Houndmills, UK: Palgrave Macmillan, 2008.

Gerstenfeld-Maltiel, Jacob. *My Private War: One Man's Struggle to Survive the Soviets and the Nazis.* London: Valentine Mitchell, 1993.

Gutman, Israel, ed. *The Encyclopedia of the Righteous Among the Nations: Rescuers of Jews during the Holocaust.* Vols. 4 and 5, *Poland*, edited by Sara Bender and Shmuel Krakowski. Jerusalem: Yad Vashem, 2004.

Gutman, Israel, and Shmuel Krakowski. *Unequal Victims: Poles and Jews during World War Two.* New York: Holocaust Library, 1986.

Hartman, John J., and Jacek Krochmal, eds. *I Remember Every Day... The Fates of the Jews of Przemyśl during World War II.* Przemyśl: Towarzystwo Przyjaciół Nauk w Przemyślu, 2002.

Heitmeyer, Wilhelm, and John Hagan. *International Handbook of Violence Research*, Boston: Kluwer Academic Publishers, 2003.

Heller, Daniel Kupfert. "The Rise of the Zionist Right: Polish Jews and the Betar Youth Movement, 1922–1935." Dissertation submitted to the Department of History and the Committee on Graduate Studies of Stanford University in partial fulfillment of the requirements for the degree of doctor of philosophy, August 2012, Stanford University.

Hoffman, Maurie. *Keep Yelling: A Survivor's Testimony*. Richmond, Australia: Spectrum Publications, 1995.

Klee, Ernst, Willi Dressen, and Volker Riess, eds. *The Good Old Days: The Holocaust as Seen by Its Perpetrators and Bystanders*. New York: William S. Konecky Associates, 1996.

Klukowski, Zygmunt. *Diary from the Years of Occupation, 1939–44*. Translated by George Klukowski. Urbana: University of Illinois Press, 1993.

Kowalski, Isaac, ed. *Anthology on Armed Jewish Resistance, 1939–1945*. New York: Jewish Combatants Publishers House, 1991.

Krakowski, Shmuel. "The Polish Underground and the Jews in the Years of the Second World War." In *Nazi Europe and the Final Solution*, edited by David Bankier and Israel Gutman, pp. 215–30. Jerusalem: Yad Vashem 2003.

———. *The War of the Doomed: Jewish Armed Resistance in Poland, 1942–1944*. New York: Holmes and Meier, 1984.

Lukas, Richard C. *Forgotten Holocaust: The Poles under German Occupation, 1939–1944*, rev. ed. New York: Hippocrene Books, 2005.

MacLean, French L. *The Cruel Hunters: SS-Sonderkommando Dirlewanger; Hitler's Most Notorious Anti-Partisan Unit*. Schiffer Military History. Atglen, PA: Schiffer, 1998.

Madejczyk, Czesław. "Deportations in the Zamość region 1942 and 1943 in the Light of German documents. *Acta Poloniae Historica* 1 (1958): 75–106.

Miron, Guy, and Shlomit Shulhani, eds., *The Yad Vashem Encyclopedia of the Ghettos during the Holocaust*. Jerusalem: Yad Vashem, 2010.

Mitcham, Samuel W., Jr. *The Men of Barbarossa: Commanders of the German Invasion of Russia, 1941*. Havertown, PA: Casemate, 2009.

Moskop, Joseph M., ed., *The Tomaszow Lubelski Memorial Book*, trans. Jacob Solomon Berger (Mahwah, NJ: Jacob Solomon Berger, 2008)

Piotrowski, Tadeusz, ed. *Genocide and Rescue in Wołyń: Recollections of the*

Ukrainian Nationalist Ethnic Cleansing Campaign against the Poles during World War II. London: McFarland, 2000.

———. *Poland's Holocaust: Ethnic Strife, Collaboration with Occupying Forces and Genocide in the Second Republic, 1918–1947*, London: McFarland, 1998.

Poprzeczny, Joseph. *Odilo Globocnik, Hitler's Man in the East*. Jefferson, NC: McFarland, 2004.

Rhodes, Richard. *Masters of Death: The SS-Einsatzgruppen and the Invention of the Holocaust*. New York: Alfred A. Knopf, 2002.

Rigg, Brian Mark. *Hitler's Jewish Soldiers: The Untold Story of Nazi Racial Laws and Men of Jewish Descent in the German Military*. Lawrence: University Press of Kansas, 2002.

Roberts, Andrew. *The Storm of War: A New History of the Second World War*. New York: Harper Collins, 2011.

Sabrin, B. F., ed. *Alliance for Murder: The Nazi-Ukrainian Nationalist Partnership in Genocide*. New York: Sarpedon, 1991.

Sanford, George. "The Katyn Massacre and Polish-Soviet Relations, 1941–43." *Journal of Contemporary History* 41, no.1 (2006): 95–111.

———. *Katyn and the Soviet Massacre of 1940: Truth, Justice and Memory*. BASEES/Routledge Series on Russian and East European Studies, no. 20. London: Routledge, 2005.

Snyder, Timothy. "'To Resolve the Ukrainian Problem Once and for All': The Ethnic Cleansing of Ukrainians in Poland, 1943–1947." *Journal of Cold War Studies* 1, no. 2 (spring 1999): 86–120.

Spector, Shmuel, editor in chief. *The Encyclopedia of Jewish Life before and during the Holocaust*. New York: NYU Press, 2001.

Tomashover Relief Committee, *TomashoverLubelski Yizkor Bukh* [Memorial book of Tomaszów Lubelski]. New York: Tomashover Relief Committee, 1965.

Tomaszewski, Irene, and Tecia Werbowski. *Code Name: Żegota; Rescuing Jews in Occupied Poland, 1942–1945; The Most Dangerous Conspiracy in Wartime Europe*. Santa Barbara, CA: Praeger, 1999.

Trepper, Leopold. *The Great Game: The Story of the Red Orchestra*. Translated by Helen Weaver. London: Michael Joseph, 1977.

Westermann, Edward B. *Hitler's Police Battalions: Enforcing Racial War in the East*. Lawrence: University Press of Kansas, 2005.

Wnuk, Rafał. "Resistance 1939–1941: The Polish Underground under Soviet Occupation and the Jews." In *Shared History, Divided Memory: Jews and Others in Soviet-Occupied Poland, 1939–1941*, edited by Elazar Barkan, Elizabeth A. Cole, and Kai Struve, 147–71. Leipzig: Leipziger Universitätsverlag, 2007.

Yones, Eliyahu. *Smoke in the Sand: The Jews of Lvov in the War Years, 1939–1944*. Jerusalem: Gefen Publishing House, 2004.

Ziemke, Earl F. *Stalingrad to Berlin: The German Defeat in the East*. United States Army Historical Series, Washington, DC: Center of Military History, 1987.

Sources in German

Bednarski, Waldemar. "Das Gesicht des Krieges in der Gemeinde Kotlice (Kreis Zamość) 1939 bis 1945" [The face of war in the municipality of Kotlice (Zamość county), 1939–1945]. In *Die polnische Heimatarmee: Geschichte und Mythos der Armia Krajowa seit dem Zweiten Weltkrieg* [The Polish Home Army: History and myth of the Armia Krajowa since the Second World War], edited by Bernhard Chiari, 411–30. Munich: Oldenbourg Verlag, 2003.

Chiari, Bernhard. "Grenzen deutscher Herrschaft: Voraussetzungen und Folgen der Besatzung in der Sowjetunion" [The boundaries of German rule: Conditions and consequences of the occupation in the Soviet Union]. In *Das Deutsche Reich und der Zweite Weltkrieg* [The German Reich and the Second World War], edited by Jörg Echternkamp. Vol. 9, bk. 2, *Ausbeutung, Deutungen, Ausgrenzung* [Exploitation, interpretations, exclusion], 877–976. Stuttgart: Deutsche Verlags-Anstalt, 2005.

———. "Die Ukraine im Spannungsfeld von Nationsbildung und deutscher Herrschaft" [The Ukraine in conflict between nation-building and German domination]. In *Das Deutsche Reich und der Zweite Weltkrieg* [The German Reich and the Second World War], edited by Jörg Echternkamp. Vol. 9, bk. 2, *Ausbeutung, Deutungen, Ausgrenzung* [Exploitation, interpretations, exclusion], 942–54. Stuttgart: Deutsche Verlags-Anstalt, 2005.

Curilla, Wolfgang. *Der Judenmord in Polen und die deutsche Ordnungspolizei, 1939–1945* [The murder of the Jews in Poland and the German Order Police, 1939–1945]. Paderborn, Germany: Ferdinand Schöningh, 2011.

Frank, Hans. *Das Diensttagebuch des deutschen Generalgouverneurs in Polen, 1939–1945* [The service diary of the German Governor-General in Poland,

1939–1945]. Edited by Werner Präg and Wolfgang Jacobmeyer. Stuttgart: Deutsche Verlags-Anstalt, 1975.

Heinemann, Isabel. *Rasse, Siedlung, deutsches Blut: Das Rasse- und Siedlungshauptamt der SS und die rassenpolitische Neuordnung Europas* [Race, settlement, German blood: The Race and Settlement Main Office of the SS and the racial political reorganization of Europe]. Göttingen: Wallstein, 2003.

Herzog, Leon. "Die verbrecherische Tätigkeit der Wehrmacht im Generalgouvernement in den Jahren 1939 bis 1945" [The criminal activities of the Wehrmacht in the General Government in the years 1939 to 1945]. *Zeitschrift für Militärgeschichte* [Journal of military history] 6 (1967): 445–58.

Hirsch, Helga. "Wir waren Besatzer in einem fremden Land: Warum Artur Singer sein Dorf in Bessarabien verlassen musste" [We were occupiers in a foreign country: Why Arthur Singer was forced to leave his village in Bessarabia]. In *Entwurzelt: Vom Verlust der Heimat zwischen Oder und Bug* [Uprooted: On the loss of the homeland between the Oder and Bug]. Hamburg: Körber-Stiftung, 2007.

Hoffmann, Jens. *Das kann man nicht erzählen: Aktion 1005; Wie die Nazis die Spuren ihrer Massenmorde in Osteuropa beseitigten* [This cannot be told: Operation 1005; How the Nazis removed the traces of their mass murder in Eastern Europe]. Hamburg: Konkret Verlag, 2008.

Mazur, Grzegorz. "Der Bund für den bewaffneten Kampf-Heimatarmee und seine Gliederung" [The Federation for armed struggle-Home Army and its structure]. In *Die polnische Heimatarmee: Geschichte und Mythos der Armia Krajowa seit dem Zweiten Weltkrieg* [The Polish Home Army: The history and the legend of the Armia Krajowa since the Second World War], edited by Bernhard Chiari, 111–49. Munich: Oldenbourg Verlag, 2003.

Mick, Christoph. *Kriegserfahrungen in einer multiethnischen Stadt: Lemberg 1914–1947* [War experiences in a multi-ethnic city: Lwów 1914–1947]. Deutsches Historisches Institut Warschau, Quellen und Studien, vol. 22. Wiesbaden: Harrassowitz Verlag, 2010.

Müller, Roland. *Stuttgart zur Zeit des Nationalsozialismus* [Stuttgart in the time of National Socialism]. Tübingen: Konrad Theiss Verlag, 1988.

Ney-Krawicz, Marek. "Die Führung der Republik Polen im Exil" [The leadership of the Republic of Poland in exile]. In *Die polnische Heimatarmee: Geschichte und Mythos der Armia Krajowa seit dem Zweiten Weltkrieg* [The Polish Home

Army: History and myth of the Armia Krajowa since the Second World War], edited by Bernhard Chiari, 151–67. Munich: Oldenbourg Verlag, 2003.

Pohl, Dieter. *Nationalsozialistische Judenverfolgung in Ostgalizien, 1941–1944: Organisation und Durchführung eines staatlichen Massenverbrechens* [National Socialist persecution of the Jews in Eastern Galicia, 1941–1944: Organization and implementation of a state mass crime]. Munich: Oldenbourg Verlag, 1997.

Roth, Markus. *Herrenmenschen: Die deutschen Kreishauptleute im besetzten Polen – Karrierewege, Herrschaftspraxis und Nachgeschichte* [Master race: the German district captains in occupied Poland – career paths, governing practice, and subsequent history]. Göttingen: Wallstein, 2009.

Wasser, Bruno. *Himmlers Raumplanung im Osten: Der Generalplan Ost in Polen, 1940–1944* [Himmler's spatial planning in the East: The General Plan for the East in Poland, 1940–1944]. Stadt Planung Geschichte [City planning history series], no. 15. Birkhäuser, 1993.

Wells, Leon Weliczker. *Ein sohn Hiobs* [A son of Job]. Munich: Hanser, 1963.

Wilhelm, Franz, and Josef Kallbrunner. *Quellen zur deutschen Siedlungsgeschichte in Südosteuropa* [Sources to German settlement history in southeast Europe]. Schriften der deutschen Akademie [Publications of the German Academy], no. 2. Munich: Ernst Reinhardt, 1936.

Witte, Peter, Michael Wildt, Martina Voight, Dieter Pohl, et al., eds. *Der Dienstkalender Heinrich Himmlers 1941–1942* [Heinrich Himmler's Desk Diary, 1941–1942]. Hamburg: Hans Christians Verlag, 1999.

Zelzer, Maria. *Weg und Schicksal der Stuttgarter Juden* [The path and fate of Stuttgart's Jews]. Stuttgart: Ernst Klett Verlag, 1964.

Sources in Hebrew

Carmy, Col. Yisrael. *B'derech lochamim* [In the way of warriors]. Tel Aviv: Maarachot–IDF Publishing House, 1960.

Sources in Polish

Argasiński, Mieczysław. *Armia Krajowa: Wolność i Niezawisłość, Lubaczów* [The Home Army (AK): Freedom and independence, Lubaczów]. Lubaczów: Komisja Historyczna przy Zarządzie Koła Światowego Związku Żołnierzy

Armii Krajowej [Historical Commission for the Management Board of the World Association of AK Soldiers], 2002.

———. *Konspiracja w powiecie lubaczowskim w latach 1939–1947* [Conspiracy in Lubaczów county in the years 1939–1947]. Zwierzyniec: Ostoja, 2010.

Armia Krajowa w Dokumentach, 1939–1945, tom 3: kwiecień 1943–lipiec 1944 [AK documents, 1939–1945, vol. 3, April 1943–July 1944]. London, 1976. Reprint, Wroclaw: Osssolineum, 1990.

Armia Krajowa w Dokumentach, 1939–1945, tom 4: lipiec 1944–październik 1944 [AK documents, 1939–1945, vol. 4, July 1944–October 1944]. London, 1977. Reprint, Wroclaw: Osssolineum, 1990.

Armia Krajowa w Dokumentach, 1939–1945, tom 5: październik 1944–lipiec 1945 [AK documents, 1939–1945, vol. 5, October 1944–July 1945]. London, 1981. Reprint, Wroclaw: Osssolineum, 1990.

Bednarski, Waldemar W. "Z dziejów okupacji Ziemi Tomaszowskiej przez Armię Czerwoną oraz terroru UB-NKWD" [The history of the occupation of the lands of Tomaszow by the Red Army and UB-NKVD terror]. *Radzynski Rocznik Humanistyczny* [The Humanities Yearbook of Radzyn Podlaski] 5 (2007): 145–55.

Berezecki, Mieczysław. "Grupa Bojowa z Lasu Dąbrowa." In Caban, *Związek Walki Zbrojnej*. Lublin: Czas, 1999.

Caban, Ireneusz. *Na dwa fronty: Obwód AK Tomaszów Lubelski w walce z Niemcami i ukraińskimi nacjonalistami* [On two fronts: The Tomaszów Lubelski district AK against the Germans and Ukrainian nationalists]. Lublin: Czas, 1999.

———. *Oddziały partyzanckie i samoobrony obwodu AK Tomaszów Lubelski* [Partisan units and self-defense in the Tomaszów Lubelski district AK]. Warsaw: O.K. Tomasz Wiater, 2000.

———. *Związek Walki Zbrojnej Armia Krajowa w Obwodzie Tomaszów Lubelski: relacje, wspomnienia, opracowania, dokumenty* [Armed Combat Union Army in the Tomaszów Lubelski district: Reports, memoirs, studies, documents]. Lublin: Czas, 1999.

Chodorska, Jolanta, ed. *Godni synowie naszej Ojczyzny: Świadectwa nadesłane na apel Radia Maryja* [Worthy sons of our country: Testimonies contributed to Radio Maria]. Vol. 2. Warsaw: Wydawnictwo Sióstr Loretanek, 2002.

Fenczak, August, Zdzisław Konieczny, and Elżbieta Forbot. *Źródła do dziejów regionu przemyskiego w latach 1944–1949* [Sources for the history of the Przemyśl region in the years 1944–1949]. Przemyśl: Wojewódzkie Archiwum Państwowe w Przemyślu, 1979.

Frank, Hans, *Okupacja i ruch oporu w dzienniku Hansa Franka, 1939–1945* [Occupation and Resistance in the diary of Hans Frank, 1939–1945]. 2 vols. Warsaw: Książka i Wiedza, 1972.

Friedman, Filip. *Zagłada Żydów lwowskich* [The extermination of the Jews of Lwów]. Łódź: Centralnej Żydowskiej Komisji Historycznej (Central Jewish Historical Commission), 1945.

Grygiel, Jan. *Związek Walki Zbrojnej: Armia Krajowa w obwodzie zamojskim 1939-1944; Szkice, wspomnienia, dokumenty* [ZWZ: The AK in the Zamość district 1939–1944; Sketches, memories, documents]. Warsaw: Panstwowe Wydawnictwo Naukowe, 1985.

Jones, Eliyahu. *Żydzi Lwówa w okresie okupacji, 1939–1945* [The Jews of Lwów during the occupation, 1939–1945]. Łódź: Oficyna Bibliofilów, 1999.

Juchniewicz, Mieczyslaw. "Kowpakowcy w Polsce" [Units led by Soviet partisan Sydir Kovpak in Poland] *Wojskowy Przeglad Historyczny* [Military history review] 3, no. 4 (1958).

Katzmann, Friedrich. *Rozwiązanie kwestii zydowskiej w dystrykcie Galicja* [The solution to the Jewish question in the district of Galicia]. Warsaw: Instytut Pamięci Narodowej, 2001.

Kirchmayer, Jerzy. *Powstanie Warszawskie* [The Warsaw uprising]. Warsaw: Książka i Wiedza, 1959.

Klukowski, Zygmunt. *Dziennik z lat okupacji Zamojszczyzny* [Diary of the occupation of the Zamość region]. Lublin: Lubelska Spółdzielnia Wydawnicza, 1959.

———. *Zamojszczyzny* [The Zamość region]. Vol. 1, *1918–1943*. Warsaw: Ośrodek Karta, 2007.

Komański, Henryk, Szczepan Siekierka, et al., *Ludobójstwo dokonane przez nacjonalistów ukraińskich na Polakach w województwie tarnopolskim, 1939–1946* [The genocide committed by the Ukrainian nationalists against the Poles in Ternopil province, 1939–1946]. Wroclaw: Nortom, 2004.

Kubrak, Zygmunt. *Ofiary Holokaustu* [Victims of the Holocaust]. Lubaczów: Towarzysto Miłośników Ziemi Lubacozwskiej, 2003.

———. *Rok 44* [Year 44]. Lubaczów: Muzeum Kresow w Lubaczowie, 2004.

Kulik, Marian. "Tragiczny epilog." In Caban, *Związek Walki Zbrojnej*. Lublin: Czas, 1999.

Libionka, Dariusz. "ZWZ-AK i delegatura rządu RP wobec eksterminacji Żydów polskich" [ZWZ-AK and the Polish government delegation of the extermination of Polish Jews]. In *Polacy i Żydzi pod okupacją niemiecką, 1939–1945* [Poles and Jews under German occupation, 1939–1945], edited by Andrzej Żbikowski, 15–208. Warsaw: Instytut Pamięci Narodowej, 2006.

"Ludobójstwo – Grabieże – Zniszczenia – Powiat Stryj" [Genocide – Looting – Destruction – district of Stryj], *Na Rubieży: Czasopismo historyczno-publicystyczne* [On the rim: Historical and current affairs magazine] 35 (1999): 43–45.

Markiewicz, Jerzy. *Paprocie zakwitły krwią partyzantów. O wielkich bitwach w Puszczy Solskiej w czerwcu 1944 roku*. Warsaw: Ludowa Spółdzielnia Wydawnicza, 1961.

Markiewicz, Jerzy. *Partyzancki kraj: Zamojszczyzna 1 i 1944–15 vi 1944* [Partisan Land: The Zamość Region January 1, 1944–June 15, 1944]. Lublin: Wydawnictwo Lubelskie, 1980.

Niećko, Józef, and Maria Szczawińska, eds. *Żelazne Kompanie Batalionów Chłopskich*. Warsaw: Chłopski Świat, 1948.

Ogryzło, Roman. "Holocaust Żydow Lubaczowskich" [The Holocaust of the Jews of Lubaczów]. *Pogranicze* 33 (August 1995).

———. "Wybrane Zagadnienia Demograficzne" [Selected demographic issues]. In *Rocznik Lubaczowski* [Lubaczów yearbook], vol. 5. Lubaczów: Towarzysto Miłośników Ziemi Lubacozwskiej, 1994.

Pobóg-Malinowski, Władysław. *Najnowsza historia polityczna Polski* [Recent Polish political history]. Vol. 3, *1939–1945*. London: Gryf, 1960.

Poleszak, Slawomir, ed., *Rok pierwszy: Powstanie i działalność aparatu bezpieczeństwa publicznego na Lubelszczyźnie, lipiec 1944–czerwiec 1945* [Year one: Establishment and operation of public security apparatus in the Lublin region, July 1944–June 1945] (Warsaw: Instytut Pamięci Narodowej, 2004).

Polish Military Historical Institute. *20 lat Ludowego Wojska Polskiego – II sesja naukowa poświęcona Wojnie Wyzwoleńcze Narodu Polskiego, 1939–1945* [Twenty years of the Polish army: Second scientific session devoted to the War of Liberation of the Polish Nation]. Warsaw: Wydawnictwo Ministerstwa Obrony Narodowej (Ministry of Defense Publishers), 1967.

Puławski, Adam. "Postrzeganie żydowskich oddziałów partyzanckich przez Armię Krajową i Delegaturę Rządu RP na Kraj" [Perceptions of Jewish partisan units of the Home Army and the Delegation of the Polish Government in Exile]. *Pamięć i Sprawiedliwość* [Memory and justice] 2, no. 4 (2003): 271–300.

Rączy, lżbieta. "Stosunki polsko-żydowskie w latach drugiej wojny światowej na Rzeszowszczyźnie" [Polish-Jewish relations during the Second World War in Rzeszów]. In *Polacy i Żydzi pod okupacją niemiecką, 1939–1945* [Poles and Jews under German occupation, 1939–1945], edited by Andrzej Żbikowski, 891–940. Warsaw: Instytut Pamięci Narodowej, 2006.

Radziwonczyk, Kazimierz. "Niemieckie Siły Zbrojne w okupowanej Polsce" [The German armed forces in occupied Poland]. *Wojskowy Przeglad Historyczny* [Military history review] 4 (1962): 60–61.

Rawski, Tadeusz, Zdzisław Stapor, and Jan Zamojski. *Wojna wyzwoleńcza narodu polskiego w latach, 1939–1945: Wezlowe problemy* [The war of Liberation of the Polish nation in the years 1939–1945: Key problems]. Warsaw: Ministerstwa Obrony Narodowej, 1963.

Róg, Tomasz. *"...i zostanie tylko pustynia": Osobowy wykaz ofiar konfliktu ukraińsko-polskiego 1939–1948*. ["...And there is only one desert": Personal list of the victims of the Ukrainian-Polish conflict, 1939–1948] Rzeszów: Gmina Cieszanów, powiat Lubaczów, 2011.

Sulimierski, Filip, Bronisław Chlebowski, and Władysław Walewski. *Slownik geograficzny królestwa polskiego i innych krajów slowianskich* [The geographical dictionary of the kingdom of Poland and other Slavic countries]. Warsaw, 1880–1902.

Szajowski, Eugeniusz. "Tylko ziemia została ta sama: Lubaczów 1942–1943" [Only the land was the same: Lubaczów 1942–1943]. In *Rocznik Lubaczowski* [Lubaczów yearbook], vol. 9–10. Lubaczów: Towarzysto Miłośników Ziemi Lubacozwskiej, 2000.

Szwagrzyk, Krzysztof, ed. *Aparat bezpieczeństwa w Polsce: Kadra kierownicza* [Security apparatus in Poland: The leadership]. Vol. 1, 1944–1956. Warsaw: Instytut Pamięci Narodowej, 2005.

———. "Żydzi w kierownictwie UB: Stereotyp czy rzeczywistość" [Jews in the leadership of the UB: Stereotype or reality]. *Biuletyn Instytutu Pamięci Narodowej* 11 (2005): 37–42.

Szymański, Tadeusz. *My ze Spalonych Wsi* [We of the burned village]. Warsaw: Ministerstwa Obrony Narodowej, 1965.

United People's Party, Chief Committee, Department of History of the People's Movement. *Materiały źródłowe do historii polskiego ruchu ludowego* [Source materials on the history of the Polish peasant movement]. Warsaw: Ludowa Spółdzielnia Wydawnicza [People's Publishing Cooperative], 1966.

Węgierski, Jerzy. *W lwowskiej Armii Krajowej* [In the Lwów AK]. Warsaw: Pax, 1989.

Wnuk, Rafał. *Lubelski Okręg AK, DSZ i WiN, 1944–1947* [Lublin District AK, DPS (Delegatura Sil Zbrojnych–Armed Forces Delegation for Poland) and WiN (Wolność i Niezawisłość–Freedom and Independence), 1944–1947]. Warsaw: Volumen, 2000.

Zaderecki, Tadeusz. "Gdy swastyka Lwowem władala" [When the swastika ruled Lwów]. Yad Vashem Archives, 06/28.

Zarzycki, Wiesław. "Kolonizacja józefińska w powiecie lubaczowskim" [Josephian colonization in Lubaczów county]. Master's thesis written under the direction of Prof. Joseph Półćwiartek, Rzeszów, 1992.

Sources in Ukrainian

Krokhmaliuk, Roman. *Zahrava na Skhodi: spohady i dokumenty z pratsi u Viĭs'koviĭ upravi "Halychyna" v 1943–1945 rokakh*. Toronto: Nakladom Bratstva, 1978.

Index of Names, Places, and Events

Note: Names and places occurring a great number of times throughout the book, such as Edmund "Mundek" Łukawiecki, Chana Bern, and Lubaczów, were not included in the index.

Acre, 277–78
activities against Nazi and Ukrainian targets, Łukawiecki partisans', 241–45
agreement (1944) between Red Army and Polish underground, 254
air raids against partisans, 236
Alter, Feiga, 108n3
ambushes of German soldiers, 245
Ansbach, 276
anti-partisan operation in Poland, German, 171
Argasiński, Mieczysław, 267n21
arrival in Israel, Mundek and family's, 277
Asbach, Hans Adolf, 99
Atlit, 277
attack by AK on German fuel train, 174–77
Auschwitz, 147

Baczewski family, 42n6
Bandera, Stepan Andriyovych, 12, 12n13, 36, 58, 89, 94, 217, 246, 250
Bartoszewski, Konrad ("Wit"), 175–77
Baum, Abram, 166
Baum, Anshel, 276
Becholek (collaborator), 187, 188
Beitz, Berthold, 247n4
Beitz, Else, 247n4
Belz, 19n2

Bełżec, 152, 174, 207
extermination camp, 83, 95, 106, 130, 148, 172, 174n5, 185, 204, 247
Berger (Hit Squad member), 16, 242
Bern, Abraham Joel, 21
Bern, Gittel Katz, 20–21, 20n6, 20n13, 22, 102, 106, 108, 113, 120, 222
Bern, Hanoch, 21, 108, 118, 120, 222
Bern, Henye, 21, 108, 120, 125, 222
Bern, Szymon (Shimon), 19, 20–22, 20n6, 21, 102, 106, 107–8, 113, 118, 120, 125
Bertak, Sasober, 32n56
Bessarabia, 147
Bialot (collaborator), 173
Biłgoraj, 4n2, 12, 95, 152, 207, 218, 222, 235, 236
Bircza, 166
Biysk, 87
Blich, Dr., 269
Blobel, Paul, 98, 98nn4–5
Bogner, Anshel (Hit Squad member), 7, 15, 16, 18, 185–88, 186, 187n, 190, 199, 205, 206, 207, 208, 214, 219, 229–31, 242–43, 250, 251, 252, 253, 255
Bogner, Bell, 186
Bogner, Gittel, 186, 188
Bogner, Isaac, 186, 188
Bogner, Neshel, 186

Bogner, Pearl Singer, 186 s
Bogner, Rebecca, 187
Bogner, Sylvia, 188
Bogner, Zalman, 186
Bór woods, 127, 128, 134, 181, 193, 211
Bornstein, Yehuda, 276
Borysław, 246, 248
Brand, Berish, 5, 6, 7, 15, 181–83, 182, 188, 190, 192, 206, 209, 219, 242, 250, 251, 252, 255
Braun, Isaac, 167
Brygidki Prison, Łukawieckis in, 59–60
Bug River, 156, 239
Bulgaria, 147
Burek, Władysław, 125
Burek family, 124, 125–26
Bytom (Beuthen), 20n13

Caban family, 88n2
Canaris, Wilhelm, 39
capturing German officers and soldiers, 95–96
Chojnice (Konitz), 20n13
Chrabec brothers, 55
Cieszanów, 20, 26, 36, 47, 240–41
Cieszanówer, Benjamin (Binem), 19
Cieszanówer, Gittel (Tova), 19
Cieszanówer, Shimon. *See* Bern, Shimon
Cieszanówer, Wolf (Zeev), 19
Cieszanówer Diner, Chana, 19, 19n4
Cieszanówer family, 120
Ciotusza, 94
Cohen, Chaja Weinberg, 22
Cohen, Moses, 22
Cohen, Zippora, 33, 34
Cohen, Zvi, 279
collaborators, Jewish 3–7, 11–18, 132
collaborators, non-Jewish
    execution, 218–21, 273
    finding, 266

Czapacha, Hryhorij, 55, 100
Czerkasy, 250

Dąbrowa woods, 79, 83, 84, 88, 148, 149, 194, 196, 208, 210, 211, 215, 218, 223, 270
Dachnów, 6, 14, 20n13, 62, 104, 128, 129, 129, 130–33, 131n13, 184–85, 222, 267
destroying a German officers' whorehouse club, 207
destruction of bridge over Osuchy Ravine, 229–31
Diamond (Judenrat member), 132
Diamond, Esti, 132
Diner, Joseph Zvi, 19n4
Długi Kąt, 174
Dniester River, 254
Dołchobyczów, 245
Dorohusk, 139
Doruhusza, 139
Drugie, Kąty, 242
Drzewicki, Andrzej, 258n8, 267n21
Dudko (priest), 37, 52

Earl of Sokolniki, 73
East Galicia, 56, 238–39, 239n4, 241, 244
Ebensee, 275, 275n47
encountering Joseph Łukawiecki Cohen in Tel Aviv, 279
England, 94
escape from Poland, Mundek and family, 275
escape to Ostrowiec, 121–24
execution of collaborators, 206, 243–44
execution of Jews
    at anti-tank ditch in Dachnów, 128, 129–33
    in Borysław, 246
    in Lwów, 52

Fishman, Perl, 188
formation of Jewish hit squad, 180–81
Franek (Polish partisan), 95
Frank, Hans, 217
Frank, Milue, 187, 299
Franuś, Franciszek ("Oszczepski"), 268, 268n24
Franuś, Michał ("Siciński"), 148, 264
Frdek-Místek, 275
Friedman, Ben Zion, 108n3
Friedman, Zigo, 32n56, 46, 70
Friedman family, 60
Funiak (Polish partisan), 95

Galicia, 28, 42n8, 53n10, 56n15, 80n4, 97–98, 143, 151, 157, 159, 169, 172, 239n4. *See also* East Galicia
Generalplan Ost, partisan reaction to, 148–49
Germany, German
    attack on partisans in Biłgoraj, 152
    invasion of Poland, 40, 156
    occupation of Lwów, 50–51, 56, 79
Gerstenfeld, Ethel, 29 , 29n38
Gerstenfeld, Jacob, 29, 29n38, 30, 31, 87, 87n13, 93n18
Gerstenfeld, Leo, 87n13, 277
Gerstenfeld, Michal, 87n11
Gerstenfeld, Rebecca (d. of Jacob), 87, 87n13
Globocnik, Odilo, 129–30, 146, 147
Gniduła, Jozef, 218n
Gocław, 24
Goldstein, Shimon, 160, 167
Gontaze, Stanisław, 173
Graywitz, Ivan, 54
Graywitz, Omlan, 54
Grochów, 24

Hanaczów, 166
Harasowski (court member), 101
Hayydok (A. Bogner's friend), 187
Heler, Mendel, 160, 167
Helman, Bernard, 183, 184, 185
Helman, Golda, 185
Helman, Hedva, 185
Helman, Isaac, 5, 7, 16–18, 183–85, *183*, 205, 208, 220, 251, 257, 259n12
Helman, Leon, 184
Helman, Moses, 183–84
Helman, Motel, 184
Helman, Pawel, 184
Helman, Tili, 185
Helman family, 184
Heydrich, Reinhardt, 97
Heyduk, Oswald, 98
Himmler, Heinrich, 53, 97, 146, 151, 153n90, 153n93, 154, 155
Hitler, Adolf, 40, 97, 153, 155
Hoffman, Maurie, 188–92, 201, *205*, 206n3, *214*, 220, 242, 251, 252, 267n21
Hoffman, Tobias, 191–92, 220, 252, 253
Hoffman family, 192
Hrubieszów, 98, 139, 235, 240
Hul, Vasyl, 54
Huta Różaniecka, 92, 152, 172

Igiel (Igel) family, 166
Isaac (Chana Bern's step-grandmother's son), 125

Jabotinsky, Ze'ev, 28, 34
Jaffa, 278
Janczyc, Roman, 271n33
Janów forest, 171
Janowska military camp, 72, 72n2
Janowskie woods, 1, 9, 92, 210, 211, 213, 214–15, 222

Jarosław, 42, 47, 156, 239
Jaworów, 216–21
Jaworski (deputy camp commander), 74n5

Kagan, Lt., 257
Kalichmacher, Meir, 160, 167
Kalinowicz, Richard, 167
Kaminka, 138
Kammer, Feiga, 103–4, 103n29, 104n30, 260
Karl Schöngarth, Karl, 56
Katukov, Mikhail Efimovich, 261
Kąty Pierwsze, 242
Katz, Abraham, 20
Katz, Henia, 20n7
Katz, Henny, 277
Katz, Henye (Henny) Reichenthal, 20
Katz, Herman, 20, 20n13, 97n1, 109, 113, 114, 277
Katz, Isaac, 277
Katz, Jonas, 20
Katz, Leo, 277
Katz, Lucy, 277
Katz, Moritz, 20, 20n13
Katz, Selma Friedland, 20n13, 109, 109n5, 113, 114, 197
Katz-Bern family, 97n1
Katzmann, Friedrich, 169
Katzmann, Fritz, 68–69, 68n1
killing of Ukrainian at Rand hideout, 249–50
killing of Vasyl Kułczycki, 112
killing of Wehrmacht soldiers near bunker, 233–34
Kisvárda, 80n5, 81
Knieja area, 171
Kohlus (ghetto director), 103
Kopcie, 22
Kopciuch, Jan, 268
Kowal, Jozef, 218n

Kowal, Katarzyna, 218n
Kozak, Anatoli, 100
Kraków, 75, 104n29, 125, 150, 165n31, 182, 269, 273, 275
Kraków-Płaszów concentration camp, 248
Krasulak, Władysław, 55
Kreisler, Fritz, 202
Krüger, Friedrich Wilhelm, 68n1, 106
Krzyżanowski, Aleksander ("Wilk"), 165n31
Kułczycki, Teodor, 100
Kułczycki, Vasyl, 36n67, 37–39, 38, 52, 54, 55, 98, 100, 101, 104, 107, 109, 112, 118, 134
Kułczycki family, 37
Kulpa, Amana, 134
Kulpa, Czesław, 10, 91
Kulpa, Jan, 10, 65, 66
Kulpa, Józef, 3, 7–12, 7n10, 8, 9, 10, 13, 43–45, 46, 49n22, 60, 63–67, 79, 82, 85–87, 90–91, 91n9, 123–24, 126–28, 172nn4–5, 131, 134, 148n59, 167, 180–81, 187, 196, 199, 205, 206, 208, 210–11, 214, 218, 273–74
Kulpa, Rozali, 10, 134n27
Kulpa, Stanisław, 10, 65, 66, 245

Landau, Felix, 60
Laszyk, Stefan, 55
Lavee (Łukawiecki), Simon, 276
Lekowitz, Wasyl, 54
Levin, Aaron, 52
Levin, Yehezkel, 52, 59
Lewicki, Jan, 101
Lipowa Camp, 62–63, 66
Lipskie forest, 171
Lipsko, 47, 49, 152, 207, 245
Lisie Jamy, 92, 183–84, 185–87, 187n, 188, 190, 236
Lobliner (Judenrat member), 78
loss of sight, Chana's, 123, 127–28
Lostinger (Judenrat member), 78

Lubaczów, occupation of, 80
    1939, 40
    1941, 57–59
Lubaczów ghettos, establishment of, 97–106
Lubaczów Jewish cemetery, 18
Lubaczowka River, 122, 23
Lubelski woods, 92
Lublin, 139, 261, 264
    area, 12n12, 135, 137, 154, 235, 236, 238, 244
    district, 40, 58, 87, 129, 138, 143, 146, 151, 239
    southeast, 156–71
Lublin-Majdanek, 147
Ludwigsburg, 20, 20n13, 97n1, 114
Luzk, 98
Łaszczów, 245
Łubiarz, Anastazja, 218n
Łubiarz, Maria, 218n
Łukawiecki, Aleksander (Menachem Mendel), 23–24, 27–28, 80–81, 81n, *80, 81*
Łukawiecki, Dora (Dorota), 8, 23–24, 23n2, 25, 34, 60, 67, 83, 87, 121
Łukawiecki, Hersh Wolf (Velvale; Henryk), 8, 22n18, 23–24, 23n22, 25, 26, 31, 34
Łukawiecki (Cohen), Joseph (s. of Shmuel David), 24–25, 33, 34, 278, 279
Łukawiecki, Joseph (s. of Hersh), 23, 26–27, 26, 28, 28, 30, 31, 34, 42–45, 42n8, 59, 67, 69, 70n, 78, 81, 82–83, 86, 121
Łukawiecki, Joseph (s. of Mundek), 269, 275
Łukawiecki, Judith-Ida, 16, 29, 86, 120, 281, 281n
Łukawiecki, Mina (Minka; Onka), 29, 86, 120–21
Łukawiecki (Cohen), Moshe, 25
Łukawiecki, Rafael (Fulek), 29, 83, 86, 87, 114

Łukawiecki, Sara ("Sarka") Mor, 24, 24
Łukawiecki, Sarah Leah Nestel, 28–29, 29n39, 30–31, 34, 60, 67, 70, 86, 121, 270
Łukawiecki, Shmuel David, 24, 24, 25–26, 34, 279
Łukawiecki (Cohen), Shoshanna, 25n26
Łukawiecki, Zofia, 81n
Łukawiecki, Zvi, 25, 25n16
Łukawiecki, Zygmunt (Zalman), 29, 45, 59, 72, 75, 77, 78, 82, 83, 85, 87, 114, 184
Łukawiecki family, 22, 26–27, 30, 30, 33–35, *41, 42, 43, 44*, 60, 64, 71, 72, 86–87, 133, 184, 276–77
    nickname "Gorzelnicy," 26n, 42, 42n4
Łukawiecki Zilberman, Leiba (Ahuva), 24, 25

Majdan Kaszelański, 176
Majdan Nepryski, 95
Majdanek, 241n14
Margol, Anna, 218n
Mariarmia woods, 18, 270
Marseille, 277
Mauthausen-Gusen concentration camp, 248
Mazury forest, 61, 79, 210
Melnyk, Andrei, 39n70
meeting the Red Army, 255–59
Michalski, Józek, 93
Mielniki, 23, 25, 26
Minsk, 97
Mircze, 241n14
Misiarz, Edward, 148
Młodów, 192
Molotov-Ribbentrop Non-Aggression Pact, 40, 42, 85n1, 87n8, 184, 246
    breaking of the, 49, 61
    and the ZWZ/AK, 142

move of Łukawiecki family from Lwów to Ostrowiec, 64, 83–84, 85–87
Munich, 276

Nadel (Mundek's school friend), 32n56
Nahariya, 277
Narol, 19, 47, 58, 87, 87nn7–8, 92, 93, 93nn18–19, 152, 207
Nestel Gerstenfeld, Rebecca, 28–29, 29n38, 31, 58, 87, 87n11, 93n18
Niwki woods, 10, 57, 66, 126
Nowe Brusno, 67
Nowe Sioło, 35–37, 35n64, 38, 39, 52, 54–55, 112
    woods, 36–37
Nowy Majdan, 218, 218n

Oleszyce, 26, 106, 152, 156
Olkowski, Jan, 272n36
Operation Barbarossa, 49, 62, 135, 144
Operation Werewolf, 170–71
order on Jews' participation in the AK resistance, 163–64
Ostrovsky, Prof., 89
Ostrowiec, 8, 9, 23, 23, 26, 27, 30, 31, 33, 42–46, 44, 60, 61, 62, 64, 79, 82–88, 105, 114, 116, 123, 125, 127, 141n22, 184, 194, 208, 211, 216, 268
Osuchy Ravine, 229
Otwock, 271–72, 274–75

Paary woods, 92, 172
Pająk, Eugeniusz, 271n34, 272n36
Pałczyński, Jan (Ivan), 55
Pardes Chana, 277
Parnas (Judenrat head), 68
Petliura, Symon Vasylyovych, 35–38, 69
Płazów, 47, 92, 156, 207, 266
    forest, 12, 14, 47, 92, 152, 207, 266

Podkowa (assault commanding officer), 176–77
pogrom in Lwów, 69–70
Pohl, Dieter, 5n6
Potoczek, 245
Potok Łosiniecki, 176
Prague, 275, 275n45
Przemyśl, 156, 239
Puszcza Solska
    district, 152
    forest, 1, 15, 46n15, 171, 172, 208, 209, 215, 229

Radom, 150
raids
    against Germans and Ukranians, 94–95
    on military supplies from abandoned Lipowa Camp, 65–66
    retaliatory against resettlements in the Zamość area, 244, 245
Rand, Isaac, 247–50
Rand, Regina, 247–50
rape attempt on Chana Bern, 179–80
rape of Chana Bern, 110
Rapy Dylańskie, 222
Rasch, Otto Emil, 52n6, 97
Rawa Ruska, 50, 57, 58, 67, 87, 87n13, 99–100, 105, 109, 114, 129, 138, 139, 152, 153, 156, 261
Reisinger, 105
reunion with relatives in Israel, 277
Riga, 97
Ringler, Mauritius, 247
Romania, 147
Rowecki, Stefan ("Grot"), 163–64
Rubin (business partner), 27
Ruda Różaniecka, 27, 42, 46, 47, 92, 152, 206, 208
    woods, 208, 209, 229, 257

Ruda Żurawiecka, 241
Rudzienko, 24

Samsonówka, 176
San River, 156, 229, 239, 268
Schenirer, Sara, 106n2
Schtelzer, Tili, 184
Schwartz, Mundek, 248
Schwartzbard, Shalom (Samuel), 69
Sedlakowska, Janina, 218
selection of forest for hiding, 194–96, 208, 209–11
Serbia, 147
Serdyński, Roman, 105, 130, 132
Serdyński, Władysław, 105, 130
Shprecher family, 69
Sieniawa, 156
Sikorski, Władysław, 140
Sikum, Władek, 36n66–67
Silberschmidt family, 106, 109
Silberschmidt girl, 106, 114, 115, 118, 132
Skoropad, Maria, 27
Skroban, Władysław, 173
Sliwa, Józef ("Kolon"), 93
Śmigły, Rydz, 133n25
Sobibór extermination camp, 129, 130, 175n
Sokal, 11, 98, 156
Sokolniki death camp, 72–78, 73, 79, 85
Sokolniki death camp, Mundek brothers in, 72, 75–78
Späth, Helmut, 105
Stalin, Joseph, 40, 61
Staub, Fryderyk "Proch", 167
Stećko, Jarosław, 52
Stein, Fishel, 5, 12, 14
Stein, Zisa, 3–7, 4n2, 6, 11–16, 18
Steinbruch family, 12, 14
Strasberg, Chana, 223,
Stryj, 26, 42, 82

Stuttgart, 20n13
Susiec, 172–77, 179
    woods, 258n8
Symko, Eliasz, 101
Szabata, Kazimierz, 218n
Szeptycki, Andrzej, 52
Szot, Stanisław, 265
Szówsko, 28
Szczyrba, Vasyl, 55
Szutka, Michal, 27
Szymański, Jan, 55

Tadeusz Bór-Komorowski ("Bór"), 152n87, 164
Taicher, Binna, 108n3
Tatar, Miszka (Michaił Atamanow), 89, 89n4
Tel Aviv, 278
Teodor, Kołosywski ("Kowalenko"), 55
Tepper, Joseph, 32
Thomas, Max, 97n2
Tomaszów Lubelski (town and area), 88n2, 94n22, 148, 149, 156, 160, 166, 167, 172, 174, 206, 207, 208, 211, 240, 241, 245, 270
Trawniki, 151, 168
trying to warn Jews of their fate, 116–18
Tshuebak (Czubak; camp commander), 74n5

UB, Mundek and the
    deserting, 271–74
    enlistment in, 266–67
    transfer to Kraków, 269, 270
Ukraine, 37, 53n9, 98, 154

vision and prayer, Chana Bern's, 222–28

Wach [or Wachet], Adam, 105
Walter, N., 105

Warda, Marian ("Polakowski"), 88, 147n53, 148–49, 206, 241, 268n26

Watmann, Baron Hugo, 27, 27n28

wedding of Mundek and Chana, 260

Weiner (Hit Squad member; partisan), 18, 242

Weiner, Zanwet, 276

Weiner family, 132n19

Wielącza, 242

Wieptz River, 156

Wirkowice, 245

Władek, Sikum, 54n13, 55, 56

Wojda, 150

Wojtowicz, Kazimierz ("Głóg"), 166

Wojtowicz brothers, 167

Wołyń, 238, 239

Zagajski, Jerzy ("Lopek"), 88, 148n60

Zalz, 105

Zamość, 98, 139, 143, 146, 147n53, 156, 168, 174, 211, 241, 242, 245

area, 56, 148, 149–51, 161, 170, 172, 207, 215, 218, 229, 235, 243, 244

Zamość action and partisan response, 146–49

Zathey, Zdzisław ("Gładzicki"), 148, 268

Zbąszynek (Neu Bentschen), 20n13

Żegowski, Ludwik, 206, 208, 216, 217, 219, 232, 242–43, 251, 252

Żegowski, Władi, 206, 208, 219, 230–31, 242, 250, 251, 255, 257

Zilberman, Leiba Cohen, 279. See also Łukawiecki Zilberman, Leiba (Ahuva)

Zinser, Hans-Walter, 100

Ziss family, 60

Zuchowski, Andrzej, 49, 49n22, 93, 93n10

Zuchowski, Marian ("Orlik"), 49n22, 93–94, 94nn21–22

Zwierzyniec, 175, 176

ZWZ (AK), Mundek in
joining, 46–49
return to, 79, 88

Żydaczów (Zhydachiv), 28, 28n37, 60, 81–82, 82n7